Public Law, Legal Services & the Legal System

Public Law, Legal Services & the Legal System

Alan Reid

Associate Professor in Law, University of Bradford

Elizabeth Smart

Solicitor, Professor of Legal Education and Head of the School of Law and Society, St Mary's University, Twickenham

Christopher R Ratcliffe

Solicitor Advocate, Senior Lecturer in Law, Nottingham Law School, Nottingham Trent University

4th edition

OXFORD
UNIVERSITY PRESS

OXFORD
UNIVERSITY PRESS

Great Clarendon Street, Oxford, OX2 6DP,
United Kingdom

Oxford University Press is a department of the University of Oxford.
It furthers the University's objective of excellence in research, scholarship,
and education by publishing worldwide. Oxford is a registered trade mark of
Oxford University Press in the UK and in certain other countries

Third Edition published in 2023
Second Edition published in 2022
First Edition published in 2021

Published in the United States of America by Oxford University Press
198 Madison Avenue, New York, NY 10016, United States of America

British Library Cataloguing in Publication Data
Data available

Library of Congress Control Number: 2024939141

ISBN 978–0–19–893303–8

Acknowledgements

Some content under Crown copyright regarding different court structures is reproduced by kind permission under the Open Government Licence (http://www.nationalarchives.gov.uk/doc/open-government-licence/).

Grateful acknowledgement is made to the Solicitor Regulation Authority for copyright material which appears in this book.

For the latest version of the SRA Standards and Regulations, please visit their website (https://www.sra.org.uk/solicitors/standards-regulations/).

Grateful acknowledgement is made to Clare Firth for permission to reproduce Figure 12.2.

Every effort has been made to trace and contact copyright holders prior to going to press. If notified, the publisher will undertake to rectify any errors or omissions at the earliest opportunity.

Contents

Table of Cases

United Kingdom

European Court of Justice

European Court of Human Rights

Table of Legislation

United Kingdom

Statutes

Statutory Instruments

Rules

Practice Directions

Codes of Conduct and Guidelines

Solicitors Disciplinary Tribunal

Solicitors Regulation Authority (SRA)

Law Society

European Legislation

Directives

International Conventions and Treaties

Exam Technique

A.1 Introduction

The functioning legal knowledge (FLK) assessments for SQE 1 comprise two assessments of 180 questions each.

The FLK assessments will cover the following subject areas:

1. Business Law and Practice; Dispute Resolution; Contract; Tort; Legal System of England and Wales; Constitutional and Administrative Law; and EU Law and Legal Services.
2. Property Practice; Wills and the Administration of Estates; Solicitors Accounts; Land Law; Trusts; Criminal Law and Practice.

The objective of the assessments, which is linked to the Statement of Solicitor Competence, is to assess the depth and breadth of your knowledge of the law of England and Wales. The assessments are not just about nuggets of knowledge but about demonstrating how well you can apply that knowledge to demonstrate the threshold competence required of a newly qualified solicitor on day one of practice.

In practice, the reality is that you will often look up information which you need to know either to confirm your thinking, to refresh your memory or, indeed, to find out about an issue with which you are unfamiliar. However, the FLK assessments are closed book. This means that, without reference to books and notes, you are answering the questions based upon your knowledge derived from your prior learning, including that provided and supported through these manuals, and through the practise questions.

Each question in the assessment contributes to the overall validity of the assessment; that is, it allows you the opportunity to demonstrate your knowledge and understanding about the application of the law. Therefore, it should be possible to infer that a successful candidate has demonstrated their competence to meet the threshold and is thus capable of being a solicitor.

The purpose of this chapter is to talk you through the assessment questions: how they are structured, what to look for and what to avoid. Be encouraged; the questions in the assessments and the questions in the question bank are written by human beings so bear in mind that the same thinking process which has been used to generate the question can be used by you to determine the correct answer. Questions are not written in a way purposefully to catch you out, as the point of a question is to assess what you *do* know, not what you *do not* know. If you have prepared thoroughly, you should be in a position to respond positively to the assessment.

A.2 Question structure

To begin, let us take a question from the SRA SQE 1 FLK sample questions published on 16 December 2019. These sample questions were published to give a guide as to what might be expected in the live assessment, and frequent reference will be made to them throughout this chapter.

The question is split into three parts, as illustrated in **Figure A.1**:

- the context;
- the stem; and
- the options.

In the course of a trial various arguments are put to the judge as to the exact meaning of a particular section of a relevant statute. When deciding the case, the judge first looks at the natural ordinary meaning of the words used. However, such an interpretation of those words results in an absurd meaning being given to the section. The judge, therefore, in coming to his decision, interprets the words in a different way which does not result in an absurd meaning. — **Context**

What method of statutory interpretation has the judge used? → **Stem**

A. The literal rule.
B. The mischief rule.
C. The extrinsic evidence rule.
D. The golden rule.
E. The intrinsic evidence rule.
— **Options**

FIGURE A.1 Example of question structure (SRA sample question 15)

A.2.1 The context

The context may be objective, for example, just a couple of generalised sentences before the stem, which puts the question to be answered and which aims to capture a particular piece of knowledge. SRA sample question number 6 demonstrates an objective context:

> **EXAMPLE**
>
> A decision is made by the Court of Appeal (Civil Division) in favour of the claimant. The defendant wishes to obtain permission to appeal.
>
> Which of the following courts have the power to grant permission to appeal?

Or, as in question 15, the context may be subjective and contain more scene-setting for the question which follows, providing details about where, who and why something happened, as represented in **Figure A.2**.

You should read the context carefully because it will contain clues which have been laid by the question writer to help you answer the question.

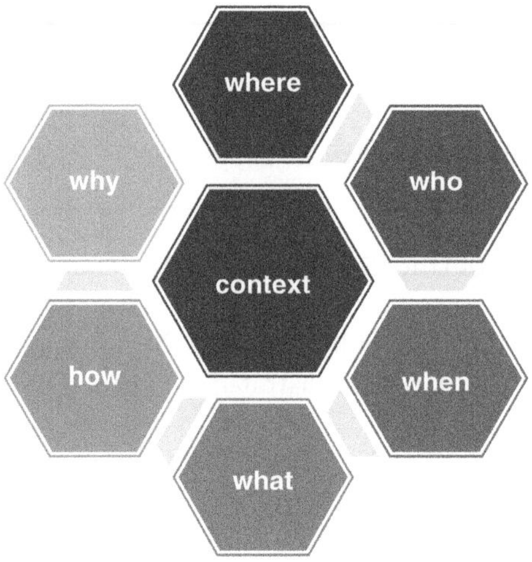

FIGURE A.2 Subjective context

Here is the question 15 context again with highlighted relevant sections which give a good idea as to what is in the question writer's mind—the rules of statutory interpretation:

EXAMPLE

In the course of a trial various arguments are put to the judge as to the *exact meaning* of a particular section of a relevant statute. When deciding the case, the judge first looks at the *natural ordinary meaning of the words* used. However, such an interpretation of those words *results in an absurd meaning* being given to the section. The judge, therefore, in coming to his decision, *interprets the words* in a different way which *does not result in an absurd meaning*.

What method of statutory interpretation has the judge used?

In this particular question, the stem itself also tells you that the question is about statutory interpretation but the stem might not always be quite so helpful. You may have to consider the facts carefully to establish which area of knowledge is being assessed; each assessment covers multiple subject areas, so you will not know what kind of question you are attempting until you read it. Having read the context carefully, you should be in the right mental zone as the context contains all of the relevant facts which are needed to give the correct answer to the stem which follows and which supports the answer.

A.2.2 **The stem**

Look at the stem very carefully—after all, it is the link to the correct answer. Given its importance, the stem should be absolutely clear, should be connected to the context and include as much information as possible to be precise about what is being asked. Stems, properly written, should pass what is known as the *cover test*. The cover test means that the correct answer should, without seeing any of the options, pop into your head as soon as you read the stem. This is a very useful step to take as it prompts your memory to offer up the right answer without being conflicted by any distracting options. If you think of what you believe to be the correct answer and then, to your surprise, you do not see it in the options, double-check that you have read the stem correctly!

TIP

When you use the practise question bank, get into the habit of using the *cover test* as a technique as it is good for revision and will improve your recollection. A good habit to have! Having read the stem thoroughly, take a moment to pause and think what answer you expect to see amongst the options. When you read through the options, if that answer appears, you know you might be on the right track but pause again before you enthusiastically tick the box and move on to the next question! Check what you believe to be the answer very carefully to make sure that it matches what you had expected to see, then look through the other options to be doubly sure that you are correct in your selection. This is especially important in relation to single best answer questions which are discussed more fully later in the chapter; bear in mind that the 'best' answer might be very close to the second best answer giving you all the more reason to look carefully at all options. Only when this process is complete should you make your selection.

A.2.2.1 Types of question

The SQE 1 FLK assessment contains what are described as single best answer questions. They are likely to be of two types. The stems for each are different although both lead to the selection of a single correct or a single best answer:

- a traditional multiple-choice question leading to a single correct answer; and
- a single best answer question leading to a single best answer.

A.2.2.2 Traditional multiple-choice questions (MCQ)

For this type of question, there must be *only one unambiguously correct answer.* The answer is supported by the stem which will be worded in such a way that it can only lead to that one correct answer and is a heavy hint that you are looking for that one correct answer. As there is just one correct answer, these questions are an ideal way to practise using the cover test (see **A.2.2**).

Stem examples:

- Which of the following . . .
- What must X do . . .
- By when . . .
- What is the next step which should be taken . . .
- What is the correct advice to give . . .
- What is the correct procedure to . . .
- What is the accurate description of . . .

In question 15, the stem is worded: 'What method of statutory interpretation has the judge used?' The language is very precise: 'What method . . .'. It is an MCQ as there can only be one unambiguously correct answer.

A.2.2.3 Single best answer questions (SBA)

A single best answer question may need a little more unravelling than a traditional MCQ. For an SBA, a range of responses might be possible or reasonable within the context of the question. However, only one will be the star option as it is the most preferable, reasonable and appropriate as the *single best answer* in the circumstances as provided by the context.

The context, here, is particularly important and is likely to require evaluation in order to determine what course of action is for the best. As there is no immediate stand-out correct answer, as for a traditional MCQ, the possible solutions require an evaluative judgement as to what is best to do in the situation. Each judgement-based option may be represented visually; see **Figure A.3** which shows how the options may be ranged from least suitable or worst option to the best option. Note that there is only *ONE* best option. You should bear in mind that the least suitable option, here B, may simply be wrong which is explanation in itself as to why it is the least suitable option!

In **Figure A.3**, A is identified as the best option on a given set of facts; B and E are identified as the least suitable options on the same set of facts with C and D somewhere in between. D is clearly challenging A for the star option spot but there is no provision to choose both options and so there will be a particular reason on the facts why option A trumps the other options.

As you can see, more thought is needed to work through and determine the best option in an SBA. The options are likely to be carefully nuanced and these types of questions demonstrate a higher degree of application in a professional context. For example, you can envisage a circumstance in which a solicitor needs to advise a client in the client's best interests. All options might present possible and plausible advice which might be given, although one option might definitely not be in the client's interests while another is recognisably the *best* advice.

Stem examples:

- Which of the following is the most appropriate ground upon which . . .
- Which of the following represents the best advice which might be given . . .
- What is the best course of action to recommend in these circumstances?

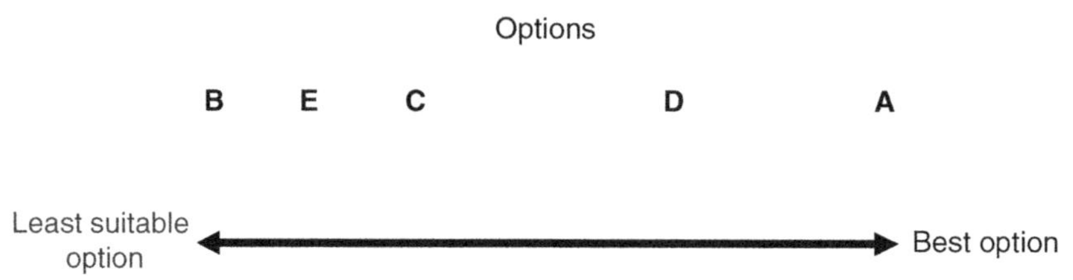

FIGURE A.3 Range of responses

- How is the court most likely to determine the claimant's application?
- What approach is the most sensible to adopt on these facts?

TIP

As you work through the practise questions in the question bank, familiarise yourself with the stem types and see how the options differ so that you are best prepared. Remember that identifying the type of question you are being asked naturally links to the type of answer which is expected. If the stem looks to be an MCQ, then the expected answer should be an unambiguously correct response; if the stem looks to be an SBA, then the expected answer will be what is best in the circumstances. The feedback which is provided to the practise questions will help you to understand why a particular best option has been identified on the facts of the question.

A.2.3 **The options**

After the stem come the five options lettered (A–E) from which you are to select your answer. Rest assured that the options will always include the right answer so there is some comfort in that! If the question has been carefully written, the answer should not stand out as being the correct answer, it should have been carefully embedded within the options which should all offer plausible alternatives to sway your choice. If you consider that the purpose of the question is to be able to infer competence, it is clear why it is unlikely that the right answer will stand out.

The remaining options are known as *distractors*, which is an apt description as they are there to distract you from the right answer. The distractors are likely to be plausibly based on common misconceptions or misunderstandings and be compatible with, and flow from, the stem. A distractor may look very similar to the right answer but will differ in a small but significant way, for example:

EXAMPLE

Which of the following is the correct explanation to provide about an unless order requiring filing and service of the defendant's list of documents by 4 pm on 21 May?

A. That unless by 4 pm on 21 May the defendant has filed and served its list of documents, the claim will be struck out.

B. That unless by 4 pm on 21 May the defendant has filed and served its list of documents, the defence will be struck out.

In this example there is a one-word difference between A and B. In the rush to answer and move on to the next question, the temptation may be to plump immediately for the first answer because it looks about right but, of course, it is wrong.

A distractor may also offer the wrong explanation for a definitive answer.

EXAMPLE

If the stem asks simply: 'Is the client entitled to take this course of action, and for what reason?', you know that the expected answer will be unambiguously correct because this is a traditional MCQ. The options might be presented as three 'Yes' options each followed by a different reason, one of which is correct, and two 'No' options each followed by a different reason.

A. Yes, because . . .

B. Yes, because . . .

C. Yes, because . . .

D. No, because . . .

E. No, because . . .

In some ways, these questions are quite helpfully structured because you might readily be able to eliminate the two 'no' options but you must still look carefully through the three remaining options to ensure that you home in on the correct reason for the 'yes' response.

> **TIP**
>
> If there are three positive options and two negative options, *do not immediately discount the negative options* and assume that one of the positive options is bound to be the right answer; the imbalance might be trying to lull you into a false sense of safety in numbers and prompt you to select a positive answer. Only eliminate options if you are sure that they are wrong.

The best distractors will also look similar to the answer in construction and length: they have symmetry. This is demonstrated in SRA sample question 15 where the options are given as:

A. The literal rule.

B. The mischief rule.

C. The extrinsic evidence rule.

D. The golden rule.

E. The intrinsic evidence rule.

A distractor must work hard to distract you from the correct answer. In the same way that a stand-out correct answer does little to assess competence, a stand-out wrong option is also unhelpful to assessors because it can be eliminated from the running and so increases the chances of a candidate getting the question right without actually knowing the answer! In the FLK assessments, there are five options and you have a 1 in 5 chance of getting the answer correct even if you guess (more on this in **A.4.1**). If two of the options are implausible, the probability of selecting the correct answer increases to 1 in 3.

In SRA sample question 6 about appeals, these are the options:

A. The Court of Appeal only.

B. The Supreme Court only.

C. The House of Lords only.

D. The Court of Appeal and the Supreme Court.

E. The Court of Appeal and the House of Lords.

There are two stand out options here, C and E, which can be eliminated as they are plainly wrong because they contain a reference to the House of Lords rather than the Supreme Court. The choice has now reduced to A, B and D.

Notice that A and B include the word 'only'. Be wary of such limiting phrasing and ask yourself whether this could possibly be correct in the context.

> **TIP**
>
> It is worth bearing in mind that options which include 'always' and 'never' are (almost) always wrong and never right. Do not discount them without some thought as such phrasing may be appropriate for the context, but bear in mind that such absolute phrasing often hints that the option is likely to be incorrect as it is inflexible and allows for no exceptions. This is often too rigid an approach in the field of law.

By this process of elimination, A and B include the word 'only' which is too absolute for the reality of those options. Therefore, only option D remains and that is the correct answer to the question.

The words 'must' and 'may' are frequently encountered in MCQs. Bearing in mind that the stem supports the answer and connects to the distractors, look carefully at whether either of those words appear in the options.

EXAMPLE

What is the likely costs order which the judge will make?

If any of the options contains the word 'must', for example:

A. The judge *must* make an order for the claimant to pay the defendant's costs in any event think carefully; costs are discretionary and, therefore, you would expect the correct answer to read:

A. The judge *may* make an order for the claimant to pay the defendant's costs in any event'.

TIP

Through use of the cover test technique, you will hopefully have in mind what you believe to be the answer and may mentally benchmark an option as soon as you see it. Do not bank that option too soon until you have reviewed the other options; use it as the measure against which the other options are considered as being correct/incorrect or better/worse. Then, eliminate options to narrow your choice further. Think logically, analyse the wording carefully and eliminate options based upon the *specific facts* you are given and not the general law, practice or procedure. The majority of questions will have a specific set of facts and the correct answer depends on those. If, after that analysis, you are still persuaded that your initial thought was correct, go ahead and bank the option!

A.3 **Worked examples**

Now that you understand how a question is constructed, you can see that there are four simple steps to take to approach each question:

Step 1. Read the context carefully, taking note of key words to identify which topic area the question is about.

Step 2. Read the stem and identify whether this is an MCQ or SBA.

Step 3. From the stem, conduct the cover test.

Step 4. Read the options and identify the distractors.

Using these steps, have a look through these worked examples and try to think one step ahead.

WORKED EXAMPLE: DISPUTE RESOLUTION

A claimant, in proceedings in which they had raised a claim and a defence to counterclaim, does not attend court on the first day of trial.

What order should the defendant ask the court to make?

A. To adjourn the trial.
B. To give judgment on the counterclaim.
C. To make a wasted costs order.
D. To strike out the claim.
E. To strike out the claim and the defence to counterclaim.

Step 1: Review the context.

A claimant, in proceedings in which *they had raised a claim and a defence to counterclaim, does not attend court* on the first day of *trial*.

Your first thoughts might be that this is a very short fact-pattern and so unlikely to be a tricky question but it packs in a considerable amount of detail. The key words have been highlighted: we know that the claimant pursues a claim but is also defending a counterclaim, and does not attend court for the trial. Of those key words, perhaps the most significant is the presence of a counterclaim, which is a claim in its own right pursued by the defendant against the claimant and which can alter the dynamic between the parties. Having got a grip on the facts, read the stem.

Step 2: Read the stem and identify whether this is an MCQ or SBA.

What order should *the defendant* ask the court to make?

Is this an MCQ or an SBA? You might be thinking that this looks like an MCQ as it begins 'What order . . .' as if only one precise and correct answer is possible. However, look again; this is an SBA. The use of the word 'should' is a hint here. It is more or less asking: what is the best thing to do in these circumstances if you were the defendant. Note that the use of the word 'should' might also appear in an MCQ to indicate what should be done correctly in the circumstances—close reading of the fact-pattern and the stem will help you to decide what you are being asked. There is also a shift of context here: the fact-pattern sets up the scenario from the claimant's perspective but the question itself is asked from the defendant's perspective.

Step 3: From the stem, conduct the cover test.

Before looking at the options, try the cover test: what pops into your head as to what order the defendant should be seeking? Anything? Do not worry if not as we can now take a look at the options.

Step 4: Read the options and identify the distractors.

Read through all of the options once. This may provide an immediate prompt as to which of the options might possibly be the answer.

A. To adjourn the trial.
B. To give judgment on the counterclaim.
C. To make a wasted costs order.
D. To strike out the claim.
E. To strike out the claim and the defence to counterclaim.

Now go back and begin the process of elimination taking each option in turn and thinking from the defendant's perspective:

A cannot be right as, although a defendant can, of course, ask the court to adjourn the trial, there is no reason for a defendant to ask the court to adjourn the trial as the court may proceed with the trial in the absence of the claimant. Why would a defendant give up the opportunity to succeed against the claimant in their absence? B looks like a possibility, but this would not dispose of the claimant's claim, only the counterclaim; but something is beginning to emerge here as to what might be best for the defendant. C seems like a good idea to make the claimant pay but this is going down the wrong track because costs orders are consequential upon an event. Some event must occur first on which to hang the costs order. Also, there is something here that is not quite right as a wasted costs order is made against the legal representatives and there is nothing on the facts to suggest that the claimant's legal representatives are at fault. Let us look at D. This does not look right as it would leave the counterclaim live so let us look closely at E: asking for an order to strike out the claim and the defence to counterclaim looks to be a good answer on these facts as although the court may proceed with the trial in the absence of a party, if the claimant does not attend the trial, the court may strike out the claim and any defence to counterclaim. Got to the best answer, E, in the end!

WORKED EXAMPLE: PROPERTY LAW

A solicitor is acting for the buyer of a house which has a registered title. The house was first registered in 2004 following a sale. The house was the subject of a further sale which was registered in 2012. The house is built on land which is near the church within a Church of England parish. There is no entry in the register as to chancel repair liability.

Which one of the following correctly describes whether the buyer's solicitor needs to carry out a chancel repair liability search?

A. No, because the title was registered under the Land Registration Act 2002.
B. Yes, because chancel repair liability takes effect as an overriding interest.
C. No, because there has been a registered transfer on sale subsequent to first registration of title.
D. No, because no entry has been made in the register in respect of any chancel repair liability.
E. Yes, because there has been no registered transfer on sale after 12 October 2013.

Step 1: Review the fact pattern.

A solicitor is acting for the buyer of a house which has a *registered* title. The house was first registered in *2004* following a sale. The house was the subject of a *further sale* which was registered in *2012*. The house is built on land which is near the church within a *Church of England* parish. There is no entry in the register as to *chancel repair liability.*

This fact-pattern sets the context for the question, which relates to a purchase of a house with registered title which is near a church. The key words and dates have been highlighted and these identify the issue—which is whether the house could be subject to chancel repair liability—and provide the important details which will be relevant to this issue. Those details include both dates and facts, so this should flag up to you that you will need to consider not just what events have taken place, but how the timing of those events could affect the outcome. With this in mind, you can now look at the stem.

Step 2: Read the stem and identify whether this is an MCQ or SBA

Which one of the following correctly describes whether the buyer's solicitor needs to carry out a chancel repair liability search?

Is this an MCQ or an SBA? The key words here are 'correctly' and 'needs', which indicate that this is an MCQ rather than an SBA. Although the focus of the question is on whether a search is considered necessary, the determining factor is objective; that is, it is based on the underlying law rather than subjective judgement as to which of several courses of action might be 'best' in the circumstances.

Step 3: From the stem, conduct the cover test.

Before looking at the options, try the cover test: what pops into your head as to whether a search might be necessary? Anything? If so, apply this when considering your answer, but do not preempt your conclusion until you have read the options. Do not worry if nothing occurs to you at this stage, as we can now take a look at the options.

Step 4: Read the options and identify the distractors.

Read through all of the options once. This may provide an immediate prompt as to which of the options might possibly be the correct answer.

A. No, because the title was registered under the Land Registration Act 2002.
B. Yes, because chancel repair liability takes effect as an overriding interest.
C. No, because there has been a registered transfer on sale subsequent to first registration of title.
D. No, because no entry has been made in the register in respect of any chancel repair liability.
E. Yes, because there has been no registered transfer on sale after 12 October 2013.

Now go back and begin the process of elimination taking each option in turn and thinking from the solicitor's perspective:

A. can be discounted because although the title was first registered in 2004, after the 2002 Act came into force, at that time chancel repair liability continued to be an overriding interest in the same way as it had previously.
B. superficially looks as though it might be correct—chancel repair liability *was* originally within the list of overriding interests. But the key word here is 'was'—it ceased to be within the list after 12 October 2013. So, again, this option can be discounted.

C. is a technical point where timing comes into play. Consider this option in conjunction with option B: when did chancel repair liability cease to be an overriding interest? In 2013—so if this transfer took place in 2009, the liability will have been binding on the transferee because it was an overriding interest at that time.

D. looks, on the face of it, as though it could be a correct option: if chancel repair liability is no longer an overriding interest and there is no entry in the register as to any liability, will the buyer not take free of it? But again, remember the importance of timing here—the buyer has not yet completed their purchase, so is there still a risk? Bear in mind that just because chancel repair liability ceased to be an overriding interest in 2013, this did not mean the liability automatically ceased to exist.

E. raises a technical point where again timing comes into play. Although there is currently no entry in the register and chancel repair liability no longer takes effect as an overriding interest after that date, the property remains subject to any existing liability until the next transfer on sale is registered. Consider whether there is a risk, at this stage of the transaction, that an application could still be made to register any such liability and the buyer would then be bound by it if they proceeded with their purchase.

Having evaluated the options, go back to the stem and check exactly what the question is asking. With this in mind, confirm the results of your evaluation and select the option you consider to be correct. In this instance, the correct option is E.

WORKED EXAMPLE: BUSINESS LAW

A woman has been appointed to the board of directors of a private limited company (with unamended model articles). It is her first directorship and she wants to understand the legal requirements relating to decisions taken by the board of directors.

Which one of the following correctly describes the requirements of the company's articles and/or the Companies Act 2006 in respect of decisions taken by the board of directors of the company?

A. Only the directors can attend board meetings.
B. If the director cannot attend a board meeting, she can appoint a proxy.
C. The directors may take decisions by way of written resolution.
D. The directors can vote at board meetings on either a show of hands or by a poll vote.
E. Minutes of the board meetings must be filed with the Registrar of Companies.

Step 1: Review the context.

A woman has been appointed to the board of directors of *a private limited company* (with unamended model articles) and seeks your advice. It is her first directorship and she wants to understand the legal requirements relating to *decisions taken by the board of directors*.

When you look at the context, you will see that this is one of those generalised style questions which seeks to test your understanding of a particular topic. The key words have been highlighted for you: we are told that the woman is seeking advice about the requirements relating to decisions taken by the board of directors of a private limited company. It is important to recognise that the question focuses entirely on board decisions. This question is not asking about shareholder decisions so you should already be thinking about the difference in formalities and procedure of the two. It is also significant that we are told about this company's constitution: it has unamended model articles. Now that you have understood the context, you must read the stem.

Step 2: Read the stem and identify whether this is an MCQ or SBA

Which one of the following correctly describes the requirements of the company's articles and/or the Companies Act 2006 in respect of decisions taken by the board of directors of the company?

Is this an MCQ or an SBA? The clue here is the use of the words 'Which one of the following' and 'correctly'. It is an MCQ as there can only be one correct answer. This stem does not ask you to advise the woman which is the best course of action when taking a decision as a director, but rather to confirm which one of the statements is a correct option.

Step 3: From the stem, conduct the cover test.

Before looking at the options, try the cover test: what pops into your head about the requirements for the decisions of the board of directors of private limited companies? What rules governing the taking of board decisions do you expect to see amongst the options? Now, move on to look at the options.

Step 4: Read the options and identify the distractors.

Carefully read through all of the options once. This may provide an immediate prompt as to which of the options might possibly be the answer.

A. Only the directors can attend board meetings.
B. If the director cannot attend a board meeting, she can appoint a proxy.
C. The directors may take decisions by way of written resolution.
D. The directors can vote at board meetings on either a show of hands or by a poll vote.
E. Minutes of the board meetings must be filed with the Registrar of Companies.

Now go back and begin the process of elimination, taking each option in turn.

A cannot be correct as others—for example, a company secretary, the company's lawyers or accountants—may also attend board meetings. Whilst they do not have a right to vote, they may attend. This option needs to be eliminated. This option also includes the word 'only'. Be alert to the use of this word as it is creating an exclusive category. It may be appropriate for a context but here it is clearly not appropriate as others may attend the meetings.

At first glance B might look like a correct answer; however, this is where a solid understanding of the differences between board decisions and shareholder decisions is important. If the director cannot attend a board meeting, she could, if the articles of association allow (and the model articles do not), appoint an alternate director to attend in her place. A proxy is the term used for someone who attends a shareholders' meeting on behalf of the shareholder, so this is not a correct option and this option needs to be ruled out. Furthermore, this option uses the word 'can'. Again, be alert to this. 'Can' means the same as to be able to do something but bear in mind that just because you can do something does not mean that you should or that it is the correct thing to do. Here, although the option is worded that the director 'can appoint a proxy' and, literally, she can do that, it would be the wrong thing to do in her position to meet requirements.

How about C? The model articles do allow the directors to take decisions either at a board meeting or in writing. This looks like it is a correct option. If you think that C is the correct answer, pause before you select the option and move on to the next question. Look through the final two options to be doubly sure that you are correct in your selection. The word 'may' is used in this option which is an expression of possibility and means that a choice may be exercised to do something or not to do something; there is no obligation to do a specific thing. Here, the directors have a choice as they may take decisions either at a board meeting *or* in writing and so C looks like a good contender for the correct answer as the option provides that the directors may take decisions by way of written resolution.

D is incorrect as directors can only vote for or against the resolution by a show of hands. A poll vote is an alternative way of voting at a general meeting of shareholders. Again, this is where a good understanding of the differences between board decisions and shareholder decisions is important. Here, again, we meet use of the word 'can'. In this context, just because the directors are physically able to vote by a show of hands does not mean that they should or that it is the correct thing to do to meet requirements.

Finally, E is incorrect as the minutes are a private record of the decisions taken by the board and there is no requirement under either the articles or the Companies Act 2006 for them to be filed with the Registrar of Companies. The use of the word 'must' creates an obligation, a necessity or requirement to do something. It may be appropriate to a given context but be alert to it being a categorical answer; there is no doubt or any choice but to do something.

Having carefully considered each of the options, go back to the stem and check exactly what the question is asking. Apply the results of your evaluation and select the option you considered to be correct. In this instance, the correct option is C.

A.4 Time management

Each FLK assessment is likely to allow five hours and six minutes to answer 180 questions; just 1.7 minutes per question. So, it is clearly important to practise your time management. You can use the practise questions however you wish but to get the most from them you might:

- use the questions to support your learning as you work through the manuals. You might read a section or a chapter of the manual and then try your hand at answering some of the questions to reinforce your learning;
- come to the questions fresh and try your hand at a random selection of questions to keep you on your toes and to embed learning over a period of time and to highlight where you may need to look again at a topic to deepen your understanding. The feedback on each question and cross-referencing with the manual will be helpful here;
- practise the questions against the clock to replicate the assessment time constraint and to be sure that you can complete the assessment within the allocated time.

A.4.1 Blind guessing against making an educated choice

This chapter would be incomplete without facing down the old chestnut that you can guess your way through a multiple-choice assessment. Statistically speaking, it has a basis in truth. Simply, there are five options and, by making a selection, you have a 1 in 5 chance of getting the answer correct. But blind guessing is a risky strategy to deploy throughout an assessment. Think of it this way: for every question answered by guessing, you have 4 chances in 5 of getting it wrong! Statistically, that would be 144 out of 180 questions wrongly answered on an FLK assessment. You may also have heard that selecting option C consistently is bound to improve your chances. This is not true. Options are often randomised so option C is no more likely to be correct than A, B, D or E.

It is far better to make an educated guess which may be necessary where you are struggling either against time, in the closing minutes of the assessment, or against a mental blank which is blocking progress. Making an educated guess involves narrowing down the options by the process of elimination leaving perhaps a choice between two or three options. You now have, respectively, a 1 in 2 or 1 in 3 chance of selecting the right answer, which has significantly improved the odds. But let us be realistic. Under time pressure, you may temporarily be at a loss even to make an educated guess. Your memory has not been prompted by reading the stem and nothing stands out when you read through the options. What should you do? Be positive and hold your nerve; recognise that this is a temporary block and there are other questions which need your attention which you will be able to answer—so get a move on to the next question. You may even find that, in working through the other questions, your memory suddenly gives up the answer which had eluded you before. Near the end of the assessment, go back to any missed questions and make an educated guess; there is no negative marking in the assessment, that is losing a mark for an incorrect answer, but, as a certainty, skipping a question loses you the chance to gain a mark.

A.5 Summary

You will now appreciate that there is a method to the process of answering questions; just as there is a method to writing them. A methodical approach brings calm to the process; knowing that there is a structured approach to the creation of a question helps you to know that the question can also be deconstructed. An understanding of how that can be done, and the step-by-step process which has been outlined, will be a guide on your shoulder when you are either working your way through the question bank or working your way through the exam paper.

Of course, 'knowing your stuff' will provide the required bedrock of functioning legal knowledge, which is at the heart of the SQE assessments. The manuals, the question banks and your own preparation and practise will help put you into the best possible position to respond to the questions in the assessments.

TIP

This tip applies throughout the entire preparation process building up to sitting the FLK assessments. From studying the manual materials, going over a tricky area of law or procedure which you do not grasp at first, practising the questions until you know (and understand) why the answer is as given, to sitting the assessment: preparation and perseverance are key. *Remember, giving up assures a fail but the difference between failing and succeeding is trying one more time!*

Good luck!

Ethics, Professional Conduct and Client Care

FUNCTIONING LEGAL KNOWLEDGE

Candidates are required to demonstrate their ability to act honestly and with integrity, and in accordance with the SRA Standards and Regulations as follows:

- the purpose, scope and content of the SRA Principles
- the purpose, scope and content of the:
  - SRA Code of Conduct for Solicitors, Registered European Lawyers and Registered Foreign Lawyers
  - SRA Code of Conduct for Firms in relation to:
    - managers in authorised firms
    - compliance officers

AUTHORITIES UNDERPINNING PRACTICE

The key authorities that underpin this area of practice are listed below. Note that for legislation you are linked to legislation.gov.uk.

Although much of the legislation on this government website is available in its amended form, the incorporation of new amendments into the text of legislation can be delayed. You should refer to legal databases to ensure you are referencing the most up-to-date legislation.

- SRA Code of Conduct 2019 for Solicitors, REL's and RFL's
  https://www.sra.org.uk/solicitors/standards-regulations/code-conduct-solicitors/
- Solicitors Regulation Authority Standards and Regulations
  https://www.sra.org.uk/solicitors/standards-regulations
- Criminal Finances Act 2017
  http://www.legislation.gov.uk/ukpga/2017/22/contents
- Data Protection Act 2018
  http://www.legislation.gov.uk/ukpga/2018/12/contents/enacted
- Legal Services Act 2007
  http://www.legislation.gov.uk/ukpga/2007/29/contents
- Money Laundering, Terrorist, Financing and Transfer of Funds (Information on the Payer) Regulations 2017 (SI 2017/692)
  http://www.legislation.gov.uk/uksi/2017/692/contents/made
- Proceeds of Crime Act 2002
  https://www.legislation.gov.uk/ukpga/2002/29/contents
- Terrorism Act 2000
  https://www.legislation.gov.uk/ukpga/2000/11/contents

B.1 Introduction

This chapter introduces ethics, professional conduct and client care in relation to solicitors and law firms. A practical understanding of ethics and professional conduct are fundamental to being a good solicitor; indeed, it is paramount that solicitors act with integrity and honesty while recognising the need to be guided by certain moral principles. Client care is covered within this chapter because it is important for all businesses, even more so for law firms. As a solicitor, you have an obligation to take care of your clients, though these are not always thought of as ethical concerns. Clients are usually facing challenging life circumstances when they contact a solicitor and they need to have trust and confidence in them to be able to deal with their matter well, whether it is part of their ethical obligations or in addition to them.

B.2 Introduction to ethics and professional conduct

Ethical principles have been recognised by the solicitors' profession for centuries. Many have argued the need to ensure a neutral partisanship: this holds that a solicitor must pursue a legal end for any client by any legal means. It is difficult, however, to balance the ethical conflicts between professional and personal morality. Ethics which arise by virtue of a solicitor's professional status are identified as professional or legal ethics. These ethics may at times be incompatible with what is morally required of non-professionals.

The Law Society was founded in 1825. At the Law Society's inception, the organisation was both the representative body and regulatory body for solicitors in England and Wales. It was only in 1960, however, that an actual text incorporating principles was published. It was called *A Guide to the Professional Conduct and Etiquette of Solicitors* and was written by the Law Society. The Solicitors' Practice Rules were then established in 1990 and were adhered to by solicitors until 1 July 2007, when the Code of Conduct 2007 was implemented.

The Solicitors Regulation Authority (SRA) is now the independent regulatory body overseeing the regulation of solicitors on behalf of the Law Society in England and Wales. It was created in January 2007, in anticipation of the Legal Services Act 2007 but also due to conflict within the profession and in an attempt to restore public trust in solicitors, which was an issue around that time. The SRA supports solicitors who are faced with moral dilemmas that arise in practice by setting out the principles and code of conduct which all solicitors and law firms in England and Wales must regulate and uphold. In the event of a conflict, the principles which safeguard the wider public interest take precedence over those relating to an individual client's interests. Solicitors should, where relevant, inform their client of the circumstances in which their duty to the court and other professional obligations will outweigh their duty to them. At the present time, the Code of Conduct 2019 is guided by trust, confidence and the protection of the public interest. It is as much about ethical values as moral principles.

B.2.1 Changes to the Code of Conduct

Since the first Code of Conduct was implemented in 2007 there have been two updates, one in October 2011 and the second, most recently, in November 2019. These are discussed in more detail later.

B.2.2 Code of Conduct 2007

The Code of Conduct 2007 was a lengthy and prescriptive code, supported by guidance. Along with the Code, there were also the Solicitors' Account Rules 1998, the SRA Recognised Bodies Regulations and the Client Financial Protection Requirements, which formed the regulatory authority to which solicitors had to adhere. Clearly, this was a lot of information placed in a number of different sources, and so it was time-consuming for solicitors to be able to understand and consult these when faced with an ethical dilemma.

B.2.3 Code of Conduct 2011 and SRA Handbook

The Code of Conduct 2011 was contained in the SRA Handbook which came into force for all firms on 6 October 2011. The purpose of the Handbook was to provide an accompanying set of rules and regulations which supported the standards and requirements which all law firms, in-house legal departments and alternative business structures were expected to uphold. There were ten Principles. They were all-pervasive and underpinned all of the Handbook requirements. The Code of Conduct chapters showed how the Principles would apply in certain contexts and focused on the quality of the service a solicitor was delivering to a client, using outcomes and indicative behaviours to generate what is known as 'outcomes focused regulation'. The 2011 Code was shorter and less prescriptive. The SRA hoped that this would offer greater flexibility as solicitors would need to use greater professional judgement to ensure compliance with the SRA. It was more detailed in some areas than others, which created uncertainty and led to some criticism. However, it did reflect the overall aim of the SRA which was to focus on the quality of what a solicitor was delivering to a client rather than prescribing how the solicitor had reached that stage.

B.2.4 Code of Conduct 2019

The SRA Standards and Regulations came into effect on 25 November 2019 and replaced the SRA Handbook. They can be found on the SRA website and, as they are published online only, they can be updated and amended regularly, so it is important to keep up to date with the website as there may have been changes since this manual was published. As well as making it easier to update, publishing the Standards and Regulations online was intended to make access to a solicitor or barrister easier for members of the public.

There was a change in this Code from a focus on indicative behaviour to one on ethical conduct, and there are now seven Principles rather than ten. There are also two types of Code of Conduct in the 2019 set of SRA Standards and Regulations.

Code of Conduct for Solicitors, Registered European Lawyers (RELs) and Registered Foreign Lawyers (RFLs) applies to those individuals who are authorised by the SRA to provide legal services.

Code of Conduct for Firms which applies to all bodies authorised by the SRA to provide legal services.

One of the reasons for creating a code for individual solicitors and another for firms is that the onus is now on a firm's management team to establish processes, structures and controls to ensure uniformity across the firm.

In light of the UK's withdrawal from the European Union (Brexit), the SRA's guidance on RFLs, initially published on 23 July 2019, was updated on 24 March 2021. See SRA Guidance: Registered Foreign Lawyers.

B.2.4.1 The Principles

The Principles, alongside the Code of Conduct, are the basis of ethical behaviour which the SRA expects individual solicitors as well as law firms, managers and employees, to uphold. The Principles were established by the SRA Enforcement Strategy which underpins all the requirements set out in the Principles, Codes, and rules and regulations. It provides a detailed explanation of the approach to taking regulatory action in the public interest. If the Principles come into conflict, those which safeguard the wider public interest and public confidence in solicitors take precedence over an individual client's interest. It is important to explain this potential situation to a client.

EXAMPLE

To demonstrate how the Principles can come into conflict, suppose a solicitor is asked to allow a witness to give evidence in support of their client, in the knowledge that the evidence is untrue. The solicitor would have to refuse to do this as the wider public interest and public confidence take precedence over the client.

The Principles are mandatory, and so a breach of these Principles may constitute professional misconduct which could result in a warning, a financial penalty, a referral to the Solicitors Disciplinary Tribunal or some level of control or disqualification from acting in certain roles. When faced with an ethical dilemma in practice, the Principles are where a solicitor should look initially for guidance.

The seven current Principles are as follows.

1. To act in a way that upholds the constitutional principle of the rule of law, and the proper administration of justice.
2. To act in a way that upholds public trust and confidence in the solicitors' profession and in legal services provided by authorised persons.
3. To act with independence.
4. To act with honesty.
5. To act with integrity.
6. To act in a way that encourages equality, diversity and inclusion.
7. To act in the best interests of each client.

EXAMPLE

In a corporate firm, a solicitor may be approached by a firm of brokers to refer all clients to them. They may be offered a large financial incentive to do this. This, however, would compromise their independence and so would not comply with the Principles above, apart from where certain conditions are met (Code of Conduct paras 5.1–5.3)). In particular to act with independence and to act in the best interests of each client. The solicitor would usually need to decline to act and suggest that the brokers provide a list of corporate firms in the area or link to the Law Society Find a Solicitor webpage, to allow the client to decide who they wished to instruct. This would avoid any risk of compromising the solicitor's independence and would allow them to continue to act in the best interests of each client who instructed them.

B.2.4.2 SRA Regulation

In line with the SRA Enforcement Strategy, the SRA seeks to:

- ensure a strong, competitive, and highly effective legal market
- ensure a focus on quality and client care
- promote a culture in which ethical values and behaviours are embedded

The SRA have a number of regulatory tools which are used in order to support compliance from law firms. The SRA Enforcement Strategy lists these as including:

- conducting thematic reviews of areas of risk
- publishing a risk outlook highlighting our priority risks
- providing advice and support through our Professional Ethics helpline and a range of toolkits and guidance
- SRA Innovate, a service which helps legal services providers to develop their business in new ways

In addition to the regulatory requirements set by the SRA Codes, Principles, rules and regulations, the SRA monitor and enforce the requirements relating to referral fees set out in s56 of the Legal Aid, Sentencing and Punishment of Offenders Act 2012. They also look at provisions relating to anti-money laundering which is mentioned at **B.3**.

B.2.5 **Compliance officers**

There are two different types of compliance officers. Compliance officers for legal practice (COLPs) and compliance officers for finance and administration (COFAs). All practices authorised by the SRA must appoint a COLP and a COFA. They are both a fundamental part of a law firm's compliance and governance arrangements as well as the culture of compliance within the firm. They have a broad number of responsibilities and may be liable for regulatory action if they fail to meet them. The Law Society Practice Note on Compliance Officers sets out a full list of the compliance officer roles, and best practice as to how breaches should be recorded and monitored.

COLPs and COFAs have a duty to report a serious breach of compliance to the SRA. This may go against the wishes of the managers of the practice. They have a duty to keep records of all breaches in order to recognise when one may be a serious breach. Managers are, however, responsible for their firm's compliance with the Code of Conduct. This responsibility is joint and several, if they share management responsibility with other managers of the firm.

EXAMPLE

A potential new solicitor applies to a firm for a job and in his additional paperwork he gives details of a physical disability which will require various reasonable adjustments to be made by his employer. The day after he submits this paperwork, the firm withdraws the job offer, giving only a brief explanation as to the reasons behind this decision. The solicitor makes a formal complaint to the firm, alleging disability discrimination.

The firm's COLP has a duty to investigate the complaint and write a report with their conclusion. If the COLP is satisfied that there is no regulation issue, then they would not need to report this.

If the COLP is, however, concerned about being misled by any staff involved in the decision then this must be reported, as a regulatory concern has arisen regarding potentially being given misleading information relating to the job offer being withdrawn.

B.2.6 **Complaints and the Legal Ombudsman**

If a client believes that their solicitor has not treated them fairly or professionally, they are entitled to complain. The main issues they may complain about are the way the case was handled or the costs for the services. If a client does complain then they will have been provided with details of how to complain by the law firm. The first step is usually to contact the solicitor to explain what the issue is and how it may be resolved. In most situations where a client complains, the matter will be resolved internally, and the complaint and file could be closed.

If the complaint has not been dealt with to the client's satisfaction or within eight weeks, then the client is entitled to complain to the Legal Ombudsman. The Legal Ombudsman deals with complaints across the entire legal profession, not just solicitors. There is a £400 fee potentially payable by the law firm which is being complained about. The aim of the Ombudsman is to use speed and informality to try and come to an agreement between the parties. If an agreement cannot be reached, then a decision is made by an officer of the Ombudsman. There are several remedies which may be available if the Ombudsman finds in favour of the complainant. There are also time limits (revised on 1 April 2023) which need to be adhered to by the client and the Ombudsman. Further details on remedies, limitations and the Legal Ombudsman can be found on the Law Society's website.

EXAMPLE

A client believes that his solicitor has not been honest with him about his chances for success and has not acted in his best interests. He feels that the solicitor encouraged him to take a matter to litigation and pay a large amount in legal fees; he subsequently lost the case and was told by the judge that he did not have a strong case in the first place. The client can lodge a complaint to the law firm but, if not satisfied with their response, then he could take it to the Legal Ombudsman.

If the client believes that a solicitor has breached the SRA Code of Conduct then they may contact the SRA direct in order to report it. Examples of breaches which a client may be concerned about include discrimination, fraud and dishonesty.

EXAMPLE

If a solicitor refused to continue acting for a client due to their religious belief, this would be a form of discrimination and thus a breach of the SRA Code of Conduct. The client could make a complaint to the law firm but, again, if not satisfied with their response then they could take it to the Legal Ombudsman and/or to the SRA.

B.2.7 **Conflicts of interest**

A solicitor has a duty to act in the best interests of their client and to make sure that these interests do not conflict with each other. This is a key area within ethics and professional conduct as it is important for public protection and for acting in relation to the client's best interests. There will be occasions when you find that your firm already acts for a client whose interests conflict with a potential new client. When this happens, then it is almost impossible to be able to act for both in their best interests. The Code of Conduct 2019 (paras 6.1–6.2) prevents a solicitor acting where a conflict of interest exists, apart from in very limited circumstances.

As the SRA Guidance on Conflicts explains (SRA Case Studies: Conflict of Interest) there are two types of conflict of interest situations. The first is a conflict between two or more clients, known as a 'conflict of interest'. The second is a conflict between the client's interests and the solicitor's interests, known as an 'own interest conflict'.

A solicitor can never act in an 'own interest conflict'; however, in certain circumstances they can act in a 'conflict of interest' situation. The best interests of the clients continuously need to be considered. There is also another conflict to consider which relates to Principle 1, to uphold the law, as solicitors are also officers of the court. There could be occasions where there is a conflict between acting in the best interests of your client (Principle 7) and your duty as an officer of the court. This is more common when conducting litigation. In this situation, a person's duty to the court would outweigh their duty to the client. An example of this is calling a witness to give evidence when the solicitor knows they are lying.

Paragraph 6.2 of the Code of Conduct 2019 outlines the circumstances where a solicitor may be able to act in a 'conflict of interest' situation:

> You do not act in relation to a matter or particular aspect of it if you have a conflict of interest or a significant risk of such a conflict in relation to that matter or aspect of it, unless:
>
> - the clients have a substantially common interest in relation to the matter or the aspect of it, as appropriate; or
> - the clients are competing for the same objective,
> - and the conditions below are met, namely that:
> - all the clients have given informed consent, given or evidenced in writing, to you acting;
> - where appropriate, you put in place effective safeguards to protect your clients' confidential information; and
> - you are satisfied it is reasonable for you to act for all the clients.

In practice, it is important to carry out a conflict check as soon as possible. Ideally, this information should be obtained from the client before the interview:

- name, address and telephone number;
- area of law on which advice is needed (eg crime, property, contract);
- name and address of any potential opponent or other involved (if applicable).

If this information is not obtained in advance of the interview, a conflict check should be done when the client arrives at the office and then the interview may progress if there is no conflict of interest. On occasions a client may not understand who the other parties are in their case and so once you recognise who they are then a conflict check must be carried out as soon as practicable. Money laundering regulations (discussed in more detail at **B3.3**), also demand information being taken into account, which supports the notion of conflict checks.

The SRA provides a helpful case study—see SRA Case Studies: Conflicts of Interest: Solicitors Regulation Authority.

EXAMPLE

There are many ways in which a conflict can arise in practice and some areas of law have more likelihood of a conflict than others. In a family law situation, a person may come to a law firm for advice when they are thinking about leaving a relationship, despite the other person being unaware of it. The advice provided could simply be a one-off appointment. A conflict would arise if at a later date the other person in the relationship came to the law firm for advice. In criminal law, a conflict could be where the criminal department of a firm represents someone accused of assaulting their wife and the wife attends the family department for advice on separation. In both instances, a solicitor would have to decline the instructions and provide details of other solicitors in their area who could assist in that area of law and/or provide them with the Law Society Find a Solicitor webpage.

B.2.8 Confidentiality

Confidentiality between a solicitor and client is one of the most important parts of their relationship. It is significant in the area of ethics and professional conduct as it is an area in which it is important that the solicitor receives all of the information from the client in order to provide the best advice, and that the client is confident that their solicitor will not release this to the public. The duty of confidentiality remains when the client retainer is terminated and even on the death of the client. Paragraphs 6.3–6.5 of the Code of Conduct 2019 state that a solicitor must keep the affairs of clients and former clients confidential apart from in limited situations. The main situations are if the client consents to the disclosure or if permitted by law.

Paragraph 6.2 the Code of Conduct 2019 outlines the situation when a solicitor may limit the information provided to a client:

> Where you are acting for a client on a matter, you make the client aware of all information material to the matter of which you have knowledge, except when:
>
> - the disclosure of the information is prohibited by legal restrictions imposed in the interests of national security or the prevention of crime;
> - your client gives informed consent, given or evidenced in writing, to the information not being disclosed to them;
> - you have reason to believe that serious physical or mental injury will be caused to your client or another if the information is disclosed; or
> - the information is contained in a privileged document that you have knowledge of only because it has been mistakenly disclosed.

Paragraph 6.5 of the Code of Conduct 2019 explains the limited circumstances when you can act for a client who has an adverse interest and where you hold confidential information:

> You do not act for a client in a matter where that client has an interest adverse to the interest of another current or former client of you or your business or employer, for whom you or your business or employer holds confidential information which is material to that matter, unless:
>
> - effective measures have been taken which result in there being no real risk of disclosure of the confidential information; or
> - the current or former client whose information you or your business or employer holds has given informed consent, given or evidenced in writing, to you acting, including to any measures taken to protect their information.

EXAMPLE

There are many ways in which an issue around confidentiality can arise in practice. In a criminal law firm, a person may come to a law firm for advice and you may overhear them on the telephone planning to sell drugs. In this case, in order to prevent a crime you would have to disclose this information to the police and would therefore be breaching confidentiality.

In a private client firm, a solicitor may have drafted a will for a lady who has now died. If her son contacts the solicitor after she has passed to ask if he has been left anything, then because of the duty of confidentiality the solicitor would be unable to tell him without the consent of the personal representatives of the will.

B.2.9 **Undertakings**

An undertaking made by a solicitor is a commitment to do or not do something that someone places reliance upon. An undertaking is binding and does not necessarily have to be made by a solicitor or use the word 'undertake'. It is often made to clients or third parties in a matter. Once the undertaking has been relied upon, then it cannot be withdrawn without the agreement of both parties.

Many areas of practice, such as conveyancing and litigation, rely on the giving and receiving of undertakings to progress matters. The solicitor giving the undertaking needs to be careful and is not obliged to give undertakings. If an undertaking is breached, then the solicitor could be sued personally for the money which was promised within the undertaking. The solicitor would have also breached the Code of Conduct and disciplinary proceedings would likely follow.

The SRA's Guidance on Undertakings, given by, or on behalf of, incorporated practice explains your obligations when undertakings are provided, by or on behalf of incorporated practices. This is because the Supreme Court decision in *Harcus Sinclair v Your Lawyers* [2021] UKSC 32 confirmed that the courts have no jurisdiction to enforce undertakings against incorporated practices. However, an incorporated practice could still face regulatory proceedings as there might have been a breach of our rules.

EXAMPLE

A solicitor is acting for a client in relation to debt matters and one large debt of £80,000 is owed by him to Jones Construction, who have written to ask for payment of the full amount within ten days. The client is in the process of selling a flat at auction, which has been valued at £100,000. The auction is in seven days and the solicitor provides an undertaking to Jones Construction to pay the £80,000 from the proceeds of sale from the flat.

The flat is only sold for £70,000 and Jones Construction has demanded the £80,000 from the solicitor. The solicitor must perform the undertaking and pay the full amount of £80,000. Failure to do so could be considered a breach of professional conduct.

In hindsight, what the solicitor should have done was to draft the undertaking but state that the payment would be limited to the amount received from the auction sale, or make it clear that they were not accepting responsibility for any personal liability.

B.2.10 **Alternate Business Structures (ABSs)**

It is worth noting that all of these regulations also bind ABSs. ABSs were introduced by the Legal Services Act 2007 and the SRA began accepting applications from prospective ABSs in January 2012. This allowed non-lawyers to own or invest in a law firm, when previously only lawyers could seek to create and operate a law firm. At the time, this was seen to be a huge change in the way law firms could function. They are still overseen by the SRA and the SRA decides whether a firm or business can become an ABS.

There are two key distinct ABS roles, those which entail the appointment of a recognised lawyer and those which do not require a qualified lawyer. There was a great deal of scepticism by many in the legal profession when the ABS was introduced. It was feared that big businesses would reduce the quality of legal work provided and that 'Tesco Law'-type businesses would emerge.

B.3 Money laundering

Money laundering is an illegal practice in which money generated from criminal activities is disguised and made to appear to have come from a legitimate source, in order to make it easier to spend the money and avoid suspicion. There are a wide variety of activities in which money may be attempted to be laundered. Examples of these are fraud, prostitution, robbery and the trafficking of drugs or people.

The purpose of anti-money laundering legislation is because solicitors' firms are often targeted in order to assist with money laundering. They can legitimise a transaction, have access to financial markets and often advise on property and business deals. It is therefore important for solicitors to understand the legislation, remain vigilant and to have the right training and processes in place in order to avoid the risk of facilitating this crime.

The Legal Sector Affinity Group (LSAG)'s Anti-Money Laundering Guidance for the legal profession, published in 2021, provides detailed guidance in this area.

Ensuring that solicitors do not facilitate money laundering is, of course, as much an ethical issue as a financial one. For more detail on money laundering regulations, see the financial services chapter in *Public Law, Legal Services & the Legal System.*

B.4 Client care

Client care is a fundamental part of the role of a solicitor. A client is required to be given information in a way that they understand and allows them to make decisions about the services they need, how their case will be handled and the options which are available to them (para 8.6 of the 2019 Code). They are also required to be provided with information about costs both at the time of engagement and as the matter progresses (para 8.7 of the 2019 Code). Most complaints from clients are either regarding not being updated about how the matter is progressing or with issues about costs.

B.4.1 General Data Protection Regulation

The UK General Data Protection Regulation (GDPR) sets out key principles, rights and obligations when processing personal data. It sits alongside the Data Protection Act 2018 and incorporates the EU GDPR, but, following Brexit, it allows the UK government the flexibility to review and amends its provisions. Personal data is essentially data that allows a living person to be directly or indirectly identified from information that is available. All solicitors hold personal data relating to both clients and employees. It is therefore crucial to be able to comply with the regulations. Knowing what personal data you have is the first step in compliance.

Further detailed guidance on the GDPR for solicitors can be found on the Law Society website.

B.4.2 The first interview

Some practical considerations are necessary in relation to client care and when meeting the client for the first time, it is important to be fully prepared. Clients may have a range of emotions depending on the areas of law you are advising on. It is important that the client is reassured, offered an appointment promptly and also that the solicitor is fully prepared for the first interview.

Before the interview, the Law Society, in its client information requirements practice note, advises that when the client attends the interview the following information must be explained to them and confirmed in writing:

- name and status of the solicitor or other person conducting the interview;
- information on the costs for the interview;
- details of who to contact if they have a complaint including the right to complain to the Legal Ombudsman, the time frame and the contact details.

This information can be prepared in a pro forma document in advance. It is important to keep a copy on file.

In the first interview, you must remember to cover all of the professional conduct issues, money laundering regulations, the GDPR and legal issues as well as to obtain the basic details from the client.

B.4.3 **Client care letter**

This letter is used by most law firms to set out the necessary client care information to a client. It is usually the first piece of correspondence you will send to your client and it is therefore an extremely important document. It must have certain regulatory information in it in order to comply with the Code of Conduct. It is usually also the retainer or contract between you and your client and is the beginning of the solicitor/client relationship. The Consumer Contracts (Information, Cancellation and Additional Charges) Regulations 2013 (SI 2013/3134) apply when you enter into a retainer with a consumer client who you have not met. This is often known as a distance contract.

B.4.4 **Fees and costs**

In most circumstances, you will have a direct retainer with the client and the client will be responsible for paying your costs. In certain areas of law, this may be different such as criminal law, family law and personal injury. In those areas, a client may be eligible for Legal Aid or there may be a 'no win, no fee' arrangement. Legal aid is the provision of assistance to people who are unable to afford legal representation and/or access to the court system. Firms must have a legal aid contract in order to be able to offer this service to clients and legal aid is only available in certain areas of law (usually family law and criminal law) and for clients who, in most cases, have a low income. More information regarding legal aid and how it is assessed can be found on the Gov.uk website.

'No win, no fee', often called a conditional fee agreement, is a legal fee arrangement whereby the client agrees to pay only if they win their case and is generally used in personal injury law. A damages-based agreement is another legal fee arrangement under which the client agrees to pay the solicitor a set percentage of the compensation they receive if they win the case.

In the situation where a client is paying your costs, there are several options available regarding how to charge a client for work. The main two ways of charging a client are by hourly rates or a fixed fee arrangement. Whichever way you do charge, it is essential to communicate this to the client and to provide the client with a likely overall cost of the matter. If the likely overall cost changes then it is important to advise the client of this as soon as possible in order to avoid any issues which may give rise to a complaint or a potential breach of the Code of Conduct.

B.4.5 **Advertising**

A solicitor cannot make an unsolicited approach to members of the public regarding the advertising of its legal services, but this does not apply to current or former clients. Any potential client referred to the firm by a current or former client will be seen as a member of the public (para 8.9 Code of Conduct for Solicitors, RELs and RFLs).

KEY POINT SUMMARY

- Ethics and professional conduct are fundamental to being a good solicitor.
- The Code of Conduct 2019 and the Principles provide the most up-to-date set of standards and requirements expected of solicitors, RELs and RFLs, and you should refer to them frequently.
- Breach of the Code of Conduct may constitute professional misconduct and could result in being fined, lead to criminal proceedings and/or being struck off from the roll of solicitors.
- It is crucial that solicitors have knowledge and understanding of the GDPR, money laundering and client care.

PART A
Introduction

CHAPTER 1
Introduction to Public Law, Legal Services and the Legal System

1.1 The purpose and context of this manual

This manual presents a discussion and explanation of the topics which cover public law, legal services and legal systems. These comprise the functioning legal knowledge required for the first of the SQE Functioning Legal Knowledge (FLK) assessments.

These topics will be assessed alongside:

- business law and practice;
- dispute resolution in contract and tort.

There are several areas covered in this *Public Law, Legal Services & the Legal System* manual. They have been included within one text as they incorporate foundations of the law and are a logical starting point to assist with learning the additional topics in the other assessed areas. The areas covered in this manual include:

- **The legal system of England and Wales and sources of law:**
  - legislation and interpretation;
  - the courts and precedent.
- **Public law, EU law and human rights:**
  - institutions of the state;
  - **separation of powers** and **rule of law**;
  - **judicial review**;
  - **public order**;
  - **the Human Rights Act 1998**;
  - **the Equality Act 2010**;
  - **EU law in the UK constitution**.
- **Legal services:**
  - **regulatory role of the SRA**.
  - financial services and **money laundering**;
  - funding options.

The topics within the legal system of England and Wales fit well alongside dispute resolution as they discuss the court hierarchy, the appeal system and jurisdiction. Constitutional and administrative law will also assist you in understanding how the law comes into force. Financial services and money laundering are an important aspect of business law and practice.

1.2 An overview of the legal system of England and Wales and sources of law

The legal system of England and Wales is one of the oldest in the western hemisphere. It can trace its origins back to the Norman Conquest of England in 1066. The Norman Conquest brought with it the concept of the **common law**. Under this system, in contrast to the legal systems of continental

Europe, decisions made by the judges in courts assumed the greatest importance in providing practical guidance for English subjects. Continental European legal systems, in contrast, were shaped by the concept of the civil law, itself based on the precepts of Roman law and latterly the French civil law. Under the civil law system, broad, general legal instructions were set out in a code, providing guidelines to be followed in a wide range of legal disputes, such as family and commercial disputes, governed by civil law codes and illegal behaviour offending the norms of society, such as theft, rape and assault being outlawed via criminal law codes.

The English legal system initially had no general overriding principles to guide it, thus the individual decisions of the judges dispensing justice locally became the main source of guidance and rules for human interaction. The risk of inconsistency inherent in such a disparate, individualised and decentralised process of adjudication required that a centralised system be created to reduce these risks. The common law system thus provided that decision-making by the judges became more consistent, coherent and competent. The consequence of this emphasis on judge-made decisions was that case law became of pivotal significance in shaping and forming the English legal system. Decisions by the judges, particularly by the judges in the highest courts of the land, became definitive pronouncements of the law and offered binding indicative guidance for the English populace to follow and to guide their future conduct. Thus, the system of binding judicial precedent was born. This system is based on the Latin maxim of *stare decisis*, that is 'the decision stands'. Judges were now legally bound to follow the earlier decisions of their peers, particularly from those judges who were their superiors. Judges will pronounce on various matters when announcing their decision. The legal reasoning behind their decision is known by its Latin maxim, the *ratio decidendi*, or for short, the *ratio*. This legal reasoning must be followed by later courts, unless the case can be distinguished; that is, the judge can show that the *ratio* does not apply to the facts of the present case.

Judges may often express their views on other legal matters peripheral to the matter in hand and these views are known by the Latin maxim '*obiter dicta*'; that is, things said by the way. These views are not binding on future judges deciding cases; however, these comments are often persuasive, having been expressed by some of the greatest legal minds in the country. Once these *obiter dicta* views are adopted by judges in a future case as the reason for deciding a case, these *obiter dicta* can be transformed into *ratio decidendi*.

The king's (or queen's) pronouncements and rulings, although legally important, were interpreted, applied and enforced by the system of royal courts that spread across the jurisdiction. Over the centuries, the bad behaviour of successive monarchs drove calls for reform of the constitution and the recognition that the Parliament, rather than God's representative in England, should be the main lawmaker for the realm. The English Civil War of the 17th century and the Glorious Revolution in 1688 ended the concept of the divine right of kings and instead emphasised the pre-eminent role of the Parliament as the ultimate lawmaker as opposed to that of the monarch.

The UK Parliament, over the past three centuries, has increasingly become more democratic in its composition and thus is now the main and pre-eminent source of law in the modern 21st-century democracy that is the UK. The UK Parliament is a sovereign legislature that can enact any law that it wishes since it is unlimited in its power. The UK Parliament will enact Acts of the UK Parliament as primary legislation and will endorse Statutory Instruments that are largely made by government ministers and are known as secondary legislation. Acts of the UK Parliament cannot be challenged by the courts and must be enforced and applied by the judiciary. The primary role of the judiciary in relation to legislation is to discover the true intention behind the UK Parliament when it enacted that law. Often, that simply means that the judges interpret the law literally. However, language is often imprecise and vague and cannot envisage all eventualities, thus judges may sometimes need to fill these ambiguous gaps. The judges are then entitled to draw on external aids to interpretation, such as debates within Parliament, grammatical rules and various canons of interpretation, in order to ensure that the law properly reflects the mischief that the law was designed to prevent.

Acts of the UK Parliament are the ultimate source of law in the UK, whilst case law or the common law is now the second most important source of law. Statutory Instruments are a primary source of law; however, they are subject to judicial review by a court where there have been defects in making that law. The increased importance of democracy for modern conceptions of the rule of law has precipitated devolution of legislative power to Scotland, Wales and Northern Ireland.

Legislation, both primary and secondary legislation—that is Acts of the UK Parliament and Statutory Instruments—and case law are considered primary sources of law. Secondary sources of law are commentaries by legal experts and writers, customary laws, the law of equity and even the case law of other common law countries.

The fact that the UK, as a sovereign state, can trace its history back through an unbroken millennium or more largely explains the uncodified nature of the UK legal system. The UK, although it has had a violent and volatile history, has not experienced constitutional upheaval of a level that has necessitated the promulgation of a written, codified constitution. Thus, the UK is one of only a tiny number of countries in the world that does not possess a specific, written constitution. The uncodified constitution of the UK is thus to be found across a wide range of historic and modern Acts of Parliament, **constitutional conventions** guiding the exercise of regal and governmental power and jurisprudence of the courts.

1.3 An overview of public law, EU law and human rights

The Human Rights Act 1998 (HRA 1998) has been in force for almost a quarter of a century and it underpins how we view and value an individual's human rights and uphold them within the law. Since its introduction, a large body of case law has developed, and solicitors need to have a working knowledge of the HRA 1998 and the European Convention on Human Rights (ECHR). It is an extremely large area of law and due regard to the most recent case law should be had in each and every case. In December 2020, the government commissioned a review appointing Sir Peter Gross as the Chair of the Independent Human Rights Act Review Panel (the Panel). The government's position is that the UK's contribution to human rights law is immense and founded in the common law tradition. Whilst there was a stated intention to remain a signatory to the European Convention on Human Rights there was nevertheless a review into its operation to keep pace with the ever-changing UK constitutional framework; as such, some refinement was called for. The Panel issued their report to the Deputy Prime Minister in October 2021, outlining identified options for consideration. The government published the Panel's report and then published its response in December 2021. The Panel considered both the relationship between domestic courts and the European Court of Human Rights and the impact of the HRA 1998 on the relationship between the judiciary, the executive and the legislature. Nevertheless, there remains intense tension between the government and the judiciary as regards the power of the judges to constrain executive and legislative power and questions are periodically raised about the UK's ongoing membership of the Council of Europe's ECHR system. **Chapter 8** on the HRA 1998 sets out the main tenets of the Convention and how they are to be applied within the context of UK legislation, providing a comprehensive overview of the main issues arising.

The Equality Act 2010 (EA 2010) came into force on 1 October 2010. The EA 2010 was designed to bring together multiple pieces of legislation into one single Act. It provides a legal framework to protect the rights of individuals and advance equality of opportunity for all, providing the UK with a discrimination law which protects individuals from unfair treatment and promotes a fairer more equal society. The EA 2010 sets out the **protected characteristics** and prohibits both **direct** and **indirect discrimination** where an individual possesses one of the protected characteristics and prohibits the **harassment** and **victimisation** of those individuals. Claims will normally be brought through the civil courts and if a claim derives from employment it can be brought in an employment tribunal. A successful claim in either the civil court or in a tribunal may result in damages and recommendations to reduce discrimination in the work environment. This is a complex area of law requiring in-depth knowledge of the provisions of the EA 2010 and how they can be enforced. **Chapter 9** on the 2010 Act details the protected characteristics contained within the Act and how they can be enforced in practice.

Public law refers to the general body of law that regulates the relationship between the individual and the state. It encompasses a range of specific categories of law, such as constitutional law, administrative law, criminal law and tax law. The state, for this purpose, includes His Majesty's Government, government departments, government agencies, public bodies, the civil service, local authorities, the police, the armed forces, prisons, the NHS, courts and tribunals and regulatory and supervisory bodies. The rule of law requires that these public entities are subject to the law and accountable under the law. Their decision-making powers must be exercised according to the law.

This does not mean just a narrow conception of the law and the legal rules applicable to their decision-making. Decisions, in order to be lawful, must also be rational, fair, just, proportionate and exercised compatibly with human rights norms. The rule of law also stipulates that the three great divisions of the state—that is the executive, the legislature and the judiciary—follow the separation of powers principle, such that they should not encroach on each other's remit. Requiring the lawmaker to make law, judges to judge cases and the executive to run the country ensures that these branches of the state concentrate on their core functions and do not stray into the territory of the other branches of state. This doctrine provides for a system of checks and balances on the exercise of power. However, in the absence of a formal, codified constitution, the separation of powers doctrine is not as strictly delineated in the UK as it is in other states with a written constitution.

Public law empowers UK citizens, non-UK citizens and corporations and other corporate entities to challenge the decisions of these public entities. Aggrieved individuals and companies may seek redress in specialist tribunals, through a statutory complaints procedure, through direct requests to the **public body**, through an Ombudsman system or ultimately via the process known as judicial review.

Judicial review is where a judge examines whether a public body's decisions or its failure to act is lawful. Judicial review is undertaken either by the Administrative Court which is part of the King's Bench Division of the High Court of Justice or in the Upper Tribunal. The system of judicial review is more a system of last resort rather than of first resort—claimants should utilise other means of securing a remedy first. This feature of judicial review also means that access to the Administrative Court or Upper Tribunal is restricted in order to prevent a flood of claims against public bodies. Judges will filter cases out on the basis of both the nature and likelihood of success of the complaint and the individual position of the claimant. Cases will only proceed where permission has been granted and claimants need to show sufficient standing or interest in the case to justify their place in court.

In judicial review, the judge will determine whether the public body acted beyond its powers, whether it exercised its discretion lawfully, whether its procedures were unfair or whether it acted irrationally or disproportionately. Where the judge determines that the public body has acted unlawfully, the court has a range of options available to it according to the nature of the breach. Thus, the court may issue: a quashing order to overturn the original decision; a prohibiting order stopping the body taking future action that would be unlawful; a mandatory order forcing the public body to take appropriate action; a declaration that definitively sets out the legal position; a declaration of incompatibility under the HRA 1998 stating the public body's action goes against the human rights of the claimant; or it may simply award monetary damages. The judge is also able to grant **injunctions** against the public body.

Public law is not just about the state and the legality of the activities of public bodies. Public law also encompasses maintenance of the King's peace. The police are primarily tasked with the role of maintaining law and order, although every citizen of the UK is also enjoined to uphold the King's peace. The Public Order Act 1986 places a number of common law offences on a statutory footing. The 1986 Act criminalises rioting, affray and violent disorder and provides for specific offences of placing people in fear of violence and behaviour that harasses, alarms or distresses people. The Act also provides for the criminalisation of certain actions that evidence hatred of people on the grounds of race, sexual orientation and religion. The Act also regulates public processions and assemblies, seeking to strike a workable balance between the need to maintain public order and open access to public highways and public spaces with the essential democratic right to gather, assemble, march and demonstrate against the government or for a legitimate cause.

The modern public law of the UK has been heavily influenced by the UK's 47-year membership of the European Union. During UK membership of the EU, the EU legislative institutions, that is the European Parliament and the Council of the European Union plus the European Commission, were able to legislate for the UK through the promulgation of secondary legislation known as **Regulations**, **Directives** and Decisions. The European Court of Justice case law was a direct source of law and the founding Treaties of the EU had to be followed and given effect in the UK legal system. The twin concepts of supremacy and direct effect of EU law meant that EU law had to have primacy over inconsistent domestic legislation, including Acts of Parliament; national judges had to interpret national law, where possible, in accordance with EUlaw; and, in the event of conflict between national law and EU law, individuals were entitled to compensation for damages sustained under the doctrine of state liability and the UK was financially liable to the EU itself for its failure to fulfil its EU law obligations.

Notwithstanding the fact that the UK left the EU on the last day of 2020 (Brexit day), EU law still plays a decreasing part in UK public law. The European Union (Withdrawal) Act 2018 cut off the power of the EU institutions to make law for the UK by repealing the European Communities Act 1972 on Brexit day. However, in order to prevent a legal vacuum and legal confusion arising, the 2018 Act froze significant aspects of EU law and incorporated that body of law into UK law as 'retained EU law'. The ability to diverge from EU rules and law was a defining feature of calls to leave the EU; thus the 2018 Act grants wide legislative powers to UK ministers to enact Statutory Instruments (commonly known as Henry VIII executive powers) to amend, revise or remove 'retained EU law' from the UK statute book.

By virtue of this power, over 100,000 amendments have been made to this corpus of law via the promulgation of over 1,000 pieces of secondary legislation. The Retained EU Law (Revocation and Reform) Act 2023 further significantly amends the nomenclature, scope and treatment of retained EU law. A whole swathe of retained EU law was expunged from the statute book on the 31 December 2023 by virtue of this act. The EU derived law that remains is now known as 'assimilated law' and possesses no special features. In particular, domestic judges are now given greater latitude to depart from assimilated case law and no longer interpret assimilated law in light of EU interpretative principles and tenets.

The European Union (Withdrawal Agreement) Act 2020 provided for the ratification of the international law agreement between the UK and the EU, the Brexit Withdrawal Agreement and for that agreement to be given legal effect in the UK. This Act provided that EU law would continue to have legal effect in the UK during the implementation period.

The European Union (Future Relationship) Act 2020 gives domestic legal effect to the EU–UK Trade and Cooperation Agreement between the UK and the EU.

1.4 An overview of legal services

Solicitors' professional and ethical responsibilities are underpinned by a need to ensure high standards of skill, competence and integrity in the provision of legal services, for the benefit and protection of clients and to support the administration of justice. The Solicitors Regulation Authority (SRA) sets the standards required of the solicitors and law firms that it regulates and has the power to take regulatory action, in the interests of protecting clients and maintaining the rule of law, against any solicitor or firm that fails to comply with the high standards required from the profession. The legal services chapters in **Part D** of the manual provide guidance on the SRA's regulatory regime.

The SRA's powers are wide-ranging. It can investigate any alleged breaches of standards and regulations and has power to impose significant sanctions and penalties against individuals and firms who fail to uphold standards. In respect of the most serious failures or breaches by solicitors, the SRA may issue disciplinary proceedings at the **Solicitors Disciplinary Tribunal** (SDT), which may result in solicitors being struck off the roll. **Part D** of the manual considers the SRA's regulatory powers, and its relationship with the SDT, in more detail.

The part also contains detail on the provision of **reserved legal activities** and on the protection which must be afforded to clients by way of compulsory **professional indemnity insurance**.

Solicitors must comply with the SRA's Standards and Regulations and act in the best interests of each client at all times. They must ensure that, as well as providing the highest standards of advice and service to their clients, they carefully consider their client's needs when advising on options to pay for legal services.

The best way for a client to pay for the legal services that they require will vary greatly depending on the nature of a client's matter and, potentially, on the individual characteristics and financial means of each client. **Part D** introduces students to a range of different funding options for legal services and to some of the circumstances in which particular funding methods may be appropriate. The chapters in that part also set out when and how solicitors must provide information about legal costs and the possible consequences of failing to provide appropriate advice.

Financial services and money laundering are important aspects of legal services and solicitors must be aware of the legislation and regulations in relation to both of these areas in order to avoid facing disciplinary action, a fine or even imprisonment. Most solicitors will provide work in relation to financial services at some point in their career. If they do, they must be able to comply with the regulations set out by the Financial Conduct Authority (FCA) and the SRA. Breach of these regulations could be classed as an offence. There are two separate offences set out under the Financial Services and Markets Act 2000, both of which can result in imprisonment and/or fines.

In addition, money laundering is a crime and something which solicitors must be aware of in order to avoid the risk of facilitating that crime. One of the purposes of anti-money laundering legislation is aimed at solicitors' firms because they are often targeted in order to assist with money laundering. They can legitimise a transaction, have access to financial markets and often advise on property and business deals.

Part D must be considered alongside the SRA's Standards and Regulations and the FCA Regulations. Applicable provisions of the Standards and Regulations are highlighted throughout the chapters.

1.5 Overview of professional conduct in public law, legal services and the legal system

In your study of the legal system and the ethics of professional conduct, you will encounter the regulatory role of the SRA in its supervision of solicitors. It is a requirement of all the SQE assessments that candidates demonstrate their ability to act honestly and with integrity, and in accordance with the SRA Standards and Regulations.

Given the breadth of the subject matter contained in this manual, students should work on the basis that all SRA Principles and provisions of the Codes of Conduct are relevant. The specific provisions of the SRA regulatory regime which are relevant to individual topics are clearly indicated within the appropriate chapters.

1.6 And onward

This introduction provides an overview of the variety of topics which cover public law, legal services and the legal system. The objective is to help you to develop your knowledge and understanding of the legal and regulatory landscape in which solicitors operate, and to introduce you to many of the important considerations and principles underpinning the provision of legal services by solicitors.

KEY POINT SUMMARY

Solicitors must ensure that at all necessary times during practice they:

- consider the best interests of each client;
- comply with the SRA's regulatory regime (including but not limited to the Principles and the Codes of Conduct);
- consider the individual circumstances of each client and matter when advising on funding options;
- observe the rule of law, acting equitably, fairly and ethically towards clients, other legal professionals, the courts and public authorities;
- only present arguable assertions and statements, present only relevant legal authorities and highlight to the court adverse case law and statutory provisions in addition to their own legal authorities;
- consider the implications of the Human Rights Act 1998;
- consider the provisions of the Equality Act 2010;
- comply with the Financial Services and Markets Act 2000 and secondary legislation when relevant;
- consider the provisions of anti-money laundering legislation including in the international context.

PART B

The Legal System of England and Wales and Sources of Law

CHAPTER 2
Legislation and Interpretation

FUNCTIONING LEGAL KNOWLEDGE

This chapter covers the following functional knowledge required to pass the SQE 1 assessments:

Legislation and interpretation
Primary legislation: the structure of an Act of Parliament
Powers and procedures for the enactment, implementation and repeal of primary and secondary legislation

Statutory interpretation:

- the literal rule
- the golden rule
- the mischief rule
- the purposive approach
- presumptions
- aids to statutory interpretation and construction

AUTHORITIES UNDERPINNING PRACTICE

The key authorities that underpin this area of practice are listed below. Note that for legislation you are linked to legislation.gov.uk.

Although much of the legislation on this government website is available in its amended form, the incorporation of new amendments into the text of legislation can be delayed. You should refer to legal databases to ensure you are referencing the most up-to-date legislation.

- Interpretation Act 1978
  https://www.legislation.gov.uk/ukpga/1978/30/contents
- European Convention on Human Rights 1950
  https://www.echr.coe.int/documents/convention_eng.pdf
- Human Rights Act 1998
  https://www.legislation.gov.uk/ukpga/1998/42/contents
- European Union (Withdrawal Act) 2018
  https://www.legislation.gov.uk/ukpga/2018/16/contents/enacted

2.1 Introduction

It is a fundamental tenet of the UK legal system that the UK Parliament is supreme. The single biggest consequence of this principle is that the power of the UK Parliament to make law is absolute. The second consequence is that Acts of the UK Parliament are the highest source of law in the UK legal system.

Acts of the UK Parliament are unlimited in their scope and range and can change any aspect of the law and the legal system. Since every Parliament is born free, any limitations placed on legislative power by a previous Parliament can be reversed. In the same way, no Act of Parliament can be immune from repeal or dictate the future type of law that can be enacted; however, there are now special Acts of Parliament known as constitutional statutes which enjoy a higher status than ordinary Acts such that their terms can only be expressly repealed and not by necessary implication (see the discussion later).

The fluid nature of the UK's uncodified constitutional structure allows for the coexistence of other legislative bodies alongside the UK Parliament. Thus, for 48 years, between 1973 and 2020, when the UK was a member of the European Union, the EU institutions enacted laws that were given legal effect within the UK by the European Communities Act 1972. Modern conceptions of local democracy have also presaged the existence of devolved legislatures in Scotland, Wales and Northern Ireland. These legislatures are not sovereign and thus their Acts can be struck down as being unconstitutional by the courts as being made ***ultra vires*** (beyond the powers of the body) or in conflict with the Human Rights Act 1998 (HRA 1998) (see **Chapter 6** on **judicial review** and **Chapter 8** on the HRA 1998).

UK membership of international organisations and the accession of the UK to international treaties requires that judges should interpret UK law in light of these international law obligations and that the jurisdiction of the UK will not normally go beyond what is permitted by international law.

Legal policy dictates that national law should be in accordance with public international law (*R v Secretary of State for the Home Department, ex p Brind* [1991] 1 AC 696). Positions contrary to international law, however, will be enforced where that intention is clear. Stronger principles apply as regards the European Convention on Human Rights (ECHR) via the HRA 1998 and as regards the compatibility of UK law with EU law during the UK's membership of the EU.

Making law is the classic role of a legislature (*River Wear Commissioners v Adamson* (1877) 2 App Cas 743). When making law, the legislature should express its intentions behind that law as clearly as possible. As regards the UK sovereign Parliament, its legislative acts are an expression of its will, and are primarily designed to regulate life and society within the UK, giving guidance to the citizenry as to what is legal and illegal, what is acceptable and what is impermissible. All legislation, by its very nature, offers broad generalisations and as such cannot provide for every eventuality. Language is subject to nuance and interpretation and thus enactments can sometimes give rise to ambiguity and legal uncertainty. The task of resolving those ambiguities and uncertainties falls to the domestic courts. In those situations, the courts must investigate the wider context of the law by reference to public policy, including legal policy and the purpose of the legislation. Construction should look at the legislation as a whole, the context in which it was enacted and should be done for the benefit of the citizenry. It is an objective exercise (Lord Nicholls in Spath Holme [2001] 2 AC 349, at 396). The result of this construction is the legal meaning of the Act (*Heydon's Case* (1584) 3 Co Rep 7).

However, in order to ensure consistency and coherency in the law, judges are bound by the confines of legislative interpretative rules and any interpretation of legislation by any other body, such as the police, local authorities, regulators, enforcement agency, government department and the legislature itself is not authoritative (*R v London Transport Executive, ex p Greater London Council* [1983] QB 484).

This chapter provides an overview of the main features of UK legislation and then discusses the interpretative framework that must be applied by judges when called upon to interpret legislation in a case before them.

2.2 **Acts of the UK Parliament**

2.2.1 **Validity of Acts of the UK Parliament**

Acts of the UK Parliament are the highest source of law in the UK legal system. As such, their validity cannot be questioned by the courts and courts must apply and enforce the terms of such enactments. More generally, by virtue of the **separation of powers** doctrine (see **Chapter 5** on the separation of powers and the **rule of law**) proceedings in Parliament cannot be questioned by any other body, such as the courts by virtue of art IX of the Bill of Rights 1689. This doctrine operates such that any irregularity, even one as serious as an allegation of fraud, cannot be used to question an Act's validity (*Edinburgh and Dalkeith Rly Co v Wauchope* (1842) 8 Cl & Fin; *British Railways Board v Pickin* [1974] AC 765 and *R (on the application of A, J, K, B and F) v Secretary of State for the Home Department* [2022] EWHC 360 (Admin)). Similarly, arguments suggesting that an Act of Parliament is contrary to reason, morality or international law will now not be entertained, given the centrality of the concept of **parliamentary sovereignty** to the contemporary UK legal system (*Bonham's (Dr) Case* (1610) 8 Co Rep 114a):

> It is not for the court to say that a Parliamentary enactment, the highest law in the country, is illegal
>
> (*Cheney v Conn (Inspector of Taxes)* [1968] 1 All ER 779 at 782 (Ungoed-Thomas J))

2.2.2 Scope, focus and nature of Acts of the UK Parliament

Acts of the UK Parliament can cover any aspect of life in the UK. Acts can be public or private or be a hybrid of the two, be general or specific, can extend to the entire territory of the UK or only apply to one or more of the four nations of the UK or to a local area. Acts can be criminal or civil in nature. They may declare the law or amend the law.

An Act of the UK Parliament is a legislative declaration from the sovereign in Parliament. The monarch gives **royal assent** to a Bill that has received the advice and consent of both Houses of Parliament.

Where an Act is a public Act, then that Act is deemed to be judicially noted; that is, the judges are presumed to know the contents of that law (s3 and Sch 2, para 2 Interpretation Act 1978; *Greenwich London Borough Council v Powell* [1989] AC 995; *The Prince's Case* (1606) 8 Co Rep 1a at 13b). By contrast, a private Act is not judicially noted and must be affirmed and proved by the claimant in a court of law.

Public Bills are Bills that affect the **public interest** and the general public at large whilst private Bills affect private interests only (Private Bills in Parliament). Private Bills are brought to Parliament by the organisation or individual that wants to change the rules that apply to them or to ask for new powers and are effectively private legislation. All government Bills are classified as public Bills because they will apply to a broad section of the population and are sponsored by the UK government. There are also Acts that affect particular private interests for the public good and are thus known as hybrid Bills (*R (HS2 Action Alliance Ltd) v Secretary of State for Transport* [2014] UKSC 3 at [57]).

EXAMPLES

Public Bill: Coronavirus Bill 2020. This Bill was a government Bill to contain the Covid-19 virus by restricting the liberty and freedom of everyone in the UK. This Bill became the Coronavirus Act 2020.

Private Bill: one of the last private Bills to be passed was the George Donald Evans and Deborah Jane Evans (Marriage (Enabling) Act 1987).

Hybrid Bill: the creation of the HS2 rail network necessitated major interference with land around the proposed route. This high-speed rail network was designed to benefit millions of people but was controversial from an environmental perspective and required significant public investment. The decision to take forward this project was one that Her Majesty's Government took, thus it was of public interest; however, it directly affected the private lives of people living alongside the route; therefore Bills designed to achieve this objective are hybrid Bills. Examples of these laws include the High Speed Rail (West Midlands–Crewe) Act 2021.

The vast majority of Acts of the UK Parliament are permanent Acts. These Acts will subsist until they are repealed by a later enactment. Some Acts are passed as temporary Acts, meaning that they expire after a set period of time, unless extended. Such temporary Acts will have a sunset clause setting out when the law expires (*Willcock v Muckle* [1951] 2 KB 844). An example of a temporary Act is the Coronavirus Act 2020 (s89 provided that operational aspects of the Act expired two years after the passing of the Act).

The majority of Acts of the UK Parliament come into effect as soon as they are passed or on the date specified within them. However, some acts are not self-operating and will only become operational when a separate external trigger is activated.

In general, Acts of Parliament should be dynamically interpreted according to current, contemporary situations and terminology. A dynamic interpretation is necessary to ensure that the law remains relevant and is not frozen in time.

EXAMPLE

The Protection of Children Act 1978, as amended, made it an offence to make indecent photographs of children. The courts interpreted the word 'make' to include the downloading of an image from the internet onto a computer screen and opening an image in an email attachment (*R v Jayson and Smith* [2002] 1 Cr App R 13).

In exceptional cases, some Acts of Parliament may need to be statically interpreted in the form of the original enactment, such that the judges must not interpret the law according to contemporary conditions.

2.2.3 **Special types of Acts of the UK Parliament**

2.2.3.1 Constitutional statutes

The UK constitution is uncodified, meaning that it is found across various **common law** principles, **constitutional conventions** and increasingly in the form of Acts of Parliament. Historically, Acts of Parliament were not subject to any rigid hierarchy of importance or significance. As the supreme source of law of the country, Acts of the UK Parliament were created equal and must be treated equally. As the jurist A V Dicey said:

> . . . neither the Act of Union with Scotland nor the Dentists Act 1878 has more claim than the other to be considered a supreme law.
>
> (*Law of the Constitution* (Macmillan, 1885), 145)

Thus, an Act of Parliament that regulates benign or insignificant issues, is a niche law or applies to a specific locality is equal, in legal superiority terms, to an Act of Parliament that has pre-eminent constitutional implications. However, this legal fiction, when it meets practical and political reality, must cede. Certain Acts of Parliament are more important constitutionally than simple regulatory laws. The question that has to be addressed is what is the significance of these important Acts of Parliament? This question started to be directly answered in the seminal case of the Metric Martyrs as regards the clash of UK weights and measures legislation with the provisions of EU law (*Thoburn v Sunderland CC* [2002] 4 All ER 156). This case suggested that some Acts of Parliament were not simply 'ordinary' statutes but were of such seismic importance that they had to be considered 'constitutional' statutes. Such special statutes could then only be expressly repealed by the clear and unambiguous terms of a later statute. It was suggested that the list of constitutional statutes was open-ended and extended to laws such as Magna Carta, the Bill of Rights 1689, the Act of Union 1707 between England and Scotland, the Reform Acts that extended the electoral franchise, the European Communities Act 1972 which took the UK into the EEC, the HRA 1998 which gave domestic legal effect to the ECHR and the laws of devolution, such as the Scotland Act 1998 and the Government of Wales Act 1998.

The answer to the question of the legal status of constitutional Acts was further refined by the Supreme Court in 2014. In the case of *R (HS2 Action Alliance Ltd) v Secretary of State for Transport* [2014] UKSC 3, the Supreme Court held that there was indeed a concept of constitutional instruments that were immune from implied repeal and further added the Petition of Right 1628, the Act of Settlement 1701 and the Constitutional Reform Act 2005 to the classification of constitutional statutes. Further, it is also generally agreed that Acts that amend the principal constitutional instruments outlined above are to be viewed themselves as constitutional instruments, such as the Parliament Acts 1911 and 1949, the Crown Proceedings Act 1947, the House of Commons Disqualification Acts 1957 and 1975, the Crown Estate Act 1961, the Senior Courts Act 1981 and the Constitutional Reform and Governance Act 2010.

Notwithstanding designation as constitutional instruments, these statutes can still be expressly repealed and replaced by a later enactment.

2.2.3.2 Acts giving effect to international conventions

As a classically dualist state, international law obligations will only be legally binding under UK law when those obligations have been brought into the UK legal system. The UK does not treat international treaties as having self-executing status; that is, that they can have automatic legal status in the country; rather the international law will need to be legally brought into the UK legal system (*Fothergill v Monarch Airlines Ltd* [1981] AC 251; *Kaur v Lord Advocate* [1980] 3 CMLR 79; and more recently *R (on the application of SC, CB and 8 children) v Secretary of State for Work and Pensions* [2021] UKSC 26 at [77])). There are three main ways in which these public international law obligations can be given legal effect in the UK legal system.

First, the Act of Parliament may directly enact the international treaty into national law. Secondly, the Act of Parliament may provide for the terms of the international treaty to have legal effect in the UK, known as indirect enactment (*The Hollandia* [1982] QB 872) and lastly relevant Acts of Parliament may simply refer to the existence of the international obligation and therefore the presumption applies that the UK Parliament enacts law in accordance with public international law.

The judges presume that the UK Parliament, in enacting law, does so in compliance with international law. Thus, where an Act is promulgated to give effect to international law, any ambiguity in meaning should be resolved in favour of that law. The judges will even look to the approach taken by other countries in complying with that international law. Nevertheless, an express intention of the UK Parliament to renege on that agreement or otherwise not comply with that international obligation will be enforced by domestic judges.

2.2.3.2.1 Financial Acts

The House of Commons has the exclusive power to raise and spend public money and thus has been given the power to make **delegated legislation** under the Provisional Collection of Taxes Act 1968. Taxes need to be levied fairly, collected honestly and not oppressively and then spent according to the will of Parliament. In constitutional terms, the Crown will demand money, the Commons will then grant it and the Lords will then assent to that grant. Thus, the House of Commons can pass budget resolutions which have the force of an Act once the relevant Finance Bill has been passed.

2.2.3.2.2 Law reform Acts

Law reform Acts are designed to modernise, update, reform or re-focus existing law. They can take the form of a consolidation Act, a codifying Act or as a miscellaneous statute which amends disparate areas of law at the same time. Reforming Acts may also remove obsolete, unnecessary or irrelevant law from the statute book. A consolidation Act will bring together all the statutory law on a subject area whilst a codifying Act will bring together both the statutory and common law that relates to a subject.

2.2.3.2.3 The process of enacting Acts of Parliament

Every Act of the UK Parliament starts life as a Bill in one of the two Houses of Parliament, that is, either the House of Commons or the House of Lords. The overwhelming majority of Bills are government Bills since it is the primary role of the executive to initiate legislative proposals. Alongside proposals for Acts of Parliament, the government produces high volumes of secondary legislation, such as Orders in Council and Statutory Instruments (SIs) (the general power to enact Statutory Instruments is set out in the Statutory Instruments Act 1946, c. 36). Statutory instruments generally fall into three categories, namely Orders, Regulations and Rules, although SIs may also be called Schemes, Directions and Declarations. The texts of these legislative proposals are prepared by draftspeople from the Office of the Parliamentary Counsel (https://www.gov.uk/government/organisations/office-of-the-parliamentary-counsel) (Drafting Guidance 2024 (https://www.gov.uk/government/publications/drafting-bills-for-parliament/2024-03-19-drafting-guidance) (Cabinet Office Guide to Making Legislation 2022, https://assets.publishing.service.gov.uk/media/62fe365fe90e0703e1bb4844/2022-08_Guide_to_Making_Legislation_-_master_version__4_.pdf).

Bills may also be initiated by other official agencies such as the Law Commission (Law Commission Act 2009).

Less commonly, individual MPs and Members of the Lords can put forward legislative proposals. These are known as **Private Members' Bills**. Unless these Bills receive the backing of the government, they will probably fall since they will not be given enough parliamentary time for their discussion and enactment. These Bills are chosen for debate via a ballot system.

A Bill will become law in the UK once both Houses of Parliament have assented to it and the monarch has granted the royal assent. Special rules apply to Bills subject to the rules of the Parliament Acts 1911 and 1949. Under these provisions, Bills can be turned into law notwithstanding the fact that the House of Lords has not assented to the Bill (*R (on the application of Jackson) v Attorney-General* [2005] UKHL 56). Once the Bill receives royal assent, the King's Printer publishes public general Acts (see **Chapter 4** on the institutions of the state).

2.2.3.2.4 The structure of an Act

Acts of Parliament are made up of a number of constituent parts (see **Figures 2.1** to **2.4**). At the start of every Act there will be the enacting formula which sets out that the process of making the law has been complied with.

EXAMPLE

The typical enacting formula is:

> Be it enacted by the King's most Excellent Majesty, by and with the advice and consent of the Lords Spiritual and Temporal, and Commons, in this present Parliament assembled, and by the authority of the same, as follows.
>
> (Erskine May, *Parliamentary Practice* (Charles Knight & Co, 1844), para 26.9)

Special rules apply to legislation such as finance Bills and Bills passed through use of the Parliament Acts 1911 and 1949. These laws utilise differently worded enacting formula since they are created using different parliamentary processes.

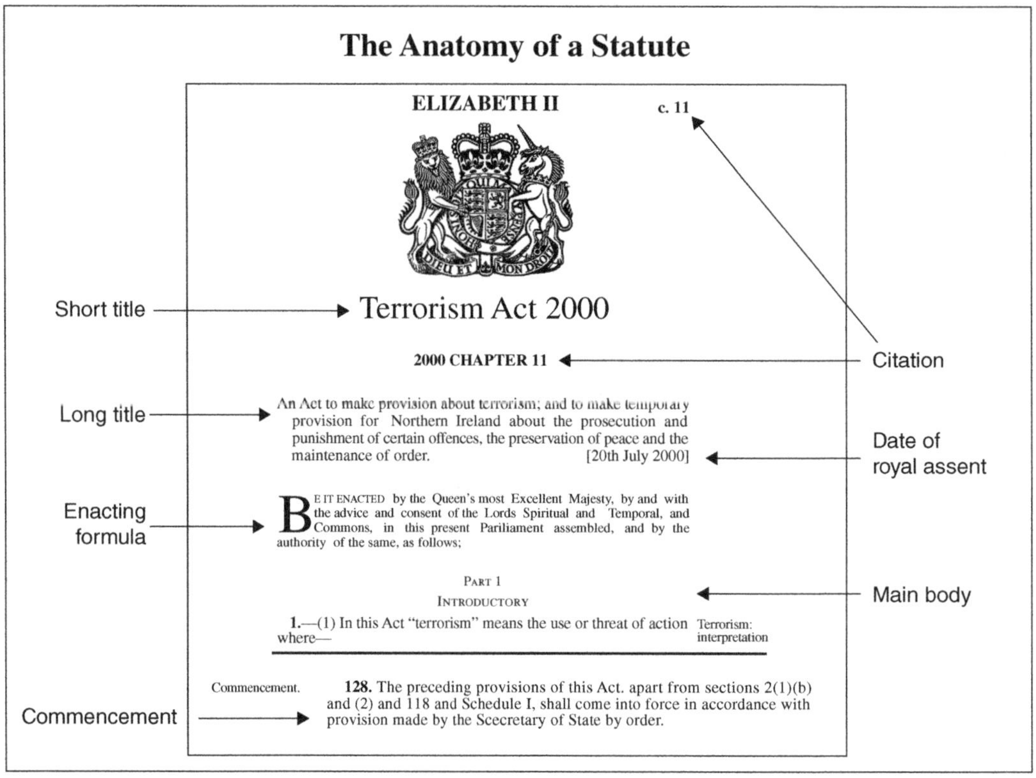

FIGURE 2.1 The anatomy of a statute

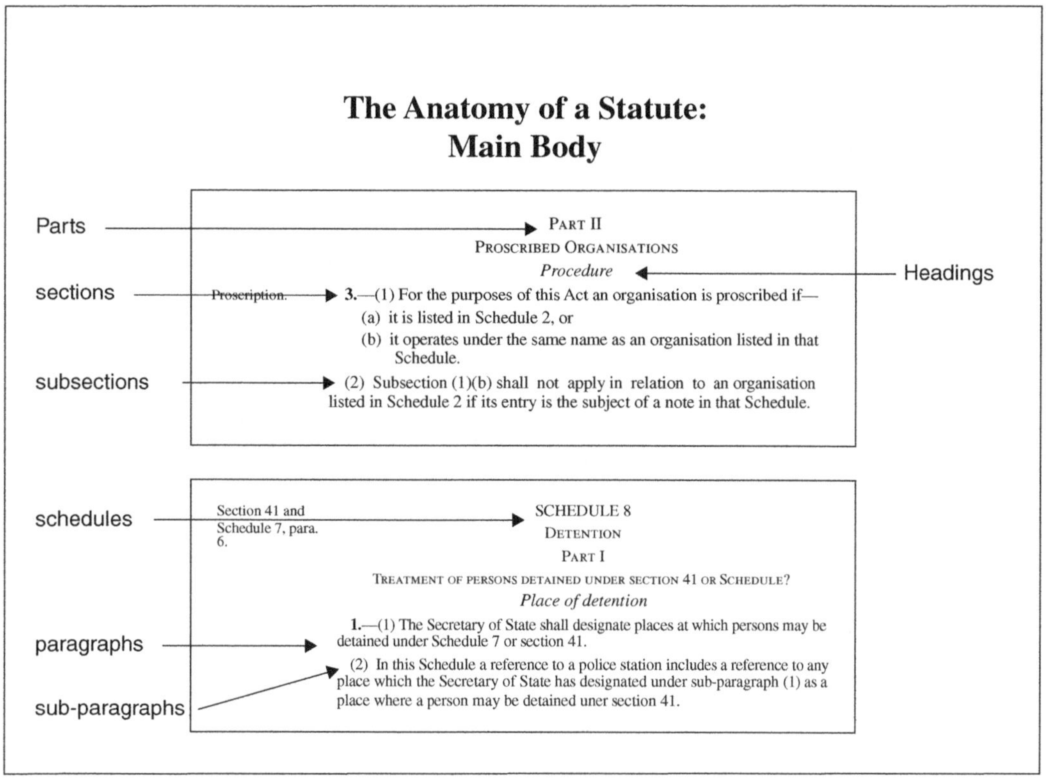

FIGURE 2.2 The anatomy of a statute: main body

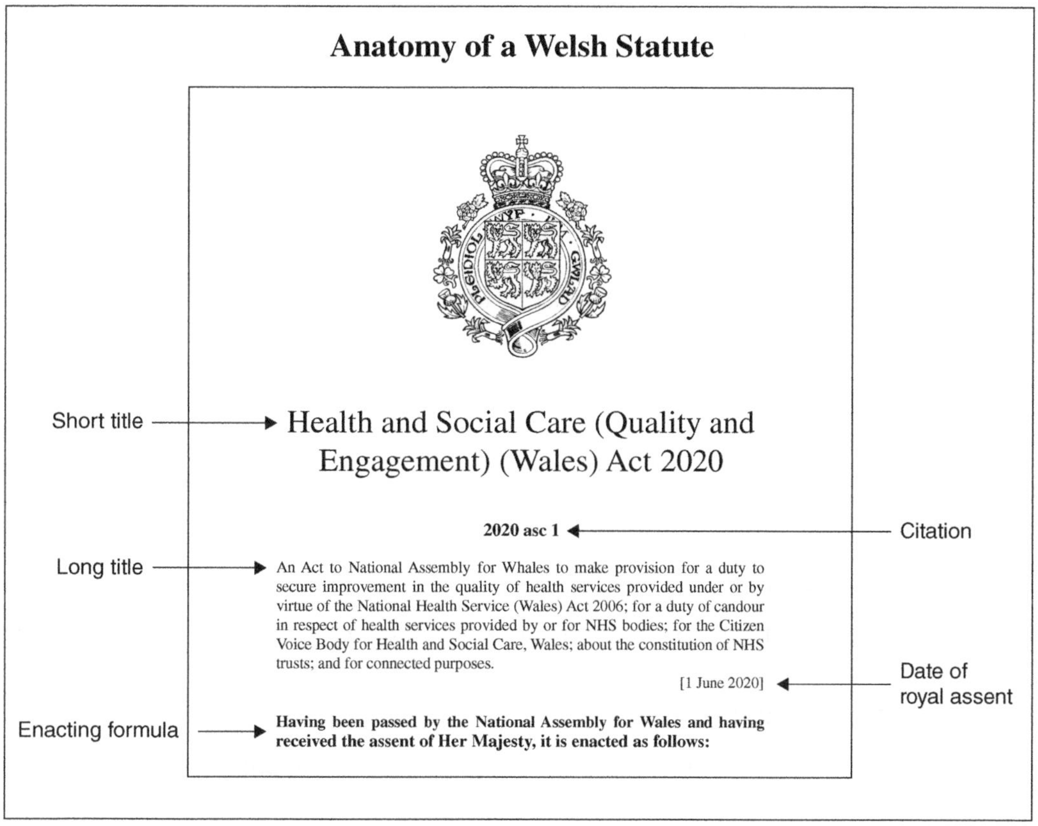

FIGURE 2.3 The anatomy of a Welsh statute

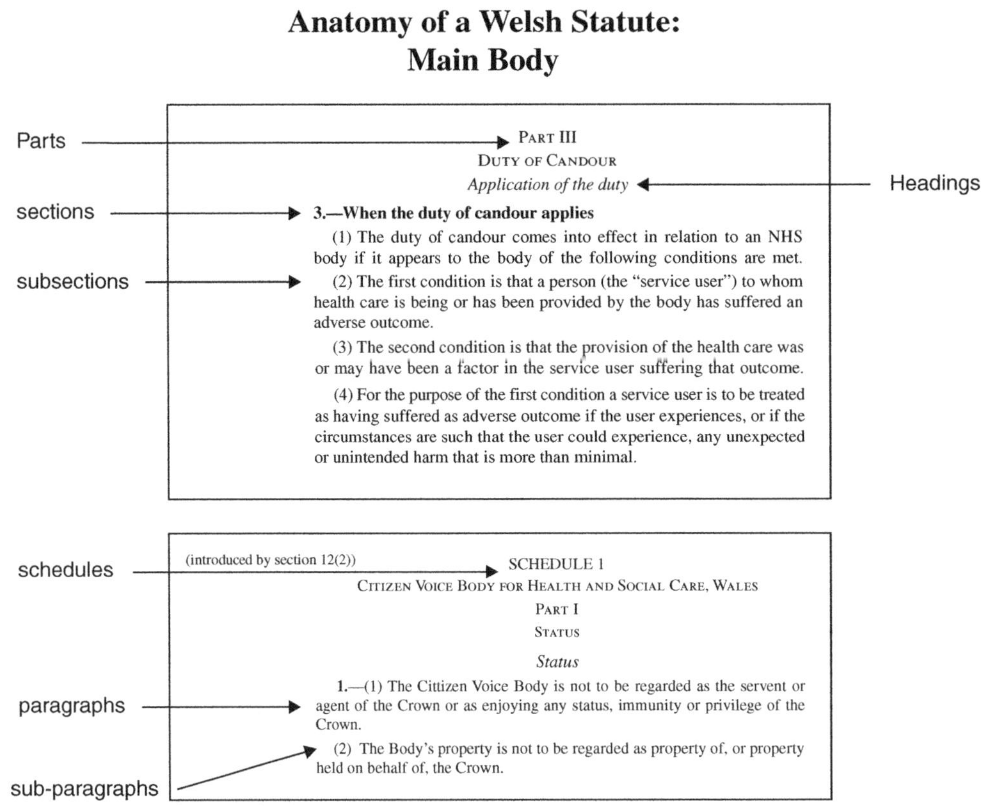

FIGURE 2.4 The anatomy of a Welsh statute: main body

2.2.3.2.5 Operative parts

The operative parts of a statute are the elements that are changing the law or creating new rules and procedures, as opposed to the preliminary and concluding parts which are essential elements in creating the law but do nothing more than that, for example the enacting formula.

The substantive parts of the Act are sections. Acts often have schedules attached to them at the end. These schedules will contain detailed or complex information or the text of an international treaty or convention. Schedules are an operative part of the Act (*Metropolitan Police Commissioner v Curran* [1976] 1 All ER 162). Schedules will often set out the laws that are being repealed by the Act and provide a list of modifications made by the Act to other laws. Modern life is complex and similarly statutes can be complicated and lengthy documents; thus Acts are commonly divided into sections with headings that identify the nature of the sections.

2.2.3.2.6 The long title

The long title of an Act appears at the very start of an Act and begins with the words 'An Act to . . .'. The long title sets out the main purposes and scope of the Act. The date of passing of an Act of Parliament directly follows the long title and appears in square brackets.

2.2.3.2.7 The short title

The short title, by contrast, is the brief name of the Act, for example the Human Rights Act 1998.

2.2.3.2.8 The chapter number

Acts will also be identifiable by the chapter number, which signifies the order of passing of Acts of Parliament in a calendar year. Thus, the HRA 1998 has a chapter number of 42 (c. 42) which means that it was the 42nd Act of Parliament to be passed in the year 1998.

An Act will be punctuated throughout its terms. The punctuation is deemed to be authoritative, although judges are prepared to alter the punctuation if considered problematic (*Allnatt London Properties Ltd v Newton* [1981] 2 All ER 290).

An Act of Parliament may come into force on the day that it receives royal assent. However, given the complexity of modern statutes and the overriding principle of legal certainty, it is common for Acts of Parliament to come into force at points in time later than the date of royal assent. Thus the Act of Parliament, having received royal assent, is law, appears on the statute book but does not have legal effect until later points in time. This time-lag is often required to allow sufficient time for citizens, law enforcement, businesses, corporations and local government and indeed central government to prepare for the impending legal changes brought by the Act. Different sections of an Act can come into force on different days and for different purposes. The process for coming into force can also differ throughout the Act with certain provisions coming into force on a set date automatically, provisions coming into force only when certain other conditions are met or coming into force by operation of ministerial discretion.

EXAMPLE

The HRA 1998 received royal assent on 9 November 1998.

Sections 18, 20 and 21(5) came into force on the same date.

The rest of the Act was to come into force on dates determined by the relevant minister.

The last remaining parts of the Act that were not in force came into force on 2 October 2000 by virtue of the Human Rights Act 1998 (Commencement No 2) Order 2000.

This time-lag of almost two years was absolutely necessary in order to give public authorities like the police, local government, the NHS and schools sufficient time to adapt to the new human rights framework by which they must act in a way compatible with human rights (see further Chapter 8 on the HRA 1998).

The modern use of ministerial power to appoint certain days for the coming into force of an Act or parts of an Act give rise to the possibility of an Act never coming into force. Some Acts may therefore provide for sunrise clauses which allow for the provisions of an Act of Parliament to automatically come into force after the expiry of a set period of time. However, these clauses are rather rare. The courts are reluctant to compel ministers to exercise their commencement powers in such a situation and are more likely to simply declare, in a judicial review case, that the minister has acted unlawfully in not adequately keeping under review the need for them to exercise their implementing powers (*R v Secretary of State for the Home Department, ex p Fire Brigades Union* [1995] UKHL 3). (See **Chapter 6 on** judicial review.)

Non-use of a statute does not mean that the statute falls into abeyance. English law does not operate the system of desuetude. However, in practical terms, if a minister were to start using provisions in a long dormant statute to issue statutory instruments, such actions would probably be deemed an unreasonable action according to the principles set out in the *Wednesbury* case.

Parliament may often provide within an Act that ministers can amend the provisions of that Act or indeed any other Act by way of Statutory Instrument (eg the European Union (Withdrawal) Act 2018, s 8(5)). Indeed, the complexity of modern life in the 21st century necessitates routine recourse to this method of legislating. Exceptionally, the terms of primary legislation may be amended by ministers without enacting secondary legislation. For example, the exact words of the coronation oath are set out in the Coronation Act 1688, however the text of the oath has been variously amended over the intervening five centuries, with only one instance of alteration being sanctioned by legislative amendment (see the discussion of the Coronation Oath in the National Archives) as set out in the House of Commons Library Research Paper on the Coronation Oath, David Torrance, 19 April 2023).

2.3 The framework for interpretation of legislation

Law is a social construct and is designed to regulate behaviour and give workable guidelines to the populace as to how to conduct their affairs. As such, legislation appears in the format of general abstractions. Legislation can never hope to address all permutations of human behaviour and actions, so unfamiliar situations and circumstances inevitably arise, calling for interpretation and application of the law to these novel situations as and when they arrive.

Fundamentally, statutory interpretation requires that the legislature's intention is the pre-eminent criteria underpinning construction of a statute. The various interpretative criteria will set out general guidance to be followed and, in the event of a conflict between the criteria, judges will weigh up and balance the criteria to determine the most appropriate interpretation (*Ralph v Carrick* (1879) 11 ChD 873).

In order to prevent the law being applied capriciously, unpredictably, inconsistently or partially, common law and statutory rules have been developed to avoid this risk. These aids to interpretation comprise various rules and presumptions to be applied. These aids can be intrinsic to the law itself or can be extrinsic aids that are beyond the strict confines of that law.

2.3.1 **Intrinsic and extrinsic aids**

Intrinsic aids are aspects of the law itself such as the statute's short and long titles and the explanatory memorandum.

Extrinsic aids are aids to interpretation that are not the law itself so include other laws like the Interpretation Act 1978, international conventions and external sources such as Hansard (the official report of parliamentary debates) and official Committee reports.

Further, judges will refer to established conventions of interpretation when tasked with determining the meaning of legislation. They will approach legislation with established canons of construction and certain presumptions. These guides and rules can be found in judicial precedent (case law) on the nature and content of legal policy, presumptions from the courts on the nature of legislation, linguistic canons of interpretation and customary and statutory rules of construction.

2.3.2 **Intrinsic aids and extrinsic aids connected to the Act itself**

2.3.2.1 Functional construction

The common law provides that Acts should be interpreted according to their function. The Act should be taken as a whole (*South West Water Authority v Rumble's* [1985] AC 609) and then each individual aspect of the Act must be interpreted in light of its nature. Thus:

> Sections set out Parliament's intention to create new legal rules, principles or offences;
>
> Schedules are integral to the Act and provide important additional information;
>
> Savings and provisos are specific to that individual section. These restrictions need to be treated carefully given the scope for them to be applied incorrectly;
>
> Long titles of Acts are simply broad statements of intent so may not offer much guidance to a judge
>
> (*Imperial Tobacco Ltd, petitioner* [2010] CSOH 134)

Short titles are similarly of limited interpretative use.

The preamble provides the reasons for enacting the law so can be useful at times. Judges will, however, prefer the substantive provisions of the Act to the preamble in the event of conflict (*Attorney-General v HRH Prince Ernest Augustus of Hanover* [1956] 1 All ER 49; *Powell v Kempton Park Racecourse Co Ltd* [1899] AC 143, HL).

A purpose clause offers some guidance but again specific sections of an Act will prevail.

A recital may offer some interpretative guidance.

References to other enactments in the Act: where the Act refers to other laws then these other enactments can be used as an interpretative guide.

Examples expressed within an Act are strongly persuasive since they provide guidance as to the legislature's approach to the provisions of the Act. However, where the example clearly goes against the intention of the legislature expressed in sections of the Act, judges will treat the example as an anomaly and prefer the section.

An Act's headings can be an interpretative aid since they indicate the scope and focus of the following parts of the Act.

Punctuation offers some interpretative assistance. It is most useful when the absence or addition of punctuation would provide for opposite constructions of a provision (*Bodden v Metropolitan Police Commissioner* [1990] 2 QB 397).

2.3.3 Informed interpretation

The common law presumes that when Parliament makes law, Parliament is fully informed and knowledgeable about the matters surrounding the topic of the law and as such the resultant law should be interpreted in a similarly comprehensive way.

Therefore, judges must look at the law in its entire context. After doing that, the judges can then investigate any questions of doubt over meaning. Interpretation of the Act should therefore be informed by the entire legislative history of that law, that is, the pre-enacting, enacting and post-enacting history of the Act (*Mykoliw v Botterill* [2010] CSOH 84).

2.3.4 Pre-enactment history

Acts of Parliament are mostly enacted to remedy some perceived mischief or problem. If a court is to determine what mischief or problem the law is to remedy, it must be aware of the pre-existing law if it exists and the need for passing the law. Where an Act uses words that have a previous legal meaning, the starting presumption is that the words will still have that meaning.

It is increasingly common now that before the UK Parliament legislates on a topic, a committee will be set up to investigate the area of concern before proposals are introduced for a new law or to reform existing law. These committees could take the form of a **Royal Commission**, a parliamentary select committee or a Law Commission report. Such reports are considered part of the pre-enactment history and thus the courts can use them as an interpretative aid.

In a similar vein, White Papers—that is, a government policy document that sets out the reasons for a legislative proposal—can be used by judges as an interpretative guide.

Modern parliamentary practice is for the vast majority of legislative proposals (Bills) to be accompanied by an Explanatory Note. These notes are prepared by the government and explain in further detail the reasons for and the intended operation of the Bill. Judges will increasingly refer to these Explanatory Notes in seeking the will of Parliament (*Kostal v Dunkley* [2021] UKSC 47).

Nevertheless, these external aids should only be utilised where they assist in elucidating the true intention of Parliament as to the purpose behind the Act of Parliament (see *R (on the application of O (a minor, by her litigation friend AO)) v Secretary of State for the Home Department* [2022] UKSC 3).

2.3.5 Enactment history

The enactment history of an Act encompasses all relevant information about its introduction as a Bill, and the records of its progress through the parliamentary legislative procedure.

Modern judges are increasingly comfortable with relying on these sources of information as an important interpretative aid. Previously, the ability of the courts to look at parliamentary proceedings as an aid to interpretation was clearly precluded under what was known as the 'exclusionary rule'. Under this rule, the only appropriate parliamentary documents that could shed light on the meaning of the Act was the actual Act itself. The final text of the Act as published and having received royal assent was the law. However, the increasing length and complexity of modern Acts of Parliament meant that such limitations of interpretation could be counterproductive and may actually conceal the true intention of Parliament.

Over time, significant inroads have been made to this rule, to the point that extraneous documents connected to the passage of the legislative proposal through Parliament are now routinely referred to by judges.

The most common and well-known exception of the exclusionary rule is that of the case of *Pepper v Hart* [1993] AC 593. The rule in *Pepper v Hart* now permits the courts to refer to Hansard as an aid to interpreting the law in question where the legal meaning of that law is ambiguous or obscure or where the literal meaning would lead to an absurd result. However, not all statements of Hansard are permitted. The only statements of Hansard that can be referred to are clear statements made by the promoter of the Bill (for government Bills, the relevant minister) that set out the mischief or problem to be remedied by the law, or otherwise display the legislative intention of the words.

The second exception to the exclusionary rule applies where the UK law being promulgated is designed to give effect to an international convention, such that parliamentary materials can be used by the courts to determine the true purpose of the statute. This rule was predominantly used for laws designed to give effect to EU law during the period of the UK's membership of the EU (*Three Rivers DC v Governor and Company of the Bank of England (No 2)* [1996] 2 All ER 363).

Lastly, under the court's inherent jurisdiction, it has the power of its own volition to refer to parliamentary materials, where deemed necessary. However, the court may not use parliamentary materials if such use would violate art IX of the Bill of Rights, that is, the rule that parliamentary proceedings should not be questioned in a court of law.

2.3.6 Post-enactment history

Once the Act has been promulgated, judges may rely on a number of sources to assist with their interpretation of the Act. Judges may draw on official statements from the government departments that promoted the Act since these documents set out their view of the Act. Similarly, judges may treat official committee reports on the meaning of an Act's provisions as persuasive authority.

2.4 Extrinsic aids

Beyond the terms of the Act itself and documents associated with the promulgation of that Act, judges will also refer to established conventions, rules and presumptions as to how to treat the words of a statute.

2.5 Rules of interpretation and construction

2.5.1 Legislative and linguistic canons of construction

Judges are tasked with discovering the meaning of legislation and the starting point is the literal meaning of the Act or Statutory Instrument in question. As Lord Steyn said in the case of *R v A (No. 2)* [2001] UKHL 25 at [44]:

'It is a general principle of the interpretation of legal instruments that the text is the primary source of interpretation: other sources are subordinate to it.' (See also *R (on the application of D4) v Secretary of State for the Home Department* [2021] EWHC 2179 (Admin).)

The most significant canon is that an Act should be read as a whole, in order to ensure consistency and to keep the words of the Act in context.

In the case where words in an Act are capable of having more than one meaning, the starting point is that the ordinary and natural meaning of the word should be preferred (*Selvey v DPP* [1970] AC 304). This may mean the most common or well-established usage of the word.

When construing statutes, judges will first look to the nature of legislation. The main task of a judge is to discover the intention of the legislature in passing that law.

The starting point for a judge is therefore to look to the literal meaning of an Act. The interpreting judge will look at the grammatical meaning of the Act itself, without reference to any external factors. The judge will refer to normal rules of grammar, syntax and punctuation and the canons of construction. This is the plain meaning or literal rule.

EXAMPLE

In *Fisher v Bell* [1961] 1 QB 394, Mr Bell was a shopkeeper who displayed a flick knife in his shop window. Under the Restriction of Offensive Weapons Act 1959, it was an offence to offer to sell such a knife. He was then prosecuted. At his trial, the judges applied the law literally to hold that he had no case to answer since his shop display, under the law of contract, was simply an 'invitation to treat' and not an offer to sell. This gap in the law was unforeseen and was remedied by Parliament in the next parliamentary session with an amendment to the 1960 Act by the Restriction of Offensive Weapons Act 1961. The amendment provided that it was an offence for a person to expose or have in their possession for the purpose of sale or hire a flick knife.

However, this rule can lead to conflict with the rule that words need to be interpreted in the context of the Act as a whole. In such a case, the interpretative requirement to read the document as a whole tends to prevail.

Judges should not attempt to further define words that are very familiar and are in widespread use.

By contrast, where an Act uses technical words in the context of a particular area of expertise, then the canon is that that word should be given its technical meaning. If the technical meaning concerns the domestic law of the court, then judicial notice is taken of that meaning and external evidence cannot be introduced as to its meaning. If the technical term relates to foreign law or matters beyond law, evidence of that meaning can be brought into court.

EXAMPLE

In determining whether a book about cocaine was obscene under the Obscene Publications Act 1959, expert testimony could be adduced in court as to the nature and effects of the drug.

Given the importance of context to interpretation, it is a canon of construction that words are to be interpreted in light of the words that surround it. This principle is commonly expressed in Latin (*noscitur a sociis*) or by the phrase 'A word is known by the company it keeps'. Thus, words are interpreted in relation to the fact that they belong to a group. However, this principle can cause difficulties where it is difficult to ascertain the group to which the word belongs and the draftspeople may have intended a different meaning to apply.

A particular problem with the application of *noscitur a sociis* is the application of the term *ejusdem generis* meaning 'of the same kind'. Where an Act has listed wide, general words alongside more restrictive words, the principle will operate to restrict those general words to only apply to matters that have the restricted character. It commonly applies where a list of examples is given alongside a general description phrase.

EXAMPLE

A fictitious law says '. . . the law applies to cars, trucks, tractors and other motor vehicles'.

Does the law apply to motorbikes?

Does the law apply to speedboats or airplanes?

Does the law apply to buses, trams or trains?

Does the law apply to combine harvesters?

The judge is faced with numerous issues in attempting to define the term 'other motor vehicles'. Cars, trucks and tractors have four wheels so motorbikes could be excluded on the basis that they only have two wheels, speedboats and airplanes could be excluded because the other vehicles are land-based and buses, trams and trains could be excluded because they are public passenger vehicles. Combine harvesters may well be included in the definition because tractors are explicitly mentioned or they could be excluded because they are highly specialised agricultural vehicles.

EXAMPLE

What does the word 'case' mean?

From a simple dictionary definition, it can mean a suitcase or a container to hold or protect something. Under the Metalliferous Mines Act 1872, gunpowder and inflammable and explosive materials could only be brought into a mine in a small case or canister. A number of mineworkers brought gunpowder into the mines in small linen bags and some of them ignited, leading to death and injury. It was held that the term 'case' in this situation could not extend to a cloth bag since the purpose of the legislation was to ensure that explosive powders were transported in containers that offered sufficient protection. Thus the action of the mineworkers was illegal (*Foster v Diphwys Casson Slate Co* (1887) 18 QBD 428).

Where an enactment uses express words then the judge is prevented from using inference to add words that would go against this meaning (*expressum facit cessare tacitum* (statement ends implication)). The best example of such a rule in practice is the well-known maxim *expressio unius est exclusio alterius* (to state one thing excludes another). Thus the judge, when faced with a list of specific terms that excludes other well-known examples, will treat that omission as a deliberate decision by the draftspeople.

EXAMPLE

The Poor Relief Act 1601 taxed 'lands, houses and coalmines'.

Does this law apply to limestone mines?

Specific mention of coalmines meant that the judge could not extend that law to other types of mine (*R v Inhabitants of Sedgely* (1831) 2 B & Ad 65).

Note that this principle has been subject to regular and sustained judicial criticism (*HM Advocate v Grant* [2007] HCJAC 71).

In the provision of a list of items, followed by general residual words, it is to be presumed that the general words do not include items of a higher rank.

EXAMPLE

Where the law says 'an officer or examiner of the court, or some other person' then that list cannot include a judge since the judge is higher in rank than an officer or examiner.

2.5.2 Common-sense construction rule

The common law also provides for the common-sense construction rule. Where there are two opposing interpretations of the Act, the courts should prefer the construction that is the most common sense, on the basis that Parliament would have intended such a result.

2.5.3 Rectifying construction rule

The courts will presume that the legislature would want judges to rectify errors in the statute. The errors that are to be rectified are where the text is garbled, there is an error in meaning, there is a missing case or a wrongly included case, there is a conflict in the text or where the statute was created on a legal error. The court will only be entitled to rectify the meaning where it is absolutely sure of the intended purpose of the enactment, sure that the draftspeople had made an error and is sure of the nature of the provision.

2.5.4 **Updating construction rule**

It is often presumed that the law should be construed on a dynamic basis in order to keep up with changes to contemporary life and society. The law, when being interpreted, should reflect technological, societal, scientific and other changes and should not be frozen in time at the date of enactment. Thus, it is said that the law is always speaking (*R (Quintavalle) v Secretary of State for Health* [2003] UKHL 13; *General Dynamics UK v Libya* [2021] UKSC 22).

EXAMPLE

The UK has a long history of undertaking censuses to ascertain information about its population so that the government can make plans for the future. The Census Act 1920 is the modern legal authority for providing for a census to be taken at regular intervals across the UK (currently every ten years). The census questions must be periodically refined to take account of societal changes, including as to changes in the conception of sex. Thus, the census question on the sex of a person may be changed to incorporate transgender rights to allow self-identification of sex different to that of birth (*Fair Play for Women v National Records for Scotland* [2022] CSOH 20).

2.5.5 **Construction by reference to the mischief (the mischief rule)**

The courts consider that when the legislature passes a law designed to address a mischief or problem, then that enactment should be interpreted in a way that suppresses that problem (*Heydon's Case* (1584) 3 Co Rep 7).

EXAMPLE

The Street Offences Act 1959 made it an offence to loiter or solicit on the street or in a public place for the purposes of prostitution. Prostitutes who solicited via a balcony from a first-floor flat argued that they did not commit the offence since they were neither on the street nor in a public place. A purely literal interpretation of the Act would not prevent the mischief, thus the judges were perfectly entitled to look beyond a mere literal meaning of the words to deduce that the actions of the prostitutes fell within the spirt of the law as preventing the mischief of public prostitution (*Smith v Hughes* [1960] 1 WLR 830).

2.5.6 **Construction against absurdity (the golden rule)**

The courts presume that the legislature does not enact law that creates an absurdity, that is, a result that is against sense and reason.

EXAMPLE

The Official Secrets Act 1920 provided for the offence of obstructing a member of HM Armed Forces in the vicinity of a prohibited place, namely in this case an RAF base. The accused staged a protest inside the airbase, therefore on a strict interpretation of the offence, being in a prohibited place meant that he could not be in the vicinity of a prohibited place. Thus, it would be an offence to protest outside the installation but not inside. This would be absurd and accordingly the legislature could not have intended such a result (*Adler v George* [1964] 1 All ER 62).

As part of this presumption against absurdity, the courts will strive to construe a statutory provision against an unworkable or impracticable result, an inconvenient result, an illogical result, a futile or pointless result or an artificial result.

2.5.6.1 Purposive construction rule

The court will presume that the legislature wants the court to construe a law to give effect to the true purpose of the law. Thus, courts may strain the meaning of the legislation if necessary. Frequently this means that the courts will not interpret the law literally where that approach would actually defeat the terms of the legislation.

EXAMPLE

In *R (Quintavalle) v Secretary of State for Health* [2003] UKHL 13, the House of Lords held that the Human Fertilisation and Embryology Act 1990 could apply to embryos made by cell nucleus replacement and not just to embryos made by fertilisation. Thus, the Act could apply to cloned embryos, even though the technology was not available at the time of the 1990 Act.

The courts, over time, have come to adopt the purposive approach as a legitimate tool of construction. This approach is increasingly adopted because the law is incredibly complex and law needs to be effective and useful as a tool of social control and guidance. Indeed, Lord Leggatt, in the Supreme Court case of *Uber v Aslam* [2021] UKSC 5, at [70], confirmed that:

> The modern approach to statutory interpretation is to have regard to the purpose of a particular provision and to interpret its language, so far as possible, in the way which best gives effect to that purpose.

2.6 **Presumptions**

When construing legislation, judges will rely on a number of presumptions.

2.6.1 **Presumption against retrospectivity**

There is a presumption that enactments that change the law only do so prospectively. Retrospective application is possible but it must be expressly stated or be by necessary implication.

In terms of criminal law and fiscal provisions, the presumption is strong. New offences, or the extension of the scope of an existing criminal offence, will ordinarily only apply to future events, especially given the reception of Art 7 ECHR into UK law via the HRA 1998. The presumption against retrospectivity is weaker in respect of procedural legislation. In the restricted cases of actual retrospective legislation, such laws will be interpreted restrictively to limit their application (*Reid v Reid* (1886) 31 ChD 402).

> . . . the reason for the presumption is that in a civilised society which acknowledges the rule of law, individual members of that society are entitled to know when they embark on a course of conduct what the legal consequences of their doing so will be, so that they may regulate their conduct accordingly.
>
> (Lord Diplock in *Inland Revenue Comrs v Joiner* [1975] 3 All ER 1050 at 1062)

2.6.2 **Presumption against avoiding the law**

The courts, when interpreting the law, will presume that their interpretation should not result in the law being evaded or circumvented. Thus, for example, sending a child to school but without paying the applicable fees was not 'causing the child to attend school' as set out in the local authority's bylaws (*London School Board v Wood* (1885) 15 QBD 415).

2.7 Statutory definitions

Given some of the linguistic problems highlighted earlier, the legislature may decide to set out statutory rules of construction for certain phrases and words. Such definitions may apply generally or be restricted to application in specified circumstances. The definition may be found in the statute itself or it may be left to be elaborated upon by later delegated legislation, in order to keep the law flexible.

Statutory definitions may clarify a common word or phrase, create a label definition that conveys a complex concept, refer to pre-existing definitions, exclude certain meanings from a definition or enlarge the meaning or provide a comprehensive definition, designed to offer an exhaustive statement of the phrase.

Interpretation Acts are special Acts that are used to simplify the drafting of other Acts of Parliament. They give definitions for common terms in order to shorten the language used, to avoid repetition and to help with the interpretation and consistency of words used in legislation. They can also provide for the legal meaning of Acts. The Interpretation Act 1978 applies to any Act passed after 1 January 1979 and to certain Acts passed before that date. The Act applies to 'assimilated ([*sic*] EU) law' and Welsh laws until 1 January 2020. The 1978 Act applies to itself.

Special interpretative rules now apply to Acts of Senedd Cymru and Welsh Statutory Instruments which receive royal assent after 1 January 2020. These laws are to be interpreted according to the interpretative rules of the Legislation (Wales) Act 2019.

2.7.1 The Interpretation Act 1978

The 1978 Act sets out a number of statutory assumptions about the geographical territorial scope of the UK, the government, its office-holders, other bodies and offices and the notion of the sovereign. It further provides presumptions as to people, their gender and their relationships. Masculine gender includes the feminine gender and vice versa. The Act is regularly updated to encompass the evolving nature of intimate human relationships. The term person extends to both bodies corporate and unincorporate. The Act sets out assumptions about legal aspects of land and its ownership and control, and for specific legal terms of art, the notion of time, distance measurement and the treatment of documents including their service.

2.8 Interpretative principles and assumptions

The courts, when undertaking their interpretative duty, will have regard to a number of general principles and assumptions. The main rules that the judges follow are set out below:

> The executive has no power to suspend the operation of an Act of Parliament (*Customs and Excise Comrs v Mechanical Services (Trailer Engineers) Ltd* [1979] 1 All ER 501).
>
> Judges cannot anticipate the coming into force of an Act of Parliament. Judges must decide a case on the basis of what the current law is and not what the law is about to be (*Wilson v Dagnall* [1972] 1 QB 509).
>
> The courts will presume that the legislature did not intend to pass a law that overrides fundamental common law rights (*R v Secretary of State for the Home Department, ex parte Simms* [2000] 2 AC 115; *Privacy International v Investigatory Powers Tribunal* [2021] EWHC 27 (Admin)).
>
> - Geographical extent of an Act of Parliament.

The 'extent' of an Act means the geographical area the law applies to. There is a presumption that Acts of the UK extend to the whole of the UK; that is, England and Wales, Scotland and Northern Ireland. This presumption still holds good despite the existence of devolution in Wales, Scotland and Northern Ireland. The geographical extent of Acts of the UK Parliament can be limited expressly or impliedly. The presumption does not prevent an Act of the UK Parliament having extraterritorial effect (see as examples the Geneva Conventions Act 1957, the War Crimes Act 1991, c. 13 and the Domestic Abuse Act 2021, c. 17).

- Application of an Act.

It is a general principle that Acts of the UK Parliament only have legal effect within the UK. Nevertheless, the UK Parliament can pass laws that have application in another sovereign state on a mutual basis, such as the immigration accord between the UK and France, and the UK Parliament may agree to pass laws that apply to British overseas territories. Extraterritorial application of UK laws can occur as regards the activities of UK citizens abroad upon their return to the UK or to foreign nationals who come within the jurisdiction of the UK, known as active and passive personality jurisdiction. Thus, for example, UK sexual offence laws may apply to UK nationals who commit sex crimes abroad and to offenders abroad who commit crimes against a UK national. Further, offenders based outside the UK can be guilty of computer misuse offences when they interfere with UK-based computer systems and components (s4 Computer Misuse Act 1990). Indeed, more generally, the increasing prevalence of information technology means that the assumption of jurisdiction over people and property beyond the UK is increasingly common.

In these cases, a significant link with the UK must be made out by the prosecution. Certain Acts of the UK Parliament may also assert universal jurisdiction on crimes committed anywhere in the world, such as torture, war crimes, genocide and crimes against humanity (HM Government Note on the investigation and prosecution of crimes of universal jurisdiction, 2018; CPS Jurisdiction Legal Guidance, September 2020, Universal Jurisdiction, House of Commons Library (2010), SN05422.pdf (parliament.uk)).

- Effect of Acts.

Acts may impose statutory duties on anyone. As such, this fact gives rise to the legal maxim that ignorance of the law is no defence (*Carter v McLaren* (1871) LR2 Sc & Div 120) even where there has been a defect in the publication of that law (*R (on the application of ZL) v Secretary of State for the Home Department* [2003] EWCA Civ 25). However, UK membership of the ECHR does require that any interferences with human rights will only be acceptable where they are 'prescribed by law' which requires that the law is both adequately accessible and is formulated with suitable precision (*Sunday Times v United Kingdom* (1979) 2 EHRR 245 and see **Chapter 8** on the HRA 1998).

Courts do not take kindly to legislative attempts to oust their jurisdiction and therefore will strictly interpret any enactment that attempts to limit that jurisdiction (*Anisminic Ltd v Foreign Compensation Commission* [1969] 2AC 147). Nevertheless, a court's jurisdiction can be excluded or limited where special procedures have been established such that claimants need apply to an administrative body, to arbitration or to a particular court or tribunal.

Judges may refer to reputable dictionaries and other reference works to determine the meaning of a term, even if the term is within judicial notice.

The legal meaning of an Act is arrived at by looking at the enactment itself and then, if warranted, by looking at external aids to interpretation (see *R (on the application of O (a minor, by her litigation friend AO)) v Secretary of State for the Home Department* [2022] UKSC 3. In particular, judges will look at the interpretative criteria and guides to legislative intention. The rule for the court is to 'ascertain the intention of Parliament as expressed in the words it has chosen' (Lord Millett in *R (Quintavalle) v Secretary of State for Health* [2003] UKHL 13 at [38] and Lord Nicholls in *R v Secretary of State for the Environment, Transport and the Regions, ex p Spath Holme Ltd* [2001] 2 AC 349[2001] 2 AC 349). In determining the intention of Parliament, modern practice is for the judges to conflate that notion with discovering the true purpose of the legislation in an objective manner (*Uber v Aslam* [2021] UKSC 5; *Rittson-Thomas v Oxfordshire County Council* [2021] UKSC 13 and *Kostal v Dunkley* [2021] UKSC 47).

If the law can be interpreted without doubt, then the legal meaning is fixed. Only where there are doubts will the courts go on to look to other interpretative criteria and aids (Lord Bingham in *R (Gillan) v Commissioner of Police of the Metropolis* [2006] UKHL 11 at [15]).

2.8.1 Opposing constructions of an enactment

Doubt as to the meaning of an Act typically arises between the two sides to a legal dispute and thus comes to be resolved in the courts. The courts will then decide which of the opposing constructions should be preferred by reference to the interpretative criteria.

2.8.2 Extracting, weighing and balancing the interpretative factors

Aids to construction must be weighted and determined by the court in order to decide which interpretation it favours.

2.8.3 Strict and liberal construction

Construction of a statute invariably involves compromises and the eventual preference of one interpretation over another. Each interpretation has consequences. If those consequences are adverse towards the subject or the state, this points towards a narrowing of that statute's operation and effect. This is known as a strict construction.

Conversely, where another interpretation of the Act would have a beneficial effect for the subject or the state, then this approach should be favoured and thus the enactment should apply to more instances, promoting a wider application of the Act. This is known as a liberal construction approach.

Therefore, in the case of an enactment coercing people, a strict interpretation will limit its application and, conversely, a measure that is liberating will often be generously construed so opening up its application to more people.

2.9 Principles of legal policy

Legal policy is pervasive, applying throughout the legal system. Essentially, it encompasses the principles that should be embodied in the legal system. The courts are able to draw on various sources in order to express legal policy. Legal policy is dynamic, changing as societal priorities, needs and attitudes change. The common law develops principles of legal policy that can be used to guide legislative intention. It is often the case that these abstract principles of general application may conflict with each other and thus judges will be tasked with determining which one has priority in the instant case.

Legal policy provides that the law should strive to serve the following principles:

2.9.1 Law should be predictable, coherent and self-consistent

Citizens should be able to understand the law and be able to regulate their conduct to remain on the side of the law. The law, as a system of rules, needs to be coherent and self-consistent. It should not be contradictory. This principle may have to yield to other principles however, such as the interpretative obligation of the HRA 1998.

2.9.2 Changes to the law should not be casual

Changes to the law should be a deliberate act of the legislature, based on measured deliberation and evaluation. This presumption is stronger in relation to changes to the common law and where the proposed change would be a major break with prior law. In these cases, changes should be done expressly, clearly and unambiguously.

2.9.3 *De minimis* principle

Legal policy implies that the law does not concern itself with trifling matters (*de minimis non curat lex*).

2.9.4 The law should be just and fair

In this regard, courts must take decisions that further the ends of justice. Judges' interpretation of the law should not lead to injustice or unfairness. This may mean that the literal interpretation of a law cannot stand if that would lead to an unjust result. The concept of fairness will weigh heavily on a judge's decision, especially when a decision either way may create injustice. In cases that involve the use of statutory discretion via officer-holders, the court will infer that Parliament intended for that power to be exercised in a similar high-principled way to decision by a judge.

2.9.5 Judges should be impartial

To ensure justice is served, the maxim *nemo judex in sua causa* applies (no one should be judge in his own cause). Over time, this maxim has grown beyond the literal meaning of the phrase to include any apparent biases, regardless of where that bias may come from and also applies to public law decision-making generally.

EXAMPLE

Lord Hoffmann adjudicated in a House of Lords case concerning the immunity of the former head of state of Chile, General Pinochet. After the judgment, it was disclosed that Lord Hoffmann was an unpaid director of Amnesty International Charitable Trust and that his wife, Lady Hoffmann, had worked for Amnesty International since 1977 in an administrative capacity. The appearance of potential bias on this basis was enough for the original decision to be set aside and for a new composition of the House of Lords to be constituted to hear the case anew (*Pinochet, In re* [1999] UKHL 1).

The existence of a pecuniary interest in a case will render the decision void, whilst any other grounds of bias will render the decision voidable.

2.9.6 Right to be heard

It is an essential feature of legal policy that in any legal dispute the other side must be heard (*audi alteram partem*). Thus, both parties to a legal dispute must have an opportunity to state their case.

2.9.7 Double jeopardy

It is a fundamental maxim of legal policy that no one should be tried twice in relation to the same events. However, certain statutory exceptions exist to this principle such that a new trial can be instigated against defendants in exceptional circumstances. For example, retrials can now be instituted for a range of serious crimes like murder, manslaughter, kidnapping, rape, armed robbery and serious drug offences under s75 of the Criminal Justice Act 2003 (*R v JFJ* [2013] EWCA Crim 569).

The general principle of double jeopardy does not prevent different sanctions being applied in respect of the same event, such as a professional disciplinary sanction in addition to a criminal sanction.

2.9.8 *Volenti non fit injuria* principle

The legal principle of *volenti* means that when a person consents to something that action cannot amount to a legal injury. The classic examples of this are extreme sports like bungee jumping and rock climbing. As a matter of public policy, however, certain actions entered into voluntarily will not absolve the participants of liability. Agreeing to be eaten or engaging in extreme sadomasochistic sex will not absolve the participants from legal action. Thus, the principle is, according to the vagaries of contemporary societal assumptions, either expressly permitted or excluded.

EXAMPLE

In *R v Brown* [1994] 1 AC 212, the House of Lords held that a number of participants in sadomasochistic sexual acts could not legally consent to the ensuing physical harm.

2.9.9 Act of God

Legal policy dictates that an act of God, that is, a natural disaster or some other calamity that is unavoidable, should not cause legal injury to anyone. To avoid unfairness, the resulting loss may be recovered by governmental funding or by the statutory imposition of an obligation to compensate on certain bodies.

2.9.10 Impotence, impossibility and necessity

Legal policy provides that people should not be punished for not doing something they could not do or could not prevent, not be punished for not doing something that was impossible or not be punished for taking action that is necessary. Thus, a drunk person should not be convicted of being found drunk on the highway as a result of police taking them from a hospital waiting room and depositing them on the road outside (*Winzar v Chief Constable of Kent* (1983) The Times, 28 March).

2.9.11 Law should serve the public interest

Thus, judges should interpret laws in a way that promotes the public benefit. From this principle flows the rule of construction that laws should be operated in good faith. '[E]very rule of law . . . which has been laid down by the courts, in that course of judicial legislation which has evolved the law of this country, has been based on considerations of public interest or policy': *Fender v St John-Mildmay* [1938] AC 1. The public interest is also served by protecting the security of the state and by safeguarding the King's peace.

2.9.12 Illegality

Legal policy provides that people alleging their own disrepute should not be entertained. Therefore, a wrongdoer should be prevented from taking legal action or raising a defence. Similarly, in equity there is a principle that people must come to court with clean hands. Further, there exists the principle that people should not benefit from their wrongdoing.

In such cases, these principles do not mean that there are no legal effects of the unlawful activity. Thus, taxes can be levied on unlawful gains and the **illegality** can be relied on where third parties were to be denied their legal rights. In assessing whether the illegal act should have legal effects, the test is whether to do so would harm the integrity of the legal system itself.

2.9.13 Protection of morality

Legal policy provides that the law, in general, should promote and protect morality. Naturally, morality changes over time and in modern life the courts are now less likely to pronounce on matters of morality.

2.10 Principles for human rights and those of citizens

Legal policy requires that the law should uphold human rights and the rights of its citizens. This principle has been strengthened by the enactment of the HRA 1998 and the specific rule of construction set out in s3 (*R v Secretary of State for the Home Department, ex p Brind* [1991] 1 AC 696; *Derbyshire CC v Times Newspapers Ltd* [1993] AC 534).

In terms of the ECHR, general legal policy upholds a number of important principles and ensures that restrictions upon those principles and rights must be strictly construed. Thus, legal policy upholds:

- The concept of family (Art 8 Respect for private life, home, family and correspondence and Art 12 Right to marry).
- The sanctity of human life and human health (Art 2 Right to life).
- Personal liberty (Art 4 Prohibition of slavery and forced labour and Art 5 Right to liberty and security).
- Religious freedom (Art 9 Freedom of thought, conscience and religion (*R v Lemon* [1979] AC 617)).
- Freedom of expression (Art 10 Freedom of expression and information). English law has a long history of upholding the principle of free speech.
- Freedom of peaceful assembly and association (Art 11 Right of assembly and association).
- Property rights and economic interests (Art 1 of Protocol 1 and *Entick v Carrington* (1765) 19 State Tr 1029).

Privacy (Art 8) is an amorphous concept and changes according to societal norms. In England and Wales, privacy is not protected directly, notwithstanding the enactment of the HRA 1998 and its absorption of Art 8 ECHR into UK law. The law of privacy is developing and now encompasses the tort of misuse of private information (*Campbell v Mirror Group Newspapers Ltd* [2004] UKHL 22; *Vidal-Hall v Google* [2015] EWCA Civ 311).

With regard to status and reputation, English law proscribes defamation (Defamation Act 2013) and thus fully accords with the requirement of Art 10 ECHR that free speech be restricted for protecting the reputation or rights of others. (Generally, see **Chapter 8** on the HRA 1998.)

2.10.1 Principle of clear penalties

People should not be penalised inadvertently, by mistake or in error.

2.10.2 Sanctity of the home

The colloquial phrase that 'an Englishman's home is his castle' is underpinned by legal policy. This maxim extends to relations between family members and protection against the entry of state officials into the home (*Balfour v Balfour* [1919] 2 KB 571; *Entick v Carrington* [1765] EWHC KB J98).

2.11 Interpretation of law to accord with specific international law

2.11.1 Interpretation of law under s3 of the Human Rights Act 1998

Since the passing of the HRA 1998, the UK courts have been required to interpret domestic law in light of the provisions of the ECHR. The 1998 Act essentially incorporated the main provisions of the ECHR into UK law.

Section 3 of the 1998 Act provides that:

> So far as it is possible to do so, primary legislation and subordinate legislation must be read and given effect in a way which is compatible with the **Convention rights**.

This section provides that the UK courts must take into account the terms of the ECHR when interpreting UK law.

EXAMPLE

One of the most expansive examples of the breadth of the interpretative obligation is the case of *Ghaidan v Godin Mendoza* [2004] UKHL 30, [2004] 2 AC 557. In this case, the Rent Act 1977 provided that a surviving husband or wife of a tenant who had died could succeed to the tenancy and thus continue to live in the property. The law did not provide for succession in the case of a homosexual partner. Ghaidan challenged this provision as being in breach of both Arts 8 and 14 ECHR. Article 8 provides for the right to respect of a person's private and family life and Art 14 provides that there should be no discrimination as regards the enjoyment of human rights, on a number of grounds, including sexual orientation. The House of Lords was prepared to read into the legislation additional wording that provided that a homosexual partner could succeed to a tenancy where, prior to the death, the partners had been living together 'as if' they were man and wife.

This case went dangerously close to displaying high levels of judicial activism, however the House of Lords was simply giving further effect to the terms of both the 1977 Act and the HRA 1998.

The case highlights the difficulties inherent with the s3 obligation. The courts are not able to effectively become the legislature and create new law by significantly rewriting legislative provisions that go against the grain of the law. However, the 1998 Act does entitle the Supreme Court (and its predecessor the House of Lords) to amend statutory provisions to reconcile the intention of Parliament in the specific law with the intention of Parliament as expressed in the 1998 Act.

The interpretative obligation of s3 is subject to limitations, the most significant being that it cannot be used to undermine the intention of Parliament (*R (Wilkinson) v Inland Revenue Commissioners* [2005] UKHL 30).

In such a case, the judges will have no option but to issue a declaration of incompatibility against that law, stating that it offends against human rights as set out in the ECHR.

(See further **Chapter 8** on the HRA 1998 and the selected cases of *R (on the application of Steinfeld and Keidan v Secretary of State for International Development* [2018] UKSC 32 and *A v Secretary of State for the Home Department* [2004] UKHL 56.)

2.11.2 The UK's membership of the EU

During the UK's membership of the European Union, domestic judges were required to interpret provisions of UK law in accordance with EU law as far as it was possible to do so (Case C-106/89, *Marleasing SA v La Comercial Internacional de Alimentacion SA*, EU:C:1990:395). This principle was known as the interpretative obligation or the concept of indirect effect. The consequences of this requirement were that if a UK law was inconsistent with EU law and that law could not be interpreted in accordance with EU law, then the courts were under an obligation to disapply that Act of Parliament (*Factortame*).

Since the expiry of the transition period on 31 December 2020, various parts of EU law have been incorporated into the UK legal system as a new species of UK law, now known as 'assimilated law' (Retained EU law (Revocation and Reform) Act 2023). When interpreting this law, UK judges can be guided by the case law of the European Court of Justice decided prior to 31 December 2020 and a number of general principles of EU law that became part of UK law (see **Chapter 10** on EU law in the UK constitution). More generally, when non-retained EU case-law is in point, it remains of persuasive authority (*Lidl GB Ltd. v Tesco Stores Ltd.* [2023] EWHC 873 (Ch)).

KEY POINT SUMMARY

- Acts of the UK Parliament are the highest source of law in the UK.
- The role of judges is restricted to interpreting those Acts in light of the will of the UK Parliament.
- Judges have no power to declare Acts of the UK Parliament illegal or unconstitutional.

- The Human Rights Act 1998 permits judges to issue a declaration of incompatibility stating that the Act goes against human rights as set out in the European Convention on Human Rights 1950, but this declaration has no impact on the Act's validity.
- Judges, when interpreting statutory law, will first look to the text of the legislation as a whole and the ordinary and natural meaning of the words of the statute to determine Parliament's intention and the true legal meaning and purpose of the Act.
- Increasingly, judges are able to draw on a wide range of resources, principles and presumptions to guide them in discovering Parliament's will when the terms of the Act are ambiguous or unclear.
- In determining the will of Parliament, judges will commonly take into account the wider purposes of the law, the legal or societal problems the law is trying to remedy or prevent and the danger of blindly following a strict, literal interpretation of the law.
- In cases of ambiguity, judges may refer to various statements made in Hansard, dictionary definitions of words, expert views, the grammar and syntax rules of language and wider fundamental precepts of the legal system as to fairness, justice, observance of the rule of law and legal consistency and coherency.
- Judges will interpret relevant domestic law generally in light of the UK's international law obligations and specifically in light of the European Convention.
- Under the rule of law and the separation of powers doctrine, judges, as unelected officials, when asked to interpret legislation, must provide clear justifications for their particular views and attitudes on the correct legal meaning of the Act since Acts of Parliament are created by the elected representatives of the legislature.

CHAPTER 3
The Courts and Precedent

FUNCTIONING LEGAL KNOWLEDGE

This chapter covers the following functioning legal knowledge required to pass the SQE 1 assessments:

The courts:

- the judiciary
- court hierarchy, the appeal system and jurisdiction
- rights of audience

Development of case law: the doctrine of precedent

AUTHORITIES UNDERPINNING PRACTICE

The key authorities that underpin this area of practice are listed below. Note that for legislation you are linked to legislation.gov.uk.

Although much of the legislation on this government website is available in its amended form, the incorporation of new amendments into the text of legislation can be delayed. You should refer to legal databases to ensure you are referencing the most up-to-date legislation.

- Constitutional Reform Act 2005
  https://www.legislation.gov.uk/ukpga/2005/4/contents
- Tribunals, Courts and Enforcement Act 2007
  https://www.legislation.gov.uk/ukpga/2007/15/contents
- *Practice Note (Judicial Precedent)* [1966] 3 All ER 77
- *Practice Direction (Citation of Authorities (2012))* [2012] 2 All ER 255

3.1 Introduction

This chapter looks at the pivotal role of the courts in creating and developing the **common law** and the doctrine of judicial precedent.

3.1.1 The courts and the common law

The courts play a pivotal role in the English legal system. They are one of the three parts of the state, the other two being Parliament and the executive. The courts are the judicial branch, whilst the legislative branch comprises the House of Commons and the House of Lords and the executive branch comprises His Majesty's Government, the civil service and the police and armed forces. The courts are independent of both these other parts of the state. The courts are the guardians of justice, upholding the **rule of law**, equality and due process and constitutional guarantees against arbitrariness and unfairness. The courts are there to independently adjudicate upon legal disputes between parties and to administer justice. Frequently, this adjudicative role will require the courts to interpret the law; that is, determine the legal meaning of Acts of Parliament, Statutory

Instruments and other legal documents such as contracts and wills. However, a more significant and frequent role of the courts is to apply the norms, rules and principles of the body of law known as the common law; that is, the law as expressed in a significant body of prior judgments.

The common law has been developed in England and Wales for over nine centuries. It starts to take shape in the 12th century and has evolved ever since. The common law system is based on the idea of a common court structure, whereby the courts across the entire nation dispense justice consistently according to the rules set out in previous judgments and old customs. This rigid reliance on previous court decisions ensured a high level of centralisation, consistency, reliability, predictability and coherence in the legal system, key traits for a respected legal system. Conversely, the civil law or continental European systems of law used the creation and development of expansive, comprehensive written codes of law to provide high levels of consistency and predictability in their courts.

In the past few centuries, the rise of the UK Parliament as the pre-eminent sovereign legislative power has meant that statutory law is now the highest source of law of the UK. This statutory law frequently replaces and overrides previous common law decisions and concepts. However, even in the 21st century, the common law remains an important and integral part of the UK legal system.

EXAMPLE

The law of murder in England and Wales is a historic creation of the common law and the definition of murder is still set out in common law and not in statute. Various other aspects of the law surrounding murder have been placed on a statutory basis, such as the mandatory sentence of life imprisonment and the abolition of the death penalty.

In contrast, the law of theft in England and Wales is now statutorily defined under s1 of the Theft Act 1968.

The courts are organised according to a strict system of hierarchy.

(See further **Chapter 2** on legislation and interpretation, **Chapter 4** on institutions of the state and **Chapter 5** on the **separation of powers** and the rule of law.)

3.1.2 **Structure of courts and tribunals**

See **Figure 3.1** for an overview of the structure of the courts and tribunals.

3.1.3 **The Supreme Court**

The Supreme Court came into operation in October 2009, replacing the House of Lords as the final court of appeal in the UK. The Supreme Court hears appeals regarding points of law that are of public or constitutional importance for the whole of the UK in civil cases, and for England and Wales and Northern Ireland in criminal cases.

3.1.4 **The Judicial Committee of the Privy Council**

The Judicial Committee of the Privy Council operates as the court of final appeal for a number of UK overseas territories, Crown dependencies and military sovereign bases and for certain Commonwealth countries. The Judicial Committee is no longer a court for any part of the UK.

3.1.5 **The senior courts of England and Wales**

The Court of Appeal and the High Court constitute the senior courts of England and Wales.

The Court of Appeal exercises an appellate jurisdiction only and is divided into two Divisions, civil and criminal.

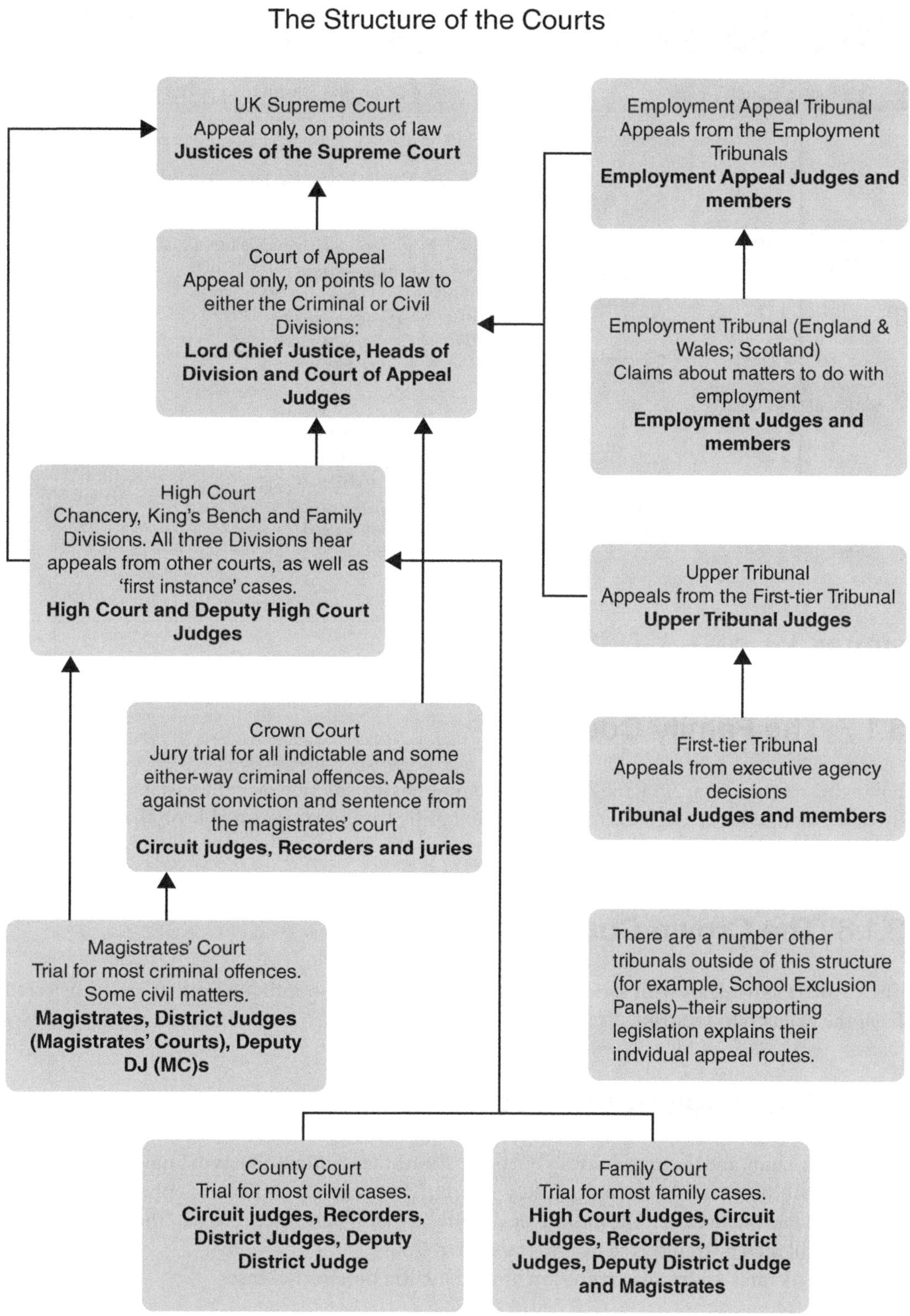

FIGURE 3.1 Courts and tribunal judiciary

The High Court (see **Figure 3.2**) hears complex and serious civil and family cases at first instance and hears appeals from lower courts. It is divided into three Divisions, namely the King's Bench Division, the Family Division and the Chancery Division. When the High Court is sitting as a Divisional Court, there will be at least two judges on the bench as opposed to just a single judge.

3.1.6 The County Court

The County Court deals with most civil cases in England and Wales.

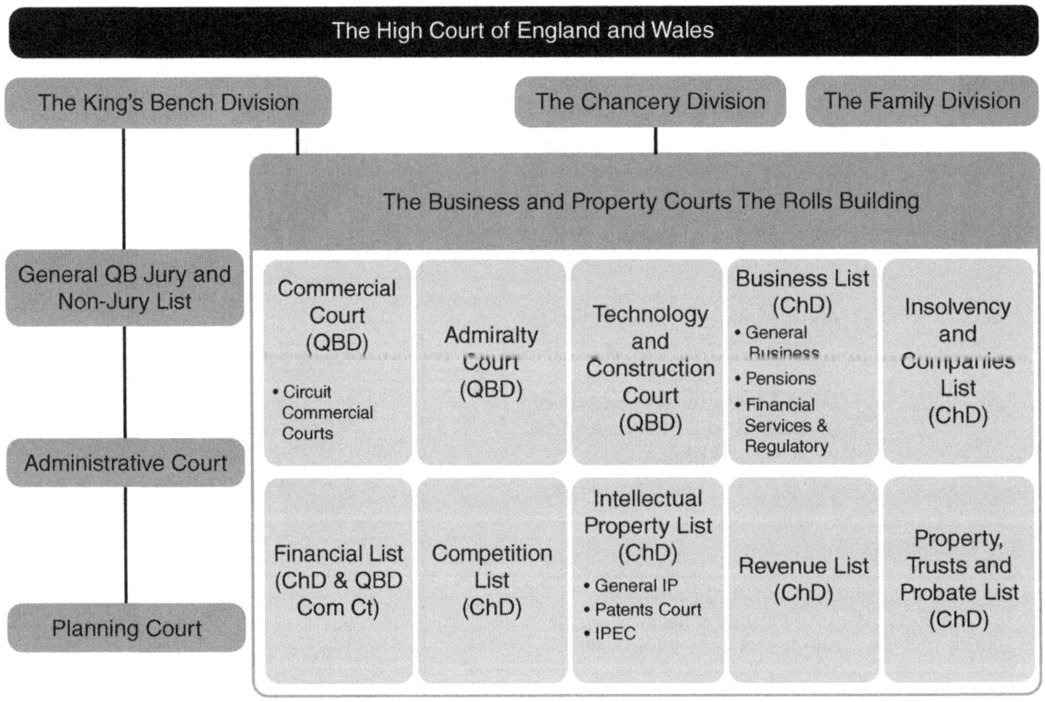

FIGURE 3.2 Structure of the High Court

3.1.7 The Family Court

Following reforms from 2014, the Family Court now has jurisdiction over the vast majority of family cases, alongside the High Court. (A guide to family law courts is available on the government website.)

3.1.8 The Crown Court

The Crown Court deals with serious criminal cases that are on indictment that are transferred from the magistrates' courts.

3.1.9 The magistrates' courts

The Crown Court and the magistrates' courts constitute the criminal courts of England and Wales. All criminal cases start in the magistrates' courts. Thus summary offences, either-way offences and indictable offences are all initially dealt with in the magistrates' courts. The more serious offences will then be transferred over to the Crown Court.

The magistrates' courts also exercise a limited jurisdiction in civil cases.

3.1.10 Tribunals

Alongside the courts, the UK legal system encompasses an extensive system of tribunals. Tribunals are specialised forums for dealing with disputes that are less formal than courts. The number of tribunals grew extensively after the Second World War, due to the rise of the welfare state, the creation of the National Health Service and growing responsibilities of local government and administration. A number of significant tribunals exist, such as the Employment Tribunal and the Employment Appeal Tribunal. The general system of tribunals comprises the First-tier Tribunal and the Upper Tribunal. Oversight of the tribunal system is secured by having the Court of Appeal hearing appeals from both the Employment Appeal Tribunal and the Upper Tribunal.

3.2 Basic features of the common law

A simple definition of the common law is that it is the law as declared by judges. In ancient times, such as the time of the Norman Conquest in 1066, disputes between landowners, neighbours, family members and traders would be dealt with by a plethora of processes and people. Decisions would be taken on spurious grounds, by partial 'judges' and were generally inconsistent and lacking in legal reasoning. King Henry II instituted a more centralised system of justice in the 12th century. This centralisation meant that court decisions shared something in 'common', namely more consistency in both the court structure across the country and the legal rules to be applied in these centres of justice.

As this system grew in stature and reputation, the idea of the 'common' law as the law of the land began to take hold. Over the centuries, the common law developed into a complex patchwork of rules and the system of court hierarchy became a pivotal aspect of the regime. In part, this was only possible due to the increasing professionalisation of recording the events that took place in court. Law reporting played an integral part in the common law becoming a logical, structured system of legal decision-making that could withstand the test of time.

The common law addresses both substantive aspects of the law, such as the definition of murder, and procedural aspects, such as court processes based on the inherent jurisdiction of the court.

In the modern conception of the English legal system, priority is now given to the enacted law of the democratic legislature, that is, the UK Parliament. Thus, common law principles or rules can be overridden by the passing of an Act of Parliament.

The fact that the common law has existed for almost a millennium is remarkable and its longevity is testament to the certainty, consistency and coherency it provides but also to its flexibility and ability to change, according to societal, economic, scientific and technological progress. The common law has to tread an extremely fine line between rigidity and flexibility. Like Goldilocks and the Three Bears, the common law cannot be too rigid and inflexible, nor too bendable, rather the common law must get the balance 'just right'. The way in which this is done is through the ability of judges to decide which cases they must follow and those which they can safely ignore.

In a simple sense, the common law is judge-made law, in the sense that it is 'made' in the courts through the cut and thrust of legal argumentation as advanced by the legal advisors of the parties before the court. However, the concept of unelected, unaccountable judges simply deciding cases on a whim or based on their prejudices is an unappealing prospect, particularly in a modern democratic state, governed by a group of elected representatives.

Thus, to survive challenge, the system of judicial precedent operates on a detailed system of legal reasoning. Judges will strive to explain their decision-making in great detail, in order to insulate their reasoning from criticism. This legal reasoning will take the form of a legal precedent, that is, the legal reason for the court making its decision, based on an in-depth review of previous cases. This legal precedent, according to the maxim of '*stare decisis*' is binding and will be followed by the courts in later, comparable cases. Rigid adherence to this doctrine has the potential to freeze the law at a particular stage of development and thereby cause injustice or unfairness. Therefore, judges will often endeavour to avoid the previous decision in order to prevent this injustice or unfairness. Such an approach, to an outsider such as a member of the public, may appear indefensible and to be little more than a game of chance or a roll of the dice. Hence, the centrality of legal reasoning to such decisions: law is a predictable system of order for regulation of society.

The common law has been criticised as being the worst form of judicial activism; that is, that judges are creating law. It may be better to describe the work of the judges as discovering the law or clarifying hidden elements of the fabric of the law. Judges may in a sense create the law where there is no prior analogous reasoning and they have to apply the law to novel situations. However, judges would reason that even here the law has simply been discovered or clarified as to its extent and application. The common law, even in this expansive sense, is sometimes limited in that judges are unable to adequately reform old law, particularly old statutes. In such cases, judges may be unable to effectively adjudicate the matter because gaps in the law may still exist or an unfavourable result has been created. Judges will then often, in *obiter dicta*, strongly suggest that law reform should be undertaken by Parliament, acting upon proposals from the Law Commission.

3.3 Finding and using the case law as legal authority

In the common law system, obviously accurate reporting of a legal case was, and is, of paramount importance in ensuring consistency and coherency in the law. Accurate reports of decided cases are of seminal importance for legal practitioners appearing before the courts, but the reports are also important for the general population as a guide for good citizenry and for the organisation of their affairs and the reports are essential reading for students of the law learning the intricacies and quirks of the English legal system.

In the Middle Ages, reporting of cases was haphazard and inconsistent as to quality, quantity and availability. Cases would generally be reported that were of prurient or other idiosyncratic interest to the recorder or to their audience and case reports were concentrated in major legal centres such as the capital. In the ensuing centuries, these issues largely subsisted. Reports would often only report the simple outcome of the case and not dwell on the legal reasoning behind the judgment and generally would be inaccurate. It is only in the 19th century that the system of law reporting vastly improves. In 1865, the Council for Law Reporting was created by the Inns of Court and the Law Society. This body became the Incorporated Council of Law Reporting for England and Wales and was instrumental in professionalising and improving the quality and scope of law reportage in England and Wales.

Reporting of cases can be undertaken by barristers, solicitors, legal academics and journalists and their reporting is recorded in various series of law reports and in newspapers. There is a hierarchy of such reports and the accepted higher ranking reports should be used in preference to the lower treated reports.

The reports from the Incorporated Council are treated with the utmost respect since they have the backing of the two main branches of the legal profession, namely barristers and solicitors. Reports are commonly identified by an abbreviation.

3.3.1 Examples from the Incorporated Council

EXAMPLE

- The Law Reports, comprising the Appeal Cases (AC), King's Bench Division (KB), Family Division (Fam) and Chancery Division (Ch).
- Weekly Law Reports (WLR).
- Industrial Case Reports (ICR).

The monopoly status of the Incorporated Council-sanctioned reports has been eaten into by a number of companies producing alternative reports.

3.3.2 Examples: private reportage

EXAMPLE

- Criminal Appeal Reports (Cr App R) published by Sweet & Maxwell.
- All England Law Reports (All ER) published by LexisNexis.

The rise of the internet saw a proliferation of alternative providers enter the market for law reports. Large corporate providers of legal information such as Sweet & Maxwell and LexisNexis, in addition to their traditional private reports, now also offer online electronic sources and databases, including their own in-house classification systems for identifying case reports.

The rise of these corporate databases and the continuing dominance of the Incorporated Council reports led to concerns that legal information was increasingly becoming only accessible to the legal profession and to those with sufficiently deep pockets. Thus, the democratising force of the internet allowed other not-for-profit providers to enter the market such as BAILII (the British and Irish Legal Information Institute). BAILII and other organisations use the internet to prepare and present unofficial reports of law cases. This proliferation of information threatened to undermine the use of citations in court, therefore Lord Woolf as Lord Chief Justice, introduced a Practice Direction in 2001 authorising the use of what is now termed a 'neutral citation' from 2001.

Under this system, every judgment from a UK court is assigned a neutral citation that signifies the date of the judgment, the court code and the case number.

EXAMPLE

- Supreme Court: UKSC
- Privy Council: UKPC
- House of Lords: UKHL
- Court of Appeal: EWCA Civ and EWCA Crim
- High Court: EWHC (Admin), EWHC (KB), EWHC (Ch) and EWHC (Fam)

As an example, the tenth case to be heard by the Supreme Court in 2024 would have the designation [2024] UKSC 10.

Legal counsel presenting their arguments in court should present their arguments according to the rules set out in *Practice Note (Citation of Cases: Restrictions and Rules)* [2001] 2 All ER 510 sub nom *Practice Direction (Citation of Authorities)* [2001] 1 WLR 1001 and *Practice Direction (Citation of Authorities (2012))* [2012] 2 All ER 255.

Reports of cases made by barristers are treated with the highest respect, nevertheless reports prepared by solicitors and other legal professionals with senior courts rights of audience are treated with a similar level of respect. Newspaper reports of cases should be referred to in the absence of the reports from legal counsel. In the absence of any reputable reports, shorthand reports and the notes of a shorthand writer or a transcript can be used.

The Civil Procedure Rules can often allow for practice directions to be used to offer guidance. Similarly, textbooks can also be discussed by legal counsel in court in order to aid interpretation but are not binding. As stated in **Chapter 2**, statements made by the government minister or promoter of a legislative Bill in Hansard, the official record of proceedings in Parliament, may now exceptionally be used as an aid to statutory construction where that law is ambiguous or obscure.

Academic citation of legal materials is often governed by the Oxford University Standard for the Citation of Legal Authorities (OSCOLA).

3.4 Judicial precedent

3.4.1 The reasons for precedent

The common law was developed in order to provide consistency, predictability and coherency to the English legal system and latterly the legal system of the UK. In the 19th century, the increasing professionalisation of the judiciary, centralised and consistent reporting of cases and greater organisation of the courts all coalesced to create the modern phenomenon of strict judicial precedence. Once the courts were organised and structured into a rigid, centralised hierarchy, rules had to be promulgated to ensure that lower courts would follow the judicial pronouncements of the higher courts on points of law. The rule was also necessary to ensure that courts of coordinate jurisdiction—that is, courts at the same horizontal plane in the court hierarchy—made consistent decisions and followed decisions of courts at the same level. This rule also extends to divisions within a court.

Indeed, the Lord Chancellor in 1972 stated that:

> The fact is, and I hope that it will never be necessary to say so again, that in the hierarchical system of courts that exists in this country, it is necessary for each lower tier, including the Court of Appeal, to accept loyally the decisions of the higher tier.
>
> (*Broome v Cassell & Co Ltd* [1972] AC 10)

3.4.2 **The hierarchy of courts**

The rigid, modern hierarchy of courts in England and Wales described earlier means that generally courts lower down in the hierarchy will be bound by the decisions of the courts above them. Thus, circuit judges will be bound by decisions of the High Court, the Court of Appeal and the Supreme Court, judges of the High Court will only be bound by decisions of the Court of Appeal and the Supreme Court and the judges of the Court of Appeal will be bound by the rulings of the Supreme Court.

The requirement to follow judicial precedent is justified on the basis that it provides, over time, that like cases will be treated alike. A consistent body of rules and systems will be established that offers invaluable guidance to judges when faced with novel questions before them. This equality of treatment promotes fairness. Precedent provides the basis for the rule of law and the principle of legality in that a legal system must offer a degree of predictability and certainty for those subject to its operation. The rule of law is also satisfied by precedent since it is important that judges do not engage in unfettered lawmaking.

Judges, when adjudicating cases, are often being asked to interpret the two main sources of law, Acts of Parliament and the common law.

When interpreting Acts of Parliament, judges should only implement and interpret the law as promulgated by the legislature since they are unelected officials, unaccountable to other organs of the state, and the modern conception of law in the UK assumes and provides that the highest source of law is that of the law promulgated by elected representatives in the legislature. As discussed in **Chapter 2**, judges may use external aids to interpret an Act of Parliament where that law is ambiguous or unclear.

When faced with a legal dispute involving the common law, the judges are given even more latitude in their role since they are entitled to interpret the common law more expansively to apply to novel situations and to adapt the common law to fit modern societal problems.

EXAMPLE

The case of *Airedale NHS Trust v Bland* [1993] 1 All ER 821 concerned Anthony Bland, who was a Liverpool FC football supporter who was crushed in the Hillsborough disaster of 15 April 1989. He suffered severe brain damage and was left unable to feed himself or feel anything. He was left in a persistent vegetative state. The legal question was whether doctors who chose to remove his feeding tube would be guilty of murder and would breach a doctor's duty of care to their patient. In the absence of an Act of Parliament explicitly allowing euthanasia, the question was left to the judges for determination. The judges unanimously held that a doctor would not be acting illegally where they removed a feeding tube from an unresponsive patient where it was in the best interests of that patient.

Precedent is also a basic human condition in that learning from the past will often lead to better decision-making in the future and past action often informs future behaviour. In that sense, the system of judicial precedent can be described as being evolutionary.

3.4.3 **Judgments**

A court is a legal body entrusted with adjudicating disputes. However, it is a very human organisation and in the English legal system particularly so. Individual judges are unique: unique in their background, upbringing, class and legal training and these factors shape a judge's thinking and approach to answering legal questions. First instance courts will invariably involve the judge sitting alone. Appellate courts and higher courts will comprise multiple members, often in odd numbering. This allows for differing views to be aired and in many cases will result in a majority decision. Thus, with a bench of five judges, you may have three judges agreeing an opinion on the law with the two others disagreeing on the law. In that case, the majority view is the opinion that decides the outcome of the case for the parties.

In civil law countries, it is common for the court, even when comprised of a number of judges, to simply deliver one judgment. It is said that the court is speaking with one voice. Even in other common law countries, such as the United States, where there are majority decisions, the judgment will be delivered by the leading judge on the majority view and that judgment has been agreed to by all the judges in the majority. In the UK legal system, individual judges are entitled to produce their own individual dictum in the eventual overall judgment of the court. Judges, even in the majority, may wish to add their own additional comments on why they decided the way they did. This is quite idiosyncratic. It was particularly a feature of the House of Lords (the predecessor to the Supreme Court), in part attributable to the fact that the House of Lords was part of the second chamber of the UK's legislature. Thus, in the past the judgment of the House was delivered by way of a series of speeches from within the chamber and typically each speech would start with a statement like 'I would dismiss the appeal' or 'I would agree the appeal'. Over time, this process became cumbersome and unwieldy and actual reading of full speeches stopped being delivered from the floor of the House in 1963. Further, it became more common that Law Lords in agreement would, if they were in full agreement, simply agree to the judgment by noting 'Having had the advantage of reading the speech(es) of . . .'. This practice has become more commonplace in the Supreme Court where it is often the case that the lead judgment will be prefaced by the name of the judge and in brackets it is added '(with whom Lords A, B and C agree)'. This is in part due to the increasing resort to Supreme Court benches of 7, 9 and 11 being constituted to hear the most significant constitutional cases (*Miller v Secretary of State for Exiting the EU* [2017] UKSC 5; *Miller v Prime Minister/Cherry v Advocate General for Scotland* [2019] UKSC 41).

This has a number of consequences. First, for example in a judgment of a five-bench court, there may be five separate decisions. Secondly, it opens up the concept that the dictum of the judge is simply seen as the verbatim report of what the judge said. That view of the judge may be excessive in word length, may be repetitive and may discuss a range of not wholly relevant material. Thus, the entire judgment of the court as reported will contain some absolutely essential pieces of information and some less important information.

The concept of *stare decisis*, outlined in this chapter, therefore only strictly relates to the operative part of the judgment; that is, the legal reasoning that justifies the decision of the court. The direct consequence flowing from this notion is that a judgment often contains essential legal reasoning justifying the decisions taken (the *ratio decidendi* (ratio)) or even multiple ratios, elements of extraneous discussion (*obiter dicta*, or things said in passing) and even sometimes the decision will have no ratio at all since it merely confirms and follows previous rulings. Only the legal reasoning, the ratio, is binding on later courts.

Thus, for lawyers, judges, law students and the general public, finding the ratio or ratios from judicial pronouncements is no easy task.

3.4.4 *Ratio decidendi*

> The common law is prized for its combination of principle and pragmatism. The doctrine of precedent is 'one of reason applied to experience'.
>
> (*Willers v Joyce* [2016] UKSC 43 at [42])

> The rules of precedent exist to provide legal certainty which is a foundation stone of the administration of justice and the rule of law. They ensure order and predictability whilst allowing for the development of the law in well-understood circumstances. They do not form a code which exists for its own sake and must, where circumstances arise, be capable of flexibility to ensure that they do not become self-defeating.
>
> (*R v Barton* [2020] EWCA Crim 575 at [103])

The very nature of the common law provides for the significance of judicial precedent. In a system predicated upon the centrality of the judge's role being to fill in gaps in the understanding of the patchwork of legal principles, rules and presumptions that apply to legal relations, certainty, predictability and uniformity assume the utmost importance.

As described earlier, the underlying rationale for the decision of the judges is known as a precedent. The principle as to why a court is bound to follow decisions in former cases (the case law) is, as discussed earlier, known as *stare decisis*. The full Latin tag is *stare rationibus decisis* and translates as 'the reasons for the decision stand'. Thus, it means that the reasoning or rationale of previous decisions should be upheld and followed.

The principle expressed to explain the decision is the *ratio decidendi*. The judges will analyse the facts of the case as presented by the parties in light of the current state of the law. The underlying pre-existing law may be statutory or based on the common law. The reasoning for the decision is based on an extraction or abstraction of the facts and application of general principles to the situation. Thus, the decision sets down guidelines for its application in the future. The specific outcome of the case is binding on the parties to the case whilst the abstract ratio underlying the decision has the force of law and is binding in the future for judges deciding cases.

The ratio may be discovered either solely within the confines of the decided case or may be taken from the context of other case law. Thus, when counsel put forward a case as authority, they are actually setting out the case as authority for a legal proposition and as such counsel must be able to express that proposition clearly and succinctly. This aspect of the definition of the ratio means that not every decided case will necessarily contain a ratio and that a decided case may contain within it multiple ratios.

The nature of judicial precedent and the ratio means that the issue of determining the meaning of the ratio falls not on the judges that made the decision but rather is one for the judges in the present case who are tasked with discovering the ratio or proposition in the earlier authorities that have been suggested to them by counsel.

Therefore, cases already decided offer clues, guidance, suggestions and options for legal counsel developing their arguments for their clients in their present case. If the lawyer successfully utilises these judgments before the judges in the present case, then the client wins their case but, more importantly, the case, especially if it has modified the pre-existing law, will now act as judicial precedent itself for future lawyers and judges to use to further develop the law in the next case, and so it goes on.

The ratio of a decision is limited by the context of the general law. Where the law has been developed since the judgment expressing the ratio, it falls on the judges hearing the instant case to determine whether the ratio is now broader or restrictive. The ratio must be consistent with the actual decision of the court. It is important to stress that when discovering the ratio, or even ratios, the judges will look to the opinions of the judges who decided the case but those opinions might not contain the ratio explicitly and the judges in the present case may disregard it as being too narrow or wide or simply inaccurate as regards the ratio. Determining the ratio is, of course, more problematic in the case of decisions made by judgments comprising a larger bench and where unanimity has not been achieved and in cases involving complex issues where there may be multiple legal issues that have arisen and thus multiple ratios at play.

3.4.5 **Example: how to determine the ratio and its scope and the concept of material facts**

EXAMPLE

The famous case of *Donoghue v Stevenson* 1932 SC (HL) 31, originating in Scotland, concerned Mrs Donoghue who went to a cafe with her friend and ordered her a ginger beer float, which is a sweet treat consisting of a glass of ginger beer topped with scoops of ice-cream. The ginger beer bottle was opaque and when it was opened a decomposed snail fell out of the bottle. Since Mrs Donoghue had not bought the drink herself but her friend had done so, the soft drink company had no contractual relationship with her so one of the legal questions for the court was whether Mrs Donoghue could bring an action for damages under the Scottish law of delict (the equivalent to English tort law). If the answer to that question was yes, that would then lead to further legal questions, such as what damage is recoverable and who is liable to compensate?

Lord Atkins expressed a number of general legal principles in his dicta. He said that a manufacturer who makes a product that does not allow for examination (ie to see inside) owes a duty of care to an ultimate consumer, that is, someone who uses the product.

Lord Atkins also discussed the neighbour principle, which means that a duty of care is owed to someone who is, in law, their neighbour, namely someone who should have been contemplated by the person when engaging in their actions.

Lord Atkin's dicta contains both the ratio and *obiter dicta*. The manufacturer's statement, after the judgment was delivered, quickly became the ratio for other courts, whilst the neighbourhood principle, because the other judges in the case did not expressly refer to it, was later viewed as just *obiter dicta*.

Is this ratio concerning manufacturers wide or narrow? What should judges in a future case do with this principle?

This principle of manufacturer liability was novel and controversial at the time and judges, when trying to discover the ratio, must also consider the wider societal and public policy issues. Interpret the principle too narrowly and this case only binds Scottish manufacturers of soft drinks to take care as regards the selling of soft drinks to females in cafes on the west coast of Scotland, if the later judges interpret these facts as being the only material facts. Interpret the principle too widely and every manufacturer of every type of good will need to take special care towards an unlimited number of people who come into contact with their goods. Under that view, significant numbers of manufacturers might choose to stop making goods under the threat of legal action, particularly where the liability extends to physical harm, and societal progress will grind to a halt.

3.4.6 Material facts of the case

The question of what is a material fact is of great importance to determining the ratio of a case. So, in this case, it was a material fact that the ginger beer float was bought by Mrs Donoghue's friend but was not consumed by her. Thus, the law of contract could not apply to the case.

The glass beer bottle being opaque and closed with a metal cap were material facts that had serious consequences for Stevenson. The cafe owner could not have known about the decomposing snail inside the bottle so could not be held responsible. Rather, the legal focus turned to the manufacturer of the soft drink. The manufacturer's processes were then the major focus of the case since he alone was responsible for ensuring the provenance of his drinks. Negligence could be reasonably inferred from the fact that the sealed units contained foreign bodies.

Later judges have endorsed a wider view of the ratio and have also treated the *obiter dicta* of the neighbourhood principle as persuasive. Treating the neighbourhood principle as persuasive in a subsequent case then allowed future judges to treat that principle as the ratio in the later case so that the neighbourhood principle is binding, until such time as it is overruled, reversed or suspended.

3.4.7 Determining material facts

Determining the material facts that justify the ratio or legal reasoning behind the decision can be a complicated matter. The extent to which judges think that a fact is material or not can have a great impact on the scope of the ratio and the narrow or wide application of that legal rule. For example, if a bystander is witness to a terrible accident in which someone is seriously injured or dies, the possibility of damages for nervous shock or psychiatric harm arises. The rules as to who can sue and for what type of damage will fundamentally depend upon the view of the judges as to what is or is not a material fact.

EXAMPLE

If the bystander was also mildly injured, the judge may determine that only people who suffer both physically and emotionally can claim, thus excluding those who only suffer psychologically.

If the bystander was related to the **victim** or knew the victim, the ability to claim may be limited to only people who have a tie of love and affection to the victim, thus excluding a large swathe of bystanders.

If the bystander only heard the crash and did not actually witness the accident, the judge may deny the bystander the right to sue. In a similar way, the judge may deny the claim where the bystander films the accident and views it through that lens.

If the bystander showed no outward distress until days or months later, the judge may refuse to allow the claim since the harm had to be suffered at the time of the crash.

In this way, the ratio may change over time generally as technology and society develop in an organic way, however the ratio will also be subject to forced change in the courts where it may be refined, narrowed, widened, limited or extended as future courts deal with broadly similar cases and the judges choose which elements of the factual matrix are material for their case.

3.4.8 Decisions as to facts

The court, when making a decision, will inevitably make a decision as to the facts before it. This opinion of the court as to facts will only bind the parties to the case and will not serve as binding on any other court. This rule also applies to statements on the facts expressed by the Supreme Court.

Material facts are, of course, of vital importance for the court deciding the case, however facts are not so important for a later court in determining the applicability of the ratio. Facts will be different for every single case and do not determine the ratio. The more important requirement is the recognition that the legal principle expressed by the ratio should apply to the case before it. If the later court is convinced that on the material facts before it and on the legal issues before it the previous case ratio is inapplicable, then that court is able to avoid that ratio. In such a case, the court is said to have distinguished that case law. What the later court is doing is ascertaining the material facts of the precedent case. Professor A L Goodhart, a leading authority on legal precedent, considers that the ratio of a case is restricted to the proposition(s) of law based on only the material facts of the case.

3.5 Options for the judges and courts

The concept of *stare decisis* and the system of judicial precedent presuppose that a court hearing a case should generally follow the precedent set out in an earlier judgment that is in point; that is, is relevant to the present case. However, determining that stance is not always apparent.

A court, in adjudicating a dispute, will invariably refer to previous case law. A previous decision may be positively treated by the court and thus follows the broad outline of the doctrine of *stare decisis*.

However, rigid adherence to the rule of *stare decisis* is not always appropriate and may lead to injustice, unfairness or arbitrariness. But, it is insufficient for the court hearing the case to simply say that it will not follow the case. The court must have a good reason for not following the case, particularly because lawyers and judges in future cases need legal guidance. The court avoiding the operation of the prior case will be at pains to justify its decision.

When a court positively deals with previous case law, it will be said to have:

- *Approved the case:* this is where the higher court considers that a case of a lower court was correctly decided.
- *Applied the case:* this simply refers to the situation where a court applies the reasoning of a previous case to its current case but where the facts are different from those of the previous case.
- *Followed the case:* this occurs where a court is bound by a previous decision of a coordinate or superior court and the material facts were substantially the same as in the present case.

Conversely, where a court has negatively dealt with previous case law, it is said that the court has:

- *Departed from the case:* this is where the Supreme Court has decided not to follow a previous judgment.

EXAMPLE

In *R (on the application of Begum) v Special Immigration Appeals Commission* [2021] UKSC 7, the Supreme Court was highly critical of the reasoning of the Court of Appeal in the case of Shamima Begum and the decision of the Home Secretary to strip her of UK citizenship because she travelled to Syria to join the terrorist group ISIL. Miss Begum sought to challenge that decision in the UK.

This would require the courts to grant leave to her to enter the UK. The Court of Appeal ordered the Home Secretary to issue her with travel documents to allow her to enter the UK for the purpose of challenging the decision to deprive her of her British nationality. The Supreme Court roundly rejected this decision of the Court of Appeal, holding that Miss Begum still constituted a major national security threat to the UK and thus should not be allowed entry to the country. The Supreme Court unanimously held that the Court of Appeal had made four errors of law. First, the Court of Appeal misunderstood the scope of appeal for challenging a decision to strip a UK national of their citizenship. Secondly, the Court of Appeal erred in substituting its view on national security for that of the Home Secretary. Thirdly, the Court of Appeal was mistaken when it decided that in a conflict between national security and the right to a fair trial, the right to a fair trial should prevail. Fourthly, the Court of Appeal misapplied the Home Secretary's extraterritorial human rights policy, treating it as a rule of law rather than as a policy guide for the exercise of discretionary power.

- *Distinguished the case:* this is where the court decides not to follow a prior case that is still perfectly sound in legal reasoning terms, and is thus still good law generally, but the present court has determined that it does not apply to the current case because the material facts are so different.
- *Disapproved of the case:* this is where a higher court may declare that it thinks a prior case heard by a lower court has been wrongly decided. The declaring court thus introduces serious doubt upon the value of that judgment and strongly suggests that the case might not be good law. In this example, the court has not expressly overruled the prior case because it was not necessary to do so. This term may also be used to describe the situation where a coordinate court disapproves of a prior decision but is prevented from overruling that decision.
- *Doubted the case:* this is where the court in its judgment expresses some doubt as to the case and suggests that the case may have been wrongly decided.
- *Not applied:* this is where the court decides not to apply a previous dicta, often because the decision is only persuasive.
- *Not followed:* this only occurs in relation to courts of coordinate jurisdiction; that is, courts on the same horizontal tier in the judicial hierarchy. The coordinate court chooses not to follow the prior decision of a court from the same level of hierarchy. This commonly occurs because the coordinate court has a choice of two or more cases from coordinate courts to decide from. Where the court is faced with two conflicting precedents, the court is able to choose which one to follow. The court will then be said to not be following the case.
- *Overruled:* this is where a higher court or the Supreme Court expressly decides that the ratio of an inferior court's decision in another case is wrong and this is bad law. Thus, the higher court has changed a precedent. Further, in the case of appeals to a higher court, the higher court will determine whether the decision of the lower court was correctly or incorrectly decided. Where the lower court got the decision 'right', the higher court will affirm the case and the judgment is good law. In a successful appeal, where the higher court determines that the lower court got the decision 'wrong', the higher court is said to have reversed the decision and that case is not good law.

Given the doctrine of parliamentary supremacy, common law decisions which are deemed to be problematic by politicians can be *superseded* by legislation, that is, an Act of Parliament is enacted with the express aim of changing the legal situation that arises by operation of the common law.

EXAMPLE

Oil fields in Burma were deliberately destroyed by UK army personnel in 1942 to prevent them falling into the hands of the Japanese. Decades after the war, the owners of the oil fields brought a claim in the Scottish courts for compensation. The House of Lords held in a 3:2 judgment that the destruction of the oil fields was tantamount to a requisitioning of the property since the action was done for the public good and thus the UK government was held liable to compensate the owners. The UK Parliament then passed the War Damages Act 1965 which retrospectively exempted the Crown from liability for lawful acts during war.

Thus, where a prior case has been reversed, overruled or superseded by legislation that case is no longer good law and cannot be used as authority.

- *Considered:* this is where a court simply refers to a previous case in its decision.

3.6 Treatment of cases from specific courts

3.6.1 Coordinate judges and the decisions of their peers

As a general principle, as explained earlier, the hierarchical structure of the English courts simply provides that the lower courts are bound to follow the judgments of the higher courts. However, that general rule is subject to certain limitations and exclusions when applied to particular categories of judges and courts and as applied to the decisions of coordinate courts. As a matter of internal logic, and for the sake of coherence, it is important that a court speaks with one voice, thus the judges of that court must be aware of the judgments of their peers and strive to act in accordance with the existing jurisprudence.

Nevertheless, neither statute nor common law requires a court to be bound by a decision of a coordinate court.

However, for the sake of legal certainty and in respect of judicial comity, or courtesy, a judge of first instance will normally be expected to follow the decision of another first instance judge. However, a judge at first instance may choose to depart from a decision of another first instance judge if they consider that that decision was wrongly decided. In the situation where there are a number of conflicting decisions of coordinate courts, a later judgment should be preferred if that decision fully considered previous decisions.

3.6.2 The High Court and its Divisions

In general, High Court judges are not strictly bound by their peers but should, for the sake of legal certainty, generally follow the decisions of their peers unless there is a powerful reason for not doing so.

A Divisional Court is generally bound by its own case law since it is undesirable that different judges of the same Division should speak with different voices.

This rule applies generally no matter the number of judges sitting, except in some criminal cases and when the court is exercising its supervisory jurisdiction such that a higher bench may depart from the case law of a lower bench. The Divisional Court may ignore previous decisions that are considered *per incuriam*; that is, the decision was made without due care to the law or the facts.

The Divisional Court may decide which of its decisions it should follow where there are two conflicting decisions.

Judgments of a Divisional Court will bind first instance judges, even of a different Division, but are not binding for the Employment Appeal Tribunal.

3.6.3 Court of Appeal

Decisions of the Court of Appeal that deal with questions of law are to be followed by both Divisional Courts and courts of first instance. The Court of Appeal is expected to follow its own decisions, except for a limited number of exceptions. This requirement to follow its previous decisions will apply until the decision is overruled by the Supreme Court.

The Court of Appeal can depart from its own decisions only in a number of specific circumstances.

First, the Court of Appeal may depart from its own decisions where there are two or more conflicting decisions that are potentially applicable. In such a case, the Court of Appeal must prefer one of them.

Secondly, if it is clear that an existing judgment of its own directly conflicts with an existing decision of the Supreme Court, then the Court of Appeal must refuse to follow that decision.

Thirdly, the Court of Appeal will not follow one of its own prior decisions where that decision is deemed to have been given *per incuriam*. However, the Court of Appeal will not lightly treat its own decisions as being *per incuriam*. The Court of Appeal will treat a prior case of its own as being *per incuriam* where the ignorance displayed in the judgment relates to an inconsistent statute or binding precedent.

The Court of Appeal, unlike the Supreme Court, is not at liberty to review its own earlier decisions. Thus, where a judgment of the Court of Appeal has misinterpreted a ruling of the Supreme Court, the Court of Appeal should still follow that wrong decision and leave the Supreme Court to resolve the issue.

In addition to the principles outlined above, in criminal cases the Court of Appeal may choose not to follow its previous decisions where the applicant is considered to be in prison unlawfully, the court considers that the law was misunderstood or misapplied and that the court is acting in its duty to set out principles and guidelines on sentencing.

One of the main functions of the Court of Appeal is to provide guidance on the quantum of damages for compensation arising from injuries. Thus, decisions of the Court of Appeal will often be cited to first instance judges.

3.6.4 **The Supreme Court**

It is a general principle that the Supreme Court binds every court below it. Even if a prior decision wrongly determined the law, that error can only be rectified by an Act of Parliament.

From the mid-19th century until 1966, the House of Lords (the judicial predecessor to the Supreme Court) was also strictly bound by its previous decisions, just like the lower courts. Given the tendency of that strict rule to stifle development of the law, in 1966 a practice statement was issued allowing for more flexibility (*Practice Statement (Judicial Precedent)* [1966] 1 WLR 1234).

Under this statement, the House of Lords (now the Supreme Court) could depart from its earlier decisions where 'it appears right to do so'.

The Supreme Court may decide to limit or question the ratio of one of its previous decisions where it deems it as being obscure, it is an outlier case in reference to other cases or legal principles or where the ratio was deemed too broad.

If the ratio is difficult to determine, the Supreme Court may refer back to a previous line of cases in order to adjudicate.

The Supreme Court is entitled to depart from its previous decisions where slavish adherence to that precedent may result in injustice or may unduly restrict development of the law.

It is to be noted that the relaxation of the binding precedence rule for the Supreme Court has not resulted in widespread use of the power. Since the practice statement was issued, case law of the House of Lords and its successor the Supreme Court addressing use of the practice statement is to be treated as precedent itself. (See Practice Direction 3 of the Supreme Court (Applications for Permission to Appeal), available on the Supreme Court's website.)

The case law connected with the operation of the practice statement provides the following guide to its use:

- The power should be used sparingly and should not be used simply because a past case is wrong or at least questionable. A case should only be overruled where the underpinning rationale has been lost and is no longer operative.
- The Supreme Court will exercise restraint in departing from its case law where such a decision risks retrospectively disturbing the foundations for a contract, fiscal set-up or property matters.
- Particular care should be taken by the Supreme Court when disturbing criminal law precedent.
- In a similar vein, the Supreme Court should avoid interfering with its decisions that are authority for a broad principle. It should not weaken a broad principle of law by introducing subtle distinctions, exceptions or limitations to the general position.
- A past decision can be overruled if its use in the present case would lead to injustice.
- The Supreme Court may avoid extremely old decisions where they have not been used in a modern context to justify legal argumentation.
- If the past judgment has been relied on for the purpose of stating the law, that case should not be easily overturned. Thus, the older the case, the more difficult it will be to disturb the settled rule. But, by the same token, recent jurisprudence is also unlikely to be overturned by the Supreme Court, given its novelty.

- The Supreme Court should be reluctant to use its power to overrule where the previous case relates to construction of a statute.
- A past decision will not be overruled in circumstances where Parliament has approved the rule and especially where Parliament had had an opportunity to change the law and did not do so.
- The power to overrule should not be used where to do so would engage the Supreme Court in effectively performing a law reform role.
- Supreme Court *obiter dicta* may possess the nature of a binding precedent in very limited circumstances where all of the justices are in agreement that a previous decision of the Court of Appeal should no longer be followed (*R v Booth; R v Barton* [2020] EWCA Crim 575).
- Where the decision is tainted by bias, that decision can be set aside (*R v Bow Street Metropolitan Stipendiary Magistrate, ex p Pinochet Ugarte (No 2)* [2000] 1 AC 119).
- The Court of Appeal is prevented from advising judges to ignore a decision of the Supreme Court on the grounds that it was *per incuriam* or unworkable. If the Court of Appeal cannot discover a ratio in a Supreme Court decision, the Court of Appeal can use its own reasoning as long as that reasoning supports the decision of the Supreme Court.
- The court seeking to justify departing from the precedent may often attempt to do so on the basis that the law has lost its meaning because of changes in social or political circumstances. In this situation, the court will decide according to the maxim *cessante ratione cessat ipsa lex* (when the rationale of the law ceases, the law also ceases).

EXAMPLE

A change in commercial practice and currency fluctuations might justify a significant change to the common law.

The old common law rule, in existence for over 350 years, was that a judgment of an English court that makes an award for payment has to be expressed in English pounds. In the case of *Miliangos* [1976] AC 443, Miliangos was a Swiss textile manufacturer who sued an English buyer of textiles who had refused to pay for the goods. Given serious fluctuations in the value of the Swiss Franc and the British pound, Miliangos faced only receiving a fraction of the actual losses he had incurred were the losses to be assessed in pounds at the date of the breach of contract. The House of Lords overruled this ancient rule and held that a UK court could express the payment to be awarded in foreign currency and that the date of exchange calculation could be the date of payment and not the date of breach of contract. The House of Lords was partly motivated to move in this direction as a direct result of persuasive, settled case law from the United States and a number of other common law countries that permitted an award of money to be calculated in foreign currency.

EXAMPLE

English judges had for a very long time declared that the common law offence of affray, that is, essentially group fighting, could only be a crime where the fighting took place outside. The ratio for this reasoning was that the action engaged in, the affray, has the potential to scare members of the public, thus the action should be treated as a public order offence. The House of Lords overturned this well-established view of the law and widened the offence to include group fighting indoors, in private (*Button v DPP, Swain v DPP* [1966] AC 591).

The common law offence of affray was abolished later in 1987, replaced with a statutory offence in s3 of the Public Order Act 1986 (see **Chapter 7** on public order).

3.7 Treatment of the construction of a statute

Courts will often be called upon to interpret the terms of an Act of Parliament as part of a legal case. The starting point for the court is to construe the actual words of the Act, however, where there is ambiguity or obscurity, the courts may be bound by prior precedent that interprets the provision.

Following the precedent of *Pepper v Hart* [1992] UKHL 3, courts may also refer to Hansard as an interpretive aid in limited circumstances (see **Chapter 2** on legislation and precedent).

3.8 Treatment of precedent from other courts and tribunals

The Employment Appeal Tribunal (EAT) must follow decisions of both the Supreme Court and the Court of Appeal. The EAT is not bound by High Court decisions or its own previous decisions but these judgments are highly persuasive.

3.8.1 Privy Council decisions

Legally, the Judicial Committee of the Privy Council is not strictly a court of the UK since its primary function now is to act as the appeal court for a number of UK overseas territories, Crown dependencies and overseas sovereign military bases and for a number of Commonwealth countries. Nevertheless, given that its membership is drawn from current and former Justices of the Supreme Court, its decisions are highly persuasive and assumed to be of great weight. The Privy Council is not bound by its previous decisions, but will only deviate from that body of law exceptionally.

3.8.2 Scottish and Northern Irish decisions

The need for convergence between the legal systems of the UK means that even though Scottish and Northern Irish jurisprudence is not binding on English courts, they must be given the utmost respect and it is desirable that the law be uniform in England and Scotland as much as possible, except of course for the position of devolved areas of competence.

Supreme Court judgments decided on a matter of principle should ordinarily apply to both jurisdictions, unless the Supreme Court holds otherwise. Clearly, the closer the law is in both countries, the greater the practice of convergence. Conversely, the greater the divergence between the countries, the less deferential the treatment of the 'foreign' case law. Thus, for areas such as revenue, taxation and constitutional law, English judges will attempt to track decisions of the Inner House of the Court of Session in Scotland and those of the Court of Appeal of Northern Ireland. In the position of the English law of trusts, English judges will rightly treat Scottish jurisprudence more sceptically given the fundamental differences in the treatment of trusts north and south of the border. More generally, where legislation applies across the UK, English courts will regularly follow the decisions of the Scottish and Northern Irish higher courts that interpret those relevant provisions.

3.8.3 Treatment of overseas decisions generally

Decisions on questions of foreign law are not binding since these are treated as questions of fact, including the case law of common law states. Decisions of foreign courts are in no way binding on an English court. However, that is not to say that they are without any significance. Decisions of foreign courts following a system of common law may act as a useful guide for the English courts, especially where that court is deciding upon a novel issue of facts, technology or scientific advances. English judges will treat decisions by the US Supreme Court with great respect. English judges will also treat decisions from the supreme courts of other significant common law systems with respect. The nature of the law at point in the English court will also affect the weight to be attached to decisions of foreign courts. For example, if commercial law, and in particular the law of carriage by sea or by air, is at the heart of the legal dispute, the English courts will pay particular attention to the judgments of US courts in order to ensure consistency in approach. Similar sentiments apply to other broad areas of law, such as damages, including issues as to remoteness of damage. However, where difference is justified, then the English judges will not be slow to refuse to apply the foreign rule.

3.8.4 Decisions of the Court of Justice of the European Union

Following the UK's departure from the European Union on 31 January 2020 and the end of the transition period on 31 December 2020, English courts and tribunals are no longer bound by any principles laid down, or decisions made, by the Court of Justice of the European Union. Further, English courts are now generally precluded from referring any legal question to the European Court of Justice. Nevertheless, an English court or tribunal is free to refer to any judgment of the Court of Justice made before or after Brexit day if relevant to the case before it. Such EU case-law will be of persuasive value only (*Lidl GB Ltd. v Tesco Stores Ltd.* [2023] EWHC 873 (Ch)).

In a similar vein, an English court or tribunal may also have regard to any decision by an EU institution where relevant.

On 31 December 2020, a significant part of EU law became an integral part of UK law by virtue of the European Union (Withdrawal) Act 2018. In particular, certain judgments of the Court of Justice made before Brexit day became part of UK law as retained EU case law. Domestic court decisions based on EU law and retained EU law were known as retained domestic case law. Following the enactment of the Retained EU Law (Revocation and Reform) Act 2023 retained case law, namely retained domestic and EU case law, are now known as assimilated case law, that is, assimilated domestic case law and assimilated EU case law. Retained EU law had a special place in the UK legal system after Brexit and was largely interpreted in the same way as EU law was when the UK was a member of the European Union. The 2023 act strips away these special features and amends s6 of the European Union (Withdrawal) Act 2018. Section 6 of the 2018 act provides for the treatment of EU-related case law in the UK court hierarchy. The amended version of s6, once fully in force, will lessen the forcefulness of that jurisprudence.

At present, the Supreme Court is not bound by any assimilated EU case law. However, the Supreme Court will only depart from retained EU case law using the same test it applies to deciding whether to depart from its own case law.

Similarly, the Court of Appeal, the Court Martial Appeal Court and the Lands Valuation Appeal Court are generally not bound by any assimilated EU case law. However, these courts will only depart from assimilated EU case law using the same test the Supreme Court applies in deciding whether to depart from its own case law.

In addition, the Court of Appeal, the Court Martial Appeal Court and the Lands Valuation Appeal Court are bound by post-transition case law which alters or applies EU case law.

The normal rules of precedent apply such that no court or tribunal is bound by any assimilated domestic case law over and above that which it would be bound by under the rule of *stare decisis*.

Under the future version of s6 of the 2018 act, the Supreme Court and higher courts, when deciding to depart from assimilated EU case law, must take into account three factors, namely, the fact that foreign court judgments are generally not binding, any relevant changes of circumstances that effect the assimilated EU case law and the extent to which the assimilated EU case law is restricting the proper development of domestic law. In addition, the future version of s6 provides for higher courts to depart from their own assimilated domestic case law if they consider it is the right thing to do, taking into account the extent to which the assimilated domestic case law is determined or influenced by assimilated EU case law that the court has departed from or would depart from, any relevant changes of circumstances and the extent to which the assimilated domestic case law is restricting the proper development of domestic law. Thus the Supreme Court and the higher courts will now find it much easier to depart from EU-related case law.

(see **Chapter 10** on EU law in the UK constitution).

3.8.5 European Court of Human Rights decisions

The European Court of Human Rights, as an international court, has no formal system of binding precedent, however it will not depart from its previous decisions unless there are compelling reasons to do so. The reluctance to depart from its own decisions stems from the need to ensure legal certainty and foreseeability, thus promoting the rule of law. Conversely, the European Court of Human Rights is prepared to depart from its decisions where to do so ensures that the European Convention on Human Rights remains a 'living instrument', responsive to societal, scientific and technological change.

Domestically, English courts and tribunals when faced with a question regarding **Convention rights** must, according to s2 of the Human Rights Act 1998, take into account any relevant judgment, decision, declaration or advisory opinion of the European Court of Human Rights and any opinion of the European Commission on Human Rights. This requirement is also supported by the UK government's international law obligation under Art 46 of the European Convention to comply with a judgment of the European Court of Human Rights.

The extent to which a domestic court should follow Strasbourg jurisprudence is determined largely on a case-by-case basis since the Strasbourg jurisprudence is only required to be taken account of. Thus, domestic judges will largely follow a clear and consistent line of Strasbourg authorities but domestic courts may also choose not to follow Strasbourg case law where it would conflict with domestic precedent (see **Chapter 8** on the Human Rights Act 1998).

The strong curial desire to follow clear and constant Strasbourg case-law is known as the mirroring principle and was clearly expressed by Lord Bingham in the *Ullah case (R v Special Adjudicator, ex p Ullah* [2004] UKHL 26). At [20] of the judgment, he pithily declared:

> The duty of national courts is to keep pace with the Strasbourg jurisprudence as it evolves over time: no more, but certainly no less.

KEY POINT SUMMARY

- The common law system as it has developed over the centuries has provided a high level of certainty, consistency and coherency into the law of England and Wales.
- A rigid hierarchy of centralised courts, if decisions are to be consistent and coherent, needs to adopt a system for ensuring high levels of predictability.
- The solution for the UK legal system was the creation of the doctrines of *stare decisis* and of *ratio decidendi*. Legally sound, well-reasoned judgments from the highest courts of the land need to be followed and respected by both coordinate courts, that is, courts at the same level in the hierarchy and those from lower down in the court hierarchy.
- The rule of law requires that legal decisions are understandable to the lay person and the citizenry generally. Judges, since they have wide decision-making powers and are unelected to their position, are required, for the purposes of accountability, to justify their decisions. The *ratio decidendi* largely performs this function. The reasons for the judgment are expressed in open court and are published in law reports, offering guidance both to professionals within the legal system and to the general public as to how the law operates.
- The system *of stare decisis* and *ratio decidendi* may become too rigid and inflexible, thus judges have a power to depart from previous decisions where necessary to avoid injustice or unfairness.
- Judges will base their legal reasoning on the material facts as presented to them in court. Material facts are facts that are absolutely essential for justifying the legal decision made. Future courts may be faced with very different circumstances that will justify deviation from the earlier position.
- Judges, when determining cases, may be inclined to comment on the difficulties with the present law, discuss hypothetical examples or may suggest how the law should be adapted for the future. These comments are often useful and insightful but are in no way binding and are referred to as *obiter dicta*, that is, things said in passing.

PART C
Public Law, EU Law and Human Rights

CHAPTER 4
The Institutions of the State

FUNCTIONING LEGAL KNOWLEDGE

This chapter covers the following functioning legal knowledge required to pass the SQE 1 assessments:

The institutions of the state

AUTHORITIES UNDERPINNING PRACTICE

The key authorities that underpin this area of practice are listed below. Note that for legislation you are linked to legislation.gov.uk.

Although much of the legislation on this government website is available in its amended form, the incorporation of new amendments into the text of legislation can be delayed. You should refer to legal databases to ensure you are referencing the most up-to-date legislation.

- Parliament Act 1911
  https://www.legislation.gov.uk/ukpga/Geo5/1-2/13
- Parliament Act 1949
  https://www.legislation.gov.uk/ukpga/Geo6/12-13-14/103/contents
- House of Lords Act 1999
  https://www.legislation.gov.uk/ukpga/1999/34/contents
- Constitutional Reform Act 2005
  https://www.legislation.gov.uk/ukpga/2005/4/contents
- The Bill of Rights 1689
  https://www.legislation.gov.uk/aep/WillandMarSess2/1/2/introduction
- Government of Wales Act 2006
  https://www.legislation.gov.uk/ukpga/2006/32/contents

4.1 Introduction

This chapter provides an overview of the main institutions of the UK as well as the devolution settlement of Wales. The **separation of powers** doctrine and the **rule of law**, discussed in greater detail in **Chapter 5**, provides that the three branches of the state—that is, the executive, the legislature and the judiciary—are limited in their roles and powers and offer a system of checks and balances to ensure that power is not abused, that no one is above the law, that everyone is equal before the law and that law lies behind the exercise of power, not arbitrary decision-making. The chapter sets out the role, composition and structure of these connected elements of the UK system of governance and the devolved system of governance in Wales.

The chapter also sets out the main features of the UK state and its constitution.

The UK, constitutionally, is a country of contrasts and contradictions. It has an uncodified, unwritten constitutional framework that offers a maximum level of flexibility, relies on political customs and norms (**constitutional conventions**) and residual sovereign power (**royal prerogative**) to work effectively. It is a representative democracy tracing its democratic roots back over nine centuries but is also a constitutional monarchy with an unelected head of state who regularly performs essential functions in the political and legal life of the nation. The UK is a unitary state that nevertheless comprises four historic, individual nations and three separate legal systems. The UK has a sovereign Parliament or supreme lawmaker for the entire territory of the UK, which is a bicameral legislature made up of the House of Commons and the House of Lords, but it also offers a system of asymmetrical devolution to the nations of the UK other than England, such that Scotland, Wales and Northern Ireland have their own subsidiary unicameral legislatures and administrations. The capital, London, has its own Assembly and an elected mayor. Certain English cities and regions also have elected mayors.

The UK subscribes to the rule of law and the separation of powers doctrine, but operates as a parliamentary executive with a fiercely independent judiciary. The day-to-day running of the country falls on the politically charged executive but also on the permanent, politically neutral, professional Civil Service. The UK is also a classically dualist state as regards international law, such that international commitments only bind the UK under international law and will only offer rights and obligations under UK law when that law has been duly incorporated into UK law by virtue of an Act of Parliament (see, eg, the dicta of the Supreme Court in the case of *R (on the application of SC, CB and 8 children) v Secretary of State for Work and Pensions* [2021] UKSC 26 at [77]). The best examples of international law obligations being integrated into the UK legal system are shown by the terms of the Human Rights Act 1998 as regards the European Convention on Human Rights 1950 (see **Chapter 8** on the Human Rights Act 1998) and the UK's 47-year membership of the European Union that was executed via the terms of the European Communities Act 1972 (see **Chapter 10** on EU law in the UK constitution).

4.2 Unique features of the UK constitution

As indicated earlier, the uninterrupted narrative of the constitutional history of the UK means that the UK's constitution is not to be found in one written, codified constitution. Rather, the UK's flexible uncodified constitution is to be found across a great swathe of legal and political provisions set out in numerous Acts of Parliament both modern and ancient, judicial precedent from the judgments of the courts and political customs, practices and maxims, collectively known as constitutional conventions. Residual power flows from the ancient royal prerogative. The UK is only one of a very small number of countries that have an uncodified constitutional system. The UK's system is described as a constitutional monarchy, whereby the monarch now plays a largely representative and ceremonial function only.

The constitution of the UK is thus the set of rules, regulations and procedures that guide the workings of government and delineate the relationship between the state and its citizens. The House of Lords has proposed the use of the following working definition to describe the UK's constitution:

> . . . the set of laws, rules and practices that create the basic institutions of the state, and its component and related parts, and stipulate the powers of those institutions and the relationship between the different institutions and between those institutions and the individual.
>
> (First Report by the Select Committee on the Constitution, 'Reviewing the Constitution: Terms of Reference and Method of Working' (HL Paper (2001–02) no 11) para 20)

The fact that across the globe only Israel, Saudi Arabia, Sweden and New Zealand share with the UK the dubious distinction of having a patchwork constitutional framework, means that the issue of codification and the creation of a written, all-encompassing constitution periodically arises (House of Commons Political and Constitutional Reform Committee Report on the UK Constitution, March 2015).

The enactment of the Human Rights Act 1998, though, with its provisions giving further effect to the European Convention on Human Rights 1950 in UK law (*R v Lyons* [2002] UKHL 44), has been put forward as a de facto constitution; however, its status as an Act of Parliament means that it is in a precarious situation and could be expressly repealed at a future date, leaving the question of codification unanswered. Indeed, discussion over whether it is desirable to have one overarching written constitutional document illustrates the flat, horizontal nature of the constitution of the UK. In an abstract sense, all Acts of Parliament have the same legal effect and priority. However, the courts have now accepted that certain Acts of Parliament are constitutional statutes that are immune from implied repeal; however, this judicial recognition does not detract from the fact that these Acts of Parliament have no special features as regards their creation or hierarchical priority over other law (see the greater discussion later, **Chapter 2** on legislation and interpretation and also the case of *R (HS2 Action Alliance Ltd) v Secretary of State for Transport* [2014] UKSC 3). However, Lord Hope in *H v Lord Advocate* [2012] UKSC 24, in *obiter* comments, suggested that constitutional statutes can be entrenched and can only be expressly repealed by clear words on the face of the later Act of Parliament purporting to repeal the constitutional statute.

Other features of the UK state and its constitution are that it has evolved over time and is thus inherently flexible and adaptable. This results in constitutional conventions assuming pivotal importance in the political system of check and balances between the organs of the state. Further, the original source of ministerial power stems from the ancient medieval power of the monarch—the royal prerogative. This flexible aspect of the British constitution is also one of its most controversial. The royal prerogative is that of the Crown. As discussed later, the notion of the Crown is wide and potentially confusing. The monarch can have a personal prerogative, the Crown in general can retain prerogative powers and in the modern UK the vast majority of prerogative powers are exercised by ministers, including the prime minister. Given the pivotal importance of democratic principles to the UK state, even where the King exercises a royal prerogative, this is usually done on the advice of his ministers such that the King is constitutionally bound to simply act on the advice given.

4.3 The royal prerogative

The royal prerogative was the king's absolute power to do anything. Over time, the monarch's power was limited and certain functions became the preserve of the legislature or of the judiciary. In terms of executive power, this power has gradually transferred over to the democratically elected Cabinet ministers.

The royal prerogative is now determined according to the **common law**, whereby the judges set out the existence, extent and limits of power. It has been described as:

> the residue of powers which remain vested in the Crown, and they are exercisable by ministers, provided that the exercise is consistent with Parliamentary legislation.
>
> (*R (Miller) v Secretary of State for Exiting the European Union* [2017] UKSC 5)

The famous jurist A V Dicey set out the royal prerogative as:

> the remaining portion of the Crown's original authority, and it is therefore . . . the name for the residue of discretionary power left at any moment in the hands of the Crown, whether such power be in fact exercised by the King himself or by his Ministers.

The prerogative is divided into three general divisions.

The first category is those of the sovereign as regards the constitution. The sovereign has the right to advise, encourage and warn ministers, to appoint the prime minister and to grant **royal assent to legislative proposals**.

The second category is that of the legal prerogatives of the Crown. The Crown is thus legally entitled to animals such as sturgeon, swans and whales. Historically, the Crown was entitled to impress men into the Royal Navy (the press gang). The Crown is also deemed to be able to do no wrong and is only bound by statute where that is expressly stated in the law or will extend to the Crown by necessary implication.

The third category contains the most extensive prerogative powers, namely those of executive powers. These powers are now routinely exercised by ministers by virtue of constitutional convention. The signing and ratifying of international conventions, diplomacy and deployment of the armed forces are all classic executive prerogative powers.

Over time, given the supremacy of Parliament, in a conflict between a statutory power that exists over an area and the residual prerogative power, the courts will defer to the statutory power and prefer that that statutory power be used (*Attorney-General v De Keyser's Royal Hotel* [1920] AC 508). Further, given the centrality of Parliament to the modern state of the UK, Parliament is entitled to pass laws that replace the residual prerogative power with a statutorily defined power. Therefore, over time, the extent, scope and application of royal prerogative reduces, primarily because it is '350 years and a civil war too late' to increase resort to the royal prerogative (*BBC v Johns* [1965] Ch 32).

This orthodox view of the complex interface between prerogative powers and statutorily defined powers has been challenged by the enactment and subsequent repeal of the Fixed-Term Parliaments Act 2011. The power to dissolve Parliament and call a general election was a classic prerogative power of the prime minister until the enactment of the Fixed-Term Parliaments Act 2011. This act removed the prerogative power of the prime minister to call an election and created five-year fixed terms. However the subsequent repeal of the 2011 act and the coming into force of the Dissolution and Calling of Parliament Act 2022 has created a curious legal situation in that the prerogative of the prime minister to call a general election has been effectively revived.

In the past, the hiring and firing of civil servants was an exercise in the royal prerogative but this power is now a statutory power in the Constitutional Reform and Governance Act 2010. This Act also added statutory parliamentary control to the ratification of international treaties.

The nature of certain prerogatives is highly political in nature and, as such, the courts are reluctant to engage in **judicial review** of the exercise of these powers since the judges are not in the best position to determine whether the political decision of the minister was legally and politically correct (*Council of Civil Service Unions v Minister for the Civil Service* [1984] UKHL 6). The first question for the court hearing claims about the legality of use of prerogative power is to determine whether the exercise of the power is **justiciable** or not; that is, capable of being reviewed by a court. Where the prerogative power is akin to a legal power, the courts will generally agree to determine the dispute, whereas where the prerogative power is operating more as a discretionary political power, the courts will tend to defer to the person or body taking the decision. As said by Lord Scarman in the GCHQ case (*Council of Civil Service Unions v Minister for the Civil Service* [1984] UKHL 9):

> Today, therefore, the controlling factor in determining whether the exercise of prerogative power is subject to judicial review is not its source but its subject matter.

The Supreme Court has also determined that it is competent to adjudicate on questions as to the legal scope of a prerogative power and not just about the actual exercise of the power (*Cherry/Miller 2* [2019] UKSC 41; see the discussion in **Chapter 6** on judicial review).

4.4 The organs of the state

4.4.1 The head of state

The current monarch, King Charles III, is the head of state of the UK and for a number of Commonwealth realm countries. King Charles III automatically became monarch after the death of his mother Queen Elizabeth II on 8 September 2022 and was officially crowned monarch in an elaborate coronation ceremony on May 2023. The monarch is the supreme executive officer of the state. He is the commander-in-chief of the armed forces of the UK—that is, the Army, the Royal Navy and the Royal Air Force—and also the Supreme Governor of the Church of England.

He is technically the font of justice and of honorary titles and awards. Declarations of war and peace and generally relations between the UK and foreign countries are undertaken in the name of the King, but exercised through his government ministers.

Historically, the monarch was the font of all power—legislative, administrative or executive and judicial—with the only real constraint on power being the need for the monarch's rule to be exercised under law. Over time, the monarch lost most of these powers with executive power transferring to the government, legislative power residing in Parliament and judicial power residing with the judges within the Royal Courts of Justice. The fact that the UK is a democracy and a constitutional monarchy means that constitutional conventions stipulate that the monarch exercises his residual power in accordance with the advice of his ministers.

The monarch acts in a personal capacity, in a representative capacity and in a formal, technical requirement capacity.

The monarch now plays no role in the dispensing of justice via the courts.

The common law provides that the monarch can do wrong on the basis that the monarch is perfect and as such no remedy lies against the King personally in civil or criminal law. However, since the Crown exercises its power through His Majesty's Government, legal actions against ministers of state are competent under the Crown Proceedings Act 1947.

The monarch performs a critical technical role in the promulgation of legislation by Parliament, the ceremonial role of the State Opening of Parliament and the operation of the prorogation of Parliament (*Cherry/Miller 2* [2019] UKSC 41). At the State Opening of Parliament, the monarch will read out the King's Speech. This speech is written by the government and sets out the legislative proposals and policies that the government intends to introduce during the course of the forthcoming parliamentary session.

It is a significant constitutional convention that the head of state has the right to be consulted, the right to encourage and the right to warn. However, he is obliged to follow the formal advice proffered to him. As part of this function, the King receives intelligence briefings from the Intelligence Services and meets the prime minister on a weekly basis in private.

4.4.2 The Crown

The term the Crown can be used interchangeably, and confusingly, to mean the monarch or the executive. Historically, the monarch was the font of all power, be it legislative, executive or judicial. Over time, the active, interventionist role of the monarch has been progressively reduced, with the majority of Crown powers now being exercised by the executive branch of the state, acting in the name of the Crown. The monarch retains some residual executive powers and possesses extremely limited legislative powers. In terms of legislation, the Crown may only enact primary legislation with the consent of Parliament and the ability to pass primary and secondary legislation relies on express statutory authority or on the prerogative power to issue Orders in Council (*R (Bancoult) v Foreign Secretary* [2008] UKHL 61).

Nevertheless, the separation of powers doctrine has not resulted in changes to the terminology used to describe the various branches of the state. So for example, in England, the senior courts are referred to as the Royal Courts of Justice and the judges in England are His Majesty's judges, the UK government is His Majesty's Government (HMG), the police uphold the King's peace and prosecutions in the higher criminal courts of England and Wales run in the name of the Crown (Rex).

The Crown was historically immune from liability and courts could not find the Crown guilty of contempt of court or raise **injunctions** against the Crown. The transfer of executive power to **ministers of the Crown** now means that they can be proceeded against for damages, injunctive relief and for contempt of court.

4.4.3 Select bodies exercising public and governmental functions

4.4.3.1 The Bank of England

The Bank of England was first set up in the last decade of the 17th century as a private bank to finance the English government. Money was required to fund the conflict between England and France. The bank was established by King William and King Mary by royal charter in 1694. The remit of the bank was to 'promote the public Good and Benefit of our People'. This objective subsists today, over three centuries later.

The bank is the central bank of the UK. The bank issues banknotes in England and Wales and regulates providers of finance, such as banks and financial firms, to promote trust in the financial system via the Prudential Regulation Authority. It was nationalised after the Second World War and was given a degree of independence from government by the Labour government in 1997. The bank is headed by a governor who works as part of a wider governance team called the Court of Directors. Policy decisions are taken by three committees, the Financial Policy Committee (FPC), the Monetary Policy Committee (MPC) and the Prudential Regulation Committee (PRC).

Through the MPC, the bank is entrusted with maintaining the purchasing power of the pound by taking action to keep inflation within set limits, currently 2%, and to take decisions as to quantitative easing; that is, the production and release of more money into the economy. The FPC is there to identify, monitor and proactively remove or reduce systemic risks within the UK financial system to maintain its resilience. The FPC is also tasked with supporting the UK government's economic policy. The PRC is the decision-making arm of the Prudential Regulation Authority.

The Bank of England's status, role and position is set out in the Bank of England Act 1998 as amended and through its charters. Given the pivotal role of the bank in the economy of the UK, its activities are closely scrutinised by the House of Common's Treasury Committee and the bank works closely with the UK Treasury, the Financial Conduct Authority and major central banks across Europe and the world, via a series of memorandums of understanding (MoUs).

4.4.3.2 Police

Policing across the UK is split into numerous localised and nationwide elements. Across the UK, there are 45 territorial police forces. In Scotland, Police Scotland is responsible for policing across the entire territory of Scotland. Policing in Northern Ireland is the responsibility of the Police Service of Northern Ireland. In Wales, policing is organised into four territorial regions, namely South Wales Police, North Wales Police, Gwent Police and Dyfed-Powys Police. England is organised into 39 separate regional police forces.

Alongside these 45 territorial forces, there are three national police forces, namely British Transport Police, which polices the UK railway network, the Civil Nuclear Constabulary, tasked with protecting the UK's non-military nuclear installations and the safe transportation of nuclear material across the UK and the Ministry of Defence Police, which is responsible for the safety and security of Ministry of Defence installations and personnel, its nuclear weapons and military-grade nuclear material.

These national and territorial forces are assisted by numerous agencies such as the National Crime Agency which is dedicated to fighting serious and organised crime, Action Fraud, the national reporting portal for fraud and cybercrime and the National Police Air service which offers air support for the 43 police forces of England and Wales.

Police accountability is assured by various means. In England and Wales, each police force area is ultimately responsible to an elected Police and Crime Commissioner (PCC). The PCC for each area is tasked with maintaining an efficient and effective police force and holds the relevant chief constable to account for the delivery of the local police and crime plan. Further accountability is ensured through the provision of Police and Crime Panels which challenge, scrutinise and support the PCCs. This system of accountability does not preclude recourse to the courts.

Complaints against the police in England and Wales are dealt with by the Independent Office for Police Conduct.

4.4.3.3 The Crown Prosecution Service

The Crown Prosecution Service (CPS) is responsible for the prosecution of the vast majority of crime in England and Wales. The CPS decides which cases are to be taken forward for prosecution, decides upon the relevant charge to be laid in the most serious or complex cases, advises the police during the initial investigatory stage, prepares cases for presentation at court and supports victims and prosecution witnesses. Prosecutors are bound, in the exercise of their powers, to act fairly, objectively and independently. Prosecutors are bound by the Code for Crown Prosecutors, that provides that someone should only be charged with a crime when there is enough evidence to provide a realistic prospect of a conviction and that the prosecution is in the **public interest**.

4.4.3.4 The Director of Public Prosecutions

The Director of Public Prosecutions (DPP) is the head of the CPS and is the third highest prosecutor in England and Wales, behind the Attorney General and the Solicitor General.

4.4.3.5 Prosecution agencies

Alongside the CPS, there exist a number of government agencies that prosecute crime, often in close conjunction with the CPS. For example, the Health and Safety Executive prosecutes breaches of health and safety legislation. The Service Prosecuting Authority is the lead prosecuting authority for criminal offences allegedly committed by serving personnel from the three armed forces. The Environment Agency will undertake prosecutions as a last resort. Trading standards officers from local authorities will prosecute traders who violate various commercial laws that uphold fair trade.

The Serious Fraud Office investigates and prosecutes incidences of serious fraud, corruption and bribery.

The Competition and Markets Authority (CMA) will prosecute companies alleged to be acting in a cartel.

A significant number of private and public organisations may institute a private prosecution, as well as private individuals under s6 of the Prosecution of Offenders Act 1985. Examples include the RSPCA and Royal Mail and, in certain cases, it will be appropriate for the CPS to take over these prosecutions (*R (on the application of Gujra) v CPS* [2012] UKSC 52).

4.4.3.6 Attorney General for England and Wales

The Attorney General for England and Wales is the chief legal advisor for the Crown. The Attorney General performs a number of public interest functions and offers advice on international relations, human rights and devolution and questions of law concerning Bills and legal policy generally. The Attorney General oversees the operation of the DPP, the Serious Fraud Office and the CPS. The Attorney General can refer unduly lenient sentences to the Court of Appeal and will bring contempt of court proceedings and cases to protect charities. The Attorney General can also submit references to the Court of Appeal for clarity on a point of law where an accused has been acquitted.

4.4.3.7 Solicitor General for England and Wales

The Solicitor General is the second highest law officer for England and Wales. The Solicitor General effectively deputises for the Attorney General and offers support to the Attorney General. The Attorney General and Solicitor General are assisted by the Attorney General's Office.

4.4.3.8 Local authorities

Local authorities across the UK carry out a number of important civic functions and deliver many important services to their residents. Local authorities are operated by elected officials and have the power to make local secondary laws such as bye-laws.

4.4.3.9 His Majesty's Armed Forces

The British Army, the Royal Navy and the Royal Air Force make up the three branches of His Majesty's Armed Forces. Members of the armed forces take an oath of allegiance to the King as the commander-in-chief, although the actual deployment of troops is, by convention, exercised by the prime minister via the prerogative. By virtue of the Bill of Rights 1689, the UK Parliament is required to enact an Armed Forces Bill at least every five years in order to maintain a permanent, standing army (Armed Forces Act 2006).

Following the political fall-out of the decision to invade Iraq by Tony Blair in 2003, there is a growing custom and convention that Parliament should be notified in advance of military operations; however, given the inherent unpredictability and flexibility in when and in what way military action will be taken, it remains the case that often Parliament will be notified afterwards (parliamentary approval for military action).

EXAMPLE

In August 2013, the then UK Prime Minister David Cameron sought parliamentary approval for air strikes against the Syrian regime of Bashar Al-Assad. He lost the vote. David Cameron's defeat was the first since Lord North's defeat in the Commons in 1782 over continued military action in the US War of Independence. In April 2018, Prime Minister Theresa May sought retrospective approval for air strikes in Syria. The air strikes were ordered after the Syrian regime was alleged to have used chemical weapons in violation of international law. The UK government won the vote.

4.4.3.10 The NHS

The National Health Service provides emergency and routine healthcare throughout the UK. Health is a devolved matter so that the NHS is organised into four regions—England, Scotland, Wales and Northern Ireland.

The NHS in England and Wales is also subdivided into a number of NHS Trusts that function across geographical lines and according to specialised functions. The provision of general medical services (general practitioner (GP) services) are run by individual GP practices that are run under contract with the NHS.

4.5 The executive

His Majesty's Government carries out the function of running the country in the name of the Crown. The executive executes law, that is, it enforces and applies the law. The sovereign legislature, the UK Parliament, passes and enacts law and the judiciary interprets that law and aspects of the common law. However, given the fluid nature of the separation of powers doctrine in the UK and the complexity of modern life, ministers of the Crown are also regularly granted extensive powers to enact delegated secondary legislation, such as Statutory Instruments (SIs) under the provisions of the relevant Act of Parliament.

The term 'executive' in its widest definition encompasses His Majesty's Government, government departments, government agencies and **public bodies**, the Civil Service that work within these bodies and also includes personnel such as the armed forces and the police.

In 21st-century UK, the complexity of modern life means that there are normally over 20 ministerial departments and 20 non-ministerial departments, with over 400 agencies and public bodies in existence. There are details available on the government's website. Also see the House of Commons Briefing Paper, 'Public Bodies 2018'.

Thus, the activities of government are spread widely across a vast number of separate bodies.

His Majesty's Government comprises ministers appointed by the Crown. The prime minister is the head of His Majesty's Government and presides over his or her Cabinet, which is made up of **Secretaries of State** who have ultimate responsibility for a wide range of policy areas.

4.5.1 The Civil Service

The Civil Service is an incredibly large diffuse organisation, encompassing officials at the highest levels of government through to employees in government departments, non-departmental public bodies (NDPBs) and executive agencies.

The executive includes ministers of non-Cabinet rank and the Civil Service; that is, the entire range of public servants who work for the public good in the government agencies, departments and public bodies. Civil servants now work under the statutory framework set out in the Constitutional Reform and Governance Act 2010. Under this Act, various codes were enacted to guide the conduct of ministers and civil servants (Cabinet Office, *Civil Service Code* (2010) and the *Ministerial Code* (2010)).

4.5.2 The prime minister

The prime minister is the head of His Majesty's Government and assumes ultimate responsibility for the decisions and policy of the government. The prime minister is appointed by the sovereign and in practice that choice is the person who commands the confidence of the House of Commons, usually by being head of the party that has more than half of the seats in the House of Commons. The prime minister in modern times is invariably a Member of Parliament. The prime minister, on appointment, will become a member of the Privy Council.

The prime minister is also in overall charge of the Civil Service and various government agencies, for example the Intelligence Services, namely the Secret Intelligence Service (SIS or MI6), the Security Service (MI5) and Government Communications Headquarters (GCHQ), although day-to-day responsibility for SIS rests with the Foreign Secretary. The prime minister selects his or her

Cabinet, represents the government in the House of Commons and is the Minister for the Union, ensuring that the government works for the four nations of the UK. Within the Cabinet, the prime minister is first among equals (*primus inter partes*). The prime minister resides at 10 Downing Street and is entitled to use the Chequers residence.

The prime minister is also the First Lord of the Treasury and is paid a salary. The title prime minister is not an official title and the role developed over time, with it generally being recognised as beginning in 1721 with the term of office of Sir Robert Walpole. The prime minister exercises power normally by convention and the office has never been placed on a statutory basis. The *Cabinet Manual* from 2011 sets out some of the main functions of the role of the prime minister (*Cabinet Manual* (2011)).

Under this document, the prime minister is described as being the 'Sovereign's principal adviser', is the head of government, takes the lead on significant matters of state, chairs Cabinet and has overall responsibility for the organisation of government. However, it is important to note that the *Cabinet Manual* is not a legal text so is not binding.

The prime minister has a number of significant royal prerogative powers relating to national security. The prime minister, acting in conjunction with the Foreign Secretary and the Defence Secretary, has the power to deploy His Majesty's Armed Forces. The prime minister is also able to declare war (and peace) and to launch a nuclear attack. In such circumstances, the prime minister will have consulted with his or her Cabinet colleagues and officials from the military prior to taking such a drastic step and will be cognisant of the UK's obligations under the United Nations Charter. The prime minister also signs and ratifies international conventions under the prerogative; however, the House of Commons now plays a role in this process via the Constitutional Reform and Governance Act 2010.

Conversely, the prime minister also renounces international treaties via the prerogative, although where the renunciation of a treaty would directly affect national law and the rights of UK citizens that decision will need to be approved by Parliament since the royal prerogative cannot be used to change national law (*Miller I* [2017] UKSC 5).

The prime minister enjoys extensive power over the appointment of individuals to head up certain public bodies, such as **royal commissions** and inquiries, and to recommend the granting of honours and peerages to the sovereign, who by convention will grant the award.

The prime minister is accountable through a number of avenues. As a Member of Parliament, the prime minister is accountable to his or her constituents and runs the risk of losing their seat at a general election. As the head of the party with the majority in Parliament (or in conjunction with other parties), he or she runs the risk of their party losing its overall majority at a general election. As the leader of their party, the prime minister must ensure party loyalty through deployment of the **Whip system** and a prime minister who loses the confidence of their party may be removed and replaced. More generally, the House of Commons may lose confidence in the prime minister and their government (confidence motions).

In 2011, the UK Parliament enacted the Fixed-Term Parliaments Act. This Act was enacted to ensure that the Conservative and Liberal Democrat coalition government could govern for a full parliamentary term. Previously, a Parliament would be dissolved through exercise of the royal prerogative by the sovereign, acting on the advice of the prime minister. Thus, Parliaments would often not last a full five years, with the prime minister being able to effectively choose the most advantageous time to dissolve Parliament and trigger the calling of a general election. The 2011 Act provided for a fixed five-year parliamentary term, with the period only being reduced in two situations. First, where at least two-thirds of MPs approved a motion to hold an early general election or, secondly, where a motion of no confidence in His Majesty's Government had been passed and 14 days elapsed without the passing of a confidence motion. The 2011 Act was a controversial law and s 7(4) of the Act provided for its own review by the end of 2020. The UK government elected in December 2019 intended, regardless of the outcome of the review instituted, to legislate to reactivate the prerogative right of the prime minister to select the date of a general election. The Parliamentary Joint Committee on the Fixed-Term Parliaments Act 2011 produced its report in March 2011 and the UK Parliament has since passed the Dissolution and Calling of Parliament Act 2022, in effect reviving the previous prerogative power.

The prime minister faces the Opposition leader and other MPs at weekly Prime Minister's Questions on the floor of the House and appears before committees of Parliament. The prime minister also faces scrutiny from the media.

Finally, scrutiny of the prime minister is also provided via the courts and the process of judicial review (see **Chapter 6** on judicial review).

4.5.3 **The Cabinet**

The prime minister is first among equals amongst his or her Cabinet; however, the prime minister is able to hire and fire ministers at will. The Cabinet is the ultimate decision-maker in government. Indeed, the Cabinet ensures that there is government by committee and not government by prime ministerial diktat. The Cabinet is bound by the concept of **collective responsibility**, such that all ministers, even if they were not present at the Cabinet meeting, are bound to support the collective decision taken and are accountable to Parliament. Collective responsibility can be waived explicitly. If a minister is no longer able to support the collective position of the government, they should resign and the prime minister remains able to sack that minister in the event that they do not so resign. Select ministers within Cabinet may be allowed by the prime minister to meet as a smaller political cabinet

The Cabinet is supported by a number of Cabinet committees and sub-committees. An example of such a committee is the National Security Council which meets weekly to discuss serious issues such as terrorism and the work of the security and intelligence agencies. Cabinet Office Briefing Room A (COBRA) meetings are special meetings convened by the prime minister and attended by a small number of ministers to deal with emergency situations.

4.5.4 **Ministers**

Ministers are in charge of discrete policy areas and head up the relevant government department. Typically, there will be over 20 government ministerial departments such as the Foreign, Commonwealth and Development Office, the Home Office, His Majesty's Treasury, the Ministry of Defence and the Ministry of Justice. Each Secretary of State is ultimately responsible for the operation of their department and is bound by the convention of individual responsibility. Individual private misconduct by the minister will result in their dismissal or the expectation that they will resign. Ministers are bound by the Ministerial Code which sets out the standards expected from ministers. However, as a convention, this rule of ministerial accountability is not always complied with.

EXAMPLE 1

Priti Patel, as Home Secretary, was alleged to have shouted at and intimidated civil servants within her department. A report into the allegations was undertaken by Sir Alex Allen, the prime minister's Head of Standards. This report found that the Home Secretary's behaviour could amount to the definition of bullying under the Ministerial Code but that she had done so unintentionally. After the publication, Prime Minister Johnson stated that he did not think the Home Secretary had bullied anyone and thus effectively sidelined the report. Sir Alex Allen chose to resign and a judicial review case was then raised at the High Court by the FDA Union, challenging the decision of the prime minister. That case was effectively dismissed in December 2021 (*R (on the application of FDA) v The Prime Minister* [2021] EWHC 3279 (Admin).

However, Priti Patel did resign in 2017 from her role as International Development Secretary, when she failed to disclose a number of private meetings she had had with politicians and business people in Israel.

EXAMPLE 2

Bullying of civil servants had more serious repercussions for Dominic Raab, the Justice Secretary and Deputy Prime Minister, in April 2023. Allegations first surfaced in November 2022 that Dominic Raab had shouted at civil servants and threw tomatoes at staff. An investigation into these, and other, allegations was ordered by Prime Minister Rishi Sunak. Adam Tolley KC produced his report on the 21 April 2023. https://www.gov.uk/government/publications/investigation-report-to-the-prime-minister Dominic Raab had no choice but to resign in light of the publication of the report because he had publicly stated that he would resign if any allegation of bullying was found to be proven in the investigative report.

EXAMPLE 3

Matt Hancock decided to resign as Health Secretary at the end of June 2021 when footage emerged of him kissing one of his aides, in breach of the social distancing rules in place during the Covid-19 pandemic.

EXAMPLE 4

Damian Green resigned as First Secretary of State in 2017 over inaccurate and misleading statements he gave to an investigation into pornography found on his House of Commons computer in 2008.

EXAMPLE 5

Liam Fox resigned as Defence Secretary in 2011 over his relationship with his close friend Adam Werritty. Mr Werritty met Dr Fox on 18 foreign business trips. Mr Werritty had received funding for these trips from a number of defence and intelligence companies.

Ministers are expected to uphold the highest standards of behaviour and to act with propriety. Ministers should act professionally at all times, should comply with the law and observe the seven Nolan standards of professional life, which are selflessness, integrity, objectivity, accountability, openness, honesty and leadership.

Ministers, as part of their role, are supposed to inform and explain their decisions, apologise for their mistakes, take remedial action to remedy the situation and ultimately resign if necessary (individual ministerial responsibility).

In the past, ministers were expected to resign over all failures within a department, however, over time, a distinction has been made between political responsibility and political accountability.

EXAMPLE 1

Neville Chamberlain was the prime minister in 1940 when the Allied Forces failed to prevent Germany invading Norway. This failure led to him resigning and being replaced by Winston Churchill.

EXAMPLE 2

In the Crichel Down affair, agricultural land was requisitioned by the government in 1938 for bombing practice by the Royal Air Force. Winston Churchill stated that the land would eventually be returned to the original owners. The land was, instead, transferred over to the Ministry of Agriculture and was leased out. After a public inquiry that exposed various shortcomings in the ministry, Sir Thomas Dugdale, as the Minister for Agriculture, resigned.

The complexity of modern life and the creation of independent agencies has meant that this strict application of the rules has given way to a more flexible approach. The creation of arm's length executive agencies and NDPBs means that the relevant minister is not directly responsible for every action of that public body, thus reducing the likelihood that the minister will resign for the failings of that organisation.

EXAMPLE 3

John Profumo, the Secretary of State for War, had an extra-marital affair with Christine Keeler. Christine was also in a relationship with a Soviet naval attaché. Thus, there was a risk of state secrets being passed to the Russians. However, a bigger issue was the fact that Profumo lied to the House of Commons in stating that he was not involved with Christine Keeler. This fact led to his resignation.

EXAMPLE 4

In 1993, Derek Lewis, the Director General of HM Prison Service, flagged up problems within the prison service. In 1995, a number of IRA prisoners escaped from prison. Home Secretary Michael Howard chose to sack Mr Lewis over the scandal rather than resigning himself.

In the same way as the Prime Minister, Ministers, when they are MPs, are subject to scrutiny by their constituents and are ultimately liable to lose their seat at the next general election and under the Recall of MPs Act 2015. Ministers face scrutiny on the floor of the House in oral questioning and both oral and written questioning takes place in various committees of the House. Ministers are also scrutinised by the media and their decisions are judicially reviewable in the courts.

4.6 The UK Parliament

The Parliament of the UK performs a number of significant constitutional tasks. Its primary function is to act as the ultimate Sovereign legislature for the entire territory of the UK. The Parliament also provides for a check on the Government's activities, by challenging its work and generally offering scrutiny of the work of ministers and the prime minister. The Parliament also operates as the nation's most significant debating forum, acting as a grand inquest for the nation, offering a space to question large-scale technological, societal and scientific challenges. The Parliament also plays an important role in approving and thereafter scrutinising the raising of public money via taxes.

In order to carry out its public role as inquisitor for the nation, scrutiniser of the work of ministers and as the lawmaker for the country, it is essential that proceedings in Parliament are not subject to challenge in the courts or by government, thus ensuring the separation of powers between the legislature, the executive and the judiciary. Parliament as a whole, and its members individually, must be able to freely speak without fear of legal repercussions and must be able to regulate its own affairs. Thus, Parliament, its members and its officials are granted parliamentary privilege against statements made in Parliament being used as the basis for a defamation action. Article 9 of the Bill of Rights 1689 guarantees freedom of speech for parliamentarians. It provides that:

> freedom of speech and debates or proceedings in Parliament ought not to be impeached or questioned in any court or place out of Parliament.

This freedom is absolute. Members of Parliament and of the Lords are able to say whatever they like in Parliament and no legal action can be instigated against them.

EXAMPLE

In 2018, Lord Hain used parliamentary privilege to name Sir Philip Green as the subject of a number of legal claims concerning inappropriate behaviour in his workplace. A court injunction was in place prohibiting the naming of the defendant due to the existence of a number of non-disclosure agreements (NDAs).

It is for the courts to determine the outer limits of this privilege and the courts have limited the application of the privilege by declaring that the privilege only extends to matters that are within the exclusive cognisance of Parliament. Thus, in *Cherry/Miller 2* [2019] UKSC 41, the Supreme Court was able to adjudicate on the legality of the proposed prorogation of Parliament because the decision to prorogate was a decision of the prime minister about the Parliament and not a decision of the Parliament. Similarly, in the case of *R v Chaytor* [2010] UKSC 52, allegations of fraud against four MPs following the expenses scandal of 2009 were held by the Supreme Court to be competent to be heard before a court of law and were not suitable for determination internally by the parliamentary standards procedures.

Reports of proceedings in Parliament are given qualified privilege under the Defamation Act 1996 as amended.

The UK Parliament is bicameral, that is it comprises two chambers, the House of Commons and the House of Lords. The House of Commons is the First Chamber of Parliament and its main function is to debate, discuss and approve new laws. To this end, a number of general committees are found in the Commons and are there to scrutinise proposed legislation in detail. There are also a number of Grand Committees of the Commons that look at proposed legislation on a regional basis. In contrast, the term Grand Committee in the lords refers to a specialised debating chamber for the Lords to debate Bills.

4.6.1 Overview of the House of Commons

The concept of Parliament stretches back to the 10th century. The early kings of England sought advice from important, powerful people and also needed their support to enforce and apply their laws and rules. Great Councils, made up of the nobility and bishops, were convened to discuss pressing problems. This concept evolved into the idea of parliament. Parliament became the main way for the king to raise taxes to fund his activities. Representation was therefore extended to the shires and boroughs in order to legitimate the raising of taxes since everyone under the jurisdiction was liable to contribute. Parliament also performed a judicial function at this time. Over centuries, Parliament assumed ever greater importance and the monarch became subject to the power of the Parliament and reliant on it to make laws. The meetings of the enlarged Parliament became unwieldy; thus it became the practice for the nobility and clergy to meet separately as the Upper Chamber, now the House of Lords, whilst the representatives of the shires and boroughs would meet as the Lower Chamber, now the House of Commons. As conceptions of democracy began to take root, the Commons became the more powerful legislative chamber of the Parliament. In the 17th century, disquiet over the arbitrary behaviour of James I and Charles I led to the beheading of Charles I, civil war and the creation of a **republic** under Oliver Cromwell. Although the monarchy was restored under Charles II, the power of the monarch was now severely curtailed and the anointing of William of Orange in the Glorious Revolution directly led to legislative limits being placed upon the power of the monarch in the form of the Bill of Rights 1689. The concept of a constitutional monarchy was born. During the past three centuries, the role of the monarch has reduced further and the rules for electing representatives to the House of Commons have been reformed to provide for universal suffrage. Under various Representation of the People Acts, the franchise is now extended to all adults over the age of 18. The electoral franchise for the UK Parliament is open to British, Irish and Commonwealth citizens over the age of 18 who are resident in the constituency and on the electoral roll. Special rules apply for people with no fixed abode, armed forces personnel posted abroad and citizens living abroad. Peers, the vast majority of prisoners and those convicted of electoral offences are ineligible to vote. The blanket rule against prisoner voting is based on the notion of 'civic death' whereby offending against the norms of society results in a loss of civic participation rights as well as a loss of liberty through incarceration. This policy was condemned by the European Court of Human Rights in the case of *Hirst (No 2)* [2005] ECHR 681 as being indiscriminate and disproportionate (see the House of Common's briefing paper, 'Prisoners' Voting Rights? Developments since 2015'). Minimal changes have been undertaken in England such that prisoners who are on home detention curfew (HDC) and prisoners in the community released on temporary licence (ROTL) can now vote. More generous reforms to the franchise as regards prisoners were made in Scotland for Scottish elections.

The House of Commons is made up of 650 representatives for the entire United Kingdom of Great Britain and Northern Ireland. To be eligible to stand as an MP, the candidate needs to be 18 or over and be a British, Irish or eligible Commonwealth citizen. Certain office-holders are prevented from standing as an MP. The main examples of roles that disqualify a person from standing are those of civil servant, judge, police officer, armed forces personnel and a peer of the House of Lords. A conviction for an offence where the sentence imposed was imprisonment for over a year and being currently bankrupt will prevent a candidate from standing as a candidate.

More generally, as a direct result of the expenses scandal in 2009, during their tenure as an MP, MPs can be subject to a process to recall their position as an elected representative. Where the MP has been convicted of a crime and sentenced to a term of imprisonment, and the time period for appeal has passed, where the MP has been suspended from the House for ten sitting days or 14 days generally, or where the MP has committed an expenses offence under the Parliamentary Standards Act 2009, a recall petition can be organised in the constituency, under the Recall of MPs Act 2015.

Following Scottish devolution, the number of representatives for Scotland was reduced. Periodic review of the size of UK constituencies is undertaken by the four Boundary Commissions for the four nations of the UK and they act according to the Rules of Redistribution in order to reflect changing demographics and to achieve a reasonable level of parity between constituency population size (see the House of Common's briefing paper, 'Constituency Boundary Reviews and the number of MPs'). For the UK general election taking place on Thursday the 4th of July 2024, Scotland and Wales lost two and eight seats respectively.

Controversy surrounds the overall size of certain constituencies since some constituencies elect an MP with a significantly lower number of votes than the average and some constituencies can only elect an MP with a higher number of voters. The most extreme example of this is the fact that the Western Isles (Na h-Eileanan an Iar) constituency has a registered electorate of around 21,000 and, at the other extreme, the Isle of Wight had a constituency of over 113,000. For the UK general election in July 2024, the Isle of Wight constituency will be split into two successor constituencies, East and West. The average UK constituency population is 71,000 and the boundary review undertaken by the Boundary Commission for England for 2023 was based on the target of a 5% tolerance of the electoral quota of 73,393 constituents (Boundary Review 2023 Which Seats will change in the UK?).

Further controversy surrounds the relationship between the size of the registered population entitled to vote and the actual population of the constituency. In most cases, there is a ratio of 4 to 3 between the total population of the constituency and the registered population. As an extreme example, in the case of the old constituency of Kensington and Chelsea, it had a population of over 150,000 but had only just over 64,000 registered voters. Thus, more than half of the population had no input into the election of their MP. Criticism has also been levelled at the system of first past the post (FPTP) whereby an election candidate only needs one vote more than their nearest rival to secure the election. In certain constituencies considered 'safe', that is where the incumbent MP has a significant majority, voters who vote for other candidates have no real power in their vote. Further, FPTP may encourage tactical voting and voters may not get to express their view on an individual electoral candidate since the choice of candidate has already been selected by the party. In such a case, the voter may not like the individual candidate but has no choice but to vote for the candidate. Periodically, there are calls for this system to be reformed to accommodate some element of proportional representation to avoid the wasting of a vote. Advocates of the present system point to its inherent simplicity, the strong link that can exist between the MP and their constituency, the ability of the system to normally produce a strong government with a significant majority and its ability to reduce the impact of extremist parties as reasons for its retention.

In the referendum on alternative voting in 2011, the UK population roundly rejected reform to the established FPTP system.

Alternative systems of voting are in place for the elections to a range of devolved administrations and for internal elections in both Houses of Parliament. Elections for the chair of a House of Commons committee, the by-election of peers and election of the Lord Speaker are all undertaken by a system of alternative vote (AV). The supplementary vote (SV) system is used for the election of English mayors and Police and Crime Commissioners. Elections for the Northern Ireland Assembly, local elections in Scotland and Northern Ireland and voting for Deputy Speakers in the House of Commons are organised under a system of single transferrable vote (STV). Elections to the Scottish and Welsh Parliaments and the London Assembly take place under the additional member system (AMS).

4.6.2 **Overview of the House of Lords**

As outlined earlier, the English Parliament started in the 11th century as an advisory council for the Anglo-Saxon kings. The Parliament then split into two distinct chambers in the 13th and 14th centuries.

Historically, the monarch, in order to maintain their pre-eminent position in the country, would bestow hereditary titles and peerages upon favoured people.

The titles granted were duke, marquess, earl, viscount and baron. This system of patronage provided that these titles came with parcels of land under the feudal system. The granting of such titles and land holdings ensured loyalty towards the monarch and offered the king a means of co-opting these peers into the system of enforcing the king's laws and rules across the kingdom. These titles would invariably be passed down the line to the male heir under the law of primogeniture. These ennobled peers were entitled to sit and participate in the work of the House of Lords and are known as Lords Temporal. The term Lords Temporal also extended, over time, to ennobled judges who sat as Law Lords in the House of Lords when sitting as the highest court of the UK. The Law Lords were life peers, such that their title did not pass to their heir. Alongside these Lords Temporal, Bishops of the Church of England were selected to sit as Lords Spiritual (see also the House of Lords In Focus publication 'Lord Spiritual in the House of Lords explained' https://lordslibrary.parliament.uk/lords-spiritual-in-the-house-of-lords-explained/). Presently there are 26 Lords Spiritual comprising the two Archbishops of Canterbury and York, the Bishops of London, Durham and Winchester and 21 other bishops from across England based on longevity of their position.

4.6.3 **Reform to the House of Lords**

Increasing discontent with the concept of hereditary privilege generally, the particular issue of hereditary privilege offering influence within the UK's legislative system, the domination of the House by white, male upper-class Lords and the ballooning of membership of the House of Lords to over 1,000 during the 20th century, led to calls to reform the unelected House of Lords.

The first modern major reform was the creation of life peers under the Life Peerages Act 1958 and the Peerage Act 1963. These Acts provided for the creation of life peerages that would not transmit to the offspring of the Lord. The 1963 Act allowed for female life peers ennobled under the 1958 Act to take up their seat in the House of Lords, allowed all Scottish hereditary peers to sit in the House and for hereditary peer holders to renounce their title.

Major reform to the House of Lords was then proposed by Prime Minister Tony Blair under his first administration. However, even with a massive 197 majority, the Labour government of 1997 only managed minimal reform. The reforms envisaged a two-stage process. The first stage would deal with the issue of hereditary peers. The reform would have removed hereditary peers entirely and the second stage would introduce elections for appointment to the newly reformed second chamber.

The first stage of reform was set out in the House of Lords Act 1999. This Act removed most of the hereditary peers; however, because of political pressure, a rump of peers was allowed to remain. In total, 667 peers were removed, 90 peers were selected to remain via a ballot system and two peers were retained due to their royal positions within the House, that is, the Earl Marshall and the Lord Great Chamberlain.

Presently, vacancies arising amongst the 90 hereditary peers are replaced by a two-process by-election system. Fifteen of the peers are office holders and are replaced by a vote of the whole House whilst the remaining 75 peers are voted in by the members of the same political grouping. The 75 peers are split as follows: 42 Conservatives, 2 Labour, 3 Liberal Democrats and 28 cross-benchers. British, Irish and Commonwealth citizens over 21 years of age who are UK resident and pay tax are eligible to apply or be nominated to become a peer. See the House of Lords briefing on membership, for more information.

The House of Lords Appointment Commission was established in 2000 to assist with this process. The Commission is an independent, advisory, non-departmental public body. The Commission recommends two non-partisan peers every year and vets the partisan nominations proposed by the political parties in order to ensure propriety. However, the appointment of life peers is subject to little control beyond this aspect of the Commission's role and, indeed, the prime minister may appoint a person who has not been approved by the Commission.

EXAMPLE

Peter Cruddas was appointed to the Lords by Prime Minister Boris Johnson in December 2020, in defiance of the view of the Lords Appointment Commission. The then Speaker of the Lords, Lord Fowler, criticised this decision and has called for reform of the appointment system.

The King formally appoints peers, although those appointments are based on the recommendations for appointment from the prime minister, exercising his or her prerogative powers. Thus, in principle, prime ministers can appoint as many peers as they like to greatly inflate the size of the House and to ensure they have a majority in the House.

Critics of the original reform were concerned that a two-stage process of reform would allow the more complicated and controversial aspects of reform to be saved for a later day and so it has proven. Since the 1999 Act, no substantive reform has been instigated. All successive governments have tried, without success, to agree, enact and implement change. The only changes that have been enacted are those of the House of Lords Reform Act 2014 and the House of Lords (Expulsion and Suspension) Act 2015. Under these Acts, lords can now retire and peers can be expelled or suspended from the House for bad behaviour.

EXAMPLE

Prior to the 2015 Act, peers could not be removed from the House of Lords following conviction of a serious crime. Lord Conrad Black of Crossharbour was convicted of fraud in the United States 2007 and simply took an extended leave of absence from the House of Lords. By doing so, he was technically entitled to later return to the House of Lords by giving three months' notice of his intention.

EXAMPLE

Lord Ahmed resigned from the House of Lords in November 2020 after an internal conduct committee report of the House of Lords found that he had taken sexual and emotional advantage of a woman (https://committees.parliament.uk/publications/3468/documents/33452/default/). Separately, in January 2022, Lord Ahmed was found guilty of the historic sexual abuse of two children in the 1970s and he was sentenced to five and a half years in jail in February 2022. Despite this catalogue of behaviour and offending, at present, he is entitled to retain his title since there is no mechanism to strip Lords of their titles following conviction, other than requesting an Act of Parliament be passed authorising the removal of the title.

Further, non-attendance of a peer for an entire session of Parliament disentitles them to attend in the next session and conviction of a peer for a serious offence also causes that peer to cease being a member of the House. In such circumstances involving a hereditary peer, a by-election must be held to elect a new peer, in order to maintain the 90-strong cohort of hereditary peers. This voting system is archaic, anachronistic and was only supposed to be a transitional arrangement; however, it has now been in place for over two decades.

The Scottish Independence referendum in September 2014 and the divisive Brexit referendum in June 2016 have highlighted further issues with the House of Lords such that further reforms have been suggested to transform the House of Lords into a Senate of the Regions and Nations in order to make the second chamber of the UK Parliament more representative of the four nations of the UK and more representative of neglected, underrepresented regions of England.

The House of Lords presently comprises 790 members eligible to vote and participate in proceedings of the House, out of a maximum membership of 827. This figure is way in excess of the numbers of elected representatives in the lower chamber House of Commons and compares unfavourably with the size of second chambers across the world, with only the Chinese People's Congress having a larger membership.

4.6.4 Scrutiny and control of the executive and the Crown by Parliament

The Houses of Parliament also perform a number of non-legislative functions. One of their major roles is to control the executive and the Crown. This can be done on the floor of both Houses through debate and through more concentrated, forensic scrutiny via the questioning of government policy via the committee structure of both Houses.

His Majesty's Government is made up of representatives coming from both Houses, thus ensuring accountability. Government ministers are subject to scrutiny through questioning by MPs and lords on the floor of the Houses via oral question times or via written questions. In a similar vein, the prime minister also faces oral questions on a weekly basis in the Commons. More general scrutiny occurs in the course of debates in both Houses. The House of Lords scrutinises the work of the government through questioning and debating. Lords may question ministers in the chamber or in writing and can require ministers to respond to debates on general issues of concern.

The House of Lords also engages in in-depth debate of contemporary issues through its numerous select committees.

Committees perform an essential scrutiny role across both Houses. In the House of Commons, departmental select committees are set up to shadow the work of government and as such generally reflect the division of government into departments. Some select committees have a broader remit and address a number of horizontal issues that cut across one or more government departments. For example, the **Public Accounts Committee** scrutinises all aspects of the value for money of government projects, programmes and services and the Public Administration and Constitutional Affairs Committee examines constitutional issues, the quality and standards of the Civil Service and the reports of the Parliamentary and Health Service Ombudsman (see the Hansard Society). Select committees can either be permanent or time-limited. An example of a time-limited select committee was the Exiting the European Union Committee which shadowed the Department for Exiting the European Union between 2016 and 2020.

Certain committees deal with specific types of documents such as the House of Commons Statutory Instruments Committee.

Both Houses have a Liaison Committee which considers a range of select committee matters. The House of Commons Liaison Committee is made up of the chairs of the select committees of the House of Commons and an additional member who chairs the committee. This committee can take evidence from the prime minister, thus providing for political accountability. The House of Lords Liaison Committee is made up of peers who are elected by the House, plus the heads of the three main political parties and the Deputy Speaker.

There are a number of joint select committees that comprise MPs and peers and therefore work across both Houses. The permanent joint committees are those of human rights, national security strategy and statutory instruments.

Proceedings of the committees can be followed online.

Parliament performs a wider scrutiny role than simply that of scrutinising legislative proposals. It is there to request and receive information from the government and scrutinise general government policy. Parliament grants the supply of money to the Crown, effectively the government, and the Commons scrutinises the spending of that public money and the raising of revenue via taxation.

The Crown will set out the financial requirements of the government as set out by the relevant ministers and thereafter set out a demand for this money.

The Commons will then grant those supplies and provide for the ways and means for that money to be raised, effectively through the raising of tax. The raising of taxes to generate public money must be done on an annual basis.

Thus, the Chancellor delivers a budget speech in the Commons every year setting out his or her plans for changing tax and setting out the conditions of the UK economy; thereafter the Finance Bill is presented for approval (see further **Chapter 2** on legislation and interpretation).

The Houses are also in charge of ensuring that parliamentary privileges are maintained and protected such that the Parliament can effectively discharge its functions.

4.7 Parliament as the legislature

The legislature in the UK is the King in Parliament, that is, the monarch and the Lords Spiritual and Temporal in the House of Lords and the elected representatives in the House of Commons. Neither the Lords nor the Commons has legal personality or corporate existence. The monarch now plays no formal role in law-making, with the role reduced to a symbolic one of granting royal assent, the last formal technical process required to transform a legislative Bill into an Act of the UK Parliament. The last time royal assent was not approved by the monarch was in 1708 when Queen Anne refused to approve the Scottish Militia Bill. This over 300-year-old convention underpins the constitutional primacy or sovereignty of the UK Parliament.

In certain cases, legislative proposals may impact on royal interests or the royal prerogative and those proposals will require the King's consent by convention. This latter role has proved to be controversial because of the number of reported instances in which it has been deemed to be necessary to provide advance notice of legislative proposals to the King, endangering the centuries-old convention of the political neutrality of the monarch (see the Queen's or Prince's Consent Pamphlet and the *Guardian* newspaper's reportage on its use).

4.7.1 Parliament

The King in Parliament is the sovereign, supreme legislature for the entirety of the UK, able to enact Acts of Parliament, the highest form of law in the UK legal system.

However, legislative power is not the absolute preserve of the King in Parliament. A number of other bodies possess limited legislative power, such as the devolved legislatures in Scotland, Wales and Northern Ireland, the King in Council, ministers exercising delegated law-making powers and local authorities and certain private bodies authorised to enact bye-laws.

4.7.2 Parliamentary sovereignty

Acts of the UK Parliament are the highest source of law in the UK legal system and thus cannot be questioned in the courts. A great number of Acts of the UK Parliament have immense constitutional significance and, over time, the Supreme Court has now accepted the idea that not all Acts of Parliament are created equal, such that there is now a hierarchy of Acts of the UK Parliament whereby constitutional statutes benefit from a higher status that offers a greater level of protection from repeal and replacement. Constitutional statutes are judicially recognised as being immune from implied repeal and can only be expressly repealed by a later Act of Parliament. Constitutional statutes are those that have constitutional significance such as Magna Carta 1215, the Petition of Right 1628, the Bill of Rights 1689, the Act of Settlement 1701, the Act of Union 1707, the Reform Acts, the Parliament Acts 1911 and 1949, the Crown Proceedings Act 1947, the House of Commons Disqualification Acts 1957 and 1975, the Crown Estate Act 1961, the Senior Courts Act 1981, the Human Rights Act 1998, the Scotland Act 1998, the Government of Wales Act 1998, the Constitutional Reform Act 2005 and the Constitutional Reform and Governance Act 2010 (see **Chapter 2** on legislation and interpretation and the case of *R (HS2 Action Alliance Ltd) v Secretary of State for Transport* [2014] UKSC 3).

The famous jurist A V Dicey stated in his seminal work *law of the Constitution* (10th edn, 1959) that:

> The principle of **parliamentary sovereignty** means neither more nor less than this, namely, that Parliament . . . has, under the English constitution, the right to make or unmake any law whatever . . . and further, that no person or body is recognised by the law as having a right to override or set aside the legislation of Parliament.

Thus, the sovereignty of Parliament means that Parliament can make laws on any matter it so wishes, every Parliament is born free and is not bound by previous laws enacted by earlier Parliaments and cannot bind future Parliaments and no Act of Parliament can be challenged as to its validity.

This broad conception of parliamentary sovereignty is bolstered, upheld and protected by the judiciary. Indeed, if this were not so, claimants before the courts would be able to launch a full-scale attack on the validity of Acts of the UK Parliament on various grounds such as morality or procedural defects.

(See **Chapter 2** on legislation and interpretation and the case of *R (HS2 Action Alliance Ltd) v Secretary of State for Transport* [2014] UKSC 3 and the previous discussion.)

However, in practical terms, the UK Parliament is subject to certain self-imposed political limitations. Thus, the Sewel Convention provides that the UK Parliament, before enacting a law within the competence of the devolved legislatures (the Scottish Parliament, Senedd Cymru and the Northern Ireland Assembly) will attempt to gain the approval of these bodies for the proposed law. However, the UK Parliament can ignore the refusal of the devolved legislature to approve the law and proceed to pass the proposed Act. The relationship between the devolved administrations and the UK government is set out in the Memorandum of Understanding from 2012. Other examples of limitations imposed by constitutional convention are that the rules of royal succession should only be changed with the consent of Commonwealth countries that retain the King as head of state, Parliament should not enact laws that have extraterritorial effect where it would actually be impossible to enforce (eg outlawing smoking on the streets of Paris) and ministers should refrain from introducing Bills to Parliament that offend against international law or international treaty obligations. This convention has not prevented UK government ministers, in the recent past, from introducing bills to Parliament that would negatively impact the UK's international law obligations under trading agreements with the European Union (the original version of the Internal Market Bill and the Northern Ireland Protocol Bill) and as regards international asylum law (the Illegal Immigration Bill).

Further, under the Human Rights Act 1998, ministers must issue a declaration of compatibility before introducing a Bill before Parliament. However, non-compatibility of an Act of Parliament with human rights does not endanger the validity of that Act, since the courts are only able to issue a **declaration of incompatibility** under s4 of the 1998 Act (see **Chapter 8** on the Human Rights Act 1998 and **Chapter 5** on the rule of law and separation of powers). In this way, the rule of law and separation of powers remain intact.

4.7.3 Government and Parliament

The government plays a pivotal role in initiating Bills to be brought forward for debate, scrutiny and subsequent approval by the two Houses of Parliament.

It is a curious feature of the UK Westminster model of parliamentary democracy that the executive, that is, the prime minister, their Cabinet and ministers also reside in the Parliament as either elected representatives in the Commons or as unelected appointees in the Lords.

It is often said that Parliament provides the executive. This facet of the relationship between the executive and the legislature can be viewed in a positive light by providing for the constitutional convention of ministerial responsibility such that ministers in His Majesty's Government will regularly be subject to parliamentary scrutiny and forensic questioning. The King will, by convention, appoint as prime minister the person who commands the majority of the House of Commons; that is, the leader of the political party that secured the most votes in a general election.

However, this closeness has been negatively described as providing for an 'elective dictatorship' whereby the Parliament is captured or dominated by the government of the day and is emasculated in its ability to properly hold the government to account (Lord Hailsham's speech, BBC, 14 October 1976).

The vast majority of legislative proposals brought before the Parliament are initiated by the executive, that is His Majesty's Government. The role of both Houses of Parliament is then to debate and scrutinise those proposals, suggesting amendments to them and then ultimately approving them and transforming them into law.

4.7.4 Speakers of the Houses of Parliament

Each House of Parliament has a speaker to act as its senior official. The speakers, on appointment, must give up their political allegiance and act in a non-partisan way. The Speaker of the House of Commons plays a pivotal and immensely powerful role in maintaining order within the House, enforcing standards of conduct and representing the House in its relationship with the Crown and the House of Lords.

The Speaker of the House of Lords is less powerful than their counterpart in the Commons because the Lords regulates itself and is able to create its own rules of procedure and the Lord

Speaker must gain consent of the House to act. The Lord Speaker role is a modern invention, being created in 2006 after the Lord Chancellor's role was significantly altered by the Constitutional Reform Act 2005.

4.7.5 The unequal relationship between the Houses of Parliament

In the early history of Parliament, the two Houses had similar powers regarding legislation. Over time, the power of the House of Lords diminished and the power of the House of Commons increased, by virtue of the recognition that the Commons has a greater call on the democratic mandate to pass law. By both convention and the statutory provisions of the Parliament Acts 1911 and 1949, the House of Commons exercises significant legislative power over financial measures and the House of Lords now only possesses a power to delay the passage of a Bill though Parliament and not a right of veto over legislative proposals. The House of Lords, under the Salisbury Convention, will not vote down legislative Bills that give effect to a government manifesto commitment.

4.7.6 House of Commons in the legislative process

Where a Bill starts in the House of Commons, the first reading is just a formal aspect of the process and proceeds without debate with just a simple reading out of the short title of the Bill and an order for the Bill to be printed.

After the first reading and printing of the Bill, the second reading commences, where members of the Commons get to debate and discuss the specific terms of the Bill on the floor of the House. At second reading, the government minister, spokesperson or MP responsible for the Bill opens the debate and the Opposition spokesperson responds. Once this debate ends, the MPs vote on whether the second reading should be granted. If agreed, the Bill will be discussed at committee stage. At committee stage, various experts and interest groups will inform the Commons about their views on the Bill and it can be amended. Where the Bill has been amended, a new version is printed and the Bill returns to the Commons for the report stage. At the report stage, MPs will debate the Bill on the floor of the House of Commons and then move on to the third reading. At third reading, MPs will have a chance to debate the Bill but will not be able to suggest amendments. If they approve the Bill, where the Bill started in the Commons, the Bill will go to the Lords for its first reading and where the Bill started in the Lords, it will go back to the Lords for the Lords to consider the Commons amendments.

4.7.7 House of Lords in the legislative process

The Second Chamber of Parliament performs a significant role in the law-making process, scrutinising the work of government and examining questions of public policy. In terms of law-making, all Bills before Parliament start off in one of the Houses of Parliament. The first reading is a formal aspect of the process and proceeds without debate with just a simple reading out of the long title of the Bill by the lord sponsoring the Bill. Once the first reading happens, the Bill is printed and the second reading commences, where members of the Lords get to debate and discuss the specific terms of the Bill on the floor of the House. After this debate, the various amendments that have been suggested in second reading are rolled together and the entire text of the Bill and proposed amendments are scrutinised in the committee stage. This discussion can theoretically last for as long as the members wish. The amended Bill then moves forward to be discussed at the report stage, where further amendments can be suggested and then it moves to the third and final reading stage. At the third stage, amendments can still be suggested in the Lords if the amendment had not been discussed at an earlier stage. If the Bill had started in the Lords, it will then go back to the Commons and the Commons will see the version of the Bill as amended by the Lords. If the Bill had started in the Commons, it will be sent to the Lords for consideration of the Lords' amendments and if there were no amendments the Bill will be sent to the monarch for royal assent. If agreement cannot be reached on the wording of the Bill, the Bill will be sent back to the other House until it is agreed. This frequent toing and froing between the two Houses is colloquially known as 'ping-pong'.

4.8 The judiciary

The judiciary and the courts are the third element of the state. The rule of law and the principle of legality demand that judges be independent of the other branches of the state. Judges generally enjoy security of tenure alongside their independence.

Independence from the other branches of the state happened slowly and incrementally over the past centuries and it was only in 2006 with the passing of the Constitutional Reform Act 2005 that this independence was laid down by statute. Under the Act, the House of Lords ceased to be the highest court of the land, replaced by the independent Supreme Court and the imposition of the legal duty on government ministers to uphold the independence of the judiciary.

Judges of the Supreme Court and the senior courts of England and Wales enjoy the highest grade of security of tenure, whilst judges lower down in the judicial hierarchy enjoy a lesser level of protection. Supreme Court justices enjoy tenure during good behaviour and can only be removed by an address of both Houses of Parliament. Justices in the senior courts enjoy tenure during good behaviour and can only be removed by the Lord Chancellor acting with the Lord Chief Justice. Senior court justices may now be compulsorily retired at 75. Inability to perform their role will also cause a justice to be removed from their position.

Misbehaviour by the judges is dealt with by the Judicial Conduct Investigations Office (JCIO). Complaints about the handling of misbehaviour by the JCIO and complaints about the Judicial Appointments Commission can be heard by the Judicial Appointment and Conduct Ombudsman.

The justices and the courts are the guardians of justice, upholding the rule of law, equality and due process and constitutional guarantees against arbitrariness and unfairness. The courts are there to independently adjudicate upon legal disputes between parties and to administer justice. Frequently, this adjudicative role will require the courts to interpret the law, that is, determine the legal meaning of Acts of Parliament, Statutory Instruments and other legal documents such as contracts and wills. However, a more significant and frequent role of the courts is to apply the norms, rules and principles of the body of law known as the common law; that is, the law as expressed in a significant body of prior judgments.

The judiciary in England and Wales can trace its history back over 1,000 years. King Henry II in the 12th century introduced the idea of a jury of 12 knights to settle land disputes and thus the jury system of being judged by your peers was born. Over the following eight centuries, the judiciary became more professionalised, became more independent from the monarch and from the parties to the case and received a salary from the public purse.

4.8.1 The Lord Chancellor and the Constitutional Reform Act 2005

The Lord Chancellor is one of the oldest offices of state, with a history stretching back almost 1,400 years.

Under the Constitutional Reform Act 2005, the Lord Chancellor's role was significantly reformed alongside fundamental reform to the judiciary in general. Prior to these reforms, the Lord Chancellor was involved in all three branches of the state. He attended Cabinet, he was the Speaker of the House of Lords and was the head of the judiciary in England and Wales.

The Lady or Lord Chief Justice is now the head of the judiciary in England and Wales and president of the courts of England and Wales. The Lady (or Lord) Chief Justice has over 400 statutory functions which can be delegated to other judicial office-holders.

The appointment of judges is now performed by the statutorily independent Judicial Appointments Commission (JAC). Judges are appointed through an open competition and the JAC is tasked with securing diversity in the judicial cohort. Decisions to appoint are made on merit.

Administration of the courts in England and Wales is overseen by His Majesty's Courts and Tribunals Service.

It is a fundamental principle that justice is conducted in the open and is transparent. Only in exceptional cases will justice be dispensed behind closed doors.

The courts are organised according to a strict system of hierarchy. See the courts structure chart on the Judiciary's website.

4.8.2 The Supreme Court

The Supreme Court came into operation in October 2009, replacing the House of Lords as the final court of appeal in the UK. The Supreme Court hears appeals regarding points of law that are of public or constitutional importance for the whole of the UK in civil cases, and for England and Wales and Northern Ireland in criminal cases.

4.8.3 The Judicial Committee of the Privy Council

The Judicial Committee of the Privy Council operates as the court of final appeal for a number of UK overseas territories, Crown dependencies and military sovereign bases and for certain Commonwealth countries. The Judicial Committee is no longer a court for any part of the UK.

4.8.4 The senior courts of England and Wales

The Court of Appeal and the High Court constitute the senior courts of England and Wales.

The Court of Appeal exercises an appellate jurisdiction only and is divided into two Divisions, civil and criminal.

The High Court hears complex and serious civil and family cases at first instance and hears appeals from lower courts.

The High Court is divided into three Divisions, namely the King's Bench Division, the Family Division and the Chancery Division. When the High Court is sitting as a Divisional Court, there will be at least two judges on the bench as opposed to just a single judge. See the structure on the Judiciary's website: https://www.judiciary.uk/you-and-the-judiciary/going-to-court/high-court/.

4.8.5 The County Court

The County Court deals with most civil cases in England and Wales.

4.8.6 The Family Court

Following reforms from 2014, the Family Court now has jurisdiction over the vast majority of family cases, alongside the High Court.

4.8.7 The Crown Court

The Crown Court deals with serious criminal cases that are on indictment that are transferred from the magistrates' courts.

4.8.8 The magistrates' courts

The Crown Court and the magistrates' courts constitute the criminal courts of England and Wales. All criminal cases start in the magistrates' courts. Thus summary offences, either-way offences and indictable offences are all initially dealt with in the magistrates' courts. The more serious offences will then be transferred over to the Crown Court.

The magistrates' courts also exercises a limited jurisdiction in civil cases.

The increasing costs of civil litigation in England and Wales have been a perennial cause of concern. Lord Woolf produced a report on access to justice in 1996 which attempted to tackle the costs, delay and complexity of civil litigation in England and Wales. These reforms were set out in the Civil Procedure Rules of 1998 which came into force a year later. However, concerns subsisted for over a decade and led to further demands for reform. Lord Justice Jackson produced his report on civil litigation in 2010. These recommendations led to the enactment of the Legal Aid, Sentencing and Punishment of Offenders Act 2012. This Act introduced reforms to the conditional fee and success fee agreements (no win, no fee) such that the success fee is no longer recoverable from the losing side but rather has to come from the claimant's damages award instead. The availability of **damages-based agreements** was extended to all civil litigation and not just for employment cases. For personal injury cases, the rule of qualified one way cost shifting operates such that a successful defendant is no longer able to claim their costs from the losing claimant. More generally, the courts are now more active in cost management of civil cases.

4.9 Tribunals

Alongside the courts, the UK legal system operates a number of significant tribunals such as the Employment Tribunal, the Employment Appeal Tribunal and the general system of tribunals comprising the First-tier Tribunal and the Upper Tribunal. The Court of Appeal may hear appeals from both the Employment Appeal Tribunal and the Upper Tribunal.

The tribunal system is by far a larger dispute resolution system than that of the courts. Indeed, in actual fact for the vast majority of the UK population, their interaction with the legal system will be more likely to be in the realm of administrative justice rather than the criminal justice, civil justice or family justice systems, given the range and extent of governmental regulation in modern life.

Tribunals proliferated after the Second World War as a cheaper, less formal and more specialised forum than courts for hearing legal disputes. However, the notion of commissioners hearing disputes started in the 18th century with the creation of the General Commissioners for Income Tax and thereafter the Insurance Commissioners set up to hear disputes under the National Insurance Act 1911. Tribunals were generally created on an ad hoc basis under the relevant legislation. The Crichel Down affair of 1954 forced the government to order a review of administrative tribunals and inquiries in 1957 under the auspices of Sir Oliver Franks. This report recommended that tribunals and inquiries be remodelled on a more judicial footing, thus improving the openness, fairness and impartiality of the adjudication process. Nevertheless, tribunals were still diverse in their composition, manner of adjudicating and procedure. These concerns subsisted for over four decades and were finally addressed by the Legatt Report of 2001. This report recommended wholesale reform of the tribunal system and led to a White Paper in 2004 and the subsequent enactment of the Tribunals, Courts and Enforcement Act 2007. Sir Andrew Legatt considered that the 'citizen and state' tribunals were not sufficiently separate from the relevant government department. Thus, tribunals should become more court like in their independence but, unlike courts, they should be as user-friendly, quick and cheap as possible. A consequence of this judicialisation of tribunals was the fusing of the courts and tribunals services into one service, His Majesty's Courts and Tribunals Service in 2011. The 2007 Act brought tribunals under one unified system that comprises two tiers, the first instance first-tier range of tribunals and the second-tier Upper Tribunals where appeals against the decisions of the First-tier Tribunal can be heard. The first tier is divided into seven chambers that deal with specific areas of competence and the upper tier is organised around four chambers. A significant volume of cases in the First-tier Tribunal are cases on asylum and immigration heard by the Immigration and Asylum Chamber.

Some tribunals remain outside this system and a separate structure applies to employment matters. Appeals from the Upper Tribunal or the Employment Appeal Tribunal on a point of law will be heard by the Court of Appeal. The tribunal system is headed by the Senior President of Tribunals, who is tasked with ensuring that the tribunal system fully accords with the statutory aims and objectives for which it was created. In addition, the Senior President of Tribunals chairs the Administrative Justice Council, a body set up to regularly review the operation of administrative justice to ensure that it remains accessible, fair and efficient and to share best practice. The council comprises members from academia, the judiciary, civil servants, ombudsmen, NGOs and the legal profession.

See the tribunals organisation chart (new website page – https://www.judiciary.uk/guidance-and-resources/tribunals-organisation-chart/) on the Judiciary's website.

4.10 Alternative dispute resolution (ADR)

Alongside the development of the tribunal system as an attractive alternative to the courts, a range of other dispute settlement systems have gained prominence in the UK legal system. In the area of commerce and business, arbitration is a popular alternative to court resolution, given that it is binding on the parties, follows legal principles and is a private system, avoiding the public scrutiny that often attends court cases. Arbitration is generally governed by the Arbitration Act 1996.

Interstate disputes are commonly referred to independent arbitration for adjudication via the terms of an international treaty. Certain disputes between the UK and the European Union will be settled by arbitration under the terms of the UK–EU Trade and Cooperation Agreement (see **Chapter 10** on EU law in the UK constitution).

Another common form of ADR is mediation, whereby the two parties are assisted by an independent mediator to come together to reach a mutually satisfactory outcome. The use of mediation is mandated for a range of family law disputes. The use of mediation in family law disputes removes the adversarial element inherent in court proceedings and promotes conciliation. It is popular also because **legal aid** is often available for mediation. Mediation is also commonly used in employment disputes under the auspices of the Advisory, Conciliation and Arbitration Service (ACAS).

4.11 The system of ombudsmen

The ombudsman system originated in Sweden in the 19th century and was designed as a bulwark against maladministration by state authorities. The term is derived from the Swedish word for agent or representative and thus the ombudsman speaks for the general public affected by the negative actions of the state institution. An ombudsman is a public servant independent of government. An ombudsman system is free from the point of the view of the complainant. An ombudsman is independent and impartial. The mere existence of an ombudsman system promotes good governance within the relevant sector or industry since the negative publicity generated by adverse decisions of the ombudsman is good motivation for competent decision-making. Further, since the system is free at point of use, the level of recourse to an ombudsman system is higher than recourse to expensive, lengthy court proceedings.

The first ombudsman in the UK was the Parliamentary Commissioner, created in 1967 by an Act of the UK Parliament of the same name. As state involvement in modern life has grown significantly, so too has the number of ombudsmen and the scope of their supervisory jurisdiction. Ombudsmen have also proliferated in the private sphere, as a method of ADR for settling certain disputes between consumers and customers and businesses.

The Parliamentary Commissioner is now called the Parliamentary and Health Service Ombudsman and is competent to hear complaints about the NHS in England as well as a broad range of UK government departments (a list of relevant UK departments and agencies is available on the Ombudsman's website). Generally, before a person can complain to an ombudsman, they need to have engaged with the institution's complaints process and only where that process is deficient or unsatisfactory can the person then file a claim with the ombudsman. In the specific case of UK government departments, agencies and bodies, there is also an additional filtering system whereby the complaint of injustice needs to be channelled through the citizen's MP. The work of the Parliamentary and Health Service Ombudsman is scrutinised by the Public Administration and Constitutional Affairs Committee. Alongside this general ombudsman, a number of specialised ombudsmen exist for hearing complaints against certain public services. Examples include the Local Government and Social Care Ombudsman, the Housing Ombudsman and the Prisons and Probation Ombudsman. A number of important sectors of society are overseen by an independent statutory office which works in a similar way to an ombudsman, such as the Office of the Independent Adjudicator for Higher Education in England.

Most public and private ombudsman in the UK are members of the Ombudsman Organisation, a professional body organisation set up to promote the resolution of disputes via an ombudsman.

As a result of devolution, there is separate provision for ombudsman services in the devolved regions of the UK. In the devolved nations, ombudsman functions are more integrated than in England. In Wales, the equivalent ombudsman is the Public Services Ombudsman for Wales (https://www.ombudsman.wales/). This ombudsman has a wider remit than that of the English Parliamentary and Health Service Ombudsman. The jurisdiction of the Public Services Ombudsman for Wales is set out on its website. Measures to reform the system of ombudsmen in England along similar lines to that pertaining in the devolved nations was proposed in 2016; however, to date these reforms have yet to be enacted or implemented.

4.12 Regulation generally

The complexity of modern life and the development of arm's length bodies functionally separate to the state to execute policy has seen a plethora of regulatory bodies set up to oversee these essential functions. Indeed, there are 553 (https://www.gov.uk/government/organisations#agencies_and_other_public_bodies) bodies listed on the UK government website that perform a profusion of public roles.

Regulators exist to supervise and regulate the work of a diverse range of bodies exercising significant power over the lives of ordinary citizens and businesses across the UK. The regulation of broadcast media is overseen by OFCOM, the Office for Communications, whilst elements of the press are regulated by a number of bodies such as IPSO (the Independent Press Standards Organisation) and IMPRESS. This system is controversial (see the House of Commons Report) since the Leveson Inquiry into press ethics set out a number of conditions that independent self-regulating bodies should adhere to. The rules to be followed were set out by a new body called the Press Recognition Panel which was set up by royal charter. Most national newspapers are members of the non-compliant IPSO system, with smaller local newspapers opting to follow the IMPRESS system which is fully compliant. A number of newspapers have refused to join either of these systems, preferring to set up their own independent systems for hearing and resolving complaints about them. The phenomenal growth of online activity and the centrality of online services to modern life has seen OFCOM tasked with regulating online harms under the Online Safety Act 2023. The classification of movies is the task of the British Board for Film Classification (BBFC).

Regulation of the energy sector is undertaken by OFGEM, the Office for Gas and Electricity Markets, a non-ministerial government department. Water services regulation is in the hands of OFWAT (the Water Services Regulation Authority).

The Civil Aviation Authority is the UK regulator for aviation, regulating the standards for pilot training and licences, equipment safety and reliability, security standards and the system for financial protection known as ATOL.

Securing a healthily competitive business environment in the UK is the responsibility of the Competition and Markets Authority (CMA).

Protection and enhancement of the environment in England is overseen by the Environment Agency whilst Cyfoeth Naturiol Cymru (Natural Resources Wales) performs the equivalent functions in Wales.

Numerous private regulators exist to maintain standards and user confidence in important professions like the law (the Solicitors Regulation Authority, the Bar Standards Board and the Chartered Institute for Legal Executives) and medicine (eg the General Medical Council, the General Dental Council and the Nursing and Midwifery Council).

Education is governed by OFQUAL, the Office for Qualifications and Examinations Regulation, OFSTED, the Office for Standards in Education, Children's Services and Skills and the Office for Students.

4.13 Commissioners

The term commissioner is a wide-ranging identifier for a number of different legal and administrative functions. Commissioners may act as executive decision-makers within a government department, they may perform a regulatory role as independent guarantors to uphold standards in a policy area or may act in a judicial or quasi-judicial capacity. Thus, for example, traffic commissioners, acting as an agency of the Department for Transport, licence and regulate heavy goods vehicles and buses and coaches and register local bus services; the Children's Commissioner for England is an NDPB that protects and upholds the rights of children; the independent Information Commissioner's Office is responsible for overseeing the data protection and freedom of information regimes of the UK; and Judicial Commissioners authorise the system of interferences with communications under the Investigatory Powers Act 2016.

4.14 Devolution

Granting devolution to Wales and Scotland and reinstating devolution in Northern Ireland was a manifesto commitment of Tony Blair's New Labour government in 1997. The Government of Wales Act 1998 created the Welsh Assembly and the Welsh government. This system was based on a conferred powers model of devolution unlike the reserved system of devolution in Scotland. Under a conferred model of devolution, the restricted powers of the devolved institutions were specifically identified in the originating legislation whereas in a reserved system of devolution, the devolved institutions are free to do anything that is not expressly reserved to the UK institutions. Devolution in Northern Ireland is a unique system based on a complex power-sharing agreement between representatives drawn from both sides of the political and religious divide. Devolution in England has been generally limited to the introduction of combined authorities, metropolitan mayors for large conurbations and the London mayor. These metropolitan mayors head up mayoral combined authorities and the London mayor heads up the Greater London Authority. The Levelling-up and Regeneration Act 2023 offers the scope for further devolution in England. The 2023 act introduces the concept of a county combined authority (CCA) for non-metropolitan areas in a similar vein to the existing combined authorities and will allow these mayors to rename themselves as a county commissioner, county governor, elected leader, governor or another title suggested by the CCA.

Thus, the system of devolution across the UK is a system of asymmetrical devolution. The devolution of power created further asymmetrical issues regarding the UK Parliament. England does not have its own Parliament, thus Scottish MPs are able to vote on legislative proposals that only apply to England, a problem known as the English question or the West Lothian question. A partial solution to this problem was the creation of English Votes for English Laws (EVEL). Under this system, Standing Orders were introduced in 2015 such that English MPs would have a veto over Bills that only affect England or England and Wales. The operation of this procedural innovation was halted during the Covid-19 pandemic and was completely abandoned in July 2021. Given extensive demographic changes across the UK, at the UK general election in July 2024, Scotland will lose two Westminster seats, Wales loses eight of its seats and England gains ten new seats.

4.14.1 Welsh institutions

The asymmetry in devolution across the UK was acutely felt in Wales since the Welsh Assembly and Welsh government possessed the weakest set of powers of all the UK nations. Over time, various reforms have partly remedied this deficiency. The Government of Wales Act 2006, the Wales Act 2017 and the Senedd and Elections (Wales) Act 2020 made significant changes to the system of Welsh devolution. The Welsh Assembly has been renamed as the Senedd, that is, the Welsh Parliament, and it and Llywodraeth Cymru (the Welsh government) are now to be a permanent feature of the UK's constitutional settlement, with their removal now contingent on the outcome of a possible future referendum of the Welsh people expressing a desire to abolish them. The upgrade in nomenclature of the Senedd reflects the fact that Welsh devolution now conforms to a reserved model of devolution, similar to the Scottish and Northern Irish systems of devolution. However, the areas of action reserved to the UK level as regards Wales are more extensive than those applicable to Scotland and Northern Ireland.

Generally, matters relating to the UK constitution, the conduct of foreign affairs and the defence of the UK, public service, political parties, the single jurisdiction of England and Wales and tribunals are reserved to the UK Parliament and His Majesty's Government. Further specific areas reserved to the UK level are set out in Pt 2 of Sch 7A to the Wales Act 2017. Thus, in Wales, matters of justice policy are reserved to the UK level, whereas justice policy is a devolved matter for Scotland and Northern Ireland. This extra level of reserved action is attributable to the historical fact that Scotland and Northern Ireland have their own separate legal systems whilst Wales is subsumed into that of England.

4.14.2 Senedd

The Senedd is made up of 60 Members, elected for a five-year term of office on a mixed-member proportional representation system. Forty members are elected on a FPTP system to represent their constituency whilst a further 20 are elected via a system of proportional representation known as the D'Hondt method to represent five broad electoral regions. This system is designed to ensure that no one political party achieves total dominance in the Senedd and to allow for representation of smaller political parties based on their overall performance across all constituencies. Thus, voters get two votes—the first vote is for the constituency representative and the second vote is for a party for regional representation. The sixth election to the Senedd took place on 6 May 2021. This election was significant since the Senedd and Elections (Wales) Act 2020 extended the franchise to 16- and 17-year-olds and to certain foreign nationals.

To be eligible for election as a Member of the Senedd, a candidate needs to be 18 years old or over and be either a UK citizen, an Irish national, a Commonwealth national or satisfy certain rules to be classified as a qualifying foreign national, or be an EU national resident in the UK. Certain professions will automatically disqualify a person from standing as a candidate such as being a judge, a civil servant or a member of the armed forces or of the police. A further wider category of public roles and professions set out in secondary legislation only precludes membership of the Senedd, thus these people can stand as a candidate and then, if successful, must resign their position in order to take up their seat. A conviction for an offence where the sentence imposed was imprisonment for over a year, conviction of certain political offences and being currently bankrupt will prevent a person standing as a candidate.

The Senedd is able to pass primary legislation, known as Acts of the Senedd Cymru. Once the provisions of the Bill have been approved by the Senedd, the Act will receive royal assent from the monarch. Bills are typically brought forward by the Welsh government although Members of the Senedd can bring forward a Member's Bill and, more rarely, private organisations can also submit private Bills for deliberation by the Senedd. Members' Bills are randomly chosen for debate by ballot. Given the change from a conferral model of devolution to that of a reserved model, the Senedd can now enact a much wider range of Acts. The Senedd is generally competent to enact legislation concerning the environment generally and, in particular, rules on agriculture, fisheries, forestry and rural development, certain aspects of culture like the arts, heritage and media, economic development, education and training, health, highways and transport, local government, tourism and the Welsh language. The Senedd has also been given responsibility for a number of taxes such as the landfill tax, the land transaction tax and business rates. The Senedd was also given further power to set different income tax bands for Welsh residents. Given the increase in powers and responsibilities of the Senedd, the Welsh government brought forward legislative proposals to increase the size of the Senedd to 96 members, making the electoral process more proportionally representative and reducing the term of the Senedd to four years (https://www.gov.wales/senedd-reform). These proposals will be gradually effectuated via the terms of theSenedd Cymru (Members and Elections) Act 2024.

Under the Sewel Convention, which is now stated in primary legislation, it is expected that the UK will not normally legislate in an area that is devolved to the other nations of the UK. Where the UK intends to do so, however, the UK will seek a legislative consent motion. Under this procedure, the Senedd may give its consent to the UK Parliament passing laws on its behalf. Nevertheless, given the overriding doctrine of UK parliamentary sovereignty, the UK Parliament is legally competent to pass laws concerning devolved matters without such consent. Indeed, the centrality of parliamentary sovereignty to the UK constitution and the political nature of the Sewel Convention means that the UK courts treat this issue as non-justiciable (*Miller I* [2017] UKSC 5).

In recent years, the UK Parliament has enacted laws concerning devolved matters as they concern Brexit without securing the consent of the Senedd, such as the European Union (Withdrawal Agreement) Act 2020 and the United Kingdom Internal Market Act 2020. Such legislative action invariably generates legal arguments about the validity of corresponding action that need to be adjudicated upon by the courts (see, eg, *R (on the application of Counsel General for Wales) v Secretary of State for Business, Energy and Industrial Strategy* [2022] EWCA Civ 118; also see **Chapter 10** for more on EU law in the UK Constitution).

4.14.3 Llywodraeth Cymru (The Welsh government)

Llywodraeth Cymru (the Welsh government) is the devolved administration for Wales and consists of the First Minister, a number of Welsh Ministers and the Counsel General. The Senedd nominates a person to fulfil the role of First Minister and the Presiding Officer of the Senedd recommends that nominee to His Majesty. The First Minister enjoys tenure at the pleasure of His Majesty.

The First Minister, once appointed, is then entitled to appoint up to 12 Welsh Ministers or Deputy Welsh Ministers drawn from the Senedd. These Ministers must be approved by His Majesty and hold office at his pleasure. The First Minister must also appoint a Counsel General who acts as the Law Officer for the Welsh Government. The Counsel General is appointed by His Majesty but can only be removed from office by His Majesty following a recommendation from the First Minister that has been agreed to by the Senedd.

The Counsel General is the main legal advisor for the Welsh government and represents the Welsh government in legal proceedings. The Counsel General is tasked with a number of statutory functions. In particular, the Counsel General is entitled to take, defend and participate in legal action to uphold and protect the public interest including measures to maintain the rule of law. These powers are exercised by the Counsel General in an independent capacity.

The Welsh government is able to pass a range of secondary legislation.

The First Minister, Welsh Ministers, Deputy Welsh Ministers and the Counsel General are all politically accountable to the Senedd for the performance of their duties.

The Counsel General can make representations about any matter affecting Wales and introduce Bills before the Senedd. The Counsel General can refer bills of the Senedd to the Supreme Court if there are questions over the competence of the Senedd to enact such law and, more generally, devolution legal issues can be raised by the Counsel General before the Supreme Court.

As a member of the Welsh government, the Counsel General can attend Cabinet meetings at the request of the First Minister.

Llywodraeth Cymru (the Welsh government) introduced legislative proposals to amend Llywodraeth Cymru (the Welsh government) as a result of the Senedd reforms as set out above. Under the proposals, as set out in the Senedd Cymru (Members and Elections) Act 2024, the number of Welsh ministers would be increased from the current 12 to 17, with the possibility of that maximum number being raised to 18 or 19 with Senedd's approval.

KEY POINT SUMMARY

- Sovereign states that are founded on democratic principles wield their power through a series of independent organs, based on a notion of a separation of powers.
- Organs of the state exercise extensive legislative, executive and judicial power.
- The modern UK consists of four nations—England, Wales, Northern Ireland and Scotland.
- The UK state offers a system of devolution for Wales, Northern Ireland and Scotland and in England as regards the mayoral system for London and a number of northern English cities.
- The unbroken narrative of modern UK history means that the UK has an uncodified constitution that fuses many elements of the exercise of state power.
- The UK is a constitutional monarchy.
- The UK comprises the UK Parliament, His Majesty's Government and the judiciary from across the three legal systems of the UK.
- Scotland, Wales and Northern Ireland have separate executive and legislative bodies that execute policy and make laws within their limited areas of competence.
- Local authorities also exercise executive and legislative power.
- The UK has a comprehensive Civil Service which administers policy for the UK and devolved Civil Services for the other nations of the UK.
- Executive power also rests with local government, executive agencies and national and regional bodies such as the police and the National Health Service.

CHAPTER 5
The Separation of Powers and the Rule of Law

FUNCTIONING LEGAL KNOWLEDGE

This chapter covers the following functional knowledge required to pass the SQE 1 assessments:

Separation of powers
Rule of law

AUTHORITIES UNDERPINNING PRACTICE

The key authorities that underpin this area of practice are listed below. Note that for legislation you are linked to legislation.gov.uk.

Although much of the legislation on this government website is available in its amended form, the incorporation of new amendments into the text of legislation can be delayed. You should refer to legal databases to ensure you are referencing the most up-to-date legislation.

- Constitutional Reform Act 2005
  https://www.legislation.gov.uk/ukpga/2005/4/contents
- The Bill of Rights 1689
  https://www.legislation.gov.uk/aep/WillandMarSess2/1/2/introduction
- House of Commons Disqualifications Act 1975
  https://www.legislation.gov.uk/ukpga/1975/24/contents

5.1 Introduction

This chapter provides an overview of two major concepts of the UK legal system; that is, those of the **separation of powers** and the **rule of law**.

The separation of powers doctrine and the rule of law, taken together, provide that three branches of state—that is, the executive, the legislature and the judiciary—are limited in their respective roles and powers and offer a system of checks and balances against abuse, that no one is above the law, everyone is equal before the law and that law lies behind the exercise of power, not arbitrary decision-making.

The constitutional structure of the UK is complex, as can be seen by briefly considering six characteristics of the constitution.

1. Unlike many jurisdictions, the UK's constitution is uncodified, meaning that the constitution is distributed across many different documents (cases, legislation etc).
2. Secondly, the UK's constitution relies on political customs and norms called **constitutional conventions** to regulate many aspects of the day-to-day operation of the constitution. These rules, being political in nature, are not generally thought to be enforceable before a court.
3. Thirdly, it is a democracy headed by an unelected head of state who possesses certain residual powers beyond merely ceremonial constitutional responsibilities.
4. Fourthly, since the UK is a form of parliamentary democracy, members of the government also sit in the Parliament, the legislature which, as discussed later, poses certain challenges for the separation of powers in the UK.

5. Fifthly, the UK's constitution is a product of a largely uninterrupted historical development. While it is true that the historical component nations of the UK have suffered numerous invasions and civil wars (consider the English Civil Wars of the 17th century and the Glorious Revolution of 1688), it is difficult to identify a revolutionary break with tradition equivalent to those seen in, for example, the United States or France in the 18th century.
6. Finally, the UK has, since the late 1990s, been developing a devolved system of government and lawmaking within the constituent nations of the country, including devolution of various governmental and legislative responsibilities.

This is by no means an exhaustive list, but it gives a flavour of the nature, scope and multiplicity of competing principles and institutions operating in what, for shorthand, we can refer to as the UK constitution. At the same time, we can see that, while on the one hand these features of the constitution, such as its uncodified nature and reliance on political constitutional conventions, offer a high degree of flexibility, on the other they can make the nature of constraints on politicians and other constitutional actors hard to define. As such, this complexity can give rise to contradiction and uncertainty when speaking in general terms, and it requires constitutional actors (including lawyers) to engage with key constitutional principles alongside the case law to derive constitutionally acceptable answers to specific constitutional questions (eg what limits, if any, are there to the prime minister's power to advise the monarch to prorogue Parliament?). We should also note that when thinking about key constitutional principles such as the separation of powers and the rule of law in isolation, it is easy to forget this complexity and oversimplify the picture. As far as is practicable, you should try to consider these principles against the background features noted earlier.

The constitution of the UK is thus the set of rules, regulations and procedures that guide the workings of government and delineate the relationship between the state and its citizens. Its inherent flexibility means that a rigidly delineated separation of powers doctrine is not possible and, indeed, is not desirable for the UK legal system. Thus, when we say that the UK subscribes to the rule of law and the separation of powers doctrine in principle, we should, at the very least, recall that in practice it operates as a parliamentary executive system whereby members of the legislature are also members of the government responsible for the day-to-day running of the country. The government is assisted in this endeavour by the permanent, politically neutral, professional Civil Service. Alongside this arrangement, an independent professional judiciary provides impartial oversight of the exercise of governmental legal powers. It is clear that, in describing even the most basic elements of the UK's constitutional framework—some key constitutional principles and the branches of the state—the position is more nuanced than it may first appear. As such, when reading this chapter, try to keep in mind the constitutional context against which the separation of powers and rule of law operate.

5.2 Introduction to the separation of powers

5.2.1 The separation of powers in historical thought

The separation of powers has a long history. The work of John Locke in the 17th century and Baron Montesquieu in the 18th century provide a good foundation for the modern understanding of the concept.

John Locke wrote his *Second Treatise of Government* in 1689 and in it he considered that for just government there needed to be separation of power between 'executive' and 'legislative' powers, that is, more generally, a separation between the king and the parliament.

Baron Montesquieu, the famous French political philosopher, in his work *L'Esprit des Lois* (The Spirit of Law) of 1748 stated that:

> When the legislative and executive powers are united in the same person, or in the same body of magistrates, there can be no liberty . . . there is no liberty if the powers of judging is not separated from the legislative and executive . . . there would be an end to everything, if the same man or the same body . . . were to exercise those three powers.

Further, he considered that:

> there would be an end to everything, if the same man, or the same body, whether of the nobles or the people, were to exercise those three powers, that of enacting laws, that of executing public affairs, and that of trying crimes or individual causes.

Lord Acton famously wrote that 'Power tends to corrupt, and absolute power corrupts absolutely. Great men are almost always bad men.' Thus, the purpose of incorporating the separation of powers into a constitutional framework is to ensure that power is not concentrated in the hands of one person or one institution. A complex interplay of actors in the state ensures that the three branches of state do not possess unlimited power, thus avoiding tyranny.

5.2.2 **Separation of powers in the UK: overview**

The UK, like most modern states, does not follow an absolutely strict separation of powers. Indeed, to do so would mean that the state could not properly function. Each branch of the state invariably possesses some responsibilities and functions which one might think should be carried out by another branch. So, for example, in the UK the executive possesses limited legislative powers (arising from the **royal prerogative** and secondary legislative powers granted by Parliament) and also sits within the legislature, the UK Parliament, where it initiates and controls the passage of almost all legislation. Walter Bagehot, in his publication *The English Constitution* (1867), stated that:

> the efficient secret of the English constitution is the nearly complete fusion of the executive and legislative powers.

However, this closeness between the executive and the Parliament has been more negatively described as providing for an 'elective dictatorship' whereby Parliament is captured or dominated by the government of the day and is emasculated in its ability to properly hold the government to account (Lord Hailsham's speech, BBC, 14 October 1976).

Thus, when we read that Lord Diplock, in *Duport Steels Ltd v Sirs* [1980] 1 All ER 529, considered that 'it cannot be too strongly emphasised that the British constitution, though largely unwritten, is firmly based upon the separation of powers', we must recognise the background constitutional context against which that statement was made.

Nevertheless, the concept of the separation of powers is fundamental to modern conceptions of a democratic state and to understanding the operation of the UK's constitution.

We can see this in the classic view on the separation of powers given by Lord Mustill in the case of *R v Home Secretary, ex p Fire Brigades Union* [1995] 2 AC 513. In this case, the **Secretary of State** refused to bring into force a statutory system for providing compensation to victims of crime, and proposed to establish an alternative system using the prerogative power. This was tantamount to repeal of the law by the executive, an action which can only be authorised by the legislature. The majority of the House of Lords held that the Secretary of State had acted unlawfully by not complying with the duty to actively consider the introduction of the scheme.

Lord Mustill (at 567) stated:

> It is a feature of the peculiarly British conception of the separation of powers that Parliament, the executive and the courts have each their distinct and largely exclusive domain. Parliament has a legally unchallengeable right to make whatever laws it thinks right. The executive carries on the administration of the country in accordance with the powers conferred upon it by law. The courts interpret the laws and see that they are obeyed.

Further:

> This requires the courts on occasion to step into the territory which belongs to the executive, not only to verify that the powers asserted accord with the substantive law created by Parliament, but also, that the manner in which they are exercised conforms with the standards of fairness which Parliament must have intended. Concurrently with this judicial function Parliament has its own special means of ensuring that the executive, in the exercise of delegated functions, performs in a way which Parliament finds appropriate. Ideally, it is these latter methods which should be used to check executive errors and excesses; for it is the task of Parliament and the executive in tandem, not of the courts, to govern the country.

Also:

> As the judges themselves constantly remark, it is not they who are appointed to administer the country. Absent a written constitution much sensitivity is required of the parliamentarian, administrator and judge if the delicate balance of the unwritten rules that has successfully evolved over recent years is not to be imperilled.

What Lord Mustill sought to convey through this discussion is that the operation of the constitution is predicated upon the observance of certain rules of practice, of expected conduct, which dictate the extent of different institutions' powers in given circumstances, and the manner in which other branches may intervene in, and regulate the exercise of, those powers.

In another case involving the prerogative power, *Attorney-General v De Keyser's Royal Hotel Ltd* [1920] AC 508, the House of Lords held that the government, in a case of requisitioning a hotel for war purposes, should be compelled to use a statutory power to do so rather than relying on the ancient royal prerogative to justify its action. This principle was particularly important where higher levels of compensation would have been payable under the statutory scheme as opposed to the general principles of the royal prerogative.

These modern cases echo long-established constitutional principles controlling the exercise of executive power by the monarch in the **common law**, as discovered and elaborated upon by the judges. For example, in the famous *Prohibitions Del Roy* (1607) 12 Co Rep 63, Sir Edward Coke CJ opined that 'the King in his own person cannot adjudge any case . . . but this ought to be determined and adjudged in some Court of Justice'. This case confirmed the separation of powers by requiring that the king no longer be involved in settling legal disputes. Further, in the *Case of Proclamations* (1611) 12 Co Rep 74, Sir Edward Coke CJ stated that 'the King hath no prerogative, but that which the law of the land allows him'. This case is authority for the view that the king's prerogative is limited by the common law, and later by statute law, such that the creation of criminal offences was no longer the power of the king. More generally, the legislature was the proper forum for making and changing law, as described below:

> the King by his proclamation or other ways cannot change any part of the common law, or statute law, or the customs of the realm.

In these historic cases, as in *Ex p Fire Brigades Union* and in *de Keyser*, we can see the discussion of the relationships between branches, and the scope and limits of their respective powers being further discussed.

5.2.3 **Checks and balances between institutions**

Staying with the royal prerogative as a means of exemplifying how the separation of powers operates in the UK, recall the discussion in **Chapter 4** that the royal prerogative was the king's absolute power to do anything. Over time, the monarch's power was limited and certain functions became the preserve of either the legislature or of the judiciary. In terms of executive power, this power has gradually transferred over to the prime minister, Cabinet and other government Ministers who, though not directly elected to these positions, derive indirect democratic authority from their seats in Parliament and the confidence of the House of Commons in their government. This reordering of power within the English constitution became the basis for the doctrine of the separation of powers for the United Kingdom.

It is clear that control of the executive has been, and continues to be, a central pillar of the separation of powers doctrine in the UK, particularly in view of the executive's dominance of the legislature. We can see this in the case on the prorogation of Parliament, *Cherry and Miller* (also referred to as *Miller 2*) mentioned more fully later. In this case, the Supreme Court was also at pains to stress that:

> The principle of Parliamentary accountability has been invoked time and again throughout the development of our constitutional and administrative law, as a justification for judicial restraint as part of a constitutional separation of powers.

Further, the principle of parliamentary accountability also explains and justifies the concept of non-**justiciability** under **judicial review** (*Mohammed (Serdar) v Ministry of Defence* [2017] UKSC 1). Under this conception of the separation of powers, matters of high politics and policy are not just inappropriate for adjudication by the courts since they do not give rise to legal questions which the courts can answer but also because these decisions of government are most properly considered and dealt with via the political accountability processes conducted in Parliament. Thus, under *Cherry and Miller/Miller 2*, an excessively long prorogation of Parliament, which would strip Parliament of its scrutiny function, offended against the separation of powers principle because it prevented scrutiny of government policy by Parliament. In a similar vein, the courts will not generally interrogate questions concerning the exercise of relations with foreign states (*R (on the application of FDA) v Prime Minister and Minister for the Civil Service* [2021] EWHC 3279 (Admin); *R (on the application of Wheeler) v Office of the Prime Minister* [2008] EWHC 1409 (Admin)).

This doctrine of separation of powers is a flexible and thus contested concept, which is subject to competing interpretations that have evolved in response to societal changes. It is true that the doctrine whereby no one person or group of persons is allowed to control the legislative, executive and judicial powers, or any two of them, has never strictly been applied in the UK since, although the powers and the functions of government are separated, membership of the three branches of the state often overlap. We can see that while the separation of powers permeates the entire UK legal system and is, rhetorically at the very least, respected by all three branches of the state, the way in which the concept manifests depends on the particular aims and animating principles of the branch under discussion. In view of this—though an understanding of the separation of powers is essential—one should avoid simplistic assessments of its relevance which do not consider the wider context in which the principle sits, including in relation to other key concepts such as parliamentary sovereignty and, as discussed in this chapter, the rule of law.

The strictest application of the separation of powers in the UK applies to the judiciary since it is strongly insulated by an extensive legislative framework and set of constitutional conventions from political interference. The judiciary, often seen as the quiet partner in this tripartite relationship, has shown itself to be forthright in protecting and defending its position as well as maintaining the rule of law and muscularly limiting governmental overreach to uphold the centrality of Parliament to the UK legal system.

EXAMPLE

***R v Chaytor* [2010] UKSC 52**

Four former MPs were charged with fraud arising from the MPs' expenses scandal of 2009. The MPs asserted that Parliament was the appropriate forum for dealing with their breaches of parliamentary standards. Parliamentary privilege under art IX of the Bill of Rights 1689 requires that proceedings in Parliament should not be impeached or questioned in any other court or place. Nonetheless, since the limits of parliamentary privilege are a question of law, the courts can determine what falls within and outwith the scope of privilege. The Supreme Court held that the MPs' actions were not protected by privileges, and that allegations of fraud should be dealt with by the ordinary criminal law, and thus could and should be determined in a normal court of law.

However, the UK's inherently flexible constitution and its amalgamation of certain functions in the constitution has been regularly subject to judicial criticism at the European Court of Human Rights.

EXAMPLE

***T and V v United Kingdom* [1999] ECHR 171**

The killers of toddler Jamie Bulger, T and V, who were themselves children at the time of the murder, were convicted and sentenced for this heinous crime. However, the Home Secretary, at the time of the judgment, was responsible for setting the tariff element of the custodial sentence. As the Home Secretary is a member of the executive, he was directly, and understandably, influenced by the public's horror at this crime, and set the tariff at a high level. However, sentencing is more properly a function for the judiciary and as such the Home Secretary's involvement in sentencing was a violation of the Art 6 right to a fair trial under the European Convention on Human Rights (ECHR). The tariff should have been set by an independent and impartial court or tribunal.

See also *R v Secretary of State for the Home Department, ex p Pierson* [1998] AC 539.

5.3 Introduction to the rule of law

5.3.1 Definitions of the concept of the rule of law

As with the separation of powers, it is difficult to provide a simple definition of the rule of law. It is a contested context when discussed in general terms, and requires close consideration of its relationship to other constitutional principles, prevailing institutional expectations and the case law when we consider its application in specific contexts. However, to begin with we can say that the rule of law is a political, constitutional, philosophical and legal concept that, at its simplest, sets out how a society should be governed, controlled and ruled. The concept is recorded in the work of Aristotle in ancient Greece and across other ancient civilisations such as the Roman Empire, across the ancient Islamic world and in China.

Aristotle believed that:

> It is more proper that law should govern than any one of the citizens: upon the same principle, if it is advantageous to place the supreme power in some particular persons, they should be appointed to be only guardians, and the servants of the laws.

This phrase emphasises that the power to take decisions should be based on law and not on the whims of individual leaders and powerful people. That is, the rule of law is concerned with eliminating the exercise of arbitrary—baseless—power and ensuring that the exercise of power is controlled by a system of rules. Absent such a structure, powerful leaders would be able to take advantage of weaker individuals and act capriciously, mendaciously, unjustly or unfairly. So, those exercising power in a society based on the rule of law are only exercising that power by virtue of the office they occupy for the time being, and remain bound by the law because the law creates their office and defines the scope and limits of its powers. This understanding of the rule of law also accords with the term democracy since it translates from the Greek as the power of the people. This indicates that the legitimacy of the legal framework—the rules of law—is derived from the population, who are sovereign and remain at liberty to organise amongst themselves an alternative to the status quo. We should recall, however, that in many ways understanding constitutional legal legitimacy as being predicated on a democratic system of government is a relatively modern concept. As we shall see later, this understanding of the rule of law falls into what we might refer to as the 'thick' understanding of the concept; the thin account operates on a less value-laden basis.

5.3.2 History of the rule of law in the UK

In the history of England, and latterly the UK, the rule of law has developed incrementally through promulgation of contracts between the monarch and his or her subjects, the enactment of statutory laws limiting the powers of kings and queens, the establishment of Parliament and later the significant expansion in the electoral franchise, the development of Parliament as the sovereign legislative power and judicial pronouncements that define and clarify the rules of the common law. More recently, the thinking of political philosophers, eminent jurists and international law commitments have shaped modern societies' views of what the rule of law should encapsulate.

Though it is not the first step in controlling power through law in England, perhaps one of the most famous early examples of the control of royal power was the signing of Magna Carta in 1215 at Runnymede, near London. This saw King John's power limited as regards the barons, the aristocratic class, and thus can be seen as a notable step towards ensuring the rule of law since the document insisted that the king was now subject to legal limitations. Though King John sought to repudiate the agreement soon after it was signed, the importance of Magna Carta, as far as the rule of law is concerned, lies in the articulation of the notion that there were limits to royal power, and that power had to be exercised within those limits.

As has been indicated, Magna Carta did not settle the question of how power should be controlled and distributed. Tensions between the monarch and his or her subjects, more particularly the aristocratic and landed classes, continued to ebb and flow over the ensuing centuries. Matters came to a head, however, in the 17th century when disquiet over the arbitrary behaviour of Charles I led to a protracted period of civil war between those aligned with the monarch (the largely catholic Royalists) and those with Parliament (the largely protestant Parliamentarians or 'Roundheads') ending with the defeat of the Royalists, the regicide by beheading of Charles I, and the creation of a **republic** under Oliver Cromwell. Although the monarchy was briefly restored under Charles II and James II, the collapse of the reinstated monarchy in the face of similar royal attitudes to power, Parliament and religious belief—ending with James II's flight to France—was a key constitutional moment in the UK's history. Parliament convened of its own volition and invited William of Orange and his wife Mary (James II's protestant daughter) to take the throne. This series of events is known as the Glorious Revolution. As part of the bargain struck between William and Mary and Parliament, legislative limits were placed upon the power of the monarch in the form of the Bill of Rights 1689. The Bill of Rights 1689 limited the divine right of kings to rule absolutely and provided that the Parliament was now the main source of legislative power. Other legislation followed, including the Act of Settlement 1701 which, among other things, allowed Parliament to dictate the royal line of succession to the throne and to regulate the dismissal of judges, both of which had previously been the prerogative of the monarch.

From these two examples we can see that the regulation of power through law, and latterly particularly the law promulgated by Parliament, has been a motivating factor in the development of the UK's constitution.

5.3.3 Diceyan view of the rule of law

With this historical context in mind, we can turn to consider how the rule of law has come to be understood in the modern period. To do this we must begin, as was the case with the discussion **of parliamentary sovereignty**, with the Victorian jurist, A V Dicey. Dicey set out a vision of the rule of law which has influenced the development of the concept in the UK. For Dicey, the rule of law encompasses three main components:

First, regular or ordinary law is the predominant or supreme power rather than the exercise of special administrative power, which Dicey equated with arbitrary power, largely due to his misunderstanding of how the French legal system of the time operated. This sentiment is captured in the following statement:

> No man is punishable or can be lawfully made to suffer in body or goods except for a distinct breach of law established in the ordinary legal manner before the ordinary courts of the land.
>
> (Dicey, *The Law of the Constitution* (10th edn, 1959), 188)

Under this proposition, the ordinary law, as created by the recognised lawmaker, provides the rules for judgement on the population and for the protection and enforcement of their rights. Thus, for Dicey, the rule of law is different from a system of government that simply grants powerful decision-makers wide discretionary or arbitrary powers.

Secondly, there should be equality before the law. 'Every man, whatever be his rank or condition, is subject to the ordinary law of the realm and amenable to the jurisdiction of the ordinary tribunals.'

Thus, there should be no special forums for deciding cases for people in power, nor should the powerful be able to operate beyond the law. Everyone is subject to the full force of the same, ordinary law from government ministers to the ordinary person on the street.

Thirdly, the inalienable rights of individuals come from the common law and are strongly protected by the courts. These rules form the basis for the unwritten, uncodified rules of the constitution of the UK. Thus, for Dicey, the rule of law permeates the entire structure of the UK's legal system. The diverse range of case law that sets out these individual rights was a bulwark against other branches of the state removing or limiting these rights since the entire edifice of the common law would need to be expunged. Dicey considered that an essential negative characteristic of a written constitutional system was that it could easily be replaced in the event of revolution.

The work of Dicey, although influential, was a product of its time and has been subject to criticism. For example, he had a simplistic understanding of the growing complexity of the state—perhaps because of his political beliefs—and so failed to see that the rise of specialist courts and tribunals, now accepted as a positive development in delivering justice, was not only inevitable but was already underway in the period.

Nonetheless, though we might criticise Dicey, his work does articulate the foundation from which it can now be taken that the rule of law requires that there must be lawful authority for the decisions taken by the executive, and that the judiciary is responsible for developing and protecting common law rights. Curiously, Dicey did not consider the implications of his account of parliamentary sovereignty in the light of his discussion of the rule of law. He only considered that, for the UK, the validity of legal action comes from statutory law, the royal prerogative or from the common law. That power must then be exercised by the proper person or institution. Action beyond that will be deemed unlawful and against the rule of law.

EXAMPLE

Entick v Carrington (1765) 19 State Tr 1029 provides an example of the classic Diceyan operation of the rule of law.

Carrington and three other king's messengers broke into the house of John Entick, who they believed was the writer and distributor of various seditious pamphlets. They were acting on the orders of Lord Halifax, the Secretary of State, a government minister. To enter the premises of someone without legal authority is a trespass. The case confirmed that the state could only enter premises by authority of the law and that individuals are free to act except where the law expressly limits their freedom. Thus, the state needs to legally justify its actions and point to the relevant legal source of its power. In the absence of such legal authority, the state and its officials are acting unlawfully.

We were earlier discussing the idea of democratic legitimacy underpinning the rule of law, but at this stage it will be clear that both in the historical examples noted in the preceding section, and in relation to Dicey, democratic legitimacy is not considered to be a central component of the rule of law. Dicey's rather narrow conception of the rule of law says nothing about the substance of the power it grants or its exercise. Thus, the most egregious of laws, such as the racist, murderous, laws of Nazi Germany, including the legislative framework underpinning the Final Solution, might be compatible with this 'thin' version of the rule of law—the law was validly enacted, expressed the will of the sovereign power and was capable of being enforced. The argument over the validity of such law can be found in the seminal debate between H L A Hart and Lon L Fuller (see, eg, H L A Hart, 'Positivism and the Separation of Law and Morals' and Lon L Fuller, 'Positivism and Fidelity to Law—A Reply to Professor Hart' (1958) 71(4) Harv L Rev 593–672). However, the essence of the division encapsulated in this debate is that either: (a) validity of law is not dependent on the compliance of law with certain fundamental rights and values, and need only be passed according to established legal processes (the 'thin' account); or that (b) law can only be valid if, in addition to being properly passed, it complies with fundamental rights and values. In any event, this brief account and our consideration of Dicey tell us that Dicey's conception does not provide a complete answer to the question 'what is the rule of law?'

5.3.4 Wider view of the rule of law

The rule of law, in another wider sense, goes to the heart of what a legal system should do.

A legal system is a system for regulating the conduct and affairs of a territorially defined state and should offer guidance to all its inhabitant as to how they should organise their lives. Therefore, if the primary role of law is to regulate and guide conduct, the law should possess certain attributes. The legal philosopher Joseph Raz suggested that laws, in order to comply with the rule of law, need to be prospective not retrospective, relatively stable and based upon open, general and clear rules. The jurist Lon L Fuller, though also accepting these aspects of the rule of law, further argued that legal orders are made by men for a purpose; namely, first to ensure order and, second, to achieve certain general, common goals. Whereas Raz focuses on the internal characteristics of valid law, Fuller's approach looks to how law can be validly used within society. As an end in itself and as an instrument to reach these societal goals, legal orders must abide by the minimum standards of the rule of law, howsoever defined, to be effective. This branch of jurisprudence is controversial because of its discussion of morality in the structure, organisation and lawfulness of legal systems. For example, and as noted earlier, legal positivists like H L A Hart, particularly in his book *The Concept of Law*, argue that the question of what is law is separate to the question of law's morality or innate goodness and its purposes. You can read more about these conceptual differences in Craig's 'Formal and substantive conceptions of the rule of law: an analytical framework' [1997] Public Law 467.

Nonetheless, almost all legal theorists, whether they subscribe to the positivist or natural law school, the formalist or substantive account, the thin or thick versions of the rule of law, agree that, as a minimum, the legal system needs to have an independent judiciary, open access to the courts and where law enforcement has discretionary power that power should not be exercised contrary to the purpose of that law. However, even with these rules, a morally suspect regime could still be said to be complying with the rule of law. Thus, other standards may need to be incorporated into theories of law in order to prevent oppressive, discriminatory or otherwise 'bad' laws from being enacted.

We can see an example of these additional standards being incorporated in Lord Bingham's model of the rule of law, explained in his book *The Rule of Law* (2011). His model identifies eight broad principles underpinning the modern rule of law, which can be summarised as.

1. The law should be accessible and predictable.
2. Legal questions should be determined according to law not by the exercise of discretion.
3. The law should apply equally to all, except where objective differences justify differentiation.
4. Public officers must exercise their powers in good faith, fairly, for the purpose for which the powers were conferred - reasonably and without exceeding their power's limits.
5. The law should seek to protect fundamental human rights.
6. The state must provide a way of resolving disputes which parties cannot themselves resolve, quickly and without high cost.
7. Adjudicative procedures should be fair.
8. The state must comply with its obligations in international law as in national law.

There are important differences between Bingham's account and those of, for example, positivist scholars, since his approach incorporates key values—such as the protection of fundamental human rights, and the concept of substantive fairness—which eliminate the possibility of certain 'bad' laws from being enacted in compliance with the rule of law.

5.3.5 **Differing conceptions of the rule of law**

As can be seen from this brief overview, the rule of law is a controversial concept and is subject to multiple interpretations. Academics, lawyers, judges and jurists disagree on the outer limits of the concept. A 'thin' interpretation of the rule of law would limit its application to formal, technical aspects of the law and the legal system. Thus, a thin interpretation would simply require that the norms of the legal system be clear such that individuals know the rules, the norms are prospective or forward-looking and the norms are non-contradictory such that the legal system makes sense as a whole.

An overly narrow, thin, interpretation of the rule of law is problematic since the focus on the technical, formal aspects of the law means that issues concerning the substance of the law will be overlooked. Thus, from this positivist view, in extremis, as long as the law is properly created according to the formal rules of the legal system (ie the established legislative process is followed), that law is valid and enforceable. From this perspective, a thin rule of law does nothing to protect the population from the worst excesses of the sovereign power. This narrow conception of the rule of law is neutral on the substantive terms of a properly enacted law and thus offers no mechanism to void or condemn that law. In this limited sense, the discriminatory and murderous laws of Nazi Germany were lawfully enacted so were legally valid according to a thin rule of law (notwithstanding that the international community rightly condemned these legal measures through the Nuremberg Trials and other actions).

Conversely, a substantive or 'thick' conception of the rule of law encompasses a wider review of the law, taking in additional concepts such as morality, fairness and a greater respect and role for individual liberties within the legal system. However, this wider conception suffers from its own problems since questions of fairness, justice and morality are inherently subjective and open to multiple interpretations, whereas the question of what is validly enacted law in a formal sense is a more objective question. Thus, this thick conception of the rule of law raises the question as to who gets to decide on the nature of these external checks on the validity of the legal system. Moreover, the 'thick' conception can also tend to overlook the complexity and contestability of related concepts upon which it might rely—for example, superficially the separation of powers appears to complement the operation of a 'thick' rule of law (eg an independent judiciary, limitations on governmental and legislative power according to fundamental rights) but, as we have seen, such concepts are not themselves objectively defined. There is not a neutral account of the separation of powers to supplement our understanding of the rule of law.

5.3.6 The international and regional dimension to the rule of law

World history is replete with examples of gross violations of human rights and human dignity that have been undertaken in the name of the law and under the rule of law. Slavery in the British and other European Empires and in America, the apartheid regime of South Africa and the system of national socialism in Germany are just three famous examples of legal regimes that authorised the most egregious violations of human rights under systems of legal regulation. The horrors of the Second World War prompted the development of regimes to protect human rights (eg the UN Universal Declaration of Human Rights and the ECHR) and have led to a more expansive view of the rule of law. The United Nations Universal Declaration of Human Rights 1948 (UDHR), for example, contains an express reference to the rule of law. The preamble to the UDHR states that:

> Whereas it is essential, if man is not to be compelled to have recourse, as a last resort, to rebellion against tyranny and oppression, that human rights should be protected by the rule of law.

Thus, today the rule of law is often framed as a tool against anarchy and lawlessness since oppressed citizens are more likely to demonstrate, rebel and engage in civil disobedience and violent disorder, and are more likely to accept as legitimate a legal regime which adheres to modern conceptions of the rule of law.

More generally, the United Nations considers the rule of law to be essential to the recognition and enjoyment of human rights. The UN Secretary-General considers that the rule of law necessitates that legal processes, legal institutions and the substantive norms of a legal system conform with human rights. In particular, this means that a legal system subscribes to the core principles of equality under the law, accountability before the law and fairness as regards the protection and enforcement of rights.

The Human Rights Council of the United Nations has taken a leading role in promoting and protecting the rule of law. The Council has produced a number of significant resolutions on the administration of justice, the integrity of the judicial system and more generally on the interface between human rights, democracy and the rule of law.

After the establishment of the United Nations, the Council of Europe was set up in 1949 to ensure peace throughout the continent of Europe. The Statute of the Council of Europe provides, in its preamble, that the principles of individual freedom, political liberty and the rule of law underpin the basis of all genuine democracies. Further, Art 3 of the Statute requires that every member of the Council of Europe must accept the principles of the rule of law and of the enjoyment by all persons within its jurisdiction of human rights and fundamental freedoms and collaborate sincerely and effectively in the realisation of the aims of the Council of Europe. The primary function of the Council of Europe was the promulgation and ratification of the ECHR. The ECHR upholds the rule of law in both a thick and thin perspective. The preamble refers to the rule of law as a common feature of its Member States and also provides more substantively that the rule of law underpins the achievement of the substantive rules of the Convention.

Indeed, the rule of law is an essential component of the ECHR. The European Commission for Democracy through Law, otherwise known as the Venice Commission, has provided a rule of law checklist.

Under this checklist, the laws of the Member States of the Council of Europe should comply with the following benchmark minimum standards: legality, legal certainty, prevention of abuse of powers, equality and non-discrimination and access to justice, including the independence and impartiality of the judiciary and the concept of a fair trial.

The case law of the Convention requires that legal limitations on the rights of the Convention must be set out in law, either through a legislative provision or be reasonably foreseeable through the operation of case law to enable citizens to adjudge their conduct as being legal or illegal and, secondly, those limitations must be substantively in accordance with the law by being necessary in a democratic society and being a proportionate response to the threat posed to the state

(*Handyside v United Kingdom* [1976] ECHR 5). Being 'in accordance with the law' means both that there is a legal rule setting out the limitation or restriction and also that that restriction substantively respects the rule of law. (See **Chapter 8** on the Human Rights Act 1998 and *Craig v HMA* [2022] UKSC 6.) It is important to note that certain rights protected by the Convention cannot be abrogated by law—for example, under Art 3 there is an absolute prohibition on torture, inhuman or degrading treatment. It is not possible for a state to legally sanction treatment contrary to Art 3, no matter what emergency might be facing the nation.

The Report of the International Commission of Jurists, *Declaration of Delhi: The Rule of Law in a Free Society* (1959), emphasises the rule of law as a principle of good governance.

Both the International Commission of Jurists (ICJ) and the European Court of Human Rights treat the notion of the rule of law as a living instrument, whereby it needs to be adjudged by contemporary standards and not become fossilised and preserved as a historical relic.

In 1955, the ICJ also produced its Athens Declaration, which stated that:

1. The State is subject to the law.
2. Governments should respect the rights of the individual under the Rule of Law and provide effective means for their enforcement.
3. Judges should be guided by Rule of Law, protect and enforce it without fear or favour and resist any encroachments by governments or political parties on their independence as judges.
4. Lawyers of the world should preserve the independence of their profession, assert the rights of the individual under the Rule of Law and insist that every accused is accorded a fair trial.

As is clear from the preceding discussion, the 'thick' conception of the rule of law has permeated many aspects of international legal regimes and treaties to which the UK and other states have subscribed. As the UK operates a dualist constitutional system—where the international and domestic regimes are distinct, such that international treaties must be implemented domestically to have legal effect—however, it is still essential to consider the domestic understanding of the rule of law in the UK. (See *Assange v Government of the United States* [2024] EWHC 700 (Admin); *Fothergill v Monarch Airlines Ltd* [1981] AC 251; *Kaur v Lord Advocate* [1980] 3 CMLR 79; and more recently *R (on the application of SC, CB and 8 children) v Secretary of State for Work and Pensions* [2021] UKSC 26 at [77].)

5.3.7 Legal presumptions of the rule of law

There is a presumption that enactments that change the law only do so prospectively. Retrospective application is possible but it must be expressly stated or by necessary implication. In the case of *Reilly (No 2) and another v The Secretary of State for Work and Pensions* [2014] EWHC 2182 (Admin), the High Court held that the enactment of an Act of Parliament (Jobseekers (Back to Work Schemes) Act 2013) designed to apply retrospectively to jobseekers seeking benefits because of an adverse judgment by the Court of Appeal was unlawful and a violation of Art 6 ECHR.

In terms of criminal law and fiscal provisions, the presumption is strong. New offences, or the extension of the scope of an existing criminal offence, will ordinarily only apply to future events, especially given the transposition of Art 7 ECHR into UK law via the Human Rights Act 1998. The presumption against retrospectivity is weaker in respect of procedural legislation. In the restricted cases of actual retrospective legislation, such laws will be interpreted restrictively to limit their application (*Reid v Reid* (1886) 31 ChD 402).

> . . . the reason for the presumption is that in a civilised society which acknowledges the rule of law, individual members of that society are entitled to know when they embark on a course of conduct what the legal consequences of their doing so will be, so that they may regulate their conduct accordingly.
>
> (Lord Diplock in *Inland Revenue Comrs v Joiner* [1975] 3 All ER 1050 at 1062)

The reasons for this view are clear. The law is not a game of chance. The rule of law provides that anyone subject to the law should be able to determine, with reasonable foreseeability, that their proposed course of action will be within the law.

A politically controversial decision on the application of the rule of law and the separation of functions between the judges, the government and Parliament was the seminal decision in *Cherry/Miller 2* as regards the prorogation of Parliament.

5.3.8 The case of Cherry/Miller 2

The power to prorogue Parliament is a classic power of the executive (see *The Prorogation Dispute of 2019: One Year On* for more details). It is a routine power exercised periodically. Indeed, it is normal for Parliament not to be permanently in session and typically Parliament will be prorogued on an annual basis for a short period to allow the government to refresh its legislative agenda before Parliament. The government will prorogue Parliament by advising the monarch to exercise their royal prerogative powers. When Boris Johnson wished to prorogue Parliament for over five weeks in 2019, his critics suggested that this prorogation was designed to prevent Parliament from sitting during the countdown to the date for the UK leaving the EU. This exercise of the royal prerogative was thought to be a classic example of non-justiciable power, since the power is a matter of high politics, and judges have historically refused to adjudicate on such political questions. However, the question of what are the outer limits of the prorogation power *is* a matter of law and thus, in that respect, is capable of being judicially reviewed. The Supreme Court went on to hold unanimously that an excessively long period of prorogation that could not be explained by the government was unlawful since it would prevent the Parliament from exercising one of its core functions beyond that of making law—the supervision and accountability of the government to Parliament.

In *Cherry/Miller 2* [2019] UKSC 41, at [34], the Supreme Court stated that:

> A decision to prorogue Parliament (or to advise the monarch to prorogue Parliament) will be unlawful if the prorogation has the effect of frustrating or preventing, without reasonable justification, the ability of Parliament to carry out its constitutional functions as a legislature and as the body responsible for the supervision of the executive. In such a situation the court will intervene if the effect is sufficiently serious to justify such an exceptional course.

Further, the Supreme Court went on to say that:

> Indeed, by ensuring that the Government does not use the power of prorogation unlawfully with the effect of preventing Parliament from carrying out its proper functions, the court will be giving effect to the separation of powers.

And that:

> the courts have protected Parliamentary sovereignty from threats posed to it by the use of prerogative powers, and in doing so have demonstrated that prerogative powers are limited by the principle of Parliamentary sovereignty.

5.3.9 The principle of legality

The principle of legality has two complimentary meanings. In the first sense, as stated in *R v Secretary of State for the Home Department, ex p Simms* [1999] UKHL 33, it regulates the relationship between parliamentary sovereignty and the expectation that parliamentary enactments will generally be expected to conform to the rule of law and respect fundamental rights. Crucially, however, this concept of legality gives way in the face of parliamentary sovereignty where Parliament uses 'express language' to make clear that it intends to go against the above-mentioned presumptions (see eg *R (on the application of AAA (Syria) and others v Secretary of State for the Home Department* [2023] UKSC 42 as regards the proposed UK–Rwanda Migration and Economic partnership and the terms of the Safety of Rwanda (Asylum and Immigration) Act 2024. This Act designates Rwanda as a safe country for the purposes of asylum, a position at variance to that expressed by the justices in the Supreme court). In practice, courts have been known to go to great lengths to interpret statutory language as being insufficiently express to counter these presumptions. This can be seen in the case of *R (on the application of Evans) v Attorney General* [2015] UKSC 21, in which Lord Neuberger (majority) was said by Lord Wilson (dissenting) to have 're-wrote' the provisions of the Freedom of Information Act in order to find against the Attorney General (see at [168]).

The second meaning of legality is more general and concerns the conduct of government under law. That is, that a government which adheres to the rule of law is expected to conform to the concept of legality. Specifically, this means that government interference with people and property must only be undertaken by exercise of a statutory power or through the common law and that clearly defined power must be exercised lawfully. Necessity does not justify, on its own, the state acting to interfere with an individual's rights or liberties (*Entick v Carrington* (1765) 19 State Tr 1029) although, in cases of urgency where the state is incapacitated, the state is justified in taking action necessary to restore the operational tools of government.

Public bodies, individuals exercising official power and the Crown itself are legal and natural persons and as such are limited by the normal rules of capacity and liability. We can see how these two ideas relate to one another. The latter requires that government conduct itself through law, and the former—in the context of the UK—provides the basis on which the democratically elected legislature may sanction a deviation from this principle. Government action, its powers and its duties are all set out according to law. Thus, any changes to those powers and duties must be accomplished by changes to the law. The supremacy of Parliament means that Parliament is legally authorised to change any aspect of the government and its operation via enactment of a new law.

The modern conception of the rule of law also encompasses control of the executive through judicial review. The courts, via judicial review, demand that the government is accountable by complying with the principle of good administration. Good administration requires both procedural and substantive legality. Thus, administrative decision-making should be guided by the following principles: legality, propriety, participatory, openness, rationality, relevancy, reasonableness, equality, reasonability, certainty, **proportionality** and in accordance with fundamental rights and the concept of legitimate expectations. Governmental decision-making, under the rule of law, should be formally, procedurally and substantively just and fair. In this way, the institutional structure needs to be moral and act as a constraint on unbridled government power.

On both meanings of legality, the question as to whether a state power or duty exists is a legal question—that is, a matter of law—and as such will be answered by the courts. The court will set out the parameters of the duty or power and will offer an effective remedy for any unlawful activity.

In the leading case of *R (UNISON) v Lord Chancellor* [2017] UKSC 51, the Supreme Court stated that:

> At the heart of the concept of the rule of law is the idea that society is governed by law. Parliament exists primarily in order to make laws for society in this country. Democratic procedures exist primarily in order to ensure that the Parliament which makes those laws includes Members of Parliament who are chosen by the people of this country and are accountable to them. Courts exist in order to ensure that the laws made by Parliament, and the common law created by the courts themselves, are applied and enforced. That role includes ensuring that the executive branch of government carries out its functions in accordance with the law. In order for the courts to perform that role, people must in principle have unimpeded access to them. Without such access, laws are liable to become a dead letter, the work done by Parliament may be rendered nugatory, and the democratic election of Members of Parliament may become a meaningless charade . . .

Therefore, the right of access to justice flows from the rule of a law as a necessary consequence of it.

It can be seen that in order to carry out this function the independence of the judiciary is essential in ensuring that the principle of legality is upheld. This idea is widely and deeply embedded in the UK's legal system. One example of this can be found in the Human Rights Act 1998 and its reception of the ECHR into UK law. Under the 1998 Act individuals who have their legal and political rights infringed are entitled to access to independent courts and tribunals in pursuit of an effective legal remedy.

5.3.10 **Civil liberties and the rule of law**

Historically, and in general terms, citizens (properly, subjects) were free to engage in any activity that was not expressly prohibited or limited by the law and, conversely, public servants and institutions could only interfere with such liberties and the private property of subjects by virtue of legal authority (*Malone v Metropolitan Police Commissioner (No 2)* [1979] 2 All ER 620). The common law thus developed protections such as the writ of habeas corpus, requiring the state to promptly present arrested criminal suspects before the courts, and other requirements such as the need for warrants to approve entry onto premises (*Entick* v *Carrington* [1765] 95 ER 807).

These common law rights are not protected in a codified constitution or a Bill of Rights. Some would argue that this perceived gap in the level of protection has been partly plugged by the reception of the ECHR into UK law by the terms of the Human Rights Act 1998 (see **Chapter 8** on the Human Rights Act 1998). More recently, the judiciary has articulated that the common law continues to develop and offer protections alongside the Human Rights Act and beyond those traditional protections seen in historical examples (see, eg, *A* v *BBC (Scotland)* [2014] UKSC 25; *R (UNISON) v Lord Chancellor* [2017] UKSC 51). In any event, it is clear that the common law and the concept of the rule of law are intertwined in constitutional and legal thought on the UK constitution.

5.4 The separation of powers and the rule of law in the UK: the role of the judiciary

As has been indicated earlier, the separation of powers and the rule of law can, and indeed should, be considered together. Looking at the judiciary is a good way to demonstrate this. The judiciary and the courts are the third branch of the state alongside the legislature and the executive. The rule of law demands that judges be independent of the other branches of the state. To facilitate this, judges generally enjoy security of tenure, protection of their salaries and pensions from political interference and an independent appointments process.

The judiciary is the guardian of justice, maintaining and upholding the rule of law (*R (on the application of Stratton) v Enfield LBC* [2022] EWHC 404 (Admin); *R (Plan B Earth) v Secretary of State for Transport* [2020] EWCA Civ 214), equality and due process, and providing constitutional guarantees against arbitrary decision-making and unfair actions by the state. The judiciary is there to adjudicate on disputes between private individuals and bodies (eg between two companies) and between private individuals and bodies and public bodies (eg between an individual citizen and a government department or between a company and a public regulatory body established by the state). The judicial process assists in upholding the rule of law, developing the common law, the interpretation of Acts of Parliament and secondary legislation and the monitoring of government decision-making to ensure that it is variously lawful, rational, reasonable, proportionate and compliant with procedural standards.

Historically, the monarch was the source of all power in the territory and over time those powers have transferred over to the legislature, the executive and the judiciary. As a link back to this historical facet of the UK constitution, notwithstanding the separation of powers doctrine, the terminology adopted to describe the various branches of the state remains unaltered. So for example, in England, the senior courts are as administered by His Majesty's Courts and Tribunals Service, the judges in England and Wales are His Majesty's judges, the UK government is His Majesty's Government (HMG), the police uphold the King's peace and prosecutions in the criminal courts of England and Wales are conducted in the name of the Crown (Rex). The King also remains an essential conceptual component of Parliament, through the idea of the King in Parliament and his role in granting **royal assent** to legislation as a necessary step in the legislative process.

The separation of powers is a constitutional principle (*Cherry/Miller 2* at [40]) and, as such, the courts should not interfere with the proceedings of the legislature (*R (Wheeler) v Office of the Prime Minister* [2008] EWHC 1409 (Admin) at [46]). In the *Miller 1* [2017] UKSC 5 case, at [42], the Supreme Court held that:

> In the broadest sense, the role of the judiciary is to uphold and further the rule of law; more particularly, judges impartially identify and apply the law in every case brought before the courts.

More generally, access to the courts is a fundamental constitutional right which can only be curtailed by clear and express statutory enactment (*R (UNISON) v Lord Chancellor* [2017] UKSC 51; *Witham v Lord Chancellor* [1998] QB 575).

Originally, judges possessed wider powers to review the law of the land. Under the rule of law, the judges in the 17th century were quick to limit the role of the king to make law. In the case of *Prohibitions Del Roy* (1607) 12 Co Rep 63, Sir Edward Coke quoted the medieval jurist Bracton to note:

> That the King ought not to be under any man but under God and the law.

Similarly, in the case of *Dr Bonham* (1610) 8 Co Rep 107, it was declared by Sir Edward Coke that Parliament could not make law that offended against morality; however, with the increasing imperative to curb the excessive, arbitrary power of the king, the concept of parliamentary supremacy developed through the common law as an alternative method to limit the use of arbitrary power. The democratic Parliament, it is argued, will produce fairer and more just law since the legislators are cognisant of the needs of the population at large and will not produce unjust law. However, this is not always the case as seen in the examples of Nazi Germany, apartheid South Africa and other fascist regimes. More recently, senior UK judges have discussed the possibility, in *obiter dicta*, that the courts would refuse to apply and enforce an abhorrent, unjust law despite the notion of parliamentary sovereignty (Lord Hope in *Attorney General v Jackson* [2005] UKHL 56). The courts have also taken a dim view of the suggestion that it would be constitutionally proper for Parliament, at the behest of government, to oust the jurisdiction of the courts to review executive action (see Lord Carnwath in *Privacy International* [2019] UKSC 22).

We can see, therefore, how a thicker conception of the rule of law poses challenges for a judiciary which, on the one hand, has a role in upholding the rule of law, while on the other, is bound to respect the sovereignty of Parliament. Under the UK doctrine of the separation of powers, the notion of parliamentary sovereignty provides that the role of judges is limited, such that they are prevented from declaring Acts of the UK Parliament as illegal:

> It is not for the court to say that a Parliamentary enactment, the highest law in the country, is illegal.
>
> (Ungoed-Thomas J in *Cheney v Conn (Inspector of Taxes)* [1968] 1 All ER 779 at 782)

See also *R (on the application of A, J, K, B and F) v Secretary of State for the Home Department* [2022] EWHC 360 (Admin).

5.4.1 **Impartial judiciary**

As discussed earlier, an independent judiciary is the hallmark of a modern democratic state. An independent judiciary ensures that the rule of law is upheld and provides for its own legitimacy and authority since the judges' decisions are accepted by the population as being decided upon by legal principles and not on spurious grounds such as the relationship between the judges and the lawmakers or politicians. In addition to this institutional independence, that is, adherence to the separation of powers principle, judges must be also impartially minded when deciding on cases and, just as importantly, judges must be *seen to be* impartial to instil confidence in the population as to the probity of judges.

To ensure justice is served, the maxim *nemo judex in sua causa* applies (no one should be judge in his own cause). Over time, this maxim has grown beyond the literal meaning of the phrase to include any apparent biases, regardless of where that bias may come from and also applies to public law decision-making generally.

EXAMPLE

Lord Hoffmann adjudicated in a House of Lords case concerning the immunity of the former head of state of Chile, General Pinochet. After the judgment, it was disclosed that Lord Hoffmann was an unpaid director of Amnesty International Charitable Trust and that his wife, Lady Hoffmann, had worked for Amnesty International since 1977 in an administrative capacity. The appearance of potential bias on this basis was enough for the original decision to be set aside and for a new composition of the House of Lords constituted to hear the case anew. (*Pinochet, In re* [1999] UKHL 1).

5.4.2 **Bias and the appearance of bias**

Continuing with the themes of judicial independence and impartiality as important features of the rule of law and separation of powers in practice, we should consider the question of bias. Bias is the quickest way to undermine faith in the judiciary, particularly where the judges are not elected and are otherwise unaccountable to the electorate (see *Porter v Magill* [2002] 2 AC 357).

Where a judicial decision is tainted by bias, that decision can and must be set aside since faith in the judges is an essential requirement for the system of an independent judiciary to survive (*R v Bow Street Metropolitan Stipendiary Magistrate, ex p Pinochet Ugarte (No 2)* [2000] 1 AC 119).

EXAMPLE

Special rules apply to legislative Bills that are subject to the rules of the Parliament Acts 1911 and 1949. Under these provisions, controversial Bills can be turned into law notwithstanding the fact that the House of Lords has not assented to the Bill (*R (on the application of Jackson) v Attorney-General* [2005] UKHL 56). As the democratically elected element of the UK Parliament, the House of Commons occupies a greater place in the parliamentary legislative system than the appointed House of Lords.

The Hunting Act 2004 was a law designed to outlaw fox hunting. Numerous Lords were opposed to this legislative proposal, thus the House of Commons required to use the Parliament Acts to push through the law against the wishes of the House of Lords. During the passing of the legislation, two of the Law Lords used their role as members of the legislature to vote on the proposal. Thus, these Law Lords were precluded from adjudicating on these cases.

5.4.3 General protections of the judiciary

Judges are paid a good salary (in 2023/4, ranging from around £100,531 to £294,821 depending on the judge's salary grouping (Judicial Salaries, https://assets.publishing.service.gov.uk/media/65129fffb23dad0012e70608/judicial-salaries-2023-2024.pdf), independently agreed to by the Senior Salaries Review Body in order to avoid allegations of corruption or bribery and to prevent government influence over judicial salaries.

For the general public, judges being independent and trustworthy ensures that when they interact with the legal system, in determining their civil rights and obligations or when they are facing criminal charges, they can be satisfied that they will receive a fair and public hearing within a reasonable time before an independent and impartial court or tribunal established by law.

Judges are inoculated from political pressure and interference by being appointed on merit and not because of their political affiliations. Judges in the UK are not elected; thus, they do not need to face an electorate and thus be subject to the need to placate that electorate. Technically, senior judges are appointed by the King on the recommendation of either the prime minister, in the case of the Supreme Court, or the Lord Chancellor, in the case of the senior courts, Crown Court and other judges such as circuit judges, recorders and district judges. However, this aspect of the appointment process is more ceremonial than substantive, since the decision to appoint is made by the independent Selection Commission for the Supreme Court and the independent Judicial Appointments Commission.

Once appointed, judges enjoy security of tenure. Judges sitting in the High Court and above enjoy tenure during good behaviour and can only be removed by an address of both Houses of Parliament. Judges sitting in the lower courts enjoy tenure during good behaviour and can only be removed by the Lord Chancellor acting with the Lord Chief Justice through disciplinary processes established in legislation. In general, the retirement age for judicial office-holders is now set at 75 under the Judicial Pensions and Retirement Act 1993 (as amended).

Misbehaviour by judges is dealt with by the Judicial Conduct Investigations Office (JCIO). Complaints about the handling of misbehaviour by the JCIO and complaints about the Judicial Appointments Commission can be heard by the Judicial Appointment and Conduct Ombudsman.

The judiciary are further protected from political pressure from both the legislature and the executive through parliamentary rules. According to *Erskine May*—the definitive guide to parliamentary conduct and procedure—ministers and MPs should not attack the character or motives of judges and should not publicly discuss or seek to influence decisions that are currently live before a court (the *sub judice* convention).

The Lord Chancellor, ministers and other individuals tasked with the administration of justice and matter relating to the judiciary must uphold the independence of the judiciary under the Constitutional Reform Act 2005 and must not seek to influence the course of judicial decision-making through preferential access to the judiciary. The Lord Chancellor, on appointment, must take an oath to respect the rule of law, defend judicial independence and to discharge their duty to provide resources for the efficient and effective support of the courts. The Lord Chancellor's obligations also extend to international courts with which the UK has agreements.

5.4.4 The Constitutional Reform Act 2005

The Constitutional Reform Act 2005 constituted a significant statutory intervention into the rule of law and the separation of powers, and had particular consequences for the administration of the judiciary. The Appellate Committee of the House of Lords was replaced by the Supreme Court of the United Kingdom. This ensured a physical separation of powers since the Appellate Committee of the House of Lords sat within the second chamber of the legislature of the UK. The Supreme Court building, Middlesex Guildhall, is sited in Little George Street, Westminster, London across from the Houses of Parliament. The Appellate Committee of the House of Lords was physically located within the parliamentary estate. This meant that the public struggled to really understand the focus and importance of the court itself, and often failed to differentiate between the twin roles of the House of Lords. Physical separation and a retro-fitted building that was designed to be an open, welcoming supreme court ensures that the public can learn more about the operation of the highest court of the land and the Supreme Court website and YouTube channel ensure that the UK population beyond London can view justice in action. The Supreme Court website does not share the gov.uk domain name, further providing for the separation of the court from the rest of the UK state. The justices of the Supreme Court retain the style of Lord or Lady in order to maintain a link to their past role in the House of Lords. While the justices are peers of the realm, they may not sit in the House of Lords while they hold judicial office. Similarly, judges cannot stand as a Member of Parliament under the House of Commons Disqualification Act 1975.

5.4.5 Protection of the judicial environment

Judicial independence is central to the separation of powers in the UK and key to the maintenance of both the rule of law and democracy.

The principal of judicial independence requires the protection of the judicial environment so that they are inoculated against political interference.

Judicial proceedings are given absolute privilege, meaning that no action in defamation can be taken against a judge for statements delivered in open court (*Munster v Lamb* (1883) 11 QBD 588). This rule applies to statements made by counsel and witnesses as well and is designed to ensure that the court gets to hear the truth.

Judges are expected to interpret legislation in line with the intention of Parliament and are also responsible for the development of common law: statutory laws are written laws passed by legislature and government of a country; common law, also known as case law, is law that has been developed in judgments made by judges over hundreds of years. Judges in the 'higher courts' such as the High Court (King's Bench Division, Chancery and Family Division), the Court of Appeal and the Supreme Court have life tenure until the mandatory retirement age of 75. This protects their independence. A resolution of both Houses of Parliament is needed to remove a judge from a higher court. Judges in 'lower' courts in England and Wales can only be removed after disciplinary proceedings. The Office of Judicial Complaints is jointly accountable to the Lord Chancellor and Lord Chief Justice. Judges are also protected by immunity from legal action in relation to their judicial functions and absolute privilege in relation to court proceedings. Absolute privilege ensures freedom of speech in court and protection for the judges from civil action.

In many ways, the judiciary are the most important element of both the separation of powers and the rule of law doctrines. The judiciary controls and limits the powers of both the Parliament and the executive and imposes a number of self-constraints on its own power to adjudicate on disputes.

KEY POINT SUMMARY

- The constitutional structure of the UK is complex because it is based on a mixture of primary legislation, case law, convention, custom and tradition, all of which fall to be interpreted through the lens of several key constitutional principles.
- When we talk about the rule of law, the separation of powers or any other principle underpinning the UK constitution (eg democratic accountability, parliamentary sovereignty), we should reflect on its relationship with other principles and the other elements which comprise the constitution.
- Although the UK does not observe a complete separation of powers between the three branches of the state in practice—because of the fusion of the executive and the legislature—the principle is still of essential importance in interpreting the proper scope and limits of institutional competences in given situations.
- As a result of relatively recent constitutional reforms, particularly the Constitutional Reform Act 2005, the separation of powers in relation to the judiciary has been enhanced. The 2005 Act set up a new Supreme Court which is physically and conceptually independent of the legislature. It also established an independent appointments process limiting governmental involvement in judicial appointments.
- The 2005 Act also contained important rhetorical protections for the rule of law, enjoining the Lord Chancellor and other members of the government to uphold the rule of law in the course of their official duties.
- There are many competing interpretations of the rule of law. All of them insist upon the observance of certain procedural requirements to create valid law, but only some of them also require that fundamental human rights and other values, like fairness, are protected.
- The principle of legality has both a specific meaning in UK case law and a general meaning. In the first case, it concerns what is required from Parliament to exceed or set aside certain constitutional expectations. In the second, it aligns with the general expectation of the rule of law that government should be conducted under law and in accordance with the rule of law (thickly or thinly defined).
- Notwithstanding that the rule of law and separation of powers can seem like nebulous concepts in the abstract, it is clear that there are many examples in the case law of how the principles apply in practice which guide judicial, governmental and parliamentary behaviour.
- Parliamentary sovereignty is—generally speaking—still held to be the animating principle of the UK's constitution, with other principles like the rule of law and separation of powers giving way in the face of Parliament's sovereignty.
- That being said, there is evidence in the case law that the courts will, for example, interpret statutory pronouncements in such a way as to make them comply with other constitutional principles (eg *Evans*), or may—though such a situation remains very much hypothetical—set aside legislation which is anathema to those principles (see eg *Jackson*).
- Judicial review is a key constitutional mechanism for examining the government's (the executive's) use of statutory, prerogative and other powers. Through this process, the courts assess whether the government has acted within the powers it was granted or exceeded them, whether it has acted rationally, reasonably and proportionately and whether it has followed the correct processes.
- Judicial review is an example of the rule of law and separation of power in action because it demonstrates the judiciary acting as a check and balance on the powers of government, where government has—where its power is statutory—derived its power from Parliament. It also, in that sense, protects the sovereignty of Parliament because it ensures the government do not go beyond what Parliament has authorised.

CHAPTER 6
Judicial Review

FUNCTIONING LEGAL KNOWLEDGE

This chapter covers the following functional knowledge required to pass the SQE 1 assessments:

Judicial review:

- the nature, process and limits of judicial review
- supervisory nature
- remedies
- decisions which may be challenged
- standing
- time limits
- grounds:
  - illegality
  - irrationality
  - procedural impropriety
  - legitimate expectation

AUTHORITIES UNDERPINNING PRACTICE

The key authorities that underpin this area of practice are listed below. Note that for legislation you are linked to legislation.gov.uk.

Although much of the legislation on this government website is available in its amended form, the incorporation of new amendments into the text of legislation can be delayed. You should refer to legal databases to ensure you are referencing the most up-to-date legislation.

- Senior Courts Act 1981
  https://www.legislation.gov.uk/ukpga/1981/54/contents
- Civil Procedure Rules
  https://www.justice.gov.uk/courts/procedure-rules/civil/rules
- Criminal Justice and Courts Act 2015
  https://www.legislation.gov.uk/ukpga/2015/2/contents
- Human Rights Act 1998
  https://www.legislation.gov.uk/ukpga/1998/42/contents
- Judicial Review and Courts Act 2022
  https://www.legislation.gov.uk/ukpga/2022/35/contents
- The Administrative Court Judicial Review Guide 2023
  https://www.judiciary.uk/courts-and-tribunals/high-court/administrative-court/administrative-court-judicial-review-guide-2022/

6.1 Introduction

This chapter provides an overview of the **judicial review** process. Judicial review, as its name suggests, is the power of the courts to review the lawfulness of various decisions taken by **public bodies** or bodies exercising public functions.

In addition to overseeing positive action by decision-makers, the system of judicial review also encompasses scrutiny of the failure to act by a public body or body exercising public functions (see generally the terms of the Civil Procedure Rules, where it is stated that 'judicial review' is 'a decision, action or failure to act in relation to the exercise of a public function', Civil Procedure Rules (CPR) rule 54.1).

The system of judicial review is separate from the system of appeals within the court hierarchy. The system of judicial review is not an appeal system, rather it is designed to ensure that decisions that have been taken are not *ultra vires* (ie lawful, in the sense of being within the proper confines of the law and powers granted to the decision-maker), are rational and reasonable, **proportionate** and in compliance with stated processes and procedural protections. Judicial review is not an appeal. Appeals test the appropriateness of a decision through a reappraisal of how an earlier, lower level decision-maker applied the law to the facts of the case. Judicial review is concerned with ensuring that the decision-maker had the power to make the decision, acted rationally in the application of those powers, that correct processes were followed and so on. The courts are mindful that first instance decision-makers: (a) are normally possessed of greater institutional competence to make the decision in question than the courts; and (b) in many cases have been authorised by Parliament to make that decision. Thus, judicial review is a supervisory power whereby the courts ensure that the exercise of public functions is conducted lawfully and fairly.

In broad terms, then, the task of the court in judicial review proceedings is limited to determining whether the decision-maker acted lawfully, not whether the court would have made *the same* decision itself (as discussed later, the ground of proportionality blurs the position somewhat). The court is there to investigate whether the decision-making authority has exceeded or abused its powers, made an error of law, breached the rules of natural justice or reached a decision which no reasonable decision-maker could have reached.

Recourse to judicial review has grown significantly since the end of the Second World War. For an overview of the number of judicial review cases over the first 20 years of the century, see **Figure 6.1**. Further information is also available from the Ministry of Justice's Judicial Review Interactive Data Tool, available at; https://judicial-reviews-app.apps.live.cloud-platform.service.justice.gov.uk/.

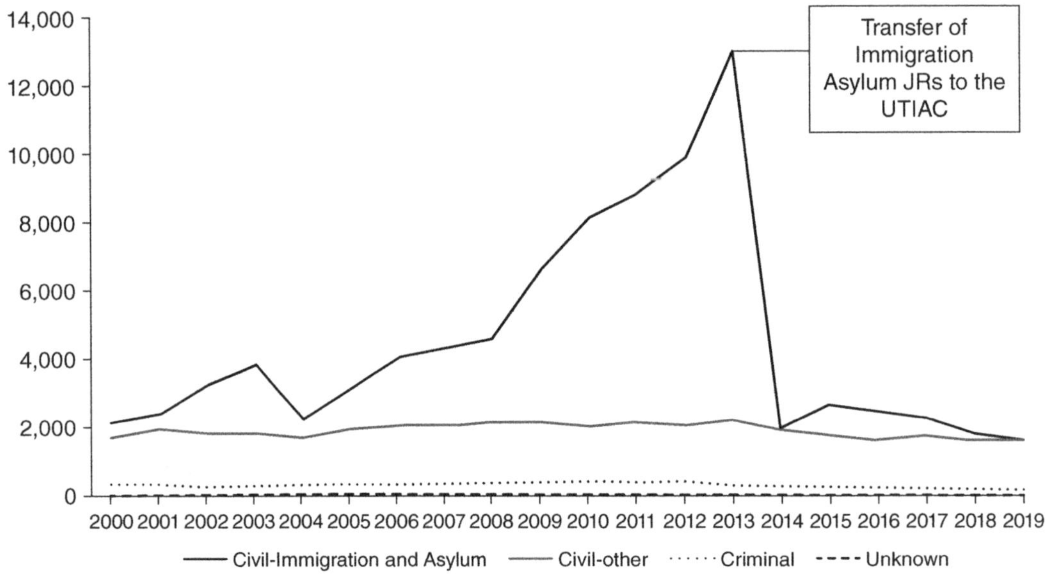

FIGURE 6.1 Judicial review cases 2000–19

Source: Civil Justice Statistics, Ministry of Justice.

In many respects, this is unsurprising given the growth of governmental involvement in the ordinary life of the UK and its citizens through executive decision-making following the significant expansion of the state since the 1940s. The growth in government powers has, understandably, been matched by increasing supervision of these powers by judges. Alongside the greater involvement of the state in regulating the everyday life of its citizenry, governmental and quasi-governmental regulatory functions have been entrusted to various private organisations through 'contracting out' processes (see **Chapter 4** on state institutions). To avoid an accountability black hole, such decisions are also subject to supervision. Thus, judicial review additionally incorporates the supervision of private bodies when they are exercising public functions. The classic case on this point is *Ex p Datafin* [1987] QB 815, in which a privately established body in the City of London regulated takeovers and mergers between companies. The court observed that, if such a body did not exist, the government would have established one to perform this essential governmental function. This type of body is plainly different to, for example, bodies regulating sporting endeavours, like the Jockey Club in *Ex p Aga Khan* [1993] 1 WLR 909 or the Football Association in *Ex p Football League* [1993] 2 All ER 833, which—though they are of great interest to many members of the public—do not exercise recognisably governmental functions. The system of judicial review also helps to ensure that decision-making generally is improved by the ever-present threat of legal challenge to decisions.

Judicial review performs many functions, all of which are justified by its core constitutional role: ensuring that the **rule of law** is maintained and upheld. Indeed, Lady Hale stated in the case of *R (Cart) v Upper Tribunal* [2011] UKSC 28 that:

> the scope of judicial review is an artefact of the **common law** whose object is to maintain the rule of law—that is to ensure that, within the bounds of practical possibility, decisions are taken in accordance with the law, and in particular the law which Parliament has enacted, and not otherwise.

This demonstrates that judicial review is a judge-made remedy designed to 'restrain the excess or abuse of power' (see *R v Secretary of State for the Home Department, ex p Brind* [1991] AC 696).

Judicial review is limited in its availability and its function. As discussed earlier, judicial review is not an appeals process. The judges will generally not substitute their decision for that of the decision-maker. Rather, the judges will simply determine whether the decision was validly taken.

Judicial review is seen as a system of last resort. Essentially, if there are other avenues available to challenge, complain or constrain a decision, then those options should be used instead (*R (Archer) v Commissioners for Her Majesty's Revenue and Customs* [2019] EWCA Civ 1021). Where these options are ineffectual or otherwise unavailable, then judicial review is appropriate.

Judicial review is also limited in terms of who can challenge and be challenged, on what basis and within what time frame. If access to judicial review were unregulated, the danger is that anyone would be able to resort to judicial review merely to complain about a decision with which they disagreed. Thus, in order to stem the tide of judicial review cases, there are various procedures which must be followed and restrictions on access to review.

6.2 The procedure to bring a judicial review

Judicial review consists of a two-stage process which is itself preceded by a pre-action process. The pre-action protocol requires the parties to attempt to exhaust other remedies before resorting to judicial review (although they are still bound by the time limits in rule 54.5(1) CPR, and see later at **6.3.4**).

6.2.1 The pre-action process

You can view the full pre-action protocol online; reference should also be made to CPR, Part 54A but it can be summarised in the following way. As in any pre-action process, the protocol in the context of judicial review is designed to help parties determine the nature of the issues in dispute and decide how they want to address them, to provide a framework to resolve the identified issues without resort to the judicial process and thus to control costs, and—if legal action is unavoidable—ensure this is commenced in an efficient manner (see protocol, para 2). There are certain situations, especially urgent cases, where it would be neither practical nor appropriate to follow the protocol (protocol, para 6), but in any case 'all claimants will need to satisfy themselves whether they should follow the protocol, depending upon the circumstances of the case' (protocol, para 7). Counsel need to be very careful that they do not abuse the streamlined urgency procedures (*In the Matter of the Court's Exercise of the Hamid Jurisdiction: Re an Application for Judicial Review* [2021] EWHC 1895 (Admin)). The protocol also contains provisions for communication between the parties (protocol, paras 13–25) and for alternative dispute resolution (ADR) procedures (protocol, paras 9–12).

In an attempt to promote resolution of the issues before the case comes to court, prior to the court proceedings the parties are encouraged to consider whether ADR may be preferable (for more on ADR, see **Chapter 4** on state institutions). This is Stage One of the protocol. If no ADR is agreed to be suitable, Stage Two of the protocol requires the claimant to send a pre-action letter of claim to the defendant or defendants. The relevant forms and process of this pre-action protocol are available on the Justice.gov.uk website.

This letter should set out the details of the act or omission being challenged and a summary of the facts. The defendant is then usually given 14 days to respond. The defendant may request additional time; however, caution needs to be exercised with delays to the process because of the strict time limits applicable to judicial review claims.

6.2.2 The two-stage process: permission stage

Where the parties are not able to resolve their dispute via the pre-action protocol, the two-stage process noted above commences. The process is set out in detail in The Administrative Court Judicial Review Guide 2023 (updated at https://www.judiciary.uk/wp-content/uploads/2023/08/14.317_HMCTS_Administrative_Court_Guide_2023_WEB1.pdf), normally updated annually; however, it can be summarised in the following way. The applicant must seek leave from the court to bring the review—this is called the permission stage.

The claim commences when the applicant files their completed claim form and documentation, along with the requisite fee at the Administrative Court Office, along with copies of the form to all defendants in the action (see 2023 Guide, 7.2. 7.3 and 7.9). There are five venues in England and Wales at which the claim may be filed (see 2023 Guide, 7.7). Since the purpose of judicial review is allied to the notion of good governance, it is incumbent on the claimant to make full and frank disclosure of all relevant facts, even those that go against their case such as the availability of an alternative remedy or delay. This obligation of candour also extends to the defendant (*R (on the application of IAB) v. Secretary of State for the Home Department* [2024] EWCA Civ 66).

The application is then normally considered on the papers by a judge who will make an assessment about whether the application should be allowed to proceed to a full hearing, having regard to issues including the claimant's standing and the viability of the claim (see 2023 Guide, 9). This is a sifting exercise, designed to exclude unmeritorious claims. In the event that permission is refused, the claimant can thereafter request an oral hearing to state their case (see 2023 Guide, 9.4). However, an oral hearing will be refused where the court considers that the claim is totally without merit. It is possible that the judge will decide they need to hear more information before proceeding to a decision, and will hear oral argument (see 2023 Guide, 9.2.1.4).

Generally, permission will only be granted where the claimant has shown an arguable ground for judicial review and that they have a realistic prospect of success (*Sharma v Brown-Antoine* [2007] 1 WLR 780).

6.2.3 The two-stage process: hearing stage

Where the applicant is successful, their claim will proceed to a substantive hearing (see 2023 Guide, 11). If permission or leave is granted, the defendant, and any interested parties, must then submit detailed grounds of their defence.

Judicial review is an expensive undertaking and should not be entered into lightly. Similarly to other general cases before the courts, the losing side may have to pay the costs of the winning side.

Thus, this aspect of procedure may chill a claimant's enthusiasm for instituting legal claims even where the case is of merit and is clearly in the **public interest**. However, the court is able to exercise discretion in awarding costs.

Under ss 88–90 of the Criminal Justice and Courts Act 2015, the court may award what is known as a Judicial Review Costs Capping Order (JRCCO). This discretionary, exceptional order may limit or even remove the liability of the losing party to pay the other side's legal costs. Such an order can only be granted where the court is satisfied that the judicial review application is a public interest case, there is a real danger that the applicant would withdraw their claim if they were exposed to full liability for costs if they were unsuccessful and that the decision to withdraw is a reasonable one. The need to limit or absolve liability for costs is a particular concern in environmental law cases given the need to ensure that concerned citizens and public interest groups are not deterred from bringing claims.

The following sections consider some of the procedural considerations discussed earlier (eg the question of standing/interest of the applicant) in more detail, as well as the grounds of review and remedies which may flow from successful judicial review actions.

6.3 Accessing judicial review

As just noted, there are various restrictions on accessing judicial review which help to regulate the flow of applications to the court and also ensure that judicial review remains focused on its principal constitutional functions of monitoring the use of public power and the relationship between the citizen and the state in relation to decisions made by the state about said citizens. The procedural aspects which filter access to judicial review can be broken down into: (a) which bodies are amenable to judicial review; (b) who can bring a judicial review against such bodies, that is, who has standing; (c) is the issue **justiciable**; and (d) within what time must a review be brought.

6.3.1 The bodies and decisions amenable to judicial review

Decisions are generally amenable to judicial review where they are of a public law nature. Thus, the nature of the body making the decision, or failing to act, is of secondary importance to the primary requirement that the decision made is one that falls within the broad remit of public law (*R v Panel on Takeovers and Mergers, ex p Datafin* [1987] QB 815, *R (on the application Doncaster MBC) v Doncaster Sheffield Airport* [2022] EWHC 3060 (Admin) and *R (on the application of Tortoise Media) v Conservative and Unionist Party* [2023] EWHC 3088 (Admin)). Essentially, the question is whether the decision should be judicially reviewable. Nevertheless, the court will take into account the nature of the relevant body or person.

As a general rule, where the body's power stems from a statute or secondary legislation, the body's decisions will normally be judicially reviewable. Conversely, where the decision-making power of the body derives from a contract, such decisions will almost invariably be beyond the scope of judicial review. So, for example, the decisions of trade unions, business associations and social clubs will generally be excluded from judicial review. However, as noted, the starting point is the nature of the decision *not* the nature of the decision-maker.

Where elements of both of these extremes are in play, the courts will investigate both the source and nature of the power to determine the reviewability of the body's decisions. Where the body exercises power in an internal capacity, such as in domestic situations or as a private tribunal, then judicial review will be unavailable, whilst some element of public duty or function will tilt towards the possibility of judicial review.

A classic situation would be where a government department makes a decision alleged to be deficient in some way. In such a case, the presumption will be that the decision of the department will be reviewable. However, even in this simple example, it is not the case that the decision is automatically reviewable. The decision taken, or failure to take a decision, must have a public law element, governmental characteristics or similar. Thus, simple contractual or employment disputes between a government department and its suppliers and employees are often purely internal issues that do not raise public law issues, although if such events raise public law concerns, these disputes will be reviewable. As Lord Diplock explained in the GCHQ case (*Council of Civil Service Unions v Minister for the Civil Service* [1984] UKHL 6):

> For a decision to be susceptible to judicial review the decision-maker must be empowered by public law (and not merely, as in arbitration, by agreement between private parties) to make decisions that, if validly made, will lead to administrative action or abstention from action by an authority endowed by law with executive powers.

In contrast, it cannot be simply assumed that private law bodies are always immune from judicial review. Where a private body or individual takes decisions that have a public law element to them, these decisions will be reviewable, notwithstanding their private law status. In determining whether decisions of a private body or person are reviewable, the court will take account of a range of factors.

6.3.1.1 Factors taken into account

The court will take into account the significance of the public function being performed. The greater the significance and consequences of the decision, the greater the need for judicial review.

The court will apply the 'but for' test. Under this test, the court will determine whether but for the existence of the body, the functions undertaken by that body would be exercised by a public body under statute. For example, where the power is being exercised by an arm's length body, a non-departmental public body or executive agency or other body, this fact is significant since in the absence of such a body, the power would be directly exercised by a governmental body, thus the decision is highly likely to be judicially reviewable.

In determining the 'but for' test, the court may take into account the fact that the organisation is underpinned by statute, that is it was set up under legislation and the court will investigate whether the organisation is endowed with extensive or even monopolistic powers. However, these factors are not determinative but simply offer guidance (*R (Beer (trading as Hammer Trout Farm)) v Hampshire Farmers Markets* [2003] EWCA Civ 1056).

The court will investigate the implications of the decision. If the decision affects the public law rights or the legitimate expectations of a person, then that is highly likely to mean that the decision is reviewable (*Council of Civil Service Unions v Minister for the Civil Service* [1985] AC 374).

The court will examine whether the decision-making is to be exercised in a judicial way.

The court will inquire as to whether there is a private law right to challenge. *Aga Khan* [1992] EWCA Civ 7 and *R (Tucker) v Director General of the National Crime Squad* [2003] EWCA Civ 57.

EXAMPLE

The role of regulating the legality and appropriateness of adverts is undertaken by the Advertising Standards Authority (ASA). If the ASA did not exist, there would still be a need for regulation of advertising in the public interest in order to protect citizens from the harms of misleading and illegal advertising; thus, its decisions could be challenged under judicial review (*R v Advertising Standards Authority Ltd, ex p the Insurance Service Plc* [1990] 2 Admin LR 77).

Similarly, the Panel on Takeovers and Mergers performs a vital public function in protecting the rights of shareholders and wider stakeholders in the case of mergers and takeovers of UK companies (see *R v Panel on Takeovers and Mergers, ex p Datafin plc* [1987] QB 815).

Conversely, the courts have declined to exercise their judicial review function over the Football Association and the Jockey Club since, in these sporting situations, it was not obvious that the state would step in to regulate such matters in the absence of those organisations (*R v Football Association Ltd, ex p Football League Ltd* [1992] 2 All 833 and *R v Disciplinary Committee of the Jockey Club, ex p The Aga Khan* [1992] EWCA Civ 7). In the case of the Aga Khan, his horse was alleged to have won a race due to the horse having been administered a banned performance-enhancing substance. The court held that the relationship between the Aga Khan and the regulator of horseracing, the Jockey Club, was a private contractual one.

More generally, the increasing privatisation of activities that were in the past performed by the state, gives rise to the risk that accountability is diluted. Thus, it is clear that the courts will take a pragmatic and sometimes expansive view of whether they have the power to supervise the decision-making of such private organisations. The courts are now more likely to determine that the actions of a private body are judicially reviewable, particularly where the decisions have wider public impacts on business and commerce. Thus, private psychiatric hospitals, privatised water companies and social landlords may all be subject to judicial review. The range of bodies subject to judicial review is therefore an evolving concept that is adapted to the changing structure, needs and priorities of the state.

6.3.2 The rules of standing (*locus standi*)

Judicial review is not a licence for busybodies, available generally to any interested citizens who are sufficiently aggrieved by the actions or inactions of public bodies to want to raise proceedings. Rather, all legal systems have to operate under the constraints of limited resources and as such priorities have to be determined. The courts and the legal system must strike a balance between access to justice and the need not to overwhelm the legal system. The Administrative Court (the King's Bench Division) has a finite number of judges available to determine cases and as such resources need to be allocated efficiently and equitably.

In addition to regulating the types of bodies which can be judicially reviewed, the courts also determine who can bring actions against them via the rules on standing (also called *locus standi*, or the requirement to demonstrate a 'sufficient interest'). Judicial review applications are limited to those who have standing to challenge the impugned decision. An applicant must show 'sufficient interest in the matter to which the application relates' (s31(3) Senior Courts Act 1981).

A question arises as to when the question of standing should be considered. In principle, no application for judicial review may be authorised unless and until the court has granted permission, and the court will only grant leave where the applicant can show 'sufficient interest' in the matter complained of. However, the sufficiency of the applicant's interest may not be clear at the permission stage and may only be fully visible with the benefit of a substantive hearing. In view of this, the courts have adopted an increasingly liberal approach to standing on the basis that it is important that where there is a prima facie question for a public body to answer, applicants should be granted standing where no better placed applicant has presented themselves. The justification for this is that it is important to ensure that potentially unlawful conduct is scrutinised (see *R (McCourt) v Parole Board* [2020] EWHC 2320 (Admin) and *R (Jones) v Commissioner of Police for the Metropolis* [2020] 1 WLR 519). This position is encapsulated in *Ex p National Federation of the Self Employed and Small Businesses Ltd* [1982] AC 617, at 644, in which Lord Diplock opined that:

> it would . . . be a grave lacuna in our system of public law if [an applicant] were prevented by outdated technical rules of *locus standi* from bringing the matter to the attention of the court to vindicate the rule of law and get the unlawful conduct stopped.

This reasoning opened the possibility of an associational and public interest basis to standing such that concerned citizens or organisations could perform a representative role in circumstances where there are no directly affected individuals available to challenge decisions or where they think it is in the public interest to challenge a decision, policy, omission or similar (see, eg, *R v Inspectorate of Pollution, ex p Greenpeace Ltd (No 2)* [1994] 2 CMLR 548; *R v Secretary of State for Foreign and Commonwealth Affairs, ex p World Development Movement* [1995] 1 All ER 611). However, the court also needs to be alert to the danger of permitting frivolous and vexatious litigation to be instituted because such litigation interrupts the legitimate conduct of public business and is potentially anti-democratic. Indeed, it has recently been determined that public interest organisations need to be careful not to draw up their articles of association too widely so as to elide their chances of success in proving standing (*R (on the application of Good Law Project Ltd, Runnymede Trust) v The Prime Minister, Secretary of State for Health and Social Care* [2022] EWHC 298 (Admin)).

In determining standing, a number of important factor will be considered. The court will:

1. consider the importance of ensuring that the rule of law is maintained. The availability and extent of judicial review is an essential device in encouraging decision-makers to make decisions according to the law. If decision-makers know that their decisions are potentially subject to detailed scrutiny by judges, then this fact will encourage good decision-making;

2. take into account the importance of the issue that is in contention in the decision. Thus, the more important the issue, the greater the need for judicial review;
3. assess the applicant's interest in the case on the basis of a number of factors;
4. determine the relative strength, importance and merits of the grounds of challenge;
5. look at the proximity of the claimant to the impugned decision. The closer the person is to the decision, the more the court will grant standing;
6. look at the availability or otherwise of an alternative remedy;
7. consider the nature of the duty breached; if the duty is more public law-focused, the more judicial review will be necessary;
8. consider the position of the claimant, particularly as regards their role, their position, the extent of their interest in the issues and the availability or otherwise of other alternative claimants who could instigate judicial review; and
9. take into account the extent and the nature of the remedy asked (*R v Secretary of State for Foreign and Commonwealth Affairs, ex p World Development Movement* [1995] 1 All ER 611).

6.3.2.1 Interveners and third parties

The public nature of judicial review, insofar as it promotes compliance with the rule of law and promotes good governance, means that the courts are relatively relaxed in admitting interested third parties to applications for judicial review. The courts will allow 'interested parties' to join claims. An interested party is someone who is not the claimant or defendant but who is directly affected by the claim. The courts are also prepared to permit 'interveners' to participate in judicial review cases. These 'interveners' are typically campaign groups, government departments or companies which are indirectly affected by the claim. They are entitled to submit evidence to the court and to make representations. These interveners perform an important role in judicial review cases since they bring their expertise to bear upon the case.

6.3.2.2 How has the liberal test on standing been applied?

The rules on standing have been liberally interpreted to now include a range of individuals and organisations beyond the traditional, limited list of directly affected individuals. Individuals do not necessarily need to show a direct link or impact on their legal rights to justify bringing a claim. For example, a TV viewer by dint of the fact that they possess a TV licence can be permitted to make a claim against the broadcast of offensive material.

EXAMPLE

In the case of *R v The Independent Broadcasting Authority* (1985) The Times, 4 April, the well-known morality campaigner, Mary Whitehouse, was given standing to challenge the decision of the IBA to screen the controversial and highly violent movie *Scum*.

Concerned citizens may also be permitted standing where they are challenging an issue of sufficient public importance.

EXAMPLE

Thus, Lord Rees-Mogg was entitled to institute a judicial review claim questioning the legality of the Foreign Secretary's decision to ratify the Treaty on European Union in 1993 (*R v Secretary of State for Foreign and Commonwealth Affairs, ex p Rees-Mogg* [1994] QB 552).

Beyond the case of individuals, the courts are increasingly receptive to the idea of public interest groups bringing claims in a representative capacity, where they can bring their significant expertise to bear in matters of general public concern. This is particularly the case as regards environmental disputes, on the basis that both the ecological health of the planet is a concern common to all and that the biosphere has no clear advocate to state its claim.

EXAMPLE

In the case of *R v Secretary of State for Foreign and Commonwealth Affairs, ex p World Development Movement* [1995] 1 WLR 386, World Development Movement had expertise in funding large-scale aid projects so was uniquely qualified to assess the merits of the proposed construction of the power plant on the Pergau Dam in Malaysia.

Similarly, the well-known environmental charity and campaign group Greenpeace has been granted standing in numerous environmental judicial review cases. An example is the case of *R v Inspectorate of Pollution, ex p Greenpeace (No 2)* [1994] 4 All ER 329, where Greenpeace was permitted to challenge British Nuclear Fuels' decision to test a new re-processing plant.

EXAMPLE

***Osterreichischer Rundfunk v Austria* [2006] ECHR 1043**

As a last point, it is worth noting that for judicial review claims involving alleged violations of human rights, the claimant will only have standing to institute a claim where it can show that it is a victim of the alleged violation, as required by s7 of the Human Rights Act 1998. The notion of victim, for the purposes of the European Convention on Human Rights (ECHR), extends to legal persons as well as natural persons.

6.3.3 Justiciability

The work of government is wide-ranging. It makes millions of decisions a year affecting individuals, communities, local and other governmental organisations, the nations of the UK and other states beyond our borders. While the conduct of government must always be carried out under law, some of the decisions government makes are intensely political; for example, decisions on economic policy in the budget, the deployment of the armed forces and the negotiation of treaties with other states. The nature of these decisions begs the question as to whether it would be appropriate for a legal body—a court—to supervise the use of the powers which enable those decisions to be made. This is particularly so given that, historically, the UK's constitution could be said to fit the model of what is broadly called political constitutionalism. That is, the expectation that important constitutional and other decisions should be taken and scrutinised by the political branches of the state (ie Parliament and the government); hence, the doctrine of **parliamentary sovereignty** and the presence of the executive in Parliament. Though this position might be changing in part, it does tell us that the constitutional starting point is that the courts should be mindful of the nature of the questions they are capable of answering; in particular, they should only answer questions which are best decided by a legal body. This is what the question of justiciability is concerned with—does a matter raise legal questions which a court is competent to answer?

6.3.3.1 Justiciability of the prerogative

The prerogative power offers a good example of a legal power which can generate decisions, and thus questions about the conduct of those decisions, which may not be suitable for a court to answer. This is not to say that the prerogative is not justiciable, far from it (see Lord Diplock in the *GCHQ Case* [1984] UKHL 6), but simply that the prerogative power aptly demonstrates the things which must be considered in terms of justiciability.

Traditionally, prerogative powers—that is, powers that flowed from the sovereign monarch—were not challengeable in a court of law. As a matter of logic, as the ultimate decision-maker and source of power, the monarch could not be subject to any controls. It was said that these powers were non-justiciable; that is, they did not present legal questions which a court could answer. Over time, many of these powers transferred to the government to exercise on behalf of the monarch, while other powers were reconstituted on a statutory basis by Acts of Parliament. Although a welcome democratic development, the coexistence of both statutory power and residual powers created a dichotomy in accountability, with only statutory powers being subject to judicial oversight. Over the past half-century, significant inroads have been made into this position, although issues of 'high policy . . . [such as] making treaties, making war, dissolving Parliament, and [*sic*] mobilising the Armed Forces' are still considered non-justiciable prerogative powers (*R v Secretary of State for Foreign and Commonwealth Affairs, ex p Everett* [1989] 1 QB 811).

As discussed earlier, the GCHQ case (*Council of Civil Service Unions v Minister for the Civil Service* [1984] UKHL 6) was the first case where the judges were prepared to potentially review an exercise of the **royal prerogative**. Though they agreed in principle that the prerogative power was reviewable, the subject matter to which the prerogative power was applied in this case—the national security infrastructure of the state—meant that the courts were reluctant to engage in judicial review of the exercise of such power since the judges were not in the best position to determine whether the decision of the minister was correct. Thus, the judges showed deference to the minister (incidentally, the Minister for the Civil Service is traditionally the prime minister) as being in the best position to assess what national security demanded in this context.

EXAMPLE

A contemporary example of deference to a minister can be seen in the case of *R (on the application of Begum) v Special Immigration Appeals Commission* [2021] UKSC 7.

In this case, the Supreme Court was highly critical of the reasoning of the Court of Appeal in the case of Shamima Begum and the decision of the Home Secretary to strip her of UK citizenship under a statutory power because of criminal allegations against her stating that she travelled to Syria to join the terrorist group ISIL. Begum sought to challenge that decision in person in the UK. This would require the courts to grant leave to her to enter the UK. The Supreme Court was highly critical of the Court of Appeal's decision to substitute its own view of national security for that of the Home Secretary. The Home Secretary is in the best position to assess the requirements of national security.

Wider developments in other aspects of judicial review had an impact on the extent of the non-justiciability question. For example, the case of *Gillick* (*Gillick v West Norfolk and Wisbech AHA* [1986] 1 AC 112) concerned a government circular advising doctors on issuing contraception to children under 16 without the knowledge of their parents. Decisions were traditionally only amenable to judicial review when they altered someone's rights or obligations or deprived them of a benefit or advantage. In *Gillick*, the court considered that the general memorandum giving guidance on when to issue contraception could in principle be reviewed.

The difficulties of negotiating complex legal–political issues in the assessment of justiciability is exemplified by the cases of *Miller 1* and *Cherry/Miller 2* [2019] UKSC 41.

6.3.3.2 Justiciability in the *Miller* cases

It is something of an understatement to say that the UK's departure from the EU was politically charged. In view of this, one might have expected that legal challenges pertaining to the process of leaving the EU would encounter problems vis-à-vis justiciability. In two of the most significant cases to come out of the exit process thus far—though by far not the only significant cases (see, eg, *Allister's application for Judicial Review, Re* [2023] UKSC 5)—the courts were able to address the justiciability issues with little conceptual difficulty.

The case of *Miller 1* (*R (Miller) v Secretary of State for Exiting the European Union* [2017] UKSC 5) concerned whether the government could commence the countdown to leaving the EU without parliamentary authorisation. The Supreme Court declared that the prerogative power to resile from an international treaty did not apply to the specific case of withdrawal of the UK from the EU where exercise of that prerogative power would alter the domestic law of the land. Leaving the EU would result in major changes to UK law and it is a fundamental principle that the royal prerogative cannot be used to effect legal change. Starting a countdown timer commencing the Art 50 process using the prerogative power would ultimately lead to a change in the domestic law. Legal change must be done through an Act of Parliament. The justiciability question is evident—the matter is highly politically charged—but there was a clear legal question for the court to answer: did the government have the power to initiate the countdown timer? There was also a key legal–constitutional principle at issue, since misuse of the prerogative power to alter the domestic law of the land would compromise the principle of parliamentary sovereignty. The fact that a matter is political does not automatically make it non-justiciable if there are legal questions which a court is competent to answer, and which it is appropriate for them to answer.

This much is clear from the case of *Cherry/Miller 2* in which the Supreme Court determined that it was competent to adjudicate on questions as to both the legal scope of a prerogative power to prorogue Parliament, not merely the actual exercise of the power in a specific case. The court held that:

> no question of justiciability . . . can arise in relation to whether the law recognises the existence of a prerogative power, or in relation to its legal limits. Those are by definition questions of law. Under the **separation of powers**, it is the function of the courts to determine them.

Where the government failed to give any reasons for the prorogation, this meant that its exercise was unlawful, particularly when the length of time of the prorogation was exceptional and effectively prevented Parliament from exercising its task of holding the executive to account.

6.3.3.3 Ouster clauses

It is worth addressing **ouster clauses** while we also have in mind justiciability since ouster clauses seek to render matters which might otherwise be justiciable non-justiciable by virtue of a statutory enactment. In short, the government makes use of its dominance in Parliament to pass legislation which seeks to restrict the courts' ability to judicially review executive action. Historically, such restrictions have been confined to the decisions of particular decision-making bodies (eg in *Anisminic* [1969] 2 AC 147, the Foreign Compensation Commission and in *Privacy International* [2019] UKSC 22, the Investigatory Powers Tribunal); however, recent trends indicate a willingness for the government to seek to expand the effect of ouster clauses (see, eg, discussion during the passage of the Internal Markets Bill 2019–21 as was).

The classic case on ouster clauses, which established the courts' highly sceptical attitude towards them, is *Anisminic*. As is evident from *Anisminic* and *Privacy International*, the fact that a statute appears to oust the jurisdiction of the courts should not be taken at face value. The effectiveness of the ouster, since it is a statutory enactment, will require interpretation by the courts.

EXAMPLE

***Anisminic Ltd v Foreign Compensation Commission* [1969] 2 AC 147**

Anisminic was a case concerning the Suez crisis in the 1950s. After the crisis, Egypt nationalised the mining interests of Anisminic, a UK company based in Egypt. Under the terms of the Foreign Compensation Act 1950, a tribunal (the Foreign Compensation Commission) was set up to determine the distribution formula for compensation that had been granted to the UK government from the Egyptian government. The Commission refused to award Anisminic any compensation because it had sold its interests to an Egyptian company and, in the Commission's view, the law did not allow disbursement to a non-UK company.

The relevant law also contained an ouster clause stating that the determinations of the Commission were not to be called into question in any court of law. The House of Lords circumvented this ouster by observing that Parliament could not have intended invalid determinations to stand, since such determinations were, of necessity, nullities. Thus, the courts could interrogate determinations in order to assess their validity. Valid determinations were protected by the ouster clause, invalid determinations were not.

Ouster clauses remain a significant point of tension between the courts, Parliament and the government (as demonstrated by the government's proposals to reform this area of the law, see eg the Judicial Review Reform Consultation and the resultant Bill, the Judicial Review and Courts

Act 2022). This is because in the first place they are statutory enactments—legislation passed by a sovereign Parliament. Secondly, they purport to insulate decisions of the executive from judicial scrutiny, contrary to the rule of law. Thirdly, in circumventing ouster clauses, the courts may uphold the rule of law, and assert a particular vision of the separation of powers, but they seem to ignore the sovereignty of Parliament. Generally case law indicates that the courts' ousters are constitutionally deeply problematic (see Lord Carnwath in *Privacy International* [2019] UKSC 22). Notwithstanding courts' general reluctance to accept ouster clauses, the ouster clause of s2 of the Judicial Review and Courts Act 2022 (and the resultant changes to s11A of the Tribunal, Courts and Enforcement Act 2007 and the Civil Procedure Rules via the Civil Procedure (Amendment) Rules 2023 SI 2023/105), which prevents courts from adjudicating on a refusal of the Upper Tribunal to grant permission to appeal from a decision of the First-Tier Tribunal (colloquially known as a 'Cart' judicial review claim (see *R (Catt) v Upper Tribunal* [2011] UKSC 28) and typically focused on immigration claims) has been judicially approved of by both the English High Court (see *R (on the application of Oceana) v Upper Tribunal (Immigration and Asylum Chamber)* [2023] EWHC 791 (Admin) and the English Court of Appeal (*R (on the application of LA (Albania) v The Upper Tribunal and the Secretary of State for the Home Department* [2023] EWCA Civ 1337).

6.3.4 Time limits

As well as regulating who can be challenged, who can bring a review and the types of issues which are reviewable, judicial review cases are also limited via very restrictive time limits. Applicants generally need to institute a claim promptly and, in any event, no later than three months after the event (rule 54.5 CPR (*R (on the application of Crompton) v South Yorkshire Police and Crime Commissioner* [2018] 1 WLR 131)). Even shorter time limits apply in judicial review cases relating to planning disputes and public procurement cases. Planning cases must be instituted within six weeks, whilst procurement cases must be lodged within 30 days. The overriding requirement to act promptly means that the maximum time limits as set out are not to be treated as ordinary time limits that allow for submission close to the deadline. Rather, a failure to submit a claim promptly even with the maximum time frame can be rejected (*R (Sustainable Development Capital LLP) v SSBEIS* [2017] EWHC 771 (Admin); *Finn-Kelcey v Milton Keynes BC* [2009] Env LR 17). The time limit begins to run from the date on which the grounds for making the claim first arose. In practice, this means the date when the impugned decision was made. The justification for this approach lies in the fact that it would be impractical if public law decisions were contested long after they were made. Consider, for example, the loss in public funds caused by outlays to progress a decision if a challenge was made many months or years after the initial decision.

Applications for judicial review in England and Wales are generally heard before the Administrative Court, which is a specialist division of the King's Bench Division of the High Court. Planning disputes are heard by the Planning Court and immigration and asylum claims are heard by the Upper Tribunal Immigration and Asylum Chamber.

6.4 Grounds of review

Having considered questions relating to how judicial review can be accessed, we can now turn to how decisions are challenged—that is, on what *grounds* can public law decisions, omissions and so on be contested at judicial review. Traditionally, there were three classic grounds of judicial review, namely **illegality**, procedural unfairness and irrationality.

Lord Diplock in the case of *Council of Civil Service Unions v Minister for the Civil Service* [1985] AC 374 set out these three non-exhaustive grounds of judicial review. He then stated that:

> further development on a case by case basis may . . . in course of time add further grounds.

In particular, he suggested that the concept of proportionality as set out under the law of the EU and the ECHR could become a separate ground of judicial review.

Since the enactment of the Human Rights Act 1998 and the increased legal effect of the ECHR within the UK legal system, compatibility of decisions with the Convention is a further, conceptually distinct—since its basis lies in statute rather than the common law—ground of judicial review.

The classification as set out earlier is somewhat artificial, since the grounds of challenge may overlap with each other and the courts will not rigidly adhere to this distinction.

6.4.1 Illegality

The question of illegality arises when a decision-maker has misdirected themselves in law, has exercised a power incorrectly or has tried to exercise a power that it did not have. This last element of the concept of illegality is known as ***ultra vires***. This is a Latin term that means 'beyond its powers' thus the body did not have the legal power to take the decision it did. That being said, all illegal actions are of necessity *ultra vires* since no unlawful decision can be *intra vires*.

The clearest example of illegality is this last element of *ultra vires*.

EXAMPLE

***Attorney-General v Fulham Corporation* [1921] 1 Ch 440**

The local authority built a communal washhouse for the local tenants and citizens to use for washing their clothes. Subsequently, the corporation started to provide a wider commercial laundry service, including a collection and delivery service via a horse and van. The court held that the corporation had no legal power to operate a commercial laundry and that it had gone beyond its statutory powers. The court issued a declaration to that effect and issued an **injunction** stopping the council from continuing to provide the service.

EXAMPLE

***R. (on the application of D4) v Secretary of State for the Home Department* [2022] EWCA Civ 33**

The Home Secretary revoked the British citizenship of a woman who had previously travelled to Syria to support ISIS and was now detained in the Roj camp in Syria. The Home Secretary effected the decision to strip D4's citizenship by simply placing a note on her Home Office file, in accordance with the terms of regulations passed in 2003. The Court of Appeal held that these regulations were *ultra vires*, thus void and of no legal effect since the British Nationality Act 1981 required actual notice to be given to the citizen. More generally, the government has removed this notice requirement via the Nationality and Borders Act 2022. The government had intended to appeal this decision to the Supreme Court, however the case was withdrawn by the mutual consent of the parties (https://www.supremecourt.uk/cases/uksc-2022-0042.html).

Whilst the UK was a member of the EU, judicial review was also available to challenge the applicability of UK Acts of Parliament and secondary legislation that was inconsistent with EU law. That is, whether law which appeared to apply to a given situation should be so applied if it contradicted EU law.

EXAMPLE

***Factortame* jurisprudence**

In the long-running saga of Factortame, the UK government, since the 1980s, was concerned about Spanish fishermen creating new companies under English law allowing them to utilise fishing quotas in UK waters. As a result of this scenario, the UK government enacted the Merchant Shipping Act 1988. This Act limited this avenue by requiring UK companies that would have had access to UK waters to have an ownership constituting at least 75% British nationality.

Thus, Spanish-owned UK companies would be denied a fishing licence by the **Secretary of State** where they fell below the 75% threshold. This rule violated the cardinal law of the EU Treaties that there should be no discrimination on the grounds of nationality.

In a number of subsequent judgments, including preliminary reference applications to the European Court of Justice (see **Chapter 10** on EU law aspects in the UK constitution), the UK courts accepted a number of significant limitations upon the UK legal system, including the concept that UK Acts of Parliament do not apply in the event of a conflict between them and a provision of EU law, the availability of damages against the state for violations of EU law and the ability of the UK courts to issue injunctions against the Crown in judicial review proceedings. After Brexit, it is still possible for challenges to be brought against Acts of Parliament on the basis that the act is incompatible with the terms of the Windsor Agreement between the UK and the EU (*Dillon's Application for Judicial Review, Re* [2024] NIKB 11 and *Northern Ireland Human Rights Commission's Application for Judicial Review* [2024] NIKB 35).

More generally, decisions of public bodies that are in conflict with Acts of Parliament or **delegated legislation** can be judicially reviewed. Further, secondary legislation can also be judicially reviewed as being inconsistent with an Act of Parliament (*R (on the application of O (a minor, by her litigation friend AO)) v Secretary of State for the Home Department* [2022] UKSC 3).

Since the enactment of the Human Rights Act 1998, decisions of public bodies and secondary legislation can also be challenged as being unlawful according to s6 of the 1998 Act (including so-called hybrid public bodies where the body in question is private but where it carries out a public function bringing that aspect of its activity within the terms of the 1998 Act). Where the challenge is in respect of an Act of Parliament, the most that the court can declare is that the legislation is incompatible with the ECHR (s4 1998 Act). Thus, the Act of Parliament remains valid. An Act of Parliament that has been found to offend against the ECHR may be amended or repealed in order to avoid that incompatibility at the discretion of Parliament (see **Chapter 8** and the case of (*Dillon's Application for Judicial Review, Re* [2024] NIKB 11)).

Illegality often occurs where inferior courts, tribunals and quasi-judicial bodies such as regulators and ombudsmen make a **jurisdictional error**. Further, a lawful power to take a decision may become unlawful when power is exercised for an improper purpose.

EXAMPLE

Wheeler v Leicester City Council [1985] AC 1054

Leicester City Council acted unlawfully when it decided to ban a rugby club from using its outdoor recreation spaces for a year because the rugby club had not intervened to prevent certain of its members from participating in a rugby tour of South Africa during the apartheid regime, which ran contrary to the general governmental diplomatic policy of not engaging with the regime. The council was generally entitled to take into account race relations when exercising its statutory powers; however, it was an abuse of that power and a failure to act fairly when it decided to ban the rugby club from its land when the club had done nothing wrong.

The decision-maker will act illegally where it takes a decision that frustrates the purpose of the legislation.

EXAMPLE

Padfield v Minister of Agriculture, Fisheries and Food [1968] AC 997

In this case, Padfield objected to the fixed price paid for his milk. The Milk Marketing Board fixed the price paid for milk across England and Wales according to a number of factors. England and Wales was divided into 11 regions and each region was given a particular formula for calculating the price paid for milk. Thus, farmers in different areas of England and Wales were paid different prices for their milk. Padfield objected to the lower price paid for milk in the south-east of England and asked the Minister of Agriculture to intervene using his discretionary power to send his complaint to a committee under the Agricultural Marketing Act 1958. The minister refused to do so. The court held that he had fettered his discretion and, in so doing, had frustrated the aims of the legislation.

It is a general principle of law that it is not possible for a person entrusted with a delegated power to re-delegate that power to another. The Latin term is *delegatus non potest delegare*. If a specific duty or task has been entrusted to a named individual or organisation, that specified individual or group must perform that function and not ask someone else to undertake it. However, a power to delegate can be provided as long as it is expressly and clearly set out.

EXAMPLE

***Allingham v Minister of Agriculture and Fisheries* [1948] 1 All ER 780**

Under the relevant law, the minister was permitted to delegate his power concerning agricultural land to an executive committee, which he did. This executive committee then charged its executive officer with setting out the terms of a direction to an owner of agricultural land to grow sugar beet. The court held that this was an impermissible sub-delegation.

Thus, a decision-maker will act illegally where it has unlawfully delegated its power to another. However, it is likewise accepted that it is simply not practical for a minister to personally take all of the decisions required to be taken day-to-day in their department. Taken in combination, these considerations are known as the *Carltona* principle.

EXAMPLE

***Carltona v Commissioner of Works* [1943] 2 All ER 560**

In this case, the decision of a civil servant was not challengeable on the basis that a decision had to be taken personally by the minister in charge and not by civil servants within the department. Rather, decisions made by officials were generally lawful if they were taken under guidance from the minister. It is unreasonable to expect that all decisions within a governmental department have to be taken personally by the minister. Such a stance is wholly unreasonable given the amount of decisions that need to be taken by government departments. Thus, it is more accurate to state that within government departments, decision-making power has been devolved to civil servants rather than it being delegated. Nonetheless, in exceptional cases, certain decisions, by law, will have to be taken personally by the minister and a failure to do so will render the decision of the official unlawful (see *R v Adams* [2020] UKSC 19).

Illegality will be made out where a body takes irrelevant considerations into account or conversely fails to take into account relevant considerations.

EXAMPLE

***R v Somerset County Council, ex p Fewings* [1995] 1 WLR 1037**

In this case, Somerset County Council sought to prevent hunting on council land. The court held that the council, in giving weight to their concerns over the suffering caused to animals through hunting in making their decision—that is, the moral and ethical questions raised by hunting—they had taken account of irrelevant considerations. The council was required to pay close attention to the limits of its legal powers.

Illegality also extends to the issue of a body fettering its discretion to act by closing its mind to alternative options.

EXAMPLE

Stringer v Minister for Housing and Local Government **[1970] 1 WLR 1281**

The Jodrell Bank radio telescope is a sensitive piece of scientific equipment. The local council had agreed to 'discourage development' (at 1289) around the telescope. However, the council subsequently interpreted this as precluding the possibility of allowing development in the Brereton Heath area. This meant that the council had prematurely limited the range of issues which it would consider in making planning decisions—it had fettered its discretion.

6.4.2 Procedural unfairness or impropriety

Illegality, with that of irrationality or *Wednesbury* **unreasonableness**, discussed later, are classic substantive grounds for assessing the legality of a decision. Procedural unfairness or impropriety was viewed as a procedural ground of challenge only; however, this ground of challenge is now both a procedural and a substantive ground of challenge. Procedural unfairness will generally arise where the decision-maker has not followed the applicable statutory procedures for taking a decision. Some of the most obvious examples are a failure to consult people or where the decision-maker did not give reasons for their decision.

We can divide the elements of **procedural impropriety** into the rule against bias, the right to be heard and the right to receive reasons for decisions.

6.4.2.1 Natural justice

The general rule against procedural unfairness is grounded in the fundamental principle that legal processes should comply with the principles of natural justice. Thus, before looking at the elements of natural justice, we should consider this concept. The concept was articulated in the case of *Ridge v Baldwin* [1964] AC 40. Ridge was the chief constable of Brighton. He was arrested with other officers on a charge of conspiring to obstruct the course of justice but was acquitted of the charge. However, his two co-defendants were found guilty and the trial judge made adverse comments about Ridge's conduct. As a result, he was then charged with corruption, but he was later acquitted of this charge as well. Nevertheless, he was summarily sacked by the local watch committee which oversaw local police forces at the time. Ridge was not informed of the reasons for his dismissal or given the opportunity to respond to those reasons. Subsequent efforts to restore the integrity of the dismissal process were unsatisfactory. The court held that the rules of natural justice (including that due process must be observed and that processes should be fair) could equally apply to this type of administrative situation as well as judicial decision-making. The decision was a gross violation of natural justice.

EXAMPLE

Procedural unfairness was successfully pled in the case of *R (Medway Council) v Secretary of State for Transport* [2002] EWHC 2516 (Admin). The Secretary of State had issued a consultation document prior to a White Paper on the future of air transport in the UK. The document only expressed options considering the expansion of Heathrow and Stansted and the possibility of a new airport in Kent. The document made no mention of a possible second runway for Gatwick airport because the local authority had an agreement with BAA, the British Airport Authority, that no second runway would be contemplated until 2019. It was held that this decision was flawed since the complete exclusion of Gatwick from the process meant that the relevant options were not all considered.

6.4.2.2 The rule against bias

Findings of actual bias are fairly uncommon (although classic cases exist, see *Dimes v Proprietors of the Grand Junction Canal* (1852) III HL Cas (Clark's) 759, 10 ER 301). Where it does exist, this will automatically render the decision illegal. Much more common is the appearance of bias.

The courts utilise the test as to whether there has been a 'real possibility' of bias as laid out succinctly by Lord Hope in the *Porter v Magill* [2002] 2 AC 357 case:

> The question is whether the fair-minded and informed observer, having considered the facts, would conclude that there was a real possibility that the tribunal was biased.

Bias is anathema to the legal system because its effects go beyond impugning the decisions made in a specific case. Any appearance of bias undermines faith in the legal system and in the impartiality of the judiciary. The seriousness with which the courts take the question of bias can be seen in how the Appellate Committee of the House of Lords responded to an accusation of bias in a case concerning the former dictator of Chile, General Pinochet, on which see the example in **5.4.1**.

6.4.2.3 The right to be heard

The right to be heard is a fundamental right in criminal law cases, but is also increasingly important in civil cases, particularly as regards commercial and business matters in terms of the right to be properly consulted. For criminal law matters, it is a fundamental requirement that the defendant receives a fair trial that is in compliance with the substantive terms of Art 6 ECHR.

Flaws in a consultation, particularly consultations set out by statute, will typically ground a claim for judicial review and the courts are largely sympathetic to such claims.

EXAMPLE

***R (on the application of Buckinghamshire CC) v Secretary of State for Transport* [2013] EWHC 481 (Admin)**

HS2 Alliance, a not-for-profit organisation, was opposed to the building of the High Speed 2 rail link. Under the HS2 scheme, a high-speed rail link was to be built between London, Birmingham and cities in the north of England, including Sheffield, Leeds, Manchester and Liverpool. A significant number of homes needed to be destroyed in order to build the route and many more would have been adversely affected by their proximity to the rail line. Thus, compensation had to be offered to these homeowners.

The Administrative Court held that the Secretary of State had failed, at the first stage of the consultation, to provide enough information on the scope and nature of the blight and the discretionary compensation that would be made available to the affected homeowners. Thus, the consultees had not been treated fairly and indeed this meant that the process was so unfair as to render it unlawful.

6.4.2.4 The right to reasons

A failure to follow the rules of natural justice will also render a decision unlawful. The right to be given reasons for a decision is also an integral element of procedural fairness.

Under the common law, there is at present no general duty to give reasons for a decision (*R v Secretary of State for the Home Department, ex p Doody* [1994] 1 AC 531). In certain cases of statutory decision-making powers, the statute may expressly provide for reasons to be given. More generally, the court has the power to imply a duty to give reasons, particularly where the decision-maker is making decisions in a judicial fashion (*R v Civil Service Appeal Board, ex p Cunningham* [1991] 4 All ER 310).

Increasingly, it is a feature of public law and judicial review that decisions should be accompanied by reasons for the decision. The need to publicise reasons for a decision invariably leads to qualitatively better decision-making since the decision-maker will be subject to greater levels of scrutiny and thus concentrates the mind of the decision-maker. The giving of reasons also satisfies the principle that justice should be both done and seen to be done, and ensures that reviews and appeals against decisions can be more effectively targeted against the offending elements of the decision.

The failure to receive reasons can be a significant factor in vitiating a subsequent decision (although see **6.5.3** on the 'no substantial difference' rule). From a judicial review perspective, a failure to receive reasons from the parties means that those parties will be unable to determine for themselves whether the decision ultimately taken was lawful or unlawful.

EXAMPLE

***R (on the application of Luton BC) v Secretary of State for Education* [2011] EWHC 217 (Admin)**

The Labour government of Tony Blair created a Building Schools for the Future programme which was designed to fund the refurbishment or rebuilding of secondary schools in England during a 15-year period from 2005–20. The Coalition government of 2010, in light of the need to cut government expenditure, cancelled the programme. A number of councils found out about the cancellation of the programme via television and radio reportage of the decision of the Secretary of State. The High Court considered that the failure to consult with the local authorities affected by this decision was unlawful.

6.4.2.5 Legitimate expectations

The concept of legitimate expectations is closely aligned to that of procedural impropriety. Under this concept, the courts can examine whether a body or person has, through their previous actions or express statements, made their view on a matter so clear such that the claimant was entitled to expect that the body or person would act in a particular way.

It is abundantly clear that an expectation has to be legitimate. For example, no one can reasonably rely on an expectation that a **public authority** will act unfairly or *ultra vires*.

Legitimate expectations only ever arise in a small percentage of cases. The courts readily appreciate that public bodies, when exercising a discretionary power, should be free to make a decision as they see fit, even including changing their mind. Thus, public bodies are free to change their policies and must not fetter their decision-making power.

EXAMPLE

Residents of Westminster instituted legal action when a premises licence was issued without their knowledge. The residents concerned had had a legitimate expectation that the council would notify them of future applications for a premises licence via the council's own notification procedure. The court held that the council had to grant the licence under a statutory duty and as such this overrode any legitimate expectation that had arisen under their notification procedure (*Corporation of the Hall of Arts and Sciences v Albert Court Residents' Association* [2011] EWCA Civ 430).

The courts are rather reluctant to acknowledge a legitimate expectation and are only prepared to do so where the public body has abused its power and the claimant has reasonably relied on the expectation. Courts tend to only intervene in exceptional cases. The courts will only accept a legitimate expectation where the decision-maker has made a 'clear and unambiguous' promise that leads to reliance.

EXAMPLE

A successful claim of legitimate expectations occurred in the case of *R v North and East Devon Health Authority, ex p Coughlan* [2001] QB 213. A disabled resident of a care home had been informed by the predecessor organisation that she could live in the care home for the rest of her life. The successor health authority chose to close down the facility. The court held that Coughlan had reasonably relied on the expectation that this residential home would be her forever home.

6.4.3 Irrationality and unreasonableness

This ground of judicial review was first articulated in the seminal case of *Associated Provincial Picture House v Wednesbury Corporation* [1948] 1 KB 223. The case set out what came to be termed *Wednesbury* unreasonableness; that is, where a decision-maker makes a decision that is 'so absurd that no sensible person could ever dream that it lay within the powers of the authority' to make that decision (at 229).

The court, by way of example, referenced a hypothetical decision of an education authority to dismiss a head teacher because they had red hair. Such a decision would be so unreasonable that it could not be lawful. The court stated that in determining the reasonableness or otherwise of a decision, the court would inquire as to whether the decision-maker: (a) took into account relevant or irrelevant factors; (b) did not exercise their discretion in an absurd manner; and (c) had acted in good faith.

Although the case of *Wednesbury* outlined the concept of irrationality and unreasonableness, the court in this case held that the decision-maker had actually acted lawfully. In the case, the local authority had permitted the Sunday opening of a cinema but with the proviso that children under 15 could not attend the cinema on a Sunday. The cinema objected to the blanket nature of the condition. The cinema considered that children should have been allowed to go to the cinema when accompanied by a parent. The relevant Act of Parliament permitted the decision-maker to impose general restrictions on a cinema licence as they saw fit and as such the local authority was acting fully within the terms of the law when imposing a blanket ban on children going to the cinema on a Sunday. The wide-ranging nature of the statutory power to impose conditions saved the council's decision.

Irrationality or *Wednesbury* unreasonableness was further elaborated upon in the famous *GCHQ* case.

Lord Diplock reiterated the definition of irrationality or *Wednesbury* unreasonableness by stating that it 'applies to a decision which is so outrageous in its defiance of logic or of accepted moral standards that no sensible person who had applied his mind to the question to be decided could have arrived at it'.

Thus, it must be noted that irrationality or *Wednesbury* unreasonableness, as defined by the courts, means in practice that it is extremely difficult to successfully argue that a decision-maker has acted irrationally. One of the main reasons for this judicial restraint is that the court, in assessing irrationality or unreasonableness, is straying into territory that is more in the nature of an appeal as to the merits of the decision.

6.4.4 Proportionality

As you will recall from the opening of this chapter, in his seminal judgment in the *GCHQ* case, Lord Diplock indicated the possible development of a fourth ground of review, proportionality. Judges in the UK are already familiar with the concept of proportionality in other contexts as a result of the historical connection with the jurisprudence of the EU and the ongoing connection with the ECHR, both of which rely on proportionality as a concept. The idea of proportionality is simply that a decision-maker should not take steps which are unnecessary to achieve the outcome sought, and should only take action so far as is necessary to meet the objectives pursued. In the human rights context, this might mean that a restriction on rights would be legitimate in certain situations where a right is being balanced against a competing right—for example, the right to freedom of expression and, as a facet of that, the freedom of the press, as balanced against the right to privacy. There is a balance to be struck between these two rights in particular situations proportionate to the goals sought and the relative weight given to the rights etc.

As will become clear from the cases considered later, recent case law has come to articulate a connection between *Wednesbury* unreasonableness and proportionality—both in terms of when one or the other should apply and the different consequences flowing from them.

EXAMPLE

***Smith and Grady v United Kingdom* (2000) 29 EHRR 493**

The case of *Smith and Grady* demonstrates why the ground of proportionality in administrative settings can make a difference to the outcome reached as compared with *Wednesbury* unreasonableness. *Smith and Grady* concerned the Ministry of Defence policy against allowing people who are gay to serve in the military. Smith and Grady both had exemplary service records but it became known that they were gay. They were subjected to a deeply offensive, inappropriate investigation by military police and were discharged from the military. In the domestic courts, while the judges were clearly personally in agreement with the applicants that the policy was unjustifiable, they were not able to say that it was irrational or unreasonable in the *Wednesbury* sense of the term (see [137] and [138]). Conversely, with the concept of proportionality at hand, the European Court of Human Rights was able to conclude that the policy was not proportionate to the aims sought. Unsurprisingly, the Ministry of Defence has since rescinded the policy–which is to be welcomed.

Perhaps because of the dissatisfaction of the domestic courts' ability to respond to situations such as that found in *Smith and Grady*, more recent judgments of the Supreme Court have articulated how the principle of proportionality can be incorporated into domestic administrative law review processes. In the case of *Kennedy v Charity Commission* [2014] UKSC 20, for example, Lord Mance recognised that the high 'rigid' bar (at [51]) set by *Wednesbury* was no longer appropriate, and instead the courts should be responsive to the context of the situation in question. He said (at [51]) that:

> The common law no longer insists on the uniform application of the rigid test of irrationality once thought applicable under the so-called *Wednesbury* principle. . . . The nature of judicial review in every case depends on the context.

He went on to consider the advantages of adopting this varying intensity of review, stating (at [54]) that:

> The advantage of the terminology of proportionality is that it introduces an element of structure into the exercise, by directing attention to factors such as suitability or appropriateness, necessity and the balance or imbalance of benefits and disadvantages. There seems no reason why such factors should not be relevant in judicial review even outside the scope of Convention and EU law.

Lord Mance was not arguing for the rejection of irrationality/unreasonableness as a ground of review, but rather a reassessment of when it would be appropriate to apply that standard or that of proportionality. Subsequent case law has demonstrated that where the consequences for an applicant are especially serious, the more intensive scrutiny permitted by proportionality will be appropriate in place of unreasonableness.

EXAMPLE

***Pham v Secretary of State for the Home Department* [2015] UKSC 19**

In 1989, Pham and his family moved to the UK with his parents from Hong Kong and claimed asylum. His parents are Vietnamese citizens which, in principle, meant that he was also a Vietnamese citizen. Through the operation of the asylum process, Pham became a British citizen. At the age of 21, he is said to have travelled overseas to undertake terrorist training. The British Nationality Act 1981 provides a route to strip a person of their British citizenship where they hold dual nationality and the Home Secretary made use of this route in relation to Pham. However, the Vietnamese government refused to recognise him as a citizen. This rendered Pham stateless. Given the severity of the consequences to Pham of the Home Secretary's decision, the court thought it would not be appropriate to assess the action against the *Wednesbury* standard, and so instead turned to proportionality. The justices arrived at this position via different routes, but for our purposes the essential point is that proportionality can be applied in a domestic administrative justice setting where the consequences for the applicant are severe.

The risk of incorporating proportionality into our domestic administrative law jurisprudence is that because it entails the courts scrutinising how a decision was made, including what weight decision-makers assigned to different considerations, it runs the risk of implicating them in policy-making decisions where previously they have sought to extract themselves from this.

6.5 Remedies

As has been set out earlier, judicial review is not an appeal process and does not normally inquire into the merits of a decision. Thus, the range of remedies available are limited and are related to the nature of the judicial review case itself. At the same time, we should consider *why* people seek a judicial review in the first place. Often it is not that they want financial compensation, which is fortunate since public law damages are comparatively small as compared with other areas of the law. What they are generally seeking is to prevent something from happening that they will not be able to undo once it has happened (eg the compulsory purchase and demolition of their home) or to compel a decision-maker to do something (eg to make a decision on their application seeking access to a social security benefit or similar). That is, the purpose for seeking particular judicial review remedies is closely bound up with the tensions inherent in the vast range of governmental activity.

Judicial review is a discretionary legal process and as such the remedies are also discretionary and, as discussed later, now also constrained by certain statutory considerations. In certain instances, the court may refuse to issue a remedy or may be precluded from issuing one. The court can grant a range of orders specific to judicial review and can also offer general remedies commonly available to the court in any case that comes before it. Generally, the court has six remedies available to it when determining judicial review cases.

6.5.1 **Remedies specific to judicial review**

The court can issue three orders specific to judicial review applications depending on the nature of the issue before it (s31 Senior Courts Act 1981).

The orders are quashing orders, prohibiting orders and mandatory orders.

6.5.1.1 Quashing orders

A quashing order, as its name suggests, is an order that sets aside, or 'quashes', the decision of the body that has been declared invalid by the court. Given the nature of judicial review and the fact that it is not an appeal mechanism, this means that the court will generally order that the matter goes back to the decision-maker for it to reconsider the issue in the light of the court's ruling. Thus, there is a danger for the applicant that the decision-maker will reinvestigate the matter and take a new decision that comes to the exact same result as the original impugned decision, but via a legally correct route. This may be the case for judicial review claims that allege procedural irregularities, for once the irregularities have been resolved, the new decision process may result in the same decision being taken. In cases of illegality or irrationality, it may be that the fact of that illegality or irrationality will mean that the same outcome cannot be achieved. The applicant may also find that they are placed in a worse position because of the new decision. Thus, there is also provision that in cases where there is only one outcome of the case and forcing the decision-maker to decide anew would be unnecessary, the court may issue the quashing order and then substitute the original decision with its own decision.

The Judicial Review and Courts Act 2022 modifies the rules surrounding quashing orders. Section 1 of the Act allows courts to limit the effects of any quashing order granted. In particular, courts may temporarily suspend the operation of the quashing order to give time for the offending body to remedy the problem and courts may limit the retrospective effect of a quashing order such that acts done prior to the order remain lawful.

6.5.1.2 Prohibiting orders

A prohibiting order prevents, or 'prohibits', the decision-maker from acting beyond its powers. Such an order, logically, can only be granted prior to the decision-maker making their decision. The order acts as a restraint on future, illegal, action.

Prohibiting orders are less common now since claimants will invariably prefer to use the remedy of injunction. Nevertheless, for a modern example of a prohibiting order, see the case *Chief Constable of Kent v Taylor* [2023] EWHC 2687 KBD.

6.5.1.3 Mandatory orders

A mandatory order requires, or 'mandates', the decision-maker to fully comply with its legal duties. Thus, the decision-maker must do something, typically make a decision. Thus, it is often the case that the claimant will seek a quashing order to quash the original decision and then ask for a mandatory order forcing the decision-maker to take the decision again in compliance with the court's decision.

6.5.2 General remedies

The courts, under judicial review, are also able to grant general remedies where relevant in addition to the specific remedies of judicial review. The three general remedies available are declaration, a stay or injunction and damages.

Declarations and injunctions can only be granted when it is just and convenient to do so (s31(2) Senior Courts Act 1981).

6.5.2.1 Declaration

A declaration, as its name suggests, is simply a definitive statement by the court as to the correct legal position or statement as to the parties' rights. Declarations are generally available as a remedy and are not confined to judicial review. Declarations will not be issued where the matter is purely academic or hypothetical (*R (on the application of Counsel General for Wales) v Secretary of State for Business, Energy and Industrial Strategy* [2022] EWCA Civ 118), although in exceptional circumstances an advisory declaration concerning the legality or otherwise of future behaviour and actions may be issued where to do so would be in the public interest. Declarations can be interim in nature as well as being final.

Declarations will typically be given when other remedies are deemed inappropriate. They are also sought where the legal issues potentially affect a large number of people.

6.5.2.2 Injunctions

Injunctions are an equitable remedy; that is, it is a discretionary remedy that will compel a person or legal body to do, or refrain from doing, something. Like declarations, an injunction can be granted on an interim basis in order to preserve the status quo (see CPR, Part 25 and Practice Direction 25A) whilst the case progresses or in final form after the conclusion of the case.

Interim injunctions are generally available under the terms of the case of *American Cyanamid v Ethicon* [1975] AC 396 and the CPR, Part 25. Under this case, an interim junction is possible where the claimant has shown first, prima facie, that there is a serious issue to be tried, secondly, damages would be an insufficient remedy if the claimant were to be successful and, thirdly, on the balance of convenience, the court is satisfied that the balance tips towards the claimant and not the defendant. In public interest cases, the court must take particular care in assessing the balance of convenience between the rights of the claimant and the defendant.

In judicial review cases, an interim injunction is available under a modified version of these rules that takes into account the public law dimension.

In public law, injunctions are available to prevent the public body or body exercising public functions from acting *ultra vires* or unlawfully. An injunction may also force the body to perform its duty in a similar way to a mandatory order. Failure to comply will be treated as a contempt of court.

EXAMPLE

The case of *M v Home Office* [1994] 1 AC 377 confirmed that a minister or other officer of the Crown can be subject to injunctions, including interim injunctions and ultimately contempt of court proceedings. In the case, A was a Zairean citizen seeking political asylum. His application for asylum and for judicial review were rejected. A submitted a further claim for review and the first instance judge stated that A should not be returned to Zaire pending this new appeal. However, A was returned to Zaire. The court issued an injunction for his return but the Secretary of State cancelled his return. The House of Lords concluded that it was possible to hold a government minister or department in contempt of court in their official capacity.

6.5.2.3 Damages

Damages are only available in judicial review cases where they are specifically pled by the claimant and are sought in conjunction with another remedy. Thus, damages cannot be the sole remedy. Damages can be sought where the claimant has lodged a claim based on a private law right such as a breach of statutory duty, a claim based under the common law, such as a claim for negligence or in connection with a breach of the Human Rights Act 1998 (see **Chapter 8** on the Human Rights Act 1998).

6.5.3 The 'no substantial difference' rule

All judicial review remedies must now be considered with the 'no substantial difference' rule in mind. Section 84 of the Criminal Justice and Courts Act 2015 introduced a new provision into the Senior Courts Act 1981—s31(2A). The rule provides that:

> (2A) The High Court—
>
> (a) must refuse to grant relief on an application for judicial review, and
>
> (b) may not make an award under subsection (4) on such an application, if it appears to the court to be highly likely that the outcome for the applicant would not have been substantially different if the conduct complained of had not occurred.
>
> (2B) The court may disregard the requirements in subsection (2A)(a) and (b) if it considers that it is appropriate to do so for reasons of exceptional public interest.
>
> (2C) If the court grants relief or makes an award in reliance on subsection (2B), the court must certify that the condition in subsection (2B) is satisfied.

This means that, save in the circumstances covered by s31(2B), the court is prevented by statute from granting a remedy if the nature of the unlawful, procedurally improper, irrational/unreasonable or disproportionate conduct is such that it did not materially affect the outcome reached. It can be seen that claims under some grounds of review are more likely to be caught by these provisions than others. For example, given the provisions attaching to the reliance on proportionality in administrative law, it is highly likely that the outcome *would have* been significantly different had the complained of conduct not occurred. Conversely, a process which fails to follow the strict letter of a set procedure might well reach essentially the same conclusion, but via an incorrect route. In the latter situation, the s31(2A) rule would prevent a remedy.

The government's justification for this approach is that it relieves administrators and courts from the burden of having to deal with claims where the judicial review process will not actually alter the outcome. This reasoning is problematic since the available case law has indicated that in order to determine whether there would have been a substantially different outcome, it is normally necessary to conduct a hearing. It is also worth mentioning at this juncture that at the permission stage of review, s31(3C) requires the court to consider the same question (ie would the outcome have been substantially different but for the complained of conduct). Although for the reasons just given it is not normally possible to determine this at permission stage, and much of the judicial discussion around the 'no substantial difference' rule has taken place in the context of considering remedies.

The other obvious problem with a rule which insulates unlawful conduct from the powers available to the courts through judicial review remedies is that it appears to sanction, if not seriously unlawful conduct, at least sloppy decision-making, which cannot be good for the quality of governmental decision-making in the longer term.

6.6 The government's focus on reform of judicial review

For a number of years, the Conservative government has emphasised its commitment to significant change to the judicial review system (see Independent Review of Administrative Law, and the Government's Response to the Independent Review: https://www.gov.uk/government/consultations/judicial-review-reform). The reasons for the government's focus on change are not hard to identify. Indeed, judicial review has often been described as a growth industry. The high-profile adverse judgments in the Art 50 TEU case of *Miller 1* and the prorogation of Parliament case of *Cherry/Miller 2* and the perception amongst some ministers and commentators that there has been a rise in the number of successful judicial reviews against government departments prompted the government to order an appraisal of the system of judicial review (Judicial Review Reform). The government therefore appointed a number of eminent legal academics and practitioners to the Independent Review of Administrative Law (IRAL) panel. The panel produced its final 195-page report in March 2021, *The Independent Review of Administrative Law*, which is freely available to view via the government website.

The panel concluded that the system of judicial review is largely effective and fit for purpose and only suggested limited reforms. However, the panel did criticise the increasing tendency of the courts to engage in value judgements concerning the merits or otherwise of decisions, and suggested that the system of judicial review should accord more deference towards the powers of the executive and Parliament to deal with morality and policy matters. Nevertheless, the government's proposal for reform went beyond the recommendations of the Independent Review and attracted criticism from academic commentators. Undeterred, the government pressed ahead and successfully steered the Judicial Review and Courts Bill through both Houses of Parliament. The resultant Judicial Review and Courts Act 2022 introduced a number of significant changes to judicial review. Significantly, the act introduced the concept of suspended and prospective quashing orders and, by reversing the seminal decision of *Cart* from 2011, removed decisions of the Upper Tribunal from the purview of judicial review.

6.7 The appropriateness of judicial review

The consequence of judicial review being classified as a procedure of last resort is that frequently cases may not be appropriate for determination by judicial review and hurdles may be put in front of applicants preventing a claim going forward.

First, the rules on standing may preclude a claimant from pursuing a claim. Secondly, the existence of another form of redress will generally preclude recourse to judicial review. Thirdly, where the case has become academic—that is, it is no longer determinative of the rights and duties of the parties in the case—then the court will refuse to hear the case, although exceptionally the courts may hear such claims where it would be in the public interest to do so.

Next, under the Senior Courts Act 1981, where the outcome of judicial review would not materially change their legal position, judicial review applications will be refused.

Finally, it is incompetent for a judicial review claim to be taken against decisions of the superior courts.

KEY POINT SUMMARY

- Judicial review is not concerned with the merits of a decision but with process.
- Judicial review is a remedy of last resort. Where other remedies are available they should be used.
- Access to judicial review is governed by a range of procedural filters including a pre-action protocol, time limits, rules on standing and rules on the bodies against whom reviews may be brought.
- A range of bodies can be subject to judicial review. Decisions of public bodies and organisations which exercise powers that involve elements of public law are reviewable.
- Persons with sufficient interest in a decision are able to apply for judicial review. Over the years, the test for standing has been relaxed.
- The classic grounds for judicial review are illegality, irrationality or *Wednesbury* unreasonableness and procedural impropriety. In addition to this, proportionality is also now considered to be a ground available in administrative law in certain circumstances. The grounds of judicial review may overlap with one another and are not rigid and fixed.
- There are a range of remedies available at judicial review, although this availability may be impacted by the 'no substantial difference' rule.
- The government has successfully effected reform to the judicial review system via the Judicial Review and Courts Act 2022. These reforms permit courts to issue suspended and prospective quashing orders and reverses the rule of *Cart* so that decisions of the Upper Tribunal are no longer judicially reviewable.

CHAPTER 7
Public Order

FUNCTIONING LEGAL KNOWLEDGE

This chapter covers the following functional knowledge required to pass the SQE 1 assessments:

Public order law:

- processions
- assemblies
- breach of the peace

AUTHORITIES UNDERPINNING PRACTICE

The key authorities that underpin this area of practice are listed below. Note that for legislation you are linked to legislation.gov.uk.

Although much of the legislation on this government website is available in its amended form, the incorporation of new amendments into the text of legislation can be delayed. You should refer to legal databases to ensure you are referencing the most up-to-date legislation.

- Anti-Social Behaviour, Crime and Policing Act 2014
  https://www.legislation.gov.uk/ukpga/2014/12/contents/enacted
- Crime and Disorder Act 1998
  https://www.legislation.gov.uk/ukpga/1998/37/contents
- Criminal Justice and Public Order Act 1994
  https://www.legislation.gov.uk/ukpga/1994/33/contents
- European Convention on Human Rights 1950
  https://www.echr.coe.int/documents/convention_eng.pdf
- Highways Act 1980
  https://www.legislation.gov.uk/ukpga/1980/66
- Human Rights Act 1998
  https://www.legislation.gov.uk/ukpga/1998/42/contents
- Policing and Crime Act 2017
  https://www.legislation.gov.uk/ukpga/2017/3/contents/enacted
- Police Reform and Social Responsibility Act 2011
  https://www.legislation.gov.uk/ukpga/2011/13/contents/enacted/data.htm
- Public Meeting Act 1908
  https://www.legislation.gov.uk/ukpga/Edw7/8/66/section/1
- Public Order Act 1986
  https://www.legislation.gov.uk/ukpga/1986/64
- Serious Crime Act 2007
  https://www.legislation.gov.uk/ukpga/2007/27/contents
- Police, Crime Sentencing and Courts Act 2022
  https://www.legislation.gov.uk/ukpga/2022/32/contents/enacted
- Public Order Act 2023
  http://www.legislation.gov.uk/ukpga/2023/15/enacted
- UK Government Public Order Bill Factsheet
  https://www.gov.uk/government/publications/public-order-bill-overarching-documents/public-order-bill-factsheet

7.1 Introduction

The UK is a parliamentary democracy that traces its uninterrupted history back over a millennium. The UK is rightly proud of its openness, tolerance, commitment to the **rule of law** and its democratic credentials. In the pursuit of democracy, the UK has been a forthright defender of the right to freedom of expression, both within its shores and beyond. Democracy is only effective where the citizenry are allowed to express themselves freely and for the voice of the people to be heard by those in positions of authority. The right to freedom of expression, the right to debate, the right to discuss, the right to argue and to cause offence is an essential facet of any democratic country. This freedom operates over the internet, across social media platforms, in the broadcast and publishing media and is given to individuals and corporations alike. However, freedom of expression means nothing if there is no audience or there is just a lone voice. Thus, the legal system must also provide for voices to be amplified, through offering the right to gather together to share experiences and, where even that larger voice is unheard, for non-violent protests, demonstrations, marches, rallies and pickets to take place to force the government and businesses to sit up and take notice.

More widely, the threat of violence in public spaces is a central feature of policing activity in the UK. The citizenry of the UK are entitled to go about their normal day-to-day life without an ever-present fear of violence from other citizens and groups of citizens. Thus, the police generally safeguard the King's peace, allowing citizens to feel safe in the towns, villages and cities across the country. The police are empowered to maintain the King's peace through **common law** powers such as under the concept of breach of the peace and through various statutory powers to deal with rioting, affray, violent disorder and anti-social behaviour.

Ever since the early origins of the common law of England, individual civil liberties have been at its heart. Generally, citizens were free to engage in any activity that was not expressly prohibited or limited by the law and, conversely, public servants and institutions could only interfere with civil liberties and property of the citizens by virtue of legal authority (*Malone v Metropolitan Police Commissioner (No 2)* [1979] 2 All ER 620).

These common law rights have never been codified into a written, codified constitution or a Bill of Rights; however, this perceived gap in the level of protection has been partly plugged by the reception of the European Convention on Human Rights 1950 (ECHR) into UK law by the terms of the Human Rights Act 1998 (HRA 1998) (see **Chapter 8** on the HRA 1998).

Now the HRA 1998, under s6, requires all public authorities to act in a way that is compatible with the rights of the ECHR. Thus, in particular, public authorities must ensure that the right to liberty and security under Art 5, the right to freedom of thought under Art 9, the right to freedom of expression under Art 10 and the right to freedom of assembly and association under Art 11 ECHR are upheld by them. These Articles of the Convention, alongside the negative obligation to avoid interferences with these rights, also imposes a positive obligation on the institutions of the state to take positive action to ensure the enjoyment of these rights. Nevertheless, most **Convention rights** are qualified rights, such that the rights provided can be legitimately interfered with, where the restriction or limitation is set out in law, is necessary in a democracy and is proportionate to the aim. Legitimate reasons for interfering with these rights include the grounds of national security, public safety, prevention of crime and disorder and the rights and freedoms of others (see **Chapter 8** on the HRA 1998 and a briefing paper published by the House of Commons, Police powers: protest).

The positive obligation to actively ensure the rights of the Convention must be tempered with the need to maintain public order and to preserve the King's peace. This obligation is a central function of the police force alongside their general obligation to enforce the law (*R v Commissioner of Police of the Metropolis, ex p Blackburn (No 1)* [1968] 2 QB 118).

> There is no doubt that the police owe a positive duty in public law to protect members of the public from harm caused by third parties . . . [T]he police have a duty to take all steps which appear necessary for keeping the peace, for preventing crime and for protecting from criminal injury . . . [A] party threatened with violence from another is entitled to protection, whatever the rights and wrong of their dispute.
>
> (Hale LJ (as was) in *Michael v Chief Constable of South Wales Police* [2015] UKSC 2 at [195])

The centrality of the maintenance of the King's peace to the fabric of British society means that ordinary citizens are also co-opted with the police into the obligation to uphold the peace. As Lord Diplock observed in *Albert v Lavin* [1982] AC 546 at 565:

> Every citizen in whose presence a breach of the peace is being, or reasonably appears to be about to be, committed has the right to take reasonable steps to make the person who is breaking or threatening to break the peace refrain from doing so; and those reasonable steps in appropriate cases will include detaining him against his will. At common law, this is not only the right of every citizen, it is also his duty, although, except in the case of a citizen who is a constable, it is a duty of imperfect obligation.

Indeed, a citizen may commit an offence where they refuse, without lawful excuse, to help the police in stopping a breach of the peace (*R v Brown* (1841) Car & M 314).

The peace of British society was shattered by numerous large-scale public disorder events in the 1970s and 1980s. Events like the Red Lion Square National Front marches in 1974, the Brixton and Toxteth riots in London and Liverpool in 1981 and the miners' strike of 1984–5 compelled the UK government to order a review of public order legislative provisions. The result was the promulgation of the Public Order Act 1986. This Act created a number of new statutory offences, namely those of rioting, violent disorder, affray, causing fear or provoking violence and causing **harassment**, alarm or distress.

In a democracy, the starting point is that citizens must be free and able to make their views known to the lawmakers and to people in authority. Citizens can lawfully express their views through peaceful demonstrations, large-scale gatherings and itinerant processions.

Indeed, over the more recent history of the UK, people have peacefully marched and demonstrated against nuclear weapons, fuel price rises, hunting with dogs, the Iraq War, at the G20 meetings, student tuition fee rises and the Bedroom Tax. Even more recently, mass demonstrations and marches have taken place over the question of Scottish independence, Brexit, Extinction Rebellion, Black Lives Matter, the state visit of President Trump, the Coronavirus lockdown, Insulate Britain, Just Stop Oil, the Russian invasion of Ukraine and the ongoing conflict between Israel and Hamas. A healthy democracy needs an active and vocal population, willing to express their views.

However, such large-scale gatherings of people who are passionately animated about a matter of concern to them have the potential to descend into violence and can intimidate other people in the vicinity. Large gatherings of people may also encourage the consumption of alcohol and drugs and possession of offensive weapons and pyrotechnics. Large-scale sporting and cultural events may also prove problematic for the police. Legislation has been enacted to criminalise and regulate such behaviour.

The right to protest and the right to freedom of expression are fundamental rights long protected within the English legal system. These rights are protected by both the common law and the terms of the HRA 1998. Under the 1998 Act, the ECHR is given domestic legal effect. Article 10 ECHR guarantees citizens their freedom of expression and Art 11 ECHR provides for the freedom of assembly and association. Freedom of expression is:

> an essential foundation of democratic society and one of the basic conditions for its progress and for each individual's self-fulfilment.
>
> (*Steel and Others v United Kingdom* (1998) 28 EHRR 603 at [101])

Similarly, the European Court of Human Rights has consistently held that:

> the right to freedom of assembly is a fundamental right in a democratic society and, like the right to freedom of expression, is one of the foundations of such a society.
>
> (*Kudrevicius v Lithuania* [2015] ECHR 906 at [91])

States, according to the European Court of Human Rights, are obliged to take reasonable and appropriate measures to allow peaceful demonstrations (*Plattform 'Ärzte für das Leben' v Austria* (1988) 13 EHRR 204 at [34]). Thus, since the passing of the HRA 1998, the right to peaceful protest and assembly is a positive right enjoyed by the populace, rather than a negative obligation imposed on the state to tolerate.

Nevertheless, the freedom to express yourself and the freedom to associate with others and assemble in groups are qualified rights under the ECHR and as such can be limited where the restrictions are prescribed by law, are necessary in a democratic society and are proportionate to those limitations (*Wingrove v United Kingdom* (1997) 24 EHRR 1).

The freedom of assembly and association can be restricted on a number of essential grounds, such as in the interest of national security or public safety, for the prevention of disorder or crime, for the protection of health or morals or for the protection of the rights and freedoms of others. The freedom of expression can be restricted on the same grounds as the freedom of assembly right and can further be limited on the grounds of territorial integrity, for preventing the disclosure of information received in confidence or for maintaining the authority and impartiality of the judiciary.

Restrictions on free speech and the freedom of assembly and association taken on the grounds of public health protection took on a new significance in the era of the Covid-19 pandemic and the passing of the Coronavirus Act 2020.

The HRA 1998 requires, under s3, that domestic legislation be interpreted by the judges, as far as possible, in a Convention-compliant way (*Munim Abdul v DPP* [2011] EWHC 247 (Admin)).

The courts have a pivotal role to play in determining where the line should be drawn between active citizenship and the inevitable law enforcement response. The police must ensure that their actions do not unduly impact on the key human rights of freedom of expression and of association and assembly. The police are guided in this task by the College of Policing operating manuals. Public order policing is guided by six Core Principles that outline the policing style and tone to be adopted, the need for communication and joined up decision-making, competent and clear command structures, proportionality of the police response and effective capacity and capability.

Significant change to public order legislation has been effected by the terms of the Policing, Crime, Sentencing and Courts Act 2022 and the Public Order Act 2023.

7.1.2 **Public Order Act 2023**

The Public Order Act 2023 introduced major innovations to the law regulating public order (see the UK Government Public Order Bill Factsheet). The Act reformed s1 of the Police and Criminal Evidence Act 1984, commonly known as the law of stop and search. These reforms gave the police a new ground to stop and search anyone if they have a reasonable suspicion that they are carrying items that are made, adapted or intended to be used for protest related offences. This provision builds on the powers of the police to deal with protestors as delineated in the case of *Howarth v Commissioner of Police for the Metropolis* [2011] EWHC 2818 (Admin). Further, senior police officers are given the power to stop and search people without suspicion in certain designated areas for a specified period of time during a protest.

The Act also criminalises a number of protest tactics, such as locking on to a person, object or building (s1), or going equipped to lock on (s2), interfering with key national infrastructure (s7), causing serious disruption by tunnelling (s3) and obstructing major transport works (s6).

The courts are now able to impose a new Serious Disruption Prevention Order (SDPO) on someone over 18 who has a prior protest conviction and who they consider is likely to commit further protests (ss20–33 of the Act). SDPOs can be sought by the prosecution after conviction for a protest-related offence and on application by the police by way of complaint. In the case of a police application, the court has to be satisfied that the subject of the complaint has, on the balance of probabilities, committed at least two separate protest related offences or protest-related contempt of court offences in the past five years. In calculating the five-year period, the court must not take into account conduct of the person that took place when the subject was 15 or under or conduct taking place before the coming into force of s21 of the Public Order Act 2023, namely 5 April 2024 (see further, Home Office draft statutory guidance on SDPOs (https://www.gov.uk/government/publications/serious-disruption-prevention-orders/serious-disruption-prevention-orders-draft-statutory-guidance-accessible).

7.2 **The Public Order Act 1986: key provisions**

Mass demonstrations and gatherings by the public are the lifeblood of the democracy that is the United Kingdom of Great Britain and Northern Ireland. As briefly alluded to earlier, public marches, demonstrations and public meetings have a long history in this country from the Peasants Revolt of the 14th century, Abolitionists against the slave trade in the 18th century, the

Luddites and the Chartists of the 19th century, marches in the 20th century such as those by the Suffragettes, anti-poverty marches, labour and trade union marches like the Jarrow march, anti-racism marches like the Mangrove Nine, anti-war and pro-peace marches against the Vietnam War and the proliferation of Nuclear Weapons, the miners' strike, Poll Tax demonstrations and the Troubles in Northern Ireland, through to 21st-century grievances and events such as Fathers 4 Justice, Make Poverty History, student tuition fee protests, the Countryside Alliance, Occupy Movement, Stop The War Coalition, anti-fracking protests, Black Lives Matter, Extinction Rebellion, Insulate Britain and Just Stop Oil and protests against the Russian invasion of Ukraine and the Israel–Hamas conflict.

Mass gatherings and the mass movement of people across the country on a march pose significant public order concerns for the police. Thus, the Public Order Act 1986 imposes obligations on organisers of and participants in assemblies and marches and grants the police statutory powers to deal with such events.

The Crown Prosecution Service, when deciding whether to prosecute, will follow the guidance set out in the Code for Crown Prosecutors. Guidance on Protests, Demonstrations and Campaigns (https://www.cps.gov.uk/legal-guidance/offences-during-protests-demonstrations-or-campaigns) and Public Order Offences incorporating the Charging Standard are available on their website.

7.2.1 **Public processions (marches)**

7.2.1.1 Definition

A public procession is a body of people moving along a route open to the public, such as a public highway or a place that the public have access to, demonstrating support for or opposition to the views or actions of a person or group of people, to publicise a cause or campaign or mark or commemorate an event (ss11 and 16 Public Order Act 1986; *Flockhart v Robinson* [1950] 2 KB 498 at 502; *R (on the application of Jones) v Metropolitan Police Commissioner* [2019] EWHC 2957 (Admin)). The presumption in law is that a public procession is lawful. This presumption holds good even where the notification requirements have not been followed.

7.2.2 **Advance notice of a procession**

The general rule is that the local police must be given written notice of the planned procession at least six clear days before it is due to start, unless it is not reasonably practicable to do so. The notice must set out the proposed date and start time, the proposed route and the organiser's details. Written notice is not required for processions commonly or customarily held in the relevant police area or for funeral processions.

It is an offence for the organisers of a public procession to fail to provide notification or to provide prior notification details that do not match with the actual date, time or route of the procession (s11(7)(a), (b) Public Order Act 1986). It is a defence if the defendant did not know of the failure and did not suspect or have a reason to suspect that the notice requirements had not been complied with, or did not know of the different date, time or route, due to circumstances beyond their control or the difference was actually done in collaboration with the police (s11(8), (9) Public Order Act 1986).

7.2.3 **Power to impose conditions on processions**

Advance written notice of a procession is required so that the police can anticipate and plan for problems that may arise during the procession. If the police think the procession may cause serious public disorder, serious damage to property, serious disruption to community life, intimidate others or create noise that seriously disrupts the activities of a nearby organisation or significantly impacts people in the vicinity, they can impose conditions on the procession (s12 Public Order Act 1986).

Conditions typically imposed on the organisers of, or participants in, the procession are those that alter the route, or proposed route, ban entry to certain public places and limit the duration of the procession or the number of people attending (ss12(2) and 14 Public Order Act 1986; *R (Jones and others) v Metropolitan Police* [2019] EWHC 2957 (Admin)). Thus, in extremis, conditions issued can bring an end to the procession (*Austin v Commissioner of Police of the Metropolis* [2005] EWHC 480 (QB)).

Conditions can be imposed in advance of the procession and also during the procession itself. Conditions can only be imposed where the most senior police officer present at the procession, or the chief police officer in cases of future processions, reasonably believes that the procession may result in serious public disorder, serious damage to property, serious disruption to the life of the community, the intimidation of others or the noise generated by the procession causes serious disruption to the activities of a nearby organisation or has a significant impact on people in the vicinity. Conditions can be imposed on a public procession even where the proposed route is a spontaneously chosen route. The concept of serious disruption to the life of the community has been expanded by the Public Order Act 2023 to include slow marching, a tactic beloved of various climate emergency protest groups like Just Stop Oil.

EXAMPLE

Regular mass cycle rides would take place around London on the last Friday night of the month. Anyone could turn up at the regular meeting point and cycle around London with others. Such a mass meeting did not require prior notification given that it was a regular event (*Kay v Commissioner of Police of the Metropolis* [2008] UKHL 69). On Friday 27 July 2012, London hosted the Olympic Games Opening Ceremony. Given the security and disruptive risks to the Olympics, the Metropolitan Police were authorised to notify the organisers of Critical Mass London that they must not cycle north of the Thames (*Powlesland v DPP* [2013] EWHC 3846 (Admin)).

In the event that the police act unreasonably in imposing unrealistic or draconian conditions, their actions would be ***ultra vires*** and challengeable via **judicial review** (see **Chapter 6** on judicial review and the following discussion as to assemblies).

It is an offence for an organiser of, or a participant in, a procession to knowingly fail to comply with any conditions imposed in the direction.

EXAMPLE

In the case of *Van EK and Jukes v DPP* [2013] EWHC 195 (Admin), the two defendants were at a march against education cuts in London. The police had imposed a condition that protestors follow the set route. The route was set to ensure that the protestors did not go near Trafalgar Square, where an anti-capitalist demonstration camp had been set up. The two defendants asked to leave the procession and join the camp. They were told by the police that they could leave the procession but only for the purpose of leaving the protest. Another police officer saw people getting agitated so let the two defendants go but reminded them of the s12 conditions. Van Ek and Jukes were then allowed to leave and proceeded to go straight to the camp at Trafalgar Square. It was held that they were still 'taking part' in the overall protest so had failed to comply with the conditions stipulated and so were guilty.

It is a defence to show that a failure to comply was due to factors beyond a person's control (s14 Public Order Act 1986). It is an offence to incite another to ignore any conditions imposed (s12(6), (10) Public Order Act 1986).

The Police, Crime, Sentencing and Courts Act 2022 removes the requirement for the offence of non-compliance with a condition to be committed knowingly and instead replaces it with a requirement that the person knew or ought to have known about the existence of the condition. This provision is designed to circumvent protesters' tactics of covering their ears and ripping up the written list of conditions when being informed of the conditions by police. This Act also allows the police to impose conditions on a procession where it would seriously disrupt the activities of a nearby organisation or have a significant impact on persons in the vicinity. The concept of serious disruption controversially extends to the notion of noise, a sine qua non of peaceful protest.

7.2.4 **Power to ban processions**

If the police think the risk of serious disorder cannot be managed by imposing conditions on the procession, they can apply to the local authority for an order banning processions for up to three months (s13 Public Order Act 1986). The local authority can only grant such an order with the consent of the **Secretary of State**. In London, the Metropolitan Police and the City of London Police can ask the Secretary of State directly for an order banning processions. This discretionary power is not exercised lightly.

EXAMPLE

In September 2011, the Home Secretary banned the English Defence League (EDL) from engaging in any marches throughout Tower Hamlets, four other London boroughs and in the City of London, for a month. At the same time, counter demonstrations against the EDL were also banned for a month (Freedom of Information Request: Applications for a Banning Order under the Public Order Act 1986).

7.2.5 **Assemblies in public places**

A gathering of people is treated very differently in law from a procession or march, primarily because the impact on public order of a gathering is much less. As such, a static assembly cannot be banned unlike a procession or march; however, since the passing of the Public Order Act 1986, conditions can now be attached to the conduct of an assembly.

English law presently defines an assembly as a gathering of more than two people in a public place that is wholly or partly open to the air and such a gathering can be stationary or mobile (s16 Public Order Act 1986; *DPP v Roffey* [1959] Crim LR 283, 123 JP 241, DC). The term public place is widely defined to encompass any highway and any place open to the public for free, on payment of a fee or otherwise by permission. Controversially, s79 of the Policing, Crime, Sentencing and Courts Act 2022 introduced the concept of a 'one-person' protest into s14ZA of the Public Order Act 1986. The Act allows conditions to be imposed on such an individual when their solo protest is considered so noisy as to constitute serious disruption to the activities of an organisation in the vicinity, or otherwise has a significant impact on people in the vicinity, such as causing harassment, intimidation, alarm or distress.

7.2.6 **Power to impose conditions on assemblies**

An assembly can be subject to various conditions imposed by the most senior police officer present at the assembly, where that officer reasonably believes that the conditions are necessary to prevent serious public disorder, serious damage to property, serious disruption to community life or to prevent the intimidation of others. Conditions can also be imposed where the noise generated by the assembly may seriously disrupt the activities of a nearby organisation or significantly impact people in the vicinity (s14 Public Order Act 1986; *R (on the application of Jones) v Metropolitan Police Commissioner* [2019] EWHC 2957 (Admin)). Conditions can be imposed on the organisers of, or participants in, the assembly that affect the place where it can be held, the maximum duration or the maximum number of people in attendance (s14(1) Public Order Act 1986). Conditions can be imposed that limit the entrance and exit points of the assembly (*DPP v Jones* [2002] EWHC 110 (Admin)). As discussed earlier as regards processions, conditions imposed by the police are challengeable in a court of law under judicial review where the police have attempted to impose unreasonable conditions.

EXAMPLE

Coordinated assemblies separated by time and location but united in the same aim have been traditionally treated in law as separate assemblies for the purpose of imposing conditions, otherwise the police would be empowered to control and prohibit future assemblies that were yet to take place but were deemed by them to be sufficiently linked to an existing assembly (*R (on the application of Jones) v Metropolitan Police Commissioner* [2019] EWHC 2957 (Admin)). The orchestrated actions of the Extinction Rebellion Autumn Uprising across two weeks of October in 2019 that were held across multiple locations in London had to be considered as a series of separate public assemblies and not classed as one umbrella assembly. The police had erred in law and acted *ultra vires* when they imposed conditions that related to future, planned demonstrations.

However, in a controversial legislative amendment, the Public Order Act 2023 has now amended the law to allow the police to treat related protests as one homogeneous whole.

The Policing, Crime, Sentencing and Courts Act 2022 widens the range of justifications available to the police for imposing conditions. In particular, the government's amendments to s14 now give the police the power to impose conditions where the assembly would result in serious disruption to a nearby organisation's activities. The provisions also empower the Secretary of State to issue statutory instruments further defining and interpreting the scope of serious disruption to an organisation's activities, thus offering the possibility that the threshold as to what constitutes serious disruption may be downgraded, although the Secretary of State's first attempts at downgrading the definition have been declared unlawful (*R. (on the application of National Council for Civil Liberties) v Home Secretary* [2024] EWHC 1181 (Admin)). The Act also gives the police the power to impose a start and end time for an assembly. More generally, the Public Order Act 2023 extends the power to control assemblies and one-person protests to the British Transport Police and the Ministry of Defence Police.

The police can also seek interim **injunctions** from the courts under the Anti-Social Behaviour, Crime and Policing Act 2014 in order to prevent people from participating in certain events in the course of a notified procession or assembly (*Chief Constable of Bedfordshire v Golding* [2015] EWHC 1875 (QB); *Birmingham CC v Afsar (No 3)* [2019] EWHC 3217 (QB)). Given the positive obligation on the state under Art 11 ECHR to facilitate assemblies, recourse to these draconian measures will only be acceptable as a last resort.

More generally, the 2014 Act provides for civil injunctions; that is, court orders against people who engage, or threaten to engage, in anti-social behaviour.

7.2.6.1 Trespassory assembly on private land

The right to assembly and association under Art 11 ECHR presupposes that such demonstrations and marches take place in public spaces, including on the highway. Demonstrations on the public highway are legitimate and will only ever become unlawful where they result in an unreasonable obstruction. It is the case that many day-to-day activities cause an obstruction or inconvenience to traffic, thus only unreasonable obstructions during an assembly or march are classed as unlawful.

Assemblies, or gatherings, that take place on private land are treated very differently by the law since they impact on private property rights and the police have to also consider the right to peaceful enjoyment of property under Art 1 of Protocol 1 ECHR.

An assembly is a trespassory assembly, where there are more than 20 people present on private land or land to which the public has limited access (s14A(9) Public Order Act 1986). The police possess powers to prohibit assemblies that take place on private land and land where such an assembly is likely to be held without the permission of the landowner or will exceed the limits of that permission or is beyond the limits of the public's right of access. The question of the extent to which the public have access to the land and the limits of that access were central to the case of *DPP v Jones* [1999] 2 AC 240. In this case, 21 people took part in a demonstration on the highway near Stonehenge. The demonstration was peaceful and did not create an obstruction on the highway; however, it did take place on a part of the highway subject to an order under the Public Order Act 1986 that prohibited trespassory assemblies. Two of the protestors who were convicted appealed and the House of Lords, by a majority, held that reasonable activities that did not constitute a public or private nuisance could take place on the highway, notwithstanding the designation of part of the highway. Thus, this case confirmed that lawful use of the highway is not restricted to mere passing and repassing: the public can make use of the highway for any reasonable purpose.

The chief police officer can apply to the local authority for an order prohibiting such assemblies for a specified period where they reasonably believe that the assembly may cause serious disruption to community life or where there is a risk of serious damage to land or buildings or monuments on the land which are of historic, archaeological, architectural or scientific importance. The local authority may grant such an order with the consent of the Secretary of State.

It is an offence for a person to organise such an assembly, participate in such an assembly or incite others to take part in the assembly (ss14A and 14B Public Order Act 1986).

The police have the power to stop people travelling to a trespassory assembly. A uniformed constable is empowered to stop a person who they reasonably believe is on their way to a trespassory assembly and further direct that person not to proceed towards the assembly. It is a summary offence to fail to comply with such instructions (s14C Public Order Act 1986).

7.2.6.2 Protests and activities in and around Parliament

In the recent past, special restrictive rules applied to London as regards processions and assemblies. However, the Coalition government of 2010 repealed these laws and provided that the general rules set out in the Public Order Act 1986 should apply, with the proviso that a special zone be created around Parliament and its environs, to allow more restrictive rules to apply to planned protests and activities (Police Reform and Social Responsibility Act 2011, Part 3; *R (on the application of Gallastegui) v Westminster City Council and Others & (1) Commissioner of Police of the Metropolis (2) Secretary of State for the Home Department (Interested Parties)* [2013] EWCA Civ 28). Thus, it is prohibited to use amplified noise equipment, to erect or use a tent or other structure for sleeping or staying in and to use sleeping equipment, in the specified controlled zones. The police have the power to direct people to cease doing any of the actions above and have the power to confiscate any prohibited items. A constable can use reasonable force in order to seize the items. Upon conviction of this offence, a court may order the forfeiture of the items concerned and can make any order it deems appropriate to prevent further prohibited activity in the controlled zone.

Notwithstanding these prohibitions, any authority responsible for land in the controlled zone is able to authorise a person to use amplified noise equipment (s147 Police Reform and Social Responsibility Act 2011).

The present UK government has re-imposed stricter controls on vehicular access in and around the Parliamentary estate via the Police, Crime, Sentencing and Courts Act 2022, ss76–77.

7.2.7 **Public meetings**

Public meetings are meetings open to the public, for free or on payment, and which take place in any public place or in a private venue, including on the highway (*Burden v Rigler* [1911] 1 KB 337). In a democracy, public meetings are important since they allow citizens to be informed and to express their views on matters of local, national and international concern. As such, intentionally disrupting a meeting by acting in a disorderly manner is an offence, as is encouraging others to do so (s1 Public Meeting Act 1908). The common law allows for disruptive attendees of the meeting to be ejected (*Laporte and another v Metropolitan Police Commissioner* [2014] EWHC 3574 (QB)).

Where police are present, the chairperson can ask the police to force the disruptor to give their name and address. Failure to do so, or to give a false name or address, is a criminal offence (s1 Public Meeting Act 1908).

It is especially important that public meetings about elections are not impeded and specific laws apply to such meetings that replicate the terms and offences discussed earlier (Representation of the People Act 1983 and Local Government Act 2000).

7.2.8 **Riot**

A riot is defined in s1 of the Public Order Act 1986 as a situation when there are more than 12 people present together who use, or threaten to use, unlawful violence for a common purpose and this collective conduct would cause a person of reasonable firmness present at the scene to fear for their own safety. Rioting can take place in public and in private. The term violence is widely interpreted to encompass violent conduct towards both property and people and includes the throwing of missiles at or towards people even where the missile does not hit anyone. Open displays of a weapon can constitute a threat of violence (*I v DPP* [2001] UKHL 10). The violence must be unlawful so violence deployed in self-defence or in order to prevent a crime is excluded (*R v Rothwell, R v Barton* [1993] Crim LR 626, CA). The offence of rioting requires the prosecution to prove that the person rioting intended to use violence or was aware that their conduct could be violent since the essential element of the offence is using violence in the presence of so many people such that their action causes or inspires fear in the general public (*R v Tyler* (1993) 96 Cr App R. 332 at 334). The seriousness of rioting behaviour is reflected in the sentence available, with the maximum term of imprisonment being ten years (*R v Sherlock* [2014] EWCA Crim 310).

7.2.9 **Violent disorder**

The offence of violent disorder is similar to that of rioting. The main difference is that violent disorder is constituted when only three or more people are present rather than the 12 required for a charge of rioting (s2 Public Order Act 1986).

EXAMPLE

A middle-aged woman pled guilty to violent disorder for her action in throwing stones during a violent demonstration about immigration in Dover. She was a left-wing demonstrator who got involved in an altercation with a right-wing demonstrator. The demonstration was characterised by people wearing dark and black clothes and various head coverings to hide their faces. Smoke bombs were frequently lobbed during the demonstration, alongside stones and other missiles (*R v Smith* [2016] EWCA Crim 2080).

Violent disorder is made out when more than three people present together use, or threaten to use, unlawful violence for a common purpose and this collective conduct would cause a person of reasonable firmness present at the scene to fear for their own safety. Violent disorder can take place in public and in private. The offence of violent disorder requires the prosecution to prove that the person intends to use or threaten violence or was aware that their conduct could be violent or threatened violence. Being 'present together' means no more than simply being in the same place at the same time. The case law shows that there is no requirement on the prosecution to prove that there was a common purpose among those using or threatening violence (*R v NW* [2010] EWCA Crim 404). The maximum sentence for this offence is five years in prison.

7.2.10 **Affray**

The offence of affray is related to the offences of rioting and violent disorder. This offence is normally an individual offence unlike the group offences of violent disorder and rioting. The offence of affray occurs when an individual, or two or more people use, or threaten to use, unlawful violence towards someone and that conduct would cause a person of reasonable firmness present at the scene to fear for their own safety (s3 Public Order Act 1986). Notwithstanding the specific terms of this offence, a court, when considering whether an affray took place, may also take into account the actual reactions of the people present at the scene of violence as long as the court properly considers whether a hypothetical person of reasonable firmness would have feared for their own safety in the circumstances (*Freeman v DPP* [2013] EWHC 610 (Admin)). Affray can take place in public and in private; however, since the focus of the offence is on the potential impact on bystanders of witnessing the violence and fearing for their own safety, violent acts or threatened violence in private can only be charged as affray where there is an actual possibility of a hypothetical bystander witnessing the events. Thus, threats of violence issued by a woman to her partner in a bathroom in a locked, secure house did not constitute affray (*R (on the application of Leeson) v DPP* [2010] EWHC 994 (Admin)). The offence of affray requires the prosecution to prove that the person intends to use or threaten violence or was aware that their conduct could be violent or threatened violence. A threat, in these circumstances, cannot be simply through words alone (s3(3) Public Order Act 1986).

7.2.11 **Fear or provocation of violence**

This category of offending is divided into two subsets, namely the use of threatening, abusive or insulting words or behaviour towards another person or the distribution or display to another person of threatening, abusive or insulting materials (s4 Public Order Act 1986). Further, this offence can be committed in four discrete ways. First, the perpetrator intended to make the targeted person believe that immediate unlawful violence would be used against them or another person by any person (*Horgle v DPP* [2015] EWHC 856 (Admin)). Secondly, the perpetrator intended to provoke the immediate use of unlawful violence by the targeted person or another. Thirdly, the perpetrator used threatening or abusive words or behaviour and the person targeted is likely to believe that unlawful violence will be used and, finally, the defendant used such words or behaviour and it was likely that unlawful violence would be provoked. Given the centrality of freedom of expression to UK society, for the offence to be made out, it is not enough that the speech or behaviour gives rise to a risk that immediate violence is feared or provoked, that the speech or behaviour gives rise to annoyance, anger, disgust or distress or that it is vigorous, distasteful, unmannerly, offensive or rude (*Parkin v Norman, Valentine v Lilley* [1983] QB 92, [1982] 2 All ER 583, DC; *Brutus v Cozens* [1973] AC 854; *R v Ambrose* (1973) 57 Cr App Rep 538, CA). Rather, the perpetrator must have intended, or been aware, that their words, behaviour or material were threatening, abusive or insulting (s6(3) Public Order Act 1986). The conduct version of the offence has an objective element to it, in as much as if the conduct is threatening, abusive or insulting, it is irrelevant whether anyone who witnessed it personally felt threatened, abused or insulted (*Parkin v Norman, Valentine v Lilley* [1983] QB 92, [1982] 2 All ER 583, DC). The offence can be committed in a public or a private place; however, there is an exception whereby it is not an offence where the words, conduct or display occurs inside a dwelling and the other person is also inside the dwelling or another dwelling (*DPP v Distill* [2017] EWHC 2244 (Admin); *Rukwira v DPP* [1993] Crim LR 882, DC). The offence can also be committed with racial or religious aggravation (s31 Crime and Disorder Act 1998; *R v SH* [2010] EWCA Crim 1931). In such a case, a defendant cannot be found guilty of two versions of the offence relating to one set of circumstances (*R (on the application of Dyer) v Watford Magistrates' Court* [2013] EWHC 547 (Admin)).

7.2.12 **Intentional harassment, alarm or distress**

Alongside the offence of fear or provocation of violence, it is an offence to intentionally cause a person harassment, alarm or distress (s4A Public Order Act 1986). It is an offence to use threatening, abusive or insulting words or behaviour, use disorderly behaviour or display threatening, abusive or insulting materials which cause a person harassment, alarm or distress. The offence can be made out where the harassment, alarm or distress manifested itself at a later point in time (*S v DPP* [2008] EWHC 438 (Admin)). The offence can be committed in a public or a private place; however, there is an exception whereby it is not an offence where the words, conduct or display occurs inside a dwelling and the other person is also inside the dwelling or another dwelling. Similarly, it is a defence for the accused to prove that they were in a dwelling and had no reason to believe that the words, behaviour or materials would be heard or seen by anyone outside the dwelling or any other dwelling. The focus of the offence is again on the impact of the actions on members of the public who witness the behaviour (*Rukwira v DPP* (1994) 158 JP 65; *Le Vine v DPP* [2010] EWHC 1128 (Admin)). Further, the defendant will not be guilty where they can prove that their conduct was reasonable (for an interesting contemporary example, where use of the term 'Tory scum' at the Conservative Party annual conference in Manchester in 2023 was held to be reasonable, see *R (on the application of the DPP) v Manchester City Magistrates' Court* [2023] EWHC 2938 (Admin)). The offence can also be committed with racial or religious aggravation (*Cain v CPS* [2022] EWHC 1466 (Admin)). Commonly, defendants will argue that in being prosecuted their right to freedom of expression under Art 10 of the ECHR is being infringed (*DPP v Ziegler* [2019] EWHC 71 (Admin)).

7.2.13 **Harassment, alarm or distress: disorderly behaviour**

Alongside the previous offence, it is also a lesser offence to use threatening or abusive words or behaviour, engage in disorderly behaviour or display threatening or abusive materials within the hearing or sight of a person who is likely to suffer harassment, alarm or distress (*Gough v DPP* [2013] EWHC 3267 (Admin); s5 Public Order Act 1986; *Campaign Against Antisemitism v DPP* [2019] EWHC 9 (Admin)). In light of the pivotal importance of the right to freedom of expression, the parameters of this offence have been reduced such that it is no longer an offence to simply engage in insulting behaviour (s57 Crime and Courts Act 2013).

The offence is made out where the person intends their words, behaviour or display of materials to be threatening, abusive or disorderly, or simply that they are aware that such actions may be threatening, abusive or disorderly (*DPP v Clarke* (1991) 94 Cr App Rep 359, DC).

EXAMPLE

In the case of Norwood (*Norwood v United Kingdom* (2004) 40 EHRR SE 111), Norwood was a member of the British National Party (BNP) who put up a BNP poster in a window in his flat that showed images of the Twin Towers in flames, the phrase 'Islam out of Britain—Protect the British people' and a struck-out image of the Islamic crescent and star. He was convicted of a racially aggravated iteration of the offence and he challenged this conviction as being an unlawful interference with his Art 10 freedom of expression under the European Convention on Human Rights at the Strasbourg Court. The European Court held that his conviction was entirely justified, given the principle under Art 17 of the Convention that no one is legally able to engage in behaviour designed to destroy or limit the exercise of the human rights of others. His action in displaying the poster was exploitative of the right to freedom of expression and could not be tolerated.

As a result, the courts have held that the prosecution, in a s5 offence, does not need to prove intention (*DPP v Smith* [2017] EWHC 3193 (Admin)). In this case, the High Court held that it was wrong for the magistrates' court to acquit on the basis that the defendant had displayed no intention to act in the manner prescribed.

The offence can be committed in public or private but not in a dwelling. Thus, depositing a threatening or abusive letter through a letter-box is not an offence under the Public Order Act but is an offence under s1 of the Malicious Communications Act 1988 (*Chappell v DPP* (1988) 89 Cr App Rep 82, DC). The offence encapsulates a wide range of behaviour, from creating a disturbance in a block of flats, rowdy behaviour at night in a street, pestering people at a bus stop, 'dogging', evangelical Christian preaching (*Overd v Chief Constable of Avon and Somerset Constabulary* [2021] EWHC 3100 (QB)) and acting in a threatening and abusive manner whilst filming healthcare professionals during the Covid-19 pandemic (*Hicks v DPP* [2023] EWHC 1089 (Admin)).

There are a number of defences available. First, it is a defence if the accused had no reason to believe that anybody was within earshot or in eyesight who was likely to be harassed, alarmed or distressed. Secondly, where such conduct took place in a dwelling and, thirdly, where the accused's behaviour was reasonable, for example in self-defence or in order to protect property (*DPP v Clarke* (1991) 94 Cr App Rep 359, DC; *Norwood v DPP* [2003] EWHC 1564 (Admin); *Norwood v United Kingdom* (2004) 40 EHRR SE 111).

7.2.14 Incitement to hatred: racial, religious and sexual orientation

The term 'racial hatred' is defined as hatred against a group of people on the grounds of colour, race, nationality (including citizenship) or ethnic or national origin (ss17 and 29 Public Order Act 1986). The term 'religious hatred' refers to hatred directed against a group of people based on their religious belief or lack of religious belief (s29A Public Order Act 1986). 'Hatred on the grounds of sexual orientation' is hatred against a group of people based on their sexual orientation and applies regardless of whether the hatred is towards persons of the same sex, the opposite sex or both (s29AB Public Order Act 1986).

7.2.15 Stirring up hatred: racial, religious and sexual orientation

The offence of stirring up racial hatred is committed where a person uses threatening, abusive or insulting words or behaviour, or displays such materials, where they intend to stir up racial hatred or in the circumstances it is likely that racial hatred will be stirred up (s18 Public Order Act 1986). The offence can also be committed where threatening words or behaviour, or displays of such materials, are used for the purpose of stirring up religious hatred or hatred on the grounds of sexual orientation (s29B Public Order Act 1986).

The offence extends to activity online and as such encapsulates the activities of internet service providers (ISPs) and netizens using social media platforms (Electronic Commerce Directive (Hatred against Persons on Religious Grounds or the Grounds of Sexual Orientation) Regulations 2010 (SI 2010/894); *R v Burns* [2017] EWCA Crim 1466). ISPs can avail themselves of the hosting, caching and mere conduit defences.

The offence is not committed where the conduct takes place entirely within a dwelling. Further, it is a defence for the accused to prove that they did not intend, or were not aware, that their words, behaviour or the written material was threatening, abusive or insulting.

7.2.16 Publishing or distributing written material

The publication or distribution of written material that is threatening, abusive or insulting is an offence under s19 of the Public Order Act 1986 where the person so doing intends to stir up racial hatred or where it can be shown that, having regard to all the circumstances, racial hatred is likely to be stirred up (*R v Burns* [2017] EWCA Crim 1466). Section 29C of the Public Order Act 1986 extends the offence to publishing or distributing threatening written material where this is done for the purpose of stirring up religious hatred or hatred on the grounds of sexual orientation.

These offences can be committed by ISPs and the offence extends to perpetrators making such materials available online via servers based outside England and Wales (*R v Sheppard* [2010] EWCA Crim 65). ISPs can avail themselves of the hosting, caching and mere conduit defences. A successful prosecution does not require the prosecution to prove that someone has actually read or heard the material.

It is a defence, in relation to the latter contextual version of the offence, to prove that the defendant was unaware of the nature of the materials and did not suspect, and had no reason to suspect, that the materials were threatening, abusive or insulting.

7.3 Breach of the peace

Breach of the peace is a curious feature of English law in that it is not classed as a criminal offence but carries with it the potential for serious interferences with individual liberty. People can be arrested under the banner of breach of the peace and the courts may bind over people to maintain the peace (Doherty and Reid, 'Breach of the Peace and Binding Over: Recent Developments and the Continuing Need for Reform' (2001) 35(2) Law Teach 267–81; *Williamson v Chief Constable of the West Midlands* [2003] EWCA Civ 337; s115 Magistrates' Courts Act 1980).

Its existence is an exception to the general focus of the common law:

> For the most part, the common law is concerned to punish those who have committed an offence and to deter them and others from doing so in the future. It does not step in beforehand to prevent people from committing offences. The duty to prevent a breach of the peace is therefore exceptional. And, if not kept within proper bounds, it could be a recipe for officious and unjustified intervention in other people's affairs.
>
> (Lord Rodger of Earlsferry in *R (on the application of Laporte) v Chief Constable of Gloucestershire* [2006] UKHL 55, [2007] 2 AC 105 at 62)

The enactment of various public order statutory offences in the Public Order Act 1986 did not affect the existence and continuance of the common law provision of breach of the peace (s40(4) Public Order Act 1986).

The classic definition of what constitutes a breach of the peace is set out in the case of *R v Howell (Errol)* [1982] QB 416.

> We are emboldened to say that there is a breach of the peace whenever harm is actually done or is likely to be done to a person or in his presence to his property or a person is in fear of being so harmed through an assault, an affray, a riot . . . or other disturbance.
>
> (Lord Justice Watkins at 427)

In this case, the defendant had been at a street party at 4 am. The police had been called and told Howell and others to leave otherwise they would be arrested. As he left, Howell swore at the police, who told him he would be arrested for disturbing public order. More swearing saw Howell duly arrested.

This expansive definition was judicially approved by the House of Lords in the case of *R (on the application of Laporte) v Chief Constable of Gloucestershire* [2006] UKHL 55, [2007] 2 AC 105 and has survived legal challenges for lack of specificity at the European Court of Human Rights (*McLeod v United Kingdom* [1998] 2 FLR 1048; *Steel v United Kingdom* (1999) 28 EHRR 603).

As stated earlier, the police are obliged to preserve the King's peace and to this end must be able to effectively enforce this duty. Thus, police officers are able to arrest people, require a person to stop doing something and to require a person to do something. The exercise of these powers is uncontroversial when exercised in relation to the actual commission of a breach of the peace but are contested when deployed to deal with an anticipated breach of the peace.

In the case of *Duncan v Jones* [1936] 1 KB 218, the defendant intended to hold a meeting on a road adjacent to a training centre. She had spoken a year earlier at the same place and a disturbance had occurred. The police were concerned that if the meeting were to take place a breach of the peace would ensue so asked her to hold the meeting somewhere else. When she refused, the officers arrested her for obstructing a police officer in the execution of their duty. The wide discretion given to the police in this case was subject to both criticism and approval. Criticism came from the fact that the defendant was being punished for doing a perfectly lawful act and any future breach of the peace would be caused by other people's reactions to her public utterances.

Nevertheless, subsequent cases affirmed the rule set out in *Duncan v Jones*, most notably *Moss v McLachlan* (1985) 149 JP 167. The facts of this case arose from the national miners' strike in 1984–5. Nottinghamshire Police, in order to prevent a future breach of the peace, created a roadblock on the M1 motorway, two miles away from local pits, which prevented striking miners from around the country joining demonstrations at these pits. At the roadblock, vehicles that the police thought contained striking miners were stopped and the occupants asked to turn back and, if these requests were ignored, the individuals were further ordered not to proceed beyond the roadblock. Non-compliance with these instructions would result in a charge of obstructing a police officer. On appeal against conviction, the Divisional Court made much of the immediacy of the risk of civil unrest and upheld the convictions.

The risk of heavy-handed, restrictive policing being applied in a subjective manner required that the police be subject to clearer limitations as to their powers. Later judgments from the English courts observed that the police would only be entitled to exercise their powers regarding breach of the peace where police officers were acting honestly and reasonably in believing that a breach of the peace was imminent (*Redmond-Bate v DPP* (1999) 163 JP 789).

The enactment of the HRA 1998 required further limitations and controls to be set on the limits to breach of the peace powers of the police. The assimilation of the ECHR into UK law by the HRA 1998 meant that breach of the peace rules would now have to be sufficiently clear in their limits, terms and scope and could not disproportionately interfere with specific human rights such as the right to liberty and security (Art 5), the right to respect for privacy (Art 8), the right to freedom of expression (Art 10) and the right to association and assembly (Art 11) (*Steel v United Kingdom* (1999) 28 EHRR 603).

A significant case on breach of the peace post-HRA 1998 is the case of *R (on the application of Laporte) v Chief Constable of Gloucestershire* [2006] UKHL 55, [2007] 2 AC 105.

The Iraq War was a controversial period in modern British history. The rationale for UK involvement in the conflict was highly contested and as a result led to numerous public demonstrations and activities directed against it. Miss Laporte was a passenger on a coach which was part of a convoy of coaches from London which were booked to transport Iraq war protesters to RAF Fairford in Gloucestershire. RAF Fairford was the European airbase for US Air Force Boeing B-52 Stratofortress bombers, which were heavily used during the Iraq War. In light of the fact that RAF Fairford had been the scene of numerous previous demonstrations and incidents, the Chief Constable of Gloucestershire ordered his police officers to use the stop and search powers of s60 of the Criminal Justice and Public Order Act 1994 to intercept the coaches and conduct searches for items that could be used violently at the proposed demonstrations. The coaches were duly intercepted, stopped and searched three miles away from the airbase. Passengers were searched and various items like face masks, hard hats, spray paint cans, scissors and a safety flare were confiscated. The passengers were ordered back on the coaches and the coaches were ordered to return to London, flanked by police motorcycle outriders to prevent the coaches from stopping in the motorway lay-bys or at motorway service stations to allow any passengers to relieve themselves. The House of Lords held that the police action in turning back the coaches was unlawful. The police themselves had formed the view that there was no 'imminent' breach of the peace, only a risk of later illegal activity, thus they were not entitled to act. Further, the action of intercepting the coaches and indiscriminately searching the passengers was a disproportionate response. The better response would have been for the police to arrest demonstrators at the future protest rather than acting prematurely.

The issue of pre-emptive police action in anticipation of a future breach of the peace arose in the Supreme Court case of *R (on the application of Hicks) v Commissioner of Police of the Metropolis* [2017] UKSC 9. This case concerned potential disruption to the wedding of Prince William and Kate Middleton on 29 April 2011. A number of people were detained by the police for the duration of the wedding in order to stop them disturbing the ceremony. Lord Toulson, at [31], declared that:

> If the police cannot lawfully arrest and detain a person for a relatively short time (too short for it to be practical to take the person before a court) in circumstances where this is reasonably considered to be necessary for the purpose of preventing imminent violence, the practical consequence would be to hamper severely their ability to carry out the difficult task of maintaining public order and safety as mass public events.

The Supreme Court highlighted the delicate balance between the need to protect citizens from the risk of arbitrary detention and the role of the police in maintaining public order and protecting people and property.

During a protest, the police are entitled to deploy various crowd-control measures, including the controversial policy of 'kettling' or 'containment' whereby groups of people can be corralled into a tightly defined space until such time as the police consider that the protestors can be safely dispersed. However, such measures are only reasonable and proportionate where they are being used to stop a breach of the peace or to prevent an imminent breach of the peace from taking place. In the case of *Austin v United Kingdom* [2012] ECHR 459, the European Court of Human Rights held that detention of protestors in a confined space for a considerable period of time was not a violation of the applicants' right to liberty under Art 5 ECHR.

7.4 The Anti-Social Behaviour, Crime and Policing Act 2014

The 2014 Act provides for civil injunctions against people who engage, or threaten to engage, in anti-social behaviour. The Act, in Pt 3, also provides for dispersal powers where the police have reasonable grounds for believing that members of the public in the local area are being harassed, alarmed or distressed or where the local area is facing crime or disorder. These dispersal powers can be deployed over a 48-hour period in order to remove or reduce the likelihood of this behaviour.

Upon conviction of an anti-social offence, the prosecutor can request that the court impose a Criminal Behaviour Order. Such an order is designed to prevent the individual from engaging in future anti-social behaviour.

The police, social landlords and local government can apply for Community Protection Notices. These notices target individuals or organisations and require them to stop negative behaviour or to take action to stop the behaviour from recurring. The relevant behaviour complained of is behaviour that is detrimental to the quality of life of the local community, is unreasonable and is persistent.

For more geographically spread anti-social behaviour, councils, following consultation with the police, can designate specified areas within their region as subject to a Public Spaces Protection Order (PSPO) (ss59–75 of the 2014 Act as amended). These orders will set out a range of conditions and restrictions that apply to the designated zone, such as banning the drinking of alcohol, limiting the number of people who can congregate or banning rough sleeping. Non-compliance with these restrictions is a criminal offence.

EXAMPLE

A PSPO was issued for the streets surrounding a woman's health clinic, in order to prevent pro-life activists from harassing women going to the clinic to receive abortion services. The activities of the pro-life activists were having a detrimental effect upon the quality of life of 'those in the locality', essentially local women of child-bearing age. A judicial review of the issuance of the PSPO was rejected. (*Dulgheriu v Ealing LBC* [2019] EWCA Civ 1490).

EXAMPLE

It is competent for a local council to issue a PSPO limiting the number of dog walkers in the proscribed area to four. Such an order was necessary in light of the rise of commercial dog walkers (*Summers v Richmond upon Thames LBC* [2018] EWHC 782 (Admin)).

Under s82 of the Police, Crime, Sentencing and Courts Act 2022, expedited PSPOs can be issued around schools and sites that provide NHS vaccines and test and trace services.

Further, the Public Order Act 2023 allows the creation of Abortion Clinic Safe Access Zones.

7.5 **Miscellaneous public order offences**

A number of laws exist to deal with miscellaneous public order offences such as drunkenness, obstruction of streets, nuisances and vagrancy.

7.5.1 **Obstructions and nuisances**

The Town Police Clauses Act 1847 prohibits the placing of obstructions on public streets and behaviour that annoys or endangers residents or passengers in vehicles. An obstruction is widely defined as something that is considered unreasonable on the street, such as an advertising hoarding (*Reed v Perrett* (1876) 1 Ex D 340) or rubble deposited on the road (*Smith v Perry* [1906] 1 KB 262).

Obstruction of the highway is also prohibited by specific laws regarding streets and highways such as the Road Traffic Regulation Act 1984 and the Highways Act 1980.

More generally, the Police, Crime, Sentencing and Courts Act 2022 abolishes the common law offence of public nuisance (s78) and replaces it with a statutory offence of intentionally or recklessly causing a public nuisance.

7.5.1.1 Vagrancy, begging and rough sleeping

It is anachronistic that the Georgian, Victorian and Edwardian legislation criminalising vagrancy is still in force in the 21st century. The Vagrancy Acts of 1824, 1838, 1898 and 1935 provide for a number of offences relating to sleeping rough and begging. Section 3 of the 1824 Act criminalises begging. Section 4 of the 1824 Act created the offences of wandering abroad, being idle and disorderly, lodging in a barn, outhouse, a deserted or unoccupied building or in a cart, wagon, under a tent or in the open air and not giving a good account of oneself. Rough sleeping is also addressed by the use of PSPOs under the Anti-Social Behaviour, Crime and Policing Act 2014 (see **7.4**). The Vagrancy Act 1824 as regards England and Wales is due to be fully repealed under the terms of s81(3) of the Police, Crime, Sentencing and Courts Act 2022, c. 32.

7.5.1.2 Drunkenness

The Criminal Justice Act 1967 sets out the summary offence of disorderly behaviour whilst drunk in a public place (s91 Criminal Justice Act 1967).

KEY POINT SUMMARY

- The state has an obligation to maintain public order for the safety of its citizens.
- Public order is maintained primarily by the police; however, in exceptional cases the military may be drafted in to restore law and order.
- People living in the democracy that is the UK have a fundamental right to freedom of expression, the right to assemble and associate in order to demonstrate and protest under the common law and under Arts 10 and 11 of the European Convention on Human Rights as given effect in the UK by the Human Rights Act 1998.
- The Public Order Act 1986, as amended, sets out the rules applicable for regulating and controlling public demonstrations, public meetings, assemblies and processions.
- The Public Order Act 1986 sets out the criminal prohibitions against rioting, violent disorder and affray as well as provisions on harassment, fear of violence and hate material.
- The Anti-Social Behaviour, Crime and Policing Act 2014 sets out various rules for dealing with anti-social behaviour.
- The common law notion of breach of the peace authorises the police to take action to stop a breach of the peace but also to pre-empt certain behaviour which would imminently create a breach of the peace.
- Significant legislative reform to policing public protests has been effected by the Conservative UK government.

CHAPTER 8
The Human Rights Act 1998: Practice Questions

FUNCTIONING LEGAL KNOWLEDGE

This chapter covers the following functional knowledge required to pass the SQE 1 assessments:

Application of the Human Rights Act 1988 to legal matters or to a client's interests
European Convention on Human Rights
Schedule 1, HRA 1998: the 'Convention rights'
Articles 1, 6, 7, 8 and 10
Duty to interpret the law in a way that is compatible with Convention rights
Potential impact on parliamentary sovereignty

AUTHORITIES UNDERPINNING PRACTICE

The key authorities that underpin this area of practice are listed below. Note that for legislation you are linked to legislation.gov.uk.

Although much of the legislation on this government website is available in its amended form, the incorporation of new amendments into the text of legislation can be delayed. You should refer to legal databases to ensure you are referencing the most up-to-date legislation.

- Human Rights Act 1998
  https://www.legislation.gov.uk/ukpga/1998/42/contents
- European Convention on Human Rights
  https://www.echr.coe.int/documents/convention_eng.pdf

8.1 Introduction

This chapter covers the operation of the European Convention on Human Rights (ECHR) and the Human Rights Act 1998 (HRA 1998) in order to develop the knowledge to advise a client on options, progress cases and practice in accordance with the law and legal system of England and Wales.

8.2 General principles

8.2.1 The Human Rights Act 1998

The HRA 1998 has made the Convention central to the practice of law in the UK.

Section 2(1) of the Act requires all courts and tribunals to take into account the Convention and decisions by the institutions of the Convention, whether the European Court of Human Rights, the Commission of Human Rights or the Council. The extent to which UK courts should be guided by Strasbourg jurisprudence is often referred to as the 'mirror principle' in that the court should follow any clear and constant jurisprudence of the European Court of Human Rights (*R (Ullah) v Special Adjudicator* [2004] 2 AC 323).

The Act creates a general statutory requirement that all legislation (past or present) be read and given effect in a way which is compatible with the Convention. It does this by providing, in s3, that all legislation, primary and secondary, whenever enacted, must be read and given effect in a way that is compatible with **Convention rights** wherever possible.

This raises the question of **parliamentary sovereignty** over which there has been much debate. Clearly, there is an international obligation on the UK under Art 46(1) ECHR to abide by the decisions of the European Court of Human Rights in any case to which it is a party. This obligation is absolute (*Chester and McGeoch v Secretary of State for Justice and another* [2013] UKSC 63). That said, s2 of the HRA 1998 simply requires UK courts to take into account decisions made in the European Court of Human Rights and s3 provides that all legislation must be read and given effect in a way which is compatible with Convention rights wherever possible. As stated by Lord Steyn in *R (Anderson) v Secretary of State of the Home Department* [2002] UKHL 46, [2003] 1 AC 837 at [59]: 'the interpretative obligation under section 3 of the 1998 Act is a strong one. It applies even if there is no ambiguity in the language in the sense of the language being capable of two different meanings.'

He further noted that it may be necessary under s3 to 'adopt an interpretation which linguistically may appear strained' and that a declaration of incompatibility was a 'measure of last resort'.

Whilst there is no categorical answer to this dichotomy, it is clear that the intention to comply exists in UK courts and the UK government has in fact amended legislation to ensure that compliance. There are contentious issues, for example prisoners' voting rights, which stray into political territory and remain problematic, but in the main parliamentary sovereignty remains a fundamental principle of UK law and practice and one which the courts and the government are required to balance with their obligations under the Convention and the HRA 1998.

8.2.2 Declaration of incompatibility

Section 4 provides that if the court is satisfied that a provision of primary legislation is incompatible with a Convention right, it may make a declaration of that incompatibility. In terms of secondary legislation, if the court is satisfied that the provision is incompatible with a Convention right, and that (revocation aside) the primary legislation concerned prevents the removal of the incompatibility, a declaration of that incompatibility may be made. A declaration does not affect the validity of the provision in respect of which it is given and is not binding on the parties to the proceedings in which it is made.

Section 10 provides the government with remedial powers following a s4 declaration of incompatibility where if, after all avenues of appeal have been exhausted, it appears to a **minister of the Crown** that a provision of UK legislation is incompatible with an obligation under the Convention, they may amend the provision to remove the incompatibility if there are compelling reasons to do so.

EXAMPLE

Bill and Susan were a heterosexual couple who lived together for several years as co-habitees. They didn't want to get married as they believed this had negative connotations regarding the role of women in society. They wished instead to enter into a civil partnership. They were informed by the local council that the Civil Partnerships Act 2004 (CPA) did not apply to different-sex couples, leaving them in the position where their only option was to marry, as opposed to a same-sex couple who would have the option of either getting married under the Marriage (Same Sex Couples) Act 2013 or entering a civil partnership under the CPA. It was argued that this breached their rights under Art 14 ECHR (non-discrimination) when read in conjunction with Art 8 (respect for private life). The Supreme Court finally made a declaration of incompatibility in 2018 and the CPA was amended to allow civil partnerships for heterosexual couples.

8.2.3 Unlawful acts by a public authority

Section 6(1) of the HRA 1998 provides that '[i]t is unlawful for a **public authority** to act in a way which is incompatible with a Convention right'. Section 6(1) is subject to subs (2), which provides that subs (1) does not apply if the authority is required so to act as a result of primary legislation or provisions made thereunder which cannot be construed in any other way. Section 6(3) includes within the definition of public authority a court or tribunal or any person certain of whose functions are functions of a public nature.

The intention of the Act was specifically to prevent interference by the state—that is, public authorities—in the rights of an individual, not to involve the Convention effectively being directly enforceable as between private citizens so as to alter their contractual rights and obligations (*Manchester City Council v Pinnock* [2011] 2 AC 104; *Hounslow London Borough Council v Powell* [2011] 2 AC 186). Any individual resident in the UK regardless of whether or not they are a British citizen or a foreign national can use the HRA 1998.

This also means that the courts have their own primary duty to give effect to the Convention unless a statute positively prevents this. It would therefore be unlawful for public authorities to act in a way which is incompatible with a Convention right. Courts themselves are included in the definition of public authorities.

Accordingly, a claim may only be brought by an individual '**victim**' (or would-be 'victim') pursuant to s7(1) of the HRA 1998 against a public authority and not against a private individual. The claim for breach must be normally brought within one year of the date of the alleged unlawful act although there is some discretion (s7(5)).

Where a petition is lodged pursuant to Art 34 ECHR, a person, non-governmental organisation or group of individuals must be able to claim 'to be the victim of a violation . . . of the rights set forth in the Convention . . .'. In order to claim to be a victim of a violation, a person must be directly affected by the impugned measure (*Burden v United Kingdom* [2008] ECHR 357).

EXAMPLE

Karen is the child of parents Sam and Ada and has been taken into local authority care; in reviewing Karen's care plan the local authority, without consultation with Sam and Ada, make the decision that she can never be returned to their care. They contend that the local authority is acting in breach of Art 8. In applying the provisions under the Act, they can argue that s6 makes it unlawful for a public authority—that is, the local authority—to act in a way which is incompatible with this right; in this case, that the decision-making process was unfair as they were not involved to a sufficient degree to adequately protect their interests. Section 7 enables them as victims of the unlawful conduct to bring court proceedings against the local authority. Section 8 provides the relief a court may grant in those proceedings which in this case would be to overturn the local authority decision.

8.2.4 Judicial remedies

Section 8(1):

> In relation to any act (or proposed act) of a public authority which the court finds is (or would be) unlawful, it may grant such relief or remedy, or make such order, within its powers as it considers to be just and appropriate.

Damages may only be awarded by a court which has the power to do so or to order the payment of compensation in civil proceedings. Damages should not be awarded unless the court, having taken into account all of the circumstances of the case, is satisfied that the award is necessary to afford just satisfaction to the person in whose favour it is made.

It is clear that all courts and tribunals must have a working knowledge of the content of the Convention and the relevant case law to any given Article in order to be able to apply it correctly in accordance with UK legislation. To apply the decisions of cases brought down by Strasbourg, the courts and tribunals need to understand how decisions at Strasbourg are actually reached, so as to give the appropriate weight to any decision. In order to be able effectively to interpret Convention legislation and case law, the courts must understand the 'European jurisprudence' that exists when the judges come to a decision in Strasbourg.

8.3 European and international doctrines

Although rights are conveyed to individuals, the rights contained within the Articles are rarely absolute and can be limited or qualified. The majority of rights are subject to limitations and qualifications; however, the right to freedom from torture is an absolute right and an act of torture could never be justified by acting in the interests of the state.

8.3.1 Limited rights

Some of the rights conveyed under the Articles of the Convention have limitations placed upon them so that in some circumstances an infringement of a guaranteed right does not amount to an infringement. The right to liberty (Art 5) and the right to a fair trial (Art 6) are examples of limited rights for these purposes.

8.3.2 Qualified rights

Some Articles contain qualified rights, and as such the Convention permits them to be infringed in certain circumstances.

Once a victim has been shown to have established a primary right, the Convention seeks to balance the rights of the individual against other public rights. However, rights such as the right to respect for private life (Art 8) and the right to freedom of expression (Art 10) may sometimes compete with one another. Equally, some rights may be in direct conflict with **public interest** considerations. These sorts of rights, which impinge on the rights and freedoms of others, are necessarily qualified, and the Convention permits them to be limited by the state.

8.3.3 How far can a state limit the rights contained within the Convention?

The Convention permits these limitations only where they are:

(a) prescribed by law;

(b) intended to achieve a legitimate objective; and

(c) necessary in a democratic society (ie proportionate to the ends to be achieved).

For example, Art 8 states that, 'Everyone has the right to respect for his private and family life, his home and his correspondence'. This is a presumed right, but a number of limitations and exceptions to it are set out in Art 8(2):

> There shall be no interference by a public authority with the exercise of this right except such as is in accordance with the law and is necessary in a democratic society in the interests of national security, public safety or the economic well-being of the country, for the prevention of disorder or crime, for the protection of health or morals, or for the protection of the rights and freedoms of others.

The precise terms of the limitations in respect of the Articles vary but the judicial method for considering them is the same:

(a) Is the interference prescribed by law?

(b) Does it serve a legitimate objective?

(c) Is it necessary in a democratic society?

8.3.3.1 Is the interference prescribed by law? The rule of law

No interference with a right protected under the Convention is permissible unless the citizen knows the basis for the interference because it is set out in ascertainable law. In the absence of any such detailed authorisation by the law, any interference, however justified, will violate the Convention—see *Malone v United Kingdom* (1984) 7 EHRR 14 where the applicant's telephone was tapped by the police. When this took place, the only authorisation was an internal code of guidance produced by the police which was not available to the public. The European Court took the view that Mr Malone was unable to assess whether or not his telephone would be listened to, or what the basis in law for the surveillance might be. The **common law** position was inadequate, as could be seen from his failure in the High Court. The interference violated the Convention because it was not prescribed by law.

8.3.3.2 Does it serve a legitimate objective?

Legitimate objectives are:

(a) the interests of public safety;

(b) national security;

(c) the protection of health and morals; and

(d) the economic well-being of the country, or the protection of the rights and freedoms of others.

8.3.3.3 Is it necessary in a democratic society? Proportionality

The Convention's approach is to decide whether a particular limitation from a right is justified in the sense of being '**proportionate** to the legitimate aim pursued'.

This means that even if a policy which interferes with a Convention right might be aimed at securing a legitimate social policy, for example the prevention of crime, this will not in itself justify the violation if the means adopted to secure the aim are excessive in the circumstances. *Soering v United Kingdom* (1989) 11 EHRR 439 stated:

> inherent in the whole of the Convention is a search for the fair balance between the demands of the general interest of the Community and the requirements of the protection of the individual's fundamental rights. (para 89)

The principle of fair balance is carried through into domestic law in determining whether a limitation is proportionate. The courts should have due regard to:

> 1. Whether its objective is sufficiently important to justify the limitation of a fundamental right;
> 2. Whether it is rationally connected to the objective;
> 3. Whether a less intrusive measure could have been used; and
> 4. Whether having regard to these matters and the severity of the consequences, a fair balance has been struck between the rights of the individual and the interests of the community
>
> (*Bank Mellat v HM Treasury (No 2)* [2013] UKSC 39)

8.3.4 The margin of appreciation

A state is allowed a certain freedom to evaluate its public policy decisions, but this is subject to review by the Strasbourg institutions. The Court has to ensure that the Member State's own political and cultural traditions are respected. When determining whether a social policy aim is legitimate therefore, or whether the means adopted to achieve it are 'necessary in a democratic society', the Commission and the Court have recognised limits as to their own competence to judge the issue. They have done this by giving the state a so-called **margin of appreciation** when assessing the extent to which a signatory has violated the Convention.

The most notable case in this area is *Handyside v United Kingdom* (1976) 1 EHRR 737. This case arose because of the intention to publish *The Little Red Schoolbook*, intended for children, but which included a chapter on sex. The books were seized by the police under the Obscene Publications Act 1959 and a forfeiture order obtained against the publishers. The publishers claimed a breach of their right to freedom of expression under Art 10.

Was the seizing of the books proportionate to the legitimate aim that the state sought to protect? The Court recognised that there was a margin of appreciation in this case which justified the interference with Art 10. It stated:

> By reason of their direct and continuous contact with the vital forces of their countries, state authorities are in principle in a better position than the international judge to give an opinion on the exact nature of these requirements as well as on the necessity of a restriction or penalty

intended to meet them. Nevertheless Article 10(2) does not give the contracting state an unlimited power of appreciation. The Court which is responsible for ensuring the observance of those states' engagements is empowered to give the final ruling on whether a restriction or penalty is reconcilable with the freedom of expression as protected by Article 10. The domestic margin of appreciation thus goes hand in hand with a European supervision.

EXAMPLE

John is charged with **harassment** of his partner, Alison. His fingerprints and DNA samples are taken. However, prior to the trial the couple set aside their differences and decide to get married. The case is then discontinued by the CPS and John asks the police to destroy his fingerprints and DNA samples which they refuse to do. He could argue that this is a breach of his rights under Art 8 to respect for private and family life. The retention is prescribed by s64 ZD of the Police and Criminal Evidence Act 1984 (PACE) and so is in accordance with the law, and the reason the power is exists is to assist with the prevention and detection of crime; that is, it is in pursuit of a legitimate aim. However, it may be possible to argue that it is not necessary in a democratic society as it is a disproportionate interference with Art 8. Section 64 is a blanket provision and does not take into account the nature or gravity of the offence or, indeed, the fact that proceedings may have been discontinued; it is not time limited and therefore there are very limited opportunities for an individual such as John to have the material destroyed.

8.3.5 Derogations and reservations

In times of war or other public emergency, it is open to a Member State to enter into derogations in respect of certain obligations. These cannot be general derogations. A derogation simply allows a state not to comply with the Article in question to the legitimate extent of the derogation. However, derogations in respect of the right to life (except arising from the lawful prosecution of war) or from the prohibitions against torture are not permitted.

Reservations differ from derogations in that they are merely conditions upon acceptance of a particular Article.

8.3.6 Equality of arms

This principle, laid down in the case of *Neuminster v Austria* (1968) 1 EHRR 91, was created in order to ensure that both parties to a case, whether in civil or criminal proceedings, were not placed at a procedural disadvantage.

EXAMPLE

Kareem and Joshua, both part-time waiters, are active members of the Extinction Rebellion movement and together they create various publications which name and shame organisations which use up the earth's resources. Shale & Co Ltd take exception to the negative impact this has on their business and state that the claims made by the pair are untrue; they have the right to sue both Kareem and Joshua under the defamation laws which exist in the UK and they have the resources to finance such litigation, knowing it is a complex area of law which may take years to resolve. Kareem and Joshua would not have the means to defend such a case and assert their Art 10 right to freedom of expression and it can be argued that the state's failure to provide them with **legal aid**, which is not normally available for such cases in the UK, will deny them their right to a fair trial under Art 6.

8.3.7 Horizontality

As mentioned earlier, s6 of the HRA 1998 incorporates courts and tribunals into the definition of public bodies. When two individuals come to court for a decision to be made about their dispute, the court needs to act compatibly with the Convention. This will therefore have an indirect effect upon the two individuals who are not themselves covered by the Convention. The court's adherence to the Convention will have a **horizontal** effect on their relationship. In *Hokkanen v Finland* (1994) 19 EHRR 139, the European Court held that where grandparents failed to abide by court orders for contact and custody in favour of the father, Art 8 imposed upon the state a positive obligation to assist, so far as possible, the father's relationship with his child.

Douglas and Others v Hello! Ltd [2001] QB 467, involving Michael Douglas and Catherine Zeta Jones, again illustrated that the court had a duty under s6 to protect their private life. The case involved proceedings against *Hello!* magazine which threatened to publish unauthorised photographs from the couple's wedding when they had in fact sold the exclusive rights to *OK!* magazine. While all three judges agreed that an **injunction** should be refused because the couple had in fact traded their right to private life like a commodity, the judgment is notable in confirming the effect that the HRA 1998 has had upon legal relations between individuals as opposed to legal relations between individuals and the state.

8.3.8 Living instrument

The Convention was drafted more than 70 years ago and, unlike usual pieces of legislation, it has not been amended, repealed or replaced by more up-to-date legislation. To use the UK model of precedent would bind the court to adhere to decisions which are outmoded and probably unfair. It is primarily for this reason that the doctrine of precedent is not a main feature of Convention case law. The Convention is a 'living instrument' and cases are decided in line with the up-to-date economic and moral conditions of the Member States. Although this creates some uncertainty when relying on previous decisions handed down, it at least ensures that the decisions are modern in their approach.

8.3.9 Protocols

Protocols can be thought of as extensions to the Convention where Member States can agree to add to the rights contained within it. The procedural method for doing this is to draw up a Protocol setting out the additional rights. The First Protocol provides for rights to the peaceful enjoyment of property, to education and to free elections. The HRA 1998 allows the government to incorporate future Protocols into national law using rules of Parliament. The rights contained within the Protocols carry as much weight as the provisions contained in the Articles themselves.

8.3.10 Where to find Convention case law

The Council of Europe publishes individual judgments and decisions under the title *Publications of the European Court of Human Rights*. Court judgments are published in Series A and the pleadings, oral arguments and documents are published in Series B.

Decisions of the Commission and judgments of the Court can be found on the European Court of Human Rights website and the HUDOC database.

Another source is the European Human Rights Reports (EHRR), which publishes all judgments and important decisions. The European Human Rights Law Review (EHRLR) appears six times a year and has a case law section which highlights interesting cases and recent decisions.

8.4 The Convention rights

This section contains commentary on the main Articles of the Convention specified by the Functioning Legal Knowledge (FLK) requirements. It should be viewed only as an introduction to some of the possible effects of the Convention and is no substitute for empirical research.

Schedule 1 to the HRA 1998 lists the Convention rights by reference to the relevant Articles of, and Protocols to, the ECHR as follows.

8.4.1 Article 2: right to life

1. Everyone's right to life shall be protected by law. No one shall be deprived of his life intentionally save in the execution of a sentence of a court following his conviction of a crime for which this penalty is provided by law.
2. Deprivation of life shall not be regarded as inflicted in contravention of this Article when it results from the use of force which is no more than absolutely necessary:
   (a) in defence of any person from unlawful violence;
   (b) in order to effect a lawful arrest or to prevent the escape of a person lawfully detained;
   (c) in action lawfully taken for the purpose of quelling a riot or insurrection.

This is a limited right: see *McCann v United Kingdom* (1995) 21 EHRR 97.

8.4.2 Article 3: prohibition of torture or inhuman or degrading treatment or punishment

No one shall be subjected to torture or inhuman or degrading treatment or punishment.

This is an absolute right although there is a minimum level of severity required before Art 3 will be contravened. The case of *Ireland v United Kingdom* (1978) 2 EHRR 25 gave guidelines as to what constituted prohibited treatment. Torture was defined as deliberate inhuman treatment causing very serious and cruel suffering; inhumane treatment or punishment as treatment or punishment which causes intense physical and mental suffering; and degrading treatment or punishment as treatment or punishment that arouses in a victim a feeling of fear, anguish and inferiority capable of humiliating and debasing the victim and possibly breaking their physical or moral resistance.

8.4.3 Article 4: prohibition of slavery and forced labour

1. No one shall be held in slavery or servitude. [This is an absolute right.]
2. No one shall be required to perform forced or compulsory labour. [This is a limited right.]
3. For the purpose of this Article the term 'forced or compulsory labour' shall not include:
   (a) any work required to be done in the ordinary course of detention imposed according to the provisions of Article 5 of this Convention or during conditional release from such detention;
   (b) any service of a military character or, in case of conscientious objectors in countries where they are recognised, service exacted instead of compulsory military service;
   (c) any service exacted in case of an emergency or calamity threatening the life or well-being of the community;
   (d) any work or service which forms part of normal civic obligations.

8.4.4 Article 5: right to liberty and security

1. Everyone has the right to liberty and security of person. No one shall be deprived of his liberty save in the following cases and in accordance with a procedure prescribed by law:
   (a) the lawful detention of a person after conviction by a competent court;
   (b) the lawful arrest or detention of a person for non-compliance with the lawful order of a court in order to secure the fulfilment of any obligation prescribed by law;
   (c) the lawful arrest or detention of a person effected for the purpose of bringing him before the competent legal authority on reasonable suspicion of having committed an offence or when it is reasonably considered necessary to prevent his committing an offence or fleeing after having done so;

(d) the detention of a minor by lawful order for the purpose of educational supervision or his lawful detention for the purpose of bringing him before the competent legal authority;

(e) the lawful detention of persons for the spreading of infectious diseases, of persons of unsound mind, alcoholics or drug addicts or vagrants;

(f) the lawful arrest or detention of a person to prevent his effecting an unauthorised entry into the country or of a person against whom action is being taken with a view to deportation or extradition.

2. Everyone who is arrested shall be informed promptly, in a language which he understands, of the reasons for his arrest and of any charge against him.
3. Everyone arrested or detained in accordance with paragraph 1(c) of this Article shall be brought promptly before a judge or other officer authorised by law to exercise judicial power and shall be entitled to trial within a reasonable time or to release pending trial. Release may be conditioned by guarantees to appear for trial.
4. Everyone who is deprived of his liberty by arrest or detention shall be entitled to take proceedings by which the lawfulness of his detention shall be decided speedily by a court and his release ordered if the detention is not lawful.
5. Everyone who has been the victim of arrest or detention in contravention of the provisions of this Article shall have an exercisable right to compensation.

This is a limited (as opposed to a qualified) right and will have most relevance to the length of detention and bail. When a defendant is charged with a criminal offence, they must appear before the magistrates who will decide whether or not there should be a release pending trial, with or without conditions, or a remand into custody. Article 5(3) states that a person should be entitled to trial within a reasonable time or to release pending trial. The case of *Wemhoff v Germany* (1968) 1 EHRR 55 stated that the defendant was entitled to both things, notwithstanding the wording, and also that the defendant should be released pending trial unless there are '*relevant and sufficient*' reasons to justify continued detention. In the UK, the Bail Act 1976 provides that the magistrates must be satisfied that there are substantial grounds for believing that a person should be deprived of their liberty and the exceptions to the prima facie right to bail are clearly set out in the Schedule to the Act.

EXAMPLE

James is arrested in connection with assault occasioning grievous bodily harm and the prosecution applies for him to be remanded in custody on the grounds that he will fail to surrender to the custody of the court. He is of previous good character and has offered a surety of £25,000. The defence appeals this on the grounds that it is unlawful detention as there were no substantial grounds for this belief. James has the right to liberty under Art 5 of the Act and whilst this is a limited right the exceptions to the prima facie right to bail are not made out. James would be able to claim for damages for false imprisonment and also bring an action under s7 of the Act in the County Court for the violation of his right to liberty.

8.4.5 Article 6: right to a fair trial

1. In the determination of his civil rights and obligations or of any criminal charge against him, everyone is entitled to a fair and public hearing within a reasonable time by an independent and impartial tribunal established by law. Judgment shall be pronounced publicly but the press and public may be excluded from all or part of the trial in the interest of morals, public order or national security in a democratic society, where the interest of juveniles or the protection of the private life of the parties so require, or to the extent strictly necessary in the opinion of the court in special circumstances where publicity would prejudice the interests of justice.
2. Everyone charged with a criminal offence shall be presumed innocent until proved guilty according to law.

3. Everyone charged with a criminal offence has the following minimum rights:
   (a) to be informed promptly, in a language which he understands and in detail, of the nature and cause of the accusation against him;
   (b) to have adequate time and facilities for the preparation of his defence;
   (c) to defend himself in person or through legal assistance of his own choosing or, if he has not sufficient means to pay for legal assistance, to be given it free when the interests of justice so require;
   (d) to examine or have examined witnesses against him and to obtain the attendance and examination of witnesses on his behalf under the same conditions as witnesses against him;
   (e) to have the free assistance of an interpreter if he cannot understand or speak the language used in court.

This Article will affect proceedings in both civil and criminal trials and in determining the scope of 'civil rights and obligations' note that the court will include in that welfare benefit appeals, as these determine civil rights (*DG v Secretary of State for Work and Pensions* (ESA) [2010] CE/1084/2010).

EXAMPLE

Sheriff is evicted from his home due to non-payment of rent and makes an application to the council that he be provided with accommodation under s193(5) of the Housing Act 1996 which places a local housing authority under a duty to rehouse those who are not made intentionally homeless. The local housing authority states that mismanagement of his finances led to him being made homeless and to that extent was intentional. Sheriff is able to argue that there is a homelessness duty which is owed to him and failure to discharge that duty is a breach of his civil rights as set out in Art 6.

8.4.5.1 Criminal proceedings

Article 6(1) provides the right to a trial within a reasonable time and guarantees the expedition in the conduct of the proceedings themselves in order to prevent a defendant from remaining uncertain about the outcome of their fate for too long, for example in *Boddaert v Belgium* (1992) 16 EHRR 42 it was held that eight weeks was unlikely to be a sufficiently long delay to breach this Article particularly when taking into account the various aspects of the proper administration of justice.

When considering the fairness of the proceedings complained of, the general approach is to review the overall process in question in order to ascertain whether there is a fully Art 6-compliant court or tribunal to give fair consideration to the case (*Bryan v United Kingdom* (1995) 21 EHRR 342 at [40]).

8.4.5.2 Article 6(2): reverse burden of proof

The case of *Salabiaku v France* (1991) 13 EHRR 379 was notable in that it stated that:

> Article 6(2) does not therefore regard presumptions of fact or law provided for in criminal law with indifference. It requires states to confine them within reasonable limits which take into account the importance of what is at stake and maintain the rights of the defence.

Article 6(2) and the presumption of innocence has already been raised as an issue in UK proceedings, in particular the case of *R v DPP, ex p Kebilene* [1999] 3 WLR 972. This case concerned ss16A and 16B of the Prevention of Terrorism Act 1989 which carries with it a reverse burden of proof. The House of Lords held, in relation to the particular provision, that it was not clear that these sections were necessarily going to be contrary to Art 6(2).

8.4.5.3 Article 6(3)(b): disclosure

Our present system of disclosure contains various anomalies which contravene a defendant's right to disclosure under the Convention. The main piece of legislation to be affected here is the Criminal Procedure and Investigations Act 1996 which deals with primary and secondary disclosure of unused material and was amended by the Criminal Justice Act 2003.

The 2003 Act amends the original two-stage test contained in the 1996 Act and replaces it with a new objective single test for the disclosure of unused prosecution material to the defence, requiring the prosecutor to disclose prosecution material that has not previously been disclosed and which might reasonably be considered capable of undermining the case for the prosecution against the accused, or of assisting the case for the accused. It replaces the present secondary disclosure material which meets the new test. The prosecutor is specifically required to review the prosecution material on receipt of the defence statement and to make further disclosure if required under the continuing duty. This has been further supplemented by the Attorney General's Guidelines 2024 which came into force from 29 May 2024 and front loads disclosure of unused material and also encourages pre-charge engagement between the police and the defence after the conclusion of the PACE interview at the police station.

8.4.5.4 Article 6 and inferences from silence

The Criminal Justice and Public Order Act 1994 introduced various inroads into the right to silence which had hitherto been absolute. Under s34, in particular, if an accused failed to mention when questioned, or charged, a fact which they later relied upon in court then such inferences as appeared proper could be drawn from that earlier silence, most notably the inference of recent fabrication. It is accepted that the mere fact of drawing inference from an accused's silence will not, of itself, involve a breach of Art 6. However, the procedural safeguards involved in situations where inferences may be drawn have been subject to close scrutiny in our national courts and have been challenged in the European Court (most notably in *Condron v United Kingdom* [2000] ECHR 191).

The Court held that there had in fact been a breach of Art 6 in that the direction given to the jury in respect of the s34 inference had been incomplete. As a matter of fairness, the judge should have directed them that if they were satisfied that the applicant's silence at the police interview could not sensibly have been attributed to their having no answer, or none that would stand up to cross-examination, it should not draw an adverse inference.

8.4.5.5 Article 6 and public interest immunity

Public interest immunity (PII) is an exclusionary rule of evidence which allows for material falling within the definition of PII to be withheld from the defence.

The procedural requirements that govern the way in which the prosecution should claim such immunity were vigorously challenged in Strasbourg in the case of *Rowe and Davis v United Kingdom* (2000) 30 EHRR 1. At trial, the prosecution decided, without informing the judge, to withhold relevant material on the grounds that it fell within the definition of PII. The Court felt that:

> Such a procedure, whereby the prosecution itself attempts to assess the importance of concealed information to the defence and weigh this against the public interest in keeping the information secret, cannot comply with Article 6(1).

The generic issue that the Court was concerned with was the fact that in the UK the prosecution may make an *ex parte* application without notice to the judge in order to obtain PII status without the defence ever being involved in the decision-making process. This is as opposed to an *inter partes* hearing, or an *ex parte* hearing with notice, where the defence is allowed to make representation in writing or in person. Whilst the latter two options are clearly quite fair, the former *ex parte* without notice application has been severely criticised by Strasbourg and the position has yet to be clarified.

In *Fitt v United Kingdom* (2000) 30 EHRR 480, it was held that the procedures adopted with regards to disclosure, in this particular case, were Art 6(1)-compliant. This was because, although the prosecution was heard *ex parte*, the defence was kept informed and permitted to make submissions and participate in those decisions as far as possible without disclosing the material the prosecution sought to withhold on PII grounds. The Court also had regard to the judge's continuing duty to monitor the situation, which it felt was an important safeguard from a defence point of view. The Court came to the same conclusion in similar terms in *Jasper v United Kingdom* (2000) 30 EHRR 441.

8.4.5.6 Article 6: unfairly obtained evidence

Traditionally, unfairly obtained evidence may be excluded under s78 of PACE and, following the implementation of the HRA 1998, it could also be held to be a violation of an individual's rights under Art 6 or Art 8, the latter sometimes resulting in the courts determining that there had consequently been a breach of Art 6.

Section 78(1) of PACE provides that the court:

> may refuse to allow evidence on which the prosecution proposes to rely to be given if it appears to the court that, having regard to all the circumstances, *including the circumstances in which the evidence was obtained*, the admission of the evidence could have such an adverse effect on the fairness of the proceedings that the court ought not to admit it. [Emphasis added.]

Where the evidence was excluded under s78 it did not automatically follow that the prosecution came to an end, or that conviction, upon appeal, was necessarily unsafe. Similarly, even where a breach of Art 6 and/or Art 8 was found, it was still possible for the Court of Appeal safely to uphold a conviction.

The case of *Teixeira de Castro v Portugal* (1998) 28 EHRR 101, while notable for its decision regarding unfairly obtained evidence, also states:

> The admissibility of evidence is primarily a matter for regulation by national law and as a general rule it is for the courts to assess the evidence before them. The Court's task under the Convention is not to give rulings as to whether the statements of witnesses were properly admitted as evidence, but rather to ascertain whether the proceedings as a whole, including the way in which evidence was taken, were fair.

The practical consequences of evidence obtained primarily as a result of intelligence-led policing have been clarified in the House of Lords, in *Attorney-General's Reference (No 3 of 2000)* [2002] 1 Cr App R 29 which dealt with the conjoined appeals of *R v G* and *R v Looseley*. What the House of Lords provides is a rationale for the courts to stay prosecutions based upon entrapment, described by Lord Hoffmann as a 'jurisdiction to prevent abuse of executive power'.

8.4.5.7 Article 6: evidence obtained by torture

Where there has been a 'flagrant denial of justice' applying the test at [258]–[262] of the ECHR judgment in *Soering v United Kingdom* (1989) 11 EHRR 439 at [113]:

> It is for the applicant to adduce evidence capable of proving that there are substantial grounds for believing that, if he is removed from a Contracting State, he would be exposed to a real risk of being subjected to a flagrant denial of justice. Where such evidence is adduced, it is for the Government to dispel any doubts about it.

This was famously applied in the case of *Othman (Abu Qatada) v United Kingdom* [2009] ECHR 855 where the applicant appealed against the decision to deport him to Jordan for trial on the basis that the evidence against him had been obtained through the use of torture. The Court had to consider whether this was such a flagrant denial of justice so as to amount to a fundamental breach of Art 6. Despite assurances provided by the Jordanian government that this evidence would not be used, the Court upheld the appeal and it was only following a treaty signed by both the UK government and the Jordanian government that he was allowed to be deported to face trial.

It should be noted that, aside from this case, in the 22 years since the *Soering* judgment the Court had never found an expulsion which would be a violation of Art 6. 'Flagrant denial of justice' is a 'stringent test of unfairness'. What is required is a breach of the principles of fair trial guaranteed by Art 6 which is 'so fundamental as to amount to a nullification, or destruction of the very essence, of the right guaranteed by that article'.

8.4.6 **Article 7: no punishment without law (no retrospective criminal offences or penalties)**

> 1. No one shall be held guilty of any criminal offence on account of any act or omission which did not constitute a criminal offence under national or international law at the time when it was committed. Nor shall a heavier penalty be imposed than the one that was applicable at the time the criminal offence was committed.
> 2. This Article shall not prejudice the trial and punishment of any person for any act or omission which, at the time it was committed, was criminal according to the general principles of law recognised by civilised nations.

There is the presumption in relation to criminal offences that there will be no retroactivity and that provisions of criminal law may be argued against if they are not clear; equally, the severity of the penalty imposed cannot be increased (*Moustaquim v Belgium* (1991) 13 EHRR 802 at [34]). There are various changes in our domestic legislation which may cause a problem in relation to retroactivity which can be more clearly explained in relation to case law.

EXAMPLE

In 1995 David is charged with raping his wife in 1989. He argues that the change in the law which made marital rape a criminal offence was not in force at the time of the alleged act and therefore to apply it to him is a breach of his rights under Art 7; to the extent that this may be the case, the fact that it was sufficiently foreseeable that the change in the law would come into effect means there is no breach of Art 7.

8.4.7 Article 8: right to respect for private and family life

1. Everyone has the right to respect for his private and family life, his home and his correspondence.
2. There shall be no interference by a public authority with the exercise of this right except such as is in accordance with the law and is necessary in a democratic society and in the interests of national security, public safety or the economic well being of the country, for the prevention of disorder or crime, for the protection of health and morals, or for the protection of the rights and freedoms of others.

Note that in the case of *X and Y v Netherlands* (1985) 8 EHRR 235, the European Court stated that Art 8:

> does not merely compel the state to abstain from interference: in addition to this primarily negative undertaking, there may be positive obligations inherent in an effective respect for private and family life. These obligations may involve the adoption of measures designed to secure respect for private life even in the sphere of relations of individuals between themselves.

This imposes a secondary duty quite separate to the main function of the Article which refers to interference by a public authority. In *McVeigh, O'Neill and Evans v United Kingdom* (1981) 25 DR 15, it was held that preventing the prisoners from communicating with their spouses was a breach of Art 8 even though they were held under anti-terrorist laws; if it was the case that such contact may facilitate an escape or the destruction or removal of evidence, then the case may well be different.

The right to respect for private and family life is only directly enforceable against a public authority not against a private individual. Although it is the case that a court may make a determination and the court comes within the definition of a public authority this is not of itself sufficient to allow individuals to enforce their rights against each other. For example, in the case of *McDonald v McDonald* [2016] UKSC 28 it was held that:

> although it may well be that article 8 is engaged when a judge makes an order for possession of a tenant's home at the suit of a private sector landlord it is not open to the tenant to contend that article 8 could justify a different order from that which is mandated by the contractual relationship between the parties, at least where, as here, there are legislative provisions which the democratically elected legislature has decided properly balance the competing interests of private sector landlords and residential tenants ... to hold otherwise would involve the Convention effectively being directly enforceable as between private citizens so as to alter their contractual rights and obligations whereas the purpose of the Convention is, as we have mentioned, to protect citizens from having their rights infringed by the state.

8.4.8 Article 9: freedom of thought, conscience and religion

1. Everyone has the right to freedom of thought, conscience and religion; this right includes freedom to change his religion or belief and freedom, either alone or in community with others and in public or in private, to manifest his religion or belief, in worship, teaching, practice and observance.

2. Freedom to manifest one's religion or beliefs shall be subject only to such limitations as are prescribed by law and are necessary in a democratic society in the interests of public safety, for the protection of public order, health or morals, or for the protection of the rights and freedoms of others.

8.4.9 Article 10: freedom of expression

1. Everyone has the right to freedom of expression. This right shall include freedom to hold opinions and to receive and impart information and ideas without interference by public authority and regardless of frontiers. This Article shall not prevent States from requiring the licensing of broadcasting, television or cinema enterprises.
2. The exercise of these freedoms, since it carries duties and responsibilities, may be subject to such formalities, conditions, restriction or penalties as are prescribed by law and are necessary in a democratic society, in the interests of national security, territorial integrity, or public safety, for the prevention of disorder or crime, for the protection of health and morals, for the protection of the reputation or rights of others, for preventing the disclosure of information received in confidence, or for maintaining the authority and impartiality of the judiciary.

This is a qualified Article which has dealt primarily with political and journalistic expression. In all cases the courts must look at the restriction on the freedom of expression, and decide whether or not there is a legitimate aim which has been prescribed by law and whether or not the restriction is proportionate to the legitimate aim.

Freedom of expression was defined in *Handyside v United Kingdom* (1976) 1 EHRR 737:

> Freedom of expression constitutes one of the essential foundations of [a democratic] society, one of the basic conditions for its progress and for the development of every man. Subject to paragraph 2 of Article 10, it is applicable not only to 'information' or 'ideas' that are favourably received and regarded as inoffensive . . . but also to those that offend, shock or disturb that State or any sector of the population. Such are the demands of pluralism, tolerance and broadmindedness without which there is no 'democratic society'.

There is strong protection of journalistic sources, as evidenced by the case of *Goodwin v United Kingdom* (1996) 22 EHRR 123 where the European Court stated:

> Protection of journalistic sources is one of the basic conditions for press freedom. Without such protection, sources may be deterred from assisting the press in informing the public on matters of public interest . . . [An order to disclose] cannot be compatible with Article 10 unless it is justified by an overriding requirement in the public interest.

> **Procedure**
>
> Section 12 of the HRA 1998 specifically sets out the procedural requirements when the court is considering freedom of expression. Specifically section 12 (2) which states that all reasonable steps should be taken to notify the respondent unless there are compelling reasons why they should not be notified. Restrain prior to the trial may not be granted unless it appears that the applicant will be successful at the trial proper and the court must have due regard to the importance of Article 10 where the material complained of appears to be journalistic, literary or artistic and the extent to which the material is available to the public or where it would be in the public interest that the material be published.

The HRA 1998 also incorporates two existing Protocols in UK legislation, the First and the Sixth. They are set out as follows.

8.4.10 Article 1, First Protocol: protection of property

> Every natural or legal person is entitled to the peaceful enjoyment of his possessions. No one shall be deprived of his possessions except in the public interest and subject to the conditions provided for by law and by general principles of international law.

The preceding provisions shall not, however, in any way impair the right of a State to enforce such laws as it deems necessary to control the use of property in accordance with the general interest or to secure the payment of taxes or other contributions or penalties.

EXAMPLE

If a public authority wants to build a road over someone's land, it must have laws in place to support this and there must also be a process in place to ensure the right checks and balances between the public interest in the building of the road and the individual's right to their land (*Howard v United Kingdom* (Application no 10825/84) 16 July 1987, unreported).

8.4.11 Article 2, First Protocol: right to education

No person shall be denied the right to education. In the exercise of any functions which it assumes in relation to education and to teaching, the State shall respect the right of parents to ensure such education and teaching in conformity with their own religious and philosophical convictions.

8.4.12 Article 3, First Protocol: free elections

The High Contracting Parties [the States] undertake to hold free elections at reasonable intervals by secret ballot, under conditions which will ensure the free expression of the opinion of the people in the choice of the legislature.

8.4.13 The Sixth Protocol

This was ratified in 1999 and effectively outlaws the death penalty.

8.5 Human Rights and the Solicitors Regulation Authority Code of Conduct (SRA Code)

Lawyers, law firms and those who work in them serve both clients and society. In serving society, you uphold the **rule of law** and proper administration of justice. In serving clients, you work in partnership with clients, making the client's business your first concern. The core duties set the standards which will meet the needs of both clients and society. Should the principles come into conflict, those which safeguard the wider public interest (such as the rule of law, and public confidences in a trustworthy solicitors' profession and a safe and effective market for regulated legal services) take precedence over an individual client's interests.

Whilst there is no specific responsibility to advise clients of their responsibility to respect human rights obligations in terms of how they act or run their businesses, it is incumbent on solicitors to increase their awareness and their client's awareness in this area in order to fulfil the overall holistic aim of the SRA Code of Conduct.

EXAMPLE

Sophie acts for a company which produces ready meals for various large supermarkets; it becomes apparent that they employ illegal immigrants to work as part of the supply chain and that they are paid less than the living wage. She should have due regard to the Modern Slavery Act 2015 and the potential civil claims her client may face in the County Court.

KEY POINT SUMMARY

- The Human Rights Act 1998 effectively incorporated the European Convention on Human Rights into UK legislation providing individuals with the ability to enforce the rights contained within it in UK courts.
- The Articles provide protection in numerous ways although the rights contained within each Article may be subject to derogations, limitations and qualifications and, where UK legislation is found to be incompatible with those rights, it may require amendment to ensure compatibility in the future.
- In order for a Member State to limit a right contained within the Convention it must be prescribed by law, intended to achieve a legitimate objective and be necessary in a democratic society, that is, proportionate to the ends to be achieved.
- The Act provides a wide range of protections in both the civil and criminal courts and, in representing a client who may have a claim, it would be prudent to note the wealth of case law which exists and in some cases the high degree of specialism required when providing legal advice.

CHAPTER 9
The Equality Act 2010

FUNCTIONING LEGAL KNOWLEDGE

This chapter covers the following functional knowledge required to pass the SQE 1 assessments:

Application of the Equality Act 2010 to legal matters or to a client's interests in relation to:

- protected characteristics
- prohibited conduct
- impact on professional conduct and the provision of legal services

AUTHORITIES UNDERPINNING PRACTICE

The key authorities that underpin this area of practice are listed below. Note that for legislation you are linked to legislation.gov.uk.

Although much of the legislation on this government website is available in its amended form, the incorporation of new amendments into the text of legislation can be delayed. You should refer to legal databases to ensure you are referencing the most up-to-date legislation.

- Equality Act 2010
  http://www.legislation.gov.uk/ukpga/2010/15/contents

9.1 Introduction

The Equality Act 2010 provides protection in the workplace, and in wider society including the provision of legal services and education, against discrimination and other prohibited conduct related to certain listed characteristics which people may possess (referred to as 'protected characteristics'). While there are some exceptions, the aim of the Act was to establish a single approach to discrimination.

This chapter will explore the main principles of discrimination including how they relate to each protected characteristic and from a practical perspective identify how these rights can be enforced to ensure equality is protected. There are exceptions and they are covered where relevant in relation to the relevant protected characteristic.

9.2 Direct discrimination

Section 13(1) provides that:

> (1) A person (A) discriminates against another (B) if, because of a protected characteristic, A treats B less favourably than A treats or would treat others.

Less favourable treatment can take a variety of different forms and there is no need to show that there has been any tangible loss although this may be the case. The less favourable treatment must be *because of* the protected characteristic and it must be less favourable than the treatment of others. Merely treating a person unreasonably will not amount to direct discrimination. If it can be shown, for example, that an employer would have treated all employees similarly badly, then there will have been no 'less favourable treatment' and, therefore, no direct discrimination.

The test to determine whether or not the less favourable treatment was because of the protected characteristic is an objective test of causation. The less favourable treatment does not have to be intended, it may indeed be quite innocent; if the test is satisfied then **direct discrimination** can be made out (*Nagarajan v London Regional Transport* [2000] 1 AC 50; *Amnesty International v Ahmed* [2009] IRLR 884).

It is not enough to show that someone has been less favourably treated in order to show direct discrimination; the treatment must have happened because of a protected characteristic (race, sex etc).

The 'because of' test is quite broad and also includes instances where the less than favourable treatment 'relates to' the protected characteristic, even though it was not done on account of the protected characteristic of the victim or that of any other particular person (*English v Thomas Sanderson Blinds Ltd* [2008] EWCA Civ 1421).

Examples of direct discrimination would be recruiting a man as opposed to a woman on the basis that women do not have the strength to do the job or rejecting a job application under the mistaken belief that the applicant is Asian or a job advert which makes it clear that gypsies need not apply.

9.2.1 **Positive action**

Positive action potentially involves taking into account an individual's membership of a protected group when selecting them for preferential treatment over someone who is not a member of that group, in order to improve equality. This constitutes more favourable treatment due to a protected characteristic and is generally unlawful under the Act.

However, ss158 and 159 of the Act set out exceptions permitting certain defined types of more favourable treatment to reduce under-representation in relation to particular activities, or in relation to recruitment and promotion.

For example, a community centre catering for ethnic people notice that the Pakistani community in the area is under-represented at sessions, and so it runs a separate session for Pakistani people only to encourage their attendance.

9.2.2 **Associative discrimination**

Associative discrimination occurs where a person is treated less favourably because of the protected characteristic (eg sex, race, sexual orientation) of another person, that is, they know or are associated with someone with a certain protected characteristic.

For example, a Muslim shopkeeper who refuses to serve a Muslim woman because she is married to a Christian, or a worker might claim that she had been less than favourably treated on account of the fact that she is the primary carer for her disabled child (and might, eg, have been taking time off to care for her child).

9.3 **Combined discrimination: dual characteristics**

Section 14 of the Act (not yet in force) provides that:

> (1) A person (A) discriminates against another (B) if, because of a combination of two relevant protected characteristics, A treats B less favourably than A treats, or would treat a person who does not share either of those characteristics.

This applies to age; disability; **gender reassignment**; race; religion or belief; sex and sexual orientation.

For example, a recruitment policy in a roofing and cladding business which excludes consideration of men over the age of 60 because they will be more likely to take sick leave due to injury. This would constitute **combined discrimination** in relation to both sex and age.

9.4 Indirect discrimination

Section 19 provides that:

> (1) A person (A) discriminates against another (B) if A applies to B a provision, criterion or practice (PCP) which is discriminatory in relation to a protected characteristic of B's.

For the purposes of subs 1, a provision, criterion or practice is discriminatory in relation to a relevant protected characteristic of B's if:

- A applies, or would apply, it to persons with whom B does not share the characteristic;
- it puts, or would put, persons with whom B shares the characteristic at a particular disadvantage when compared to persons with whom B does not share it;
- it puts, or would put, B at that disadvantage; and
- A cannot show it to be a proportionate means of achieving a legitimate aim.

In comparison to direct discrimination, **indirect discrimination** can be justified if it is a proportionate means of achieving a legitimate aim; direct discrimination cannot be justified, except in the case of age. While direct discrimination expressly requires a causal link between less favourable treatment and a protected characteristic, indirect discrimination does not. Instead it requires a causal link between a PCP applied and the particular disadvantage suffered by the group and the individual claimant (*Essop v Home Office (UK Border Agency)* [2017] UKSC 27).

While direct discrimination aims to achieve equality of treatment, indirect discrimination, in contrast, assumes equality of treatment; the PCP is applied indiscriminately to all. The prohibition against indirect discrimination aims to achieve a level playing field, so that people sharing a particular protected characteristic are not subjected to requirements which many of them could not meet unless these can be justified. It is dealing with hidden barriers which are not easy to anticipate and spot (*Essop v Home Office (UK Border Agency)* [2017] UKSC 27).

In the context of the protected characteristic of sex, an example of indirect discrimination might include an employer specifying that all workers must be at least 1.7 metres tall, which would disqualify more women than men, and therefore be potentially indirectly discriminatory towards women.

9.4.1 Objective justification

Unlike direct discrimination, a potential 'defence' to indirect discrimination is justification: where the person accused of the indirect discrimination can show that the PCP amounting to indirect discrimination was 'a proportionate means of achieving a legitimate aim'.

Proportionately means balancing the degree of impact against the justification offered (*Azmi v Kirklees MBC* [2007] IRLR 484; *City of Oxford Bus Services v Harvey* (UKEAT 0171/18/JOJ)).

EXAMPLE

Linda is forced to leave her job because her employer operates a *practice* that *all* staff must work in a shift pattern which she is unable to comply with because she needs to look after her children at particular times of day, and no allowances are made because of those needs. This puts *women* (who are shown to be more likely to be responsible for childcare) at a *particular disadvantage* when *compared* to those who do not share it, and the employer will have *indirectly discriminated* against Linda *unless the practice is proportionate to achieving a legitimate aim* and therefore can be *justified*; that is, it is *appropriate* and *reasonably* necessary.

9.5 Reasonable adjustments

The duty to make **reasonable adjustments** to eliminate barriers to access and participation for disabled people set out in s20 of the Act comprises three main requirements:

1. Where a provision, criterion or practice places a disabled person at a **substantial disadvantage** in relation to a relevant matter in comparison with a non-disabled person, there is a duty to take reasonable steps to avoid that disadvantage.
2. To take reasonable steps where a physical feature places a disabled person at a substantial disadvantage in relation to a relevant matter in comparison with a non-disabled person to avoid the disadvantage.
3. To take reasonable steps to provide auxiliary aids and services where a disabled person would otherwise be at a substantial disadvantage in comparison with a non-disabled person.

9.5.1 Substantial disadvantage

A substantial disadvantage is one which is more than minor or trivial (s212(1)) and is in comparison to a non-disabled person as opposed to a person whose circumstances are the same as the disabled person's. Whether or not it is reasonable to take a particular step will be an objective test and, once it has been established that a particular step/adjustment is reasonable, then the failure to make it will breach the duty imposed under the Act and be discriminatory. An employer cannot under s20(7) of the Act require a disabled person to pay to any extent the costs in relation to the reasonable adjustment.

Examples of making reasonable adjustments could include changes to the physical layout of an office so that it can be used by a person in a wheelchair; widening doors and lowering light switches and security access; it could also include allowing flexible working hours and putting in place regular breaks thus allowing the worker to be absent for key medical appointments or providing special equipment such as larger computer screens or voice-activated software.

9.6 Harassment

Harassment is unwanted unpleasant conduct which is common to the protected characteristics of age, disability, gender reassignment, race, religion or belief, sex and sexual orientation.

Section 26(1) provides that:

(1) A person (A) **harasses** another (B) if—

- (a) A engages in unwanted conduct related to a relevant protected characteristic, and
- (b) the conduct has the purpose or effect of:
  - (i) violating B's dignity, or
  - (ii) creating an intimidating, hostile, degrading humiliating or offensive environment for B.

9.6.1 Conduct

In deciding whether conduct had the effect of violating the victim's dignity or creating an environment that is intimidating, hostile, degrading, humiliating or offensive to the victim, the perception of the victim, the other circumstances of the case and whether it is reasonable for the conduct to have that effect must be taken into account. A victim's claimed reaction to the unwanted conduct is unlikely to qualify if it is bizarre or hypersensitive. The words or acts relied upon as harassment must be seen in context. The fact that the impact of separate incidents may accumulate and that the work environment created may therefore exceed the sum of the individual episodes should be kept in mind. If the effect on the victim satisfies the reasonableness test, it does not matter that the perpetrator did not intend their unwanted conduct to have that effect.

9.6.2 Sexual harassment

Section 26(2) provides that harassment also occurs where the perpetrator engages in 'unwanted conduct of a sexual nature' and the conduct has the 'purpose or effect' as set out above. Conduct of a sexual nature includes inappropriate physical contact, sexually suggestive remarks and sexually indecent acts in the workplace.

It is no defence to argue that the perpetrator would have behaved just the same to men, or women, or both.

9.6.3 Rejection of, or submission to, harassing behaviour

Section 26(3) goes on to provide that a person will be liable for harassment if (1) they, or any other person, engages in conduct which is unwanted by the victim, and is either of a sexual nature, or related to the protected characteristic of gender reassignment or sex, and (2) that conduct has the 'purpose or effect' as set out above, and (3) the victim either rejects the conduct or submits to it, and (4) because of the victim's rejection or submission to the conduct, that person thereafter treats the victim less favourably than they would treat the victim if the victim had not rejected or submitted to the conduct.

For example, it will be harassment for a manager whose repeated advances to a more junior female employee have been consistently rebuffed subsequently to give the woman a poor performance review because she rejected him.

9.7 Victimisation

Section 27 of the Act affords protection for those who exercise their rights under the Act or assist others to do so. The Act sets out a broad list of '**protected acts**' which includes giving evidence in support of an allegation or making an allegation. Where a person subjects another to a **detriment** because they believe rightly or wrongly that that person has committed or may commit a protected act, this will constitute **victimisation**. The tests for what constitutes a detriment are subjective. It does not require the consideration of how any comparator (ie someone who does not do the protected act) was or may have been treated. It can only include acts which are positively done to another person in response to, for example, supporting a colleague in relation to a complaint of discrimination but also where there is an omission, such as where they are deliberately overlooked for promotion or development opportunities.

9.8 Burden of proof

Section 136 of the Act prescribes a two-stage statutory burden of proof test which applies to all prohibited conduct (ie discrimination) and equality of terms (ie equal pay) claims. A tribunal must consider if there are facts from which it could decide, in the absences of any other explanation that a person (A) has contravened the Act (stage 1). The tribunal must hold that the contravention occurred, unless A shows that A did not contravene the Act (stage 2). Hence, the burden of proof is on the claimant initially to prove facts which could establish that an act of discrimination has occurred. However, at stage 1 the employment tribunal is required to consider all the evidence, not just the claimant's evidence, when deciding whether or not there are facts from which it could decide, in the absence of any other explanation, that the respondent had contravened the act. Where there are facts from which the tribunal can determine whether or not there has been discrimination in relation to a protected characteristic, the burden of proof then shifts to the respondent to show on a balance of probabilities that there has not.

9.9 Public sector equality duty

Section 149(1)–(2) provides that public authorities and those who exercise public functions (listed in Sch 19 of the Act) must have 'due regard' to the need to:

(a) eliminate discrimination, harassment, victimisation, and any other conduct which is prohibited by or under this Act;

(b) advance equality of opportunity between persons who share a relevant protected characteristic and persons who do not share it;

(c) foster good relations between persons who share a relevant protected characteristic and persons who do not share it.

In relation to the second part of the duty (i.e. the duty to advance the equality of opportunity between persons who share a relevant protected characteristic and persons who do not share it) section 149(3) requires public authorities to have due regard to the need to:

(a) remove or minimise disadvantages suffered by persons who share a relevant protected characteristic that are connected to that characteristic;

(b) take steps to meet the needs of the persons who share a relevant protected characteristic that are different from the needs of persons who do not share it;

(c) encourage persons who share a relevant protected characteristic to participate in public life or in any other activity in which participation by such persons is disproportionately low.

The steps involved in meeting the needs of disabled people that are different from the needs of persons who are not disabled include steps to take into account the disabled person's disabilities (s149(4)). In fostering good relations, there should be due regard to the need to tackle prejudice and promote understanding (s149(5)) and it should be noted that s149(6) recognises that the duties may involve treating some persons more favourably than others; but that is not to be taken as permitting conduct which would otherwise be prohibited under the Act.

The relevant protected characteristics for the purposes of this duty are age, disability, gender reassignment, pregnancy and maternity, race, religion or belief, sex and sexual orientation (s149(7)).

Paragraph 484 of the Act Explanatory Notes provides examples of how this duty could operate in practice, for example it could lead a police authority to review its recruitment procedures in order to ensure that they do not intentionally deter applicants from ethnic minorities, with the aim of eliminating unlawful discrimination, or it could lead to a local authority providing training and mentoring schemes for disabled people to help them stand as local councillors in order to advance equality of opportunity for different groups of people who have the same disability, and in particular encouraging participation in public life.

9.10 Protected characteristics

The following are the protected characteristics for the purposes of s4 of the Act:

- age;
- disability;
- gender reassignment;
- marriage and civil partnership;
- race;
- religion or belief;
- sex;
- sexual orientation;
- pregnancy and maternity.

9.10.1 **Age**

Section 5 of the Act states:

(1) In relation to the protected characteristic of age—

(a) a reference to a person who has a particular protected characteristic is a reference to a person of a particular age group.

(b) a reference to persons who share a protected characteristic is a reference to persons of the same age group.

(2) A reference to an age group is a reference to a group of persons defined by reference to age, whether by reference to a particular age or range of ages.

The Act provides that you must not be discriminated against because you either are (or are not) a certain age or in a certain age group, such as the over-20s, or because you are (or are not) a specific age or in a specific age group; or because you are associated with someone of a specific age or age group. The most obvious form of age discrimination will adversely affect those who are older, but the protection applies in relation to inequality of treatment with regard to any age, including the young. For example, a job recruitment exercise which specifies applicants must have a certain number of years' experience may indirectly discriminate against younger applicants unless that requirement is justified.

9.10.1.1 Direct age discrimination

To constitute age discrimination (s13(1)) the offending less favourable treatment must be done 'because of age'. This covers situations where the behaviour is done because of the age of the victim, but also situations where the behaviour is done because of the age of a third party, for example the victim's child or partner (associative discrimination), and situations where the discriminator thought (incorrectly) that someone (the victim or a third party) was of a particular age.

Unlike other protected characteristics (sex, race etc) direct age discrimination can be justified, that is, if it can be shown that the action concerning the person is a proportionate means of achieving a legitimate aim (s13(2)). A legitimate aim may be a good business reason, but cost alone is unlikely to be considered sufficient. The actions must be proportionate, appropriate and necessary. An employer must balance its business needs against the discriminatory effect on affected employees. Proving 'a proportionate means of achieving a legitimate aim' to a tribunal can be difficult.

For example, where it was held to be direct age discrimination to take duties away from a showroom manager because it was 'too much responsibility' for someone who was 'only 21', there was no legitimate aim for this less favourable treatment (*Shanks v Heat Source Solutions Ltd*, Case No 4103660/2019). Equally, firing a 60-year-old woman because she would not be a 'good fit' in a 'younger team' was also direct age discrimination with no objective justification (*Winschief v SRS Realisations 2017 Ltd*, Case No 1402539/2018).

However, there may be situations in the workplace where direct age discrimination may be lawful, for example *Lynch v Harkers Transport Ltd*, Case No 2501608/2018, where it was held that the aim of the policy was to comply with the requirements of the Road Traffic Act that drivers be insured and this was objectively justified as a proportionate means of achieving a legitimate aim.

As well as direct age discrimination the Act, prohibits:

- Indirect age discrimination, unless the PCP is a proportionate means of achieving a legitimate aim (see **9.4**)
- For example, a gym manager, tells employees that two more staff are needed to work on reception and adds that anyone interested needs to look 'fit and enthusiastic' as the gym is trying to persuade more young people to join. The requirements may be indirectly discriminatory unless it can be objectively justified.
- Age harassment (including because of the age of someone associated with the victim, or where the harasser perceives the victim to be in a relevant age group) (eg a manager regularly tells a 60-year-old IT designer in front of other staff that he is 'out of touch' and that the company needs 'young ideas'.
- Victimisation (eg a woman is dismissed because she suggests to her manager that he did not promote her because she is over 50).

9.10.1.2 When is it lawful to be treated differently due to age?

- When there is an occupational requirement—for example, where the BBC is making a drama about primary school children, belonging to a younger age group will be essential.
- Where an employer has a **positive action** development programme to increase the number of women in leadership roles.
- Where there is a compulsory retirement age which can be objectively justified, for example construction work.
- Where one of the exceptions in the Act applies which allows organisations to provide different treatment in employment or services based on age.
- Age-related concession or benefits, for example reduced cinema ticket prices or benefits based on length of service.
- Provision of insurance and financial services.
- National minimum wage.
- Redundancy and redundancy pay.

EXAMPLE

Robert, 57, is employed as a branch sales manager. The post of regional sales manager became vacant and he applied for it. Given his 20 plus years of service and experience Robert considers himself to be a very strong candidate. At the interview Robert is asked whether he feels he would be able to cope at his age with the travelling that would be involved in the post and the pressure of the job. Robert assures the interviewer that he is fit and healthy and well able to cope with the requirements of the post. Robert is not offered the role; the job is given to Brian who is 10 years younger and has less experience than Robert. In failing to appoint Robert to the regional sales manager post the company treated him less favourably than Brian solely because of his age, which is unlawful age discrimination contrary to s13(1) of the Act.

9.10.2 **Disability**

Section 6 of the Act states that:

A person (P) has a disability if—

(a) P has a mental or physical **impairment**, and

(b) the impairment has a substantial and long-term adverse effect on P's ability to carry out normal day-to-day activities.

'Non-disabled' persons are protected from disability discrimination and harassment only where they are perceived to have a disability or are associated with a disabled person (Case C-303/06, *Colman v Attridge Law*, EU:C:2008:415).

Statutory guidance on matters to be taken into account in determining questions relating to the definition of disability is also provided in the 'Equality Act 2010 Guidance'. Case law also provides further guidance on many specific issues that may be involved in determining whether there is a disability

9.10.2.1 Impairment

Impairment is given its ordinary and natural meaning. This can include physical or mental impairment and there is no requirement that the mental impairment be clinically recognised by the Act. The focus of the Act is the effect of the impairment as opposed to the cause, although in order to establish effect evidence of the cause may be required.

9.10.2.2 Long-term effect

This is set out in Sch 1, Pt 1, para 2 to the Act. The effect of an impairment is **long term** if it has lasted, or is likely to last, for at least 12 months or is likely to last for the rest of the person's life. Where the impairment has ceased but is likely to reoccur, it is to be treated as continuing. The duration of the effects of two consecutive but different impairments each lasting less than 12 months can be aggregated in order to decide whether or not they were long term, provided the second impairment derived from the first.

9.10.2.3 Recurring conditions

Where an impairment has in the past had a substantial adverse effect but has ceased to do so, it will be treated as continuing to have that effect if that effect is likely to recur even where there are episodic effects of less than 12 months. It is the 'substantial adverse effect' which must be likely to recur as opposed to the impairment and it need not last 12 months. This means that episodic conditions including epilepsy, certain types of depression and rheumatoid arthritis can qualify as a disability if they are likely to recur, even though the individual was not suffering substantial adverse effects at the time of the alleged discrimination.

In *Swift v CC of Wiltshire* [2004] UKEAT 0484/03/1802, [2004] IRLR 540, the Employment Appeals Tribunal (EAT) set out the approach to be taken in **recurring conditions** cases:

1. Was there at some stage an impairment?
2. Did that impairment have a substantial adverse effect on the person's ability to carry out normal day-to-day activities?
3. Did the impairment cease to have a substantial adverse effect on normal day-to-day activities, and if so, when?
4. What was the substantial adverse effect?
5. Is the same substantial adverse effect likely to recur?

9.10.2.4 Substantial adverse effect

This is something which is more than a minor or trivial effect (s212(1)). The impairment may not of itself prevent someone from carrying out normal day-to-day activities but its effect could do so—the test being a comparison between the way the person would have normally carried out those activities as opposed to how they carry them out with the impairment. Medical treatment or any other 'corrective measure' which allows a person to carry out those day-to-day activities is to be disregarded, that is, what must be measured is whether or not it is likely (ie could well happen) that if the treatment were stopped or the corrective measure taken away, the impairment would have a substantial adverse effect.

9.10.2.5 Normal day-to-day activities

These can include normal activities which are carried out by the majority of people on a day-to-day basis, such as walking, shopping, driving to work, preparing and eating food. According to the CJEU in Case C-13/05, *Chacon Navas v Euest Colectividades SA* [2007] All ER (EC) 59 the question that must be asked is whether the impairment 'hinders the full and effective participation of the person concerned in professional life over a long period of time'.

9.10.2.6 Excluded impairments

The Equality Act 2010 (Disability) Regulations 2010 (SI 2010/2128) set out certain exclusions, that is, impairments that are excluded from the definition of disability:

- addiction to or dependency on alcohol, nicotine or any other substance;
- hay fever;
- tendency to set fires;
- tendency to steal;
- tendency towards physical or sexual abuse of other persons;
- exhibitionism;
- voyeurism.

Under s13 of the Act a person directly discriminates against another person if they treat them less favourably because of a disability than they would treat others without a disability. As with other forms of direct discrimination, there will always need to be a comparison with how another or others would be treated, although the comparator may sometimes be a hypothetical rather than a real one.

9.10.2.7 Discrimination arising from disability

Section 15 of the Act provides that:

(1) A person (A) discriminates against a disabled person (B) if—

(a) A treats B unfavourably because of something arising in consequence of B's disability, and

(b) A cannot show that the treatment is a proportionate means of achieving a legitimate aim.

This does not apply where A shows that they did not know and could not reasonably have been expected to know that B had a disability.

EXAMPLE

Jonah, an employee, is disciplined for losing their temper at work. The loss of temper is out of character and arose from severe pain caused by cancer. Jonah was treated unfavourably as a result of something arising from, or as a consequence of, their disability, and therefore suffered discrimination arising from their disability. However the employer, (or other person liable) may escape liability if they can justify the treatment, that is, show the treatment was a proportionate means of achieving a legitimate aim.

The duty to make reasonable adjustments under s20 of the Act applies where a disabled person is put at a substantial disadvantage in comparison with persons who are not disabled by a provision, criterion or practice, a 'physical feature' or a failure to provide an 'auxiliary aid'.

EXAMPLE

Emily works as a tennis coach at Lodgemoor Tennis Club and was diagnosed two years ago with osteoarthritis which can give her pain in her knees although it does not prevent her from being able to carry out her job as a tennis coach. She tells you that she knows the head coaches at the club are embarrassed by the sometimes awkward gait she has due to the pain and try to keep her away from clients. She requested that her employer reduce her hours to 25 hours per week predominantly on a Thursday and Friday which were her busiest days with clients; this would allow her to manage the pain and also work with enough clients to keep her income at a manageable level. Her employer reduced her hours to 20 hours per week predominantly on a Sunday and Monday which are the quietest times whilst not requiring other tennis coaches employed there to work on those days. No business reasons were provided to Emily and she now feels that she may have to resign.

Emily has a disability. Osteoarthritis is a physical impairment which has a substantial and long-term adverse effect on her ability to carry out her normal day-to-day activities under s6 of the Act. Her disability does not prevent her from doing her job, but it does have a substantial long-term effect on how she does her job.

If Emily was treated less favourably because of her disability than her employer would have treated an employee without a disability she will have a claim for **direct disability discrimination** and she would be entitled to compensation for injury to feelings and loss of future income if she resigned.

Emily's employer did not allow Emily to reduce her working hours to 25 hours per week predominantly on a Thursday or Friday. In terms of the reasonable adjustments made by her employers, there were no business reasons provided for why Emily was not allowed to work 25 hours a week and why it should be on the two quietest days of the week as opposed to Thursday and Friday as requested. Her employers also submitted her to less than favourable treatment by giving her hours on the quietest days of the week when other coaches, who did not suffer a disability, were not required to work on those days.

9.10.3 Gender reassignment

Section 7(1) of the Act provides that:

> (1) A person has the protected characteristic of gender reassignment if the person is proposing to undergo, is undergoing or has undergone a process (or part of a process) for the purpose of reassigning the person's sex by changing physiological or other attributes of sex.

'Proposing' to includes attending initial gender reassignment counselling sessions, dressing in such a way which indicates an intention to change their gender or stating their intention to undergo such a change. There is no requirement that the process must be undertaken under medical supervision, or for the individual to have obtained a gender recognition certificate. A person does not need to undergo any medical procedures (eg hormonal treatment or surgical procedure) or to have received any medical diagnosis in order to be protected by the Act. They must simply be presenting permanently in a different binary gender (ie man or woman) to the one they were assigned at birth.

The employment tribunal in *Taylor v Landrover*, Case No 1304471/2018, has held that gender-fluid and non-binary individuals are protected by the Act. However, as a first instance tribunal decision it has no binding authority and some commentators have questioned the decision.

Section 16 of the Act contains a specific provision in relation to absences from work because of 'gender reassignment' and stipulates that a person must be treated no less favourably in relation to that type of sickness absence than ordinary sickness absence unless it is reasonable to do so.

EXAMPLE

Daniela applies for a job in a large retail company, Abco Ltd, and informed them that she would prefer to be known as Daniela as opposed to her birth name Daniel. Abco agreed although they were clear that her pay slip would have to record her birth name. Due to an error, her birth name was used on both her name badge, records and pay slip. Daniela was consistently misgendered by one colleague. Another member of staff sprayed air freshener near Daniela and one key staff member told her that she would pray for her as she had the devil in her. Daniela made formal complaints to her line manager which he investigated but reported no formal outcome or none which was conveyed to Daniela. Daniela wants to hand in her notice but has no other means of paying her rent so is reluctant to do so.

Gender reassignment is a protected characteristic under the Act. Daniela has been discriminated against by her colleagues and her line manager because of her gender reassignment. The treatment she received from her line manager was less favourable because of the gender reassignment and was intended and was therefore direct discrimination.

The incident with the works system and her name badge would not be direct discrimination as the process used to input her details was no different to the process used for any other employee.

The comments and remarks made by her colleagues constituted harassment contrary to s26 of the Act, being unwanted conduct related to gender reassignment which had the purpose and effect of violating the claimant's dignity and creating an intimidating, hostile, degrading, humiliating or offensive environment for the claimant.

9.10.4 Marriage and civil partnership

Section 8(1) of the Act provides that:

> (1) A person has the protected characteristic of marriage and civil partnership if the person is married or is a civil partner.

Marriage includes same-sex couples and refers to a person who is legally married under the Marriage Act 1949. Since December 2019, under the Civil Partnership (Opposite Sex Couples) Regulations 2019, SI 2019/1458, an opposite-sex couple can form a civil partnership in England and Wales, and are therefore treated in law (with a few exceptions) in the same way as a same-sex couple who are in a civil partnership. Those who are single, engaged to be married, co-habitees, divorced or those whose civil partnerships has been dissolved are not afforded protection by the Act.

It is direct discrimination to treat a married person less favourably than they would if they were single, but it is not unlawful to discriminate against a person because they are single—the protection is one-way. Likewise, no claim of indirect discrimination in relation to the protected characteristic of marriage or civil partnership can be brought by someone who is single, divorced, engaged etc.

9.10.5 **Race**

Section 9(1) of the Act covers the protected characteristic of race and provides that:

(1) Race includes—

(a) colour;

(b) nationality;

(c) ethnic or national origin.

9.10.5.1 Meaning of race

Any reference in the Act to a person who has the protected characteristic of race means a person of a particular 'racial group', and people who share a protected characteristic means persons of the same 'racial group'. A particular 'racial group' may comprise two or more distinct racial groups.

9.10.5.2 Ethnic origins

An ethnic group has a distinct and separate community as a result of certain characteristics. There must be a long-shared history and it must have a cultural tradition of its own. Other factors to take into consideration could be common language, literature, religion, geographical descent or a sense of being a minority or an oppressed or dominant group (*Mandla v Dowell Lee* [1983] 2 AC 548). Ethnic origins is a wide and flexible phrase and covers questions of descent, and therefore at least some situations of caste are likely to fall within that phrase (*Chandok v Tirkey* [2014] UKEAT/0190/14/KN).

9.10.5.3 National origins

This describes a person's connection by birth with a nation (*Ealing LBC v Race Relations Board* [1972] AC 342) and is separate to the concept of nationality which is concerned with the membership of a particular nation. Therefore, a person could be of Canadian national origin but be a citizen of the UK.

The Scots and the English, though not of different ethnic origins or nationality, are of different national origins and therefore the Act can apply to alleged discrimination against one group or the other—although neither the English nor the Scots as racial groups have the necessary distinctiveness or community (by virtue of certain characteristics derived from their origins alone), each possess a cohesiveness derived largely (although not exclusively) from their respective history and geography and are therefore racial groups measured by their separate and distinct national origins (*BBC Scotland v Souster* (2000) Scots CS 308)).

9.10.5.4 Types of race discrimination

Race discrimination can be direct, indirect, harassment or victimisation. An example of indirect race discrimination might be an employer specifying all workers must have blonde hair, which would disqualify more non-Caucasian than Caucasian workers.

9.10.6 **Religion or belief**

Section 10(1) and (2) of the Act covers the protected characteristic of religion or belief and provides that:

(1) Religion means any religion and a reference to religion includes a reference to a lack of religion.

(2) Belief means any religious or philosophical belief and a reference to belief includes a reference to a lack of belief.

9.10.6.1 Meaning of religion

This is not explicitly defined and, in many cases, will be obvious—for example, Christianity, Judaism, Sikhism etc. A religion may not be well known but, providing it has a clear structure and belief system, it is protected by the Act.

9.10.6.2 Meaning of belief

This can take the shape of a religious belief which, following *Eweida v United Kingdom* [2013] ECHR 37, [2013] IRLR 231, will be a 'manifestation' if it is 'intimately linked to the religion or belief' or a philosophical belief. Following *Grainger v Nicholson* [2009] UKEAT/0219/09/ZT, the 'Grainger criteria' must:

1. be genuinely held;
2. be a belief and not an opinion or viewpoint based on current information;
3. be a belief as to a weighty and substantial aspect of human life and behaviour;
4. attain a certain level of cogency, seriousness, cohesion and importance;
5. be worthy of respect in a democratic society, not be incompatible with human dignity and not conflict with the fundamental rights of others.

Gender-critical beliefs and gender identity beliefs are protected philosophical beliefs (*Forstater v CDG Europe* [2021] IRLR 706.

EXAMPLE

Maria works for a local pharmacy and has done so for three years. She made a request to work a late shift so that she could be free to celebrate All Hallows Eve as she is a practising Wiccan. Whilst the request was granted, her employer commented that Halloween was the work of the devil and non-Christian. Maria says that she was made to feel that there was something wrong with her. Two days after this incident, she was dismissed on the grounds that her employer needed to cut costs due to a downturn in sales even though two male colleagues were retained.

Maria has a potential claim for sex discrimination as she was treated differently from a comparable employee as the downturn in sales applied equally to her male colleagues. Equally, she would have a claim of direct discrimination on the grounds of religion and belief. The language used by her employer was a detriment within the meaning of s39(2)(d) of the Act. She had also received less favourable treatment in relation to her dismissal given that others had retained their employment and, given the timing of the reaction to her request and the dismissal, she would satisfy the burden of proof as set out in s136 of the Act.

9.10.7 **Sex**

Section 11 of the Act covers the protected characteristic of sex and provides that:

(a) a reference to a person who has a protected characteristic is a reference to a man or a woman;

(b) a reference to persons who share a protected characteristic is a reference to persons of the same sex.

This applies to men and women of any age including boys and girls. Women can share this characteristic with other women and men with other men.

Sex discrimination can be found to be direct, indirect, harassment or victimisation. Requiring female employees to use male designated toilet facilities which put women at risk of seeing men using urinals when accessing the toilets, has been found to be direct sex discrimination as female employees were treated less favourably than male employees (*East Shilton Town Council v Miller* [2023] EAT 5). In *Commissioner of Police of the Metropolis v Denby* [2017] UKEAT 0314/16/2410, the claimant, a male police officer, was placed under a formal criminal investigation by the Department for Professional Standards (DPS) in comparison to a female officer who was equally under investigation for similar misconduct yet was dealt with locally and not the subject of a formal DPS procedure. The Court of Appeal upheld the finding of both sex discrimination and victimisation.

9.10.8 **Sexual orientation**

Section 12 provides that:

(1) Sexual orientation means a person's sexual orientation towards—

(a) persons of the same sex;

(b) persons of the opposite sex, or

(c) persons of the same or opposite sex (ie either sex).

Discrimination of this type would normally be because someone is lesbian, gay, bisexual or heterosexual. This does not include trans people who are protected through gender reassignment unless the discrimination is because of their sexual orientation.

If a lesbian woman is treated less favourably than a gay man, that may be sex discrimination but not discrimination on the grounds of sexual orientation (*Pearce v Governing Body of Mayfield School; MacDonald v Advocate General for Scotland* [2003] UKHL 34).

Sexual orientation discrimination can be direct, indirect, victimisation or harassment. For example, requiring foster carers to abstain from homosexual behaviour would be indirect sexual orientation discrimination.

In the case of *Hubble v Brooks*, Case No 1600381/05, Mr Brooks refused to employ Mr Hubble to work in his bar in a small Welsh village. He stated there was 'no way' he could employ a gay couple and he would lose a lot of money in the pub. He pointed out that he was not prejudiced against gays but that it would severely impact his business. This was held to be a clear case of direct discrimination due to sexual orientation. The exclusion by a manager of a gay employee from team social events would amount to direct sexual orientation discrimination contrary to s13(1).

Excluding a gay employee from a family fun day because they do not have children would be indirect discrimination because of sexual orientation contrary to s19 of the Act. The requirement that employees who attend the occasion must have children is a provision criteria or practice which puts a gay man at a disadvantage when compared with non-gay men and which would likely not be a proportionate means of achieving a legitimate aim.

9.10.9 **Pregnancy and maternity**

Sections 17 (non-work cases) and 18 (work cases) of the Act prohibit discrimination against women because of their pregnancy, pregnancy-related illness or maternity. This includes discrimination due to a current or previous pregnancy, because the woman has given birth or because she is breastfeeding. In relation to non-work cases, that is, services, premises, education and associations, this prohibition applies for 26 weeks from when the woman gave birth; outside this, a woman may be protected by the sex discrimination provisions. In relation to work cases, the Act defines a period called the 'protected period' which starts when the pregnancy begins and ends at the end of the additional leave period or when she returns to work after the pregnancy if that is earlier for those women with the right to ordinary and additional maternity leave, or 2 weeks after the end of the pregnancy if she is not employed. Note that the protected period for the purposes of the Act is different from the period during which an employee is protected from redundancy. There is no requirement to consider any form of comparator to establish discrimination on the grounds of pregnancy or maternity (*Commissioner of the City of London Police v Geldart*, UKEAT/0032/19/RN). There is no possibility of associative discrimination claims or claims on the basis of perception being made under the pregnancy and maternity discrimination provision.

9.11 Professional conduct and the provision of legal services

CONDUCT POINT

Under the SRA Code of Conduct, solicitors must have regard to SRA Principle 6 and its related guidance which states that you should act in a way that encourages equality, diversity, and inclusion. SRA guidance equally highlights the importance of Principle 2 which requires you to act in a way that upholds public trust and confidence in the solicitors' profession and in legal services provided by authorised persons. The following resources should be referred to:

- SRA Code of Conduct for Firms
- SRA Code of Conduct for Solicitors, RELs and RFLs
- SRA Principles
- SRA I Guidance: The SRA's approach to equality, diversity and inclusion I Solicitors Regulation Authority
- SRA I Case study: Unfair discrimination I Solicitors Regulation Authority
- SRA I Case study: Sexual harassment I Solicitors Regulation Authority

9.11.1 Provision of legal services as a business

The Act applies whether you practise as a sole practitioner or in a solicitors' firm or in an Alternative Business Structure providing legal services. As both a provider of legal services to your clients and as an employer, you are under a duty to ensure compliance with the Act. Detailed guidance on what this means for you can be found from:

- The Equality and Human Rights Commission website and the Solicitors' Regulation Authority website
- The Law Society.

KEY POINT SUMMARY

- There are nine protected characteristics contained within the Equality Act 2010, some which contain specific exceptions and are interpreted in different ways in the context of the Act.
- There are multiple different types of conduct prohibited under the Equality Act 2010, including direct and indirect discrimination, harassment and victimisation.
- The claims will tend to arise in the context of employment law and practice on the basis of unfair dismissal, constructive dismissal or redundancy and can result in damages being awarded for loss of current and future earnings and/or for injury to feelings.
- The duties and obligations set out in the Act are relevant not only when advising clients on the merits of a particular claim but also to how a solicitor operates as a business entity. This can be evidenced through an equality and diversity policy which effectively embeds the Act into the day-to-day strategic and operational running of the business.

CHAPTER 10
EU Law in the UK Constitution

FUNCTIONING LEGAL KNOWLEDGE

This chapter covers the following functional knowledge required to pass the SQE 1 assessments:

The place of EU law in the UK constitution:

- sources of assimilated law
- categories/status/interpretation of assimilated law
- modification/withdrawal of assimilated law

Parliamentary sovereignty and assimilated law

AUTHORITIES UNDERPINNING PRACTICE

The key authorities that underpin this area of practice are listed below. Note that for legislation you are linked to legislation.gov.uk.

Although much of the legislation on this government website is available in its amended form, the incorporation of new amendments into the text of legislation can be delayed. You should refer to legal databases to ensure you are referencing the most up-to-date legislation.

- European Union (Notification of Withdrawal) Act 2017
  https://www.legislation.gov.uk/ukpga/2017/9/contents/enacted
- European Union (Withdrawal) Act 2018
  https://www.legislation.gov.uk/ukpga/2018/16/contents
- European Union (Withdrawal Agreement) Act 2020
  https://www.legislation.gov.uk/ukpga/2020/1/contents/enacted
- European Union (Future Relationship) Act 2020
  https://www.legislation.gov.uk/ukpga/2020/29/enacted/data.htm
- Retained EU Law (Revocation and Reform) Act 2023
  https://www.legislation.gov.uk/ukpga/2023/28/enacted

10.1 Introduction

This chapter provides an overview of the history of the EU, the UK's membership of the EU over 47 years and the legal relationship between the law of the EU and the UK post-Brexit.

10.1.1 The origins of the EU

Incessant conflict between the major European nations in the late 19th century and the first half of the 20th century meant that a new form of cooperation between states had to be found in order to create and maintain lasting peace on the European continent. After the Second World War, the threat of Soviet expansion from the east of Europe led to the creation of the North Atlantic Treaty Organisation (NATO) and a desire for European mutual interdependence.

Two French statesmen, Jean Monnet and Robert Schuman, drew up plans for a French–German pact for joint coal and steel production. This cooperative project was open to other European nations and was controlled and supervised by an independent authority. The plan would not only prevent France and Germany from going to war with each other again but would also provide the basis for further cooperation in other sectors which would secure economic prosperity. The Treaty of Paris 1951 created the European Coal and Steel Community. The success of this project directly led to the creation of the specialist European Atomic Energy Community (EURATOM) and the general European Economic Community (EEC) in 1957. This latter community created the idea of the single market and the customs union. Under these two concepts, the countries of the EU operate as a single legal space that guarantees the free movement of goods, people, services, establishment and capital. Over the past six decades, the areas of legal competence of the EU have expanded as well as its geographical extent to include 27 countries in Europe. The EU is a unique legal organisation.

It is 'supranational' or 'above the nation state', in the sense that the system is not a traditional intergovernmental system. Rather, the creation of the European Commission, as an independent executive authority, meant that it was a unique legal system that had power over and above that of the nations that created it. The Member States, upon accession, accepted the concept that not only did they accept mutual obligations but had voluntarily limited their own sovereign rights and transferred them to independent institutions.

10.1.2 The structure and nature of EU law

As presently constituted, the founding constitutional elements of the EU are set out in the Treaty on the Functioning of the European Union (TFEU), the Treaty on European Union (TEU) and the EU's Charter of Fundamental Rights. Under these three Treaties, the EU comprises seven institutions and numerous bodies and agencies. The seven institutions are the European Commission, the European Council, the Council of the European Union, the Court of Justice of the European Union (CJEU), the European Parliament, the Court of Auditors and the European Central Bank. These institutions work together to ensure that the EU's aims and objectives are progressively achieved.

The EU is able to pass a range of secondary legislation, the most important being **Regulations**, **Directives** and Decisions (and Art 288 TFEU).

Regulations are of general application, are binding in their entirety and are directly applicable in all Member States. The concept of direct applicability means that these secondary laws become automatically part of the law of the Member States after being passed at the EU level. These laws bind the Member States, the EU institutions and EU citizens and companies.

Directives are also legally binding as a consequence of EU law; however, they are only binding on the Member States to which they are addressed but give discretion to the Member States as to how they achieve that result. Typically, a Directive will give the Member States a number of years to arrange for domestic law to be promulgated to give effect to the terms of the Directive.

The legality of EU action and action of the Member States is guaranteed by the Court of Justice of the European Union. In determining cases before it, the Court of Justice may draw on general principles of EU law. Thus, the sources of EU law are recognised as being the primary legislation of the EU, that is the founding Treaties, secondary legislation created by the EU, the case law of the Court of Justice and the general principles of EU law.

International treaties are legal agreements or contracts between states that are binding between them. Generally, international treaties do not generate rights for the citizens of those states that can be enforced and applied in the domestic courts of the states. However, the EU legal order is a unique legal system (in Latin, *sui generis*) that does create legal rights for citizens of the EU that are enforceable in the national courts of the Member States and in the Court of Justice. Such provisions are known as directly effective EU law. EU law that is sufficiently clear and unambiguous in its terms, unconditional, that is, not subject to any qualifications, can take effect without the need for implementing or discretionary measures by the Member States or EU institutions. This feature of EU law was first set out in Case C-26/62, *Van Gend en Loos*, EU:C:1963:1.

EXAMPLE

Van Gend en Loos

Van Gend en Loos was a Dutch transport company which regularly imported the chemical urea formaldehyde into the Netherlands from Germany. The original version of the EEC Treaty provided for a transitional period for the progressive reduction and thereafter total abolition of customs duties between the Member States of the EEC. The transition period lasted for a decade between 1958 and 1968. When the Netherlands joined the EEC in 1957, Dutch customs law classified urea formaldehyde as attracting a customs duty of 3% of the value of the chemical. The Dutch rules on the classification of products for customs were altered in the early 1960s. The net effect of this rule change was that urea formaldehyde was now classified in a higher customs banding such that it attracted a customs duty of 8% of the value of the chemical. Van Gend en Loos wished to challenge this Dutch law as being against the terms of the EEC Treaty. The EEC Treaty allowed questions of EEC law raised in national courts to be sent to the European Court of Justice (ECJ) for determination. The Dutch customs authorities and Dutch government argued that the EEC Treaty did not give individuals the right to bring an action on the grounds of infringement of the Treaty. The Court of Justice disagreed, stating that it was necessary to interpret the section of the EEC Treaty in light of the spirit, general scheme and wording of the EEC Treaty. The ECJ stated that the EEC Treaty was more than an international agreement that only created obligations between states. The EEC Treaty had established a common market and institutions that had been given powers to legislate not only for its Member States but also for individuals. As the ECJ explained:

> the Community constitutes a new legal order of international law for the benefit of which the states have limited their sovereign rights, albeit within limited fields and the subjects of which comprise not only Member States but also their nationals. Independently of the legislation of the Member States, Community law therefore not only imposes obligations on individuals but is also intended to confer on them rights that become part of their legal heritage.

Thus, citizens of the Member States were entitled to bring legal actions to challenge the compatibility of Member State law with the law of the EEC. The EEC Treaty provisions on customs duties were directly effective, granting citizens of the Member States rights that were enforceable in the domestic courts of the Member States and were to be given preference over inconsistent domestic law.

Sovereign states, precisely because they are sovereign, are at liberty to unilaterally take legislative and direct action to frustrate or avoid the terms of international law agreements that they have voluntarily entered into. In order to avoid this fate for provisions of European law, the ECJ asserted, in Case C-6/64, *Costa v Enel*, EU:C:1964:66 that the unique nature of the EU meant that it was 'impossible for the States . . . to accord precedence to a unilateral and subsequent measure over a legal system accepted by them on the basis of reciprocity'.

Further, the Court stated that:

> the law stemming from the Treaty, an independent source of law, could not, because of its special and original nature, be overridden by domestic legal provisions, however framed, without being deprived of its character as Community law and without the legal basis of the Community itself being called into question.

Thus, the ECJ developed the concept of **supremacy** of EU law over inconsistent domestic law. In Case C-106/77, *Simmenthal*, EU:C:1978:49, the ECJ went a stage further, declaring that a national court must:

> . . . apply [*sic*] Union law in its entirety . . . and must accordingly set aside any provision of national law which may conflict with it, whether prior or subsequent to the Union rule.

A fundamental overriding concern of the EU is that EU law is practical and effective within the Member States of the EU. To this end, the ECJ has identified further unique features of EU law.

For example, in the event of non-implementation of a Directive by a Member State, the citizens and corporations of that state are in a less favourable position than the citizens and corporations of the rest of the EU since they have been deprived of their EU law rights because of the failures of their state. Given the need to ensure the effectiveness and practical usefulness of EU law, the ECJ held that once the deadline for implementation of a Directive had passed, a Directive may generate directly effective rights, exercisable against the state, public organisations or 'emanations of the state'. However, in the situation of private organisations requiring to comply with a Directive, direct effect cannot arise. Thus, only vertical direct effect can arise in relation to unimplemented Directives.

More widely, a Directive, and now EU law generally, imposes an interpretative obligation on the courts of the Member States to interpret domestic law in accordance with the provisions of EU law. This was first set out in Case C-106/89, *Marleasing*, EU:C:1990:395 and is known as the concept of indirect effect.

Member States of the EU may perceive certain advantages to non-compliance with EU law obligations, particularly financial cost savings. To avoid this situation, the ECJ developed the concept of state liability. Originally, this principle only applied to the failure of a Member State to comply with the terms of an EU Directive, however the principle was extended to include all instances of non-compliance with EU law obligations in the seminal case of *Brasserie/Factortame* (Joined Cases C-46/93 and C-48/93, EU:C:1996:79). Under this case, damages would be payable to individuals and corporations where a Member State fails to comply with EU law where that EU law was intended to confer rights upon those natural and legal persons, the breach of EU law was sufficiently serious and there was a direct causal link between the breach and the damage sustained by the individuals.

To further ensure the effectiveness of EU law in the Member States, the EU legal system operates a system of preliminary references under Art 267 TFEU whereby national courts and tribunals can refer questions of EU law to the ECJ to assist them in their adjudication of legal disputes before them and Member States are subject to enforcement action by the European Commission and ultimately before the ECJ for non-compliance with EU Treaty obligations (Arts 258–260 TFEU).

10.2 The UK, the EU and Brexit

The economic success of the 'European' project saw a number of European states wish to join the original six. The UK first sought to join the EEC in the early 1960s but was serially rebuffed by the French President de Gaulle. The UK was finally granted accession to the EEC along with Ireland and Denmark in 1973. The negotiations on accession were tortuous, particularly for the UK, because the European legal system is a system created by international legal agreement and this agreement was not going to be threatened by new applicant states degrading the scope and effect of European law in the Member States. Thus, the original six negotiated hard to ensure that the new Member States agreed to uphold the *effet utile* (French for useful effect) of European law in their territories. A key requirement of EU law is that all Member States, both original and new, must agree to comply with the *acquis communautaire*; that is, the entire accumulated body of EU law that exists at the time of its accession and thereafter to continue to follow the *acquis* as it evolves and expands in the future. Therefore, membership of the EU requires its Member States to dynamically adhere to EU law. The UK, like any other Member State, had to agree to accord with EU law dynamically. This obligation sits uneasily with the concept of **parliamentary sovereignty** (see **Chapters 2** and **4**). The solution was found in s2 of the European Communities Act 1972, the UK Act of Parliament taking the UK into the EEC. In particular, subs (1) of that section provided that:

> All such rights, powers, liabilities, obligations and restrictions from time to time created or arising by or under the Treaties, and all such remedies and procedures from time to time provided for by or under the Treaties, as in accordance with the Treaties are without further enactment to be given legal effect or used in the United Kingdom shall be recognised and available in law, and be enforced, allowed and followed accordingly . . .

This provision allowed for directly effective and directly applicable EU law to have legal effect in the UK and, over time, for further future concepts of EU law to be given effect in the UK. The reception of EU law into the UK legal system by the 1972 Act also meant that the jurisprudence of the ECJ and therefore its interpretation of EU law became an integral part of UK law such that EU law had to be accorded supremacy over inconsistent UK law under the *Costa v ENEL* doctrine. Subsection (2) of s2 of the 1972 Act granted UK ministers the power to make secondary legislation to give effect to EU law such as EU Directives. Section 3 of the 1972 Act also provided that judicial notice was to be taken of EU law by UK courts and that questions of EU law were to be treated by UK judges as questions of law and not fact.

Thus, EU law was given a pre-eminent place in the UK legal system by the terms of the 1972 Act. Indeed, the 1972 Act has been described as the conduit through which EU law flowed into the UK legal system and means EU law was treated as an independent and overriding source of domestic law (*Miller 1* (*R (Miller) v Secretary of State for Exiting the EU* [2017] UKSC 5)).

This novel legal position of the impact of EU law on national law, and its impact on UK parliamentary sovereignty, meant that the UK's relationship with the EU for nearly a half century was always ambivalent and highly contested.

Indeed, almost straight after the UK joined the EEC in 1973, Eurosceptics were calling for the country to leave. The first UK referendum on EU membership in 1975 produced a 67% majority vote of the UK population to stay in the common market of the EEC. Successive UK governments have equivocated from open hostility to the European project through to enthusiastic approval of it. The impact of EU law principles on cherished traditions, notions and underpinnings of the UK legal system proved to be the catalyst for increasing Euroscepticism in the late 1980s and early 1990s.

10.2.1 The Factortame saga

In the long-running saga of Factortame, the UK government, since the 1980s, was concerned about Spanish fishermen creating new companies under English law allowing them to fish in UK waters. As a result of this scenario, the UK government enacted the Merchant Shipping Act 1998. This Act limited this avenue by requiring UK companies that would have had access to UK waters, to have 75% British nationality. Thus, Spanish-owned UK companies would be denied a fishing licence where they fell below the 75% threshold. This rule violated the cardinal law of the EU Treaties that there should be no discrimination on the grounds of nationality. This provision of EU law satisfied the criteria for direct effect as set out in *Van Gend en Loos* and as such had to be complied with by all elements of the UK state; that is, the executive, the legislature and the judiciary. Thus, the UK Parliament should not pass laws that conflict with EU law, the UK government should not enforce policy that violates EU law and the UK judges should enforce EU law rights in preference to conflicting UK law. All of these aspects of the nature of EU law posed problems for the UK legal system. In particular, the courts of the UK, in trying to grant direct effect of the right to establishment for the Spanish fishermen, came up against the supremacy of the UK Parliament and the absence of Crown liability. In terms of the supremacy of the UK Parliament, UK constitutional law prevents judges from declaring Acts of Parliament illegal, suspending the application of an Act of Parliament and awarding damages for the enactment of an Act of Parliament that impinges on an individual's rights (see **Chapter 4** on the institutions of the state). However, UK judges, as judges of a Member State of the EU, had to ensure that EU law was given effect in the national legal system. In order to resolve these incompatible positions, UK judges had to make extensive use of the **preliminary ruling** system of Art 267 TFEU and refer questions on the meaning of EU law to the ECJ. The ECJ confirmed that these national barriers to EU law enforcement had to be swept aside in order to ensure the correct implementation of EU law in the UK legal system. Thus, the UK courts accepted a number of significant limitations upon the UK legal system, including the concept that UK Acts of Parliament would be disapplied in the event of conflict between them and a provision of EU law, the availability of damages against the state for violations of EU law and the ability of the UK courts to issue **injunctions** against the Crown.

10.2.2 The UK referendum and the process of leaving the EU

British governments and the general public have been generally agnostic on the esoteric, wider and symbolic value of belonging to the EU, with the pragmatic, economic advantages of being in the EU's customs union and single market initiatives generally prevailing over negative antagonism felt towards the EU. However, this settled political arrangement was torn asunder by the outcome of the UK's second referendum on EU membership that was held on 23 June 2016. The UK prime minister of the time, David Cameron, had secured an outright majority in the general election the year before and was therefore politically bound to implement the Conservative Party manifesto pledge to hold an 'in-out' referendum on the UK's continued membership of the EU.

The European Union Referendum Act 2015 set out the terms of the referendum, including the date, the terms of the franchise and the framing of the question. The combined eligible population of the UK and Gibraltar voted 52% to leave the EU. David Cameron resigned and Theresa May was appointed the new leader of the Conservative Party and thus became the second female prime minister of the UK.

Theresa May, desiring to give effect to the will of the UK population, attempted to trigger Art 50 TEU. Article 50 TEU is a relatively new provision of EU law which sets out the process for a Member State to leave the EU. The making and unmaking of international treaties is a classic exercise of **royal prerogative** by the prime minister, however the unique nature of the EU and its legal system challenged this orthodoxy. The triggering of Art 50 TEU would put in train a process that would automatically eject the Member State from the EU two years after the date of initiation of Art 50. Leaving the EU invariably meant that UK citizens and companies would lose their legal rights derived from EU law. The royal prerogative cannot be used to change the law of the land, thus the legality of use of the royal prerogative by the prime minister to take the UK out of the EU was not clear.

Gina Miller, a Guyanese–British businesswoman and ardent anti-Brexit campaigner, led a crowdfunded campaign to challenge simple use of the royal prerogative. At the end of this legal process, the Supreme Court, sitting as a full bench, declared that the royal prerogative could not be used to trigger Art 50 TEU. Rather, the prime minister would need parliamentary approval to trigger Art 50 TEU precisely because the legal status of UK citizens and companies would be fundamentally altered by this seismic change in circumstances (*Miller 1* (*R (Miller) v Secretary of State for Exiting the EU* [2017] UKSC 5)). The UK Parliament passed the European Union (Notification of Withdrawal) Act 2017 in mid-March 2017, thus authorising Theresa May to trigger Art 50 TEU, which she did on 29 March 2017.

Activation of Art 50 TEU by notification of the European Council of the UK's intention to leave, then allowed the European Commission to initiate two years of negotiations with the UK on the terms of withdrawal. The countdown to Brexit had started and was due to end at 11 pm on 29 March 2019. These negotiations would culminate in the creation of a legally binding international treaty between the UK and the EU dealing with the 'divorce' and would then allow for a second international treaty between the UK and the EU dealing with the future trade and cooperation relationship between them.

The Art 50 TEU negotiating process did not progress as smoothly as planned. Theresa May called a general election in May 2017 after a supermajority of MPs agreed to her request as required under the Fixed-term Parliaments Act 2011. That general election resulted in a hung parliament, further reducing her ability to gain parliamentary support for her version of Brexit. Nevertheless, the UK Parliament did pass the European Union (Withdrawal) Act 2018 which was designed to repeal the European Communities Act 1972. Simple repeal of the 1972 Act would have created legal chaos, thus the 2018 Act also ensured that certain aspects of EU law would subsist beyond Brexit in order to maintain legal certainty.

The 2018 Act provided that the principle of supremacy of EU law over inconsistent domestic law would be abolished on exit day along with the EU law principles of direct effect, indirect effect and state liability, preventing them from applying to future UK law. However, the Act would also freeze the majority of EU law that existed at the time of Brexit and convert that body of EU law into a new category of UK law to be known as 'retained EU law'. This new category of law prevented a legal vacuum from coming into existence in the UK as a result of the UK leaving the EU. The 2018 Act also preserved UK laws that had been made before exit day that were designed to give effect to EU law and EU obligations.

Both 'retained EU law' and UK law giving effect to EU law would not make much sense once the UK had left the EU since those laws would refer to various concepts, principles and doctrines of EU law and EU institutions, bodies and agencies that would no longer have relevance to the UK, thus the 2018 Act also created sweeping executive 'Henry VIII' powers for UK ministers and those of the devolved nations to correct these laws to ensure that the UK legal system functioned properly after Brexit. Leaving the EU had significant implications for devolution in the UK since the devolved organs of the UK were previously constrained in the exercise of their legislative and executive powers through the EU law limits set out in their respective legislative constitutional frameworks, namely the Scotland Act 1998, the Government of Wales Act 1998 and the Northern Ireland Act 1998 (see *Petition on the UK Withdrawal from the European Union (Legal Continuity) (Scotland) Bill* [2018] UKSC 64). After exit day, these limits on devolution would simply disappear whilst the new category of UK law, namely 'retained EU law' would come into existence at that point. Thus, s12 of and Sch 3 to the 2018 Act reimposed limits to devolution by requiring that the devolved organs cannot act in a way that goes against 'retained EU law' or the Withdrawal Agreement. Going forward, however, there was a danger that differentiated exercise of these amended powers in the devolved nations could endanger the coherency and consistency of the UK's own internal market. Therefore the 2018 Act inserted a new power for UK ministers to make freezing regulations that would prevent devolved organs from acting in their devolved policy areas where to do so would endanger the UK's internal market. Such regulations, due to their restrictive and constrictive effect on the devolved institutions, were time-limited. They could only be enacted within two years of exit day and will automatically expire within five years of exit day.

Section 13 of the 2018 Act also made provision for UK law to give legal effect to the UK–EU Withdrawal Agreement via a process known as a 'meaningful vote'.

Notwithstanding domestic political problems, Theresa May did manage, in November 2018, to secure a near 600-page Withdrawal Agreement and a 27-page political declaration on the future UK–EU relationship with the EU. Under this plan, the entire UK would stay in the EU's customs union as a default backstop position if the UK and EU could not agree on a new trading agreement after the end of the transition period. However, Art 50 TEU required that the leaving Member State legally approve the agreement so that the European Parliament could then subsequently approve the legal text secured by the Council of the EU. Theresa May failed three times to gain s13 parliamentary approval for her deal with the EU and thus had to agree with the EU for two extensions to the original Brexit date of 29 March 2019. The first meaningful vote on 15 January 2019 was the largest government defeat in modern history. The UK government suffered its second defeat on 12 March 2019. With the Brexit clock counting down, the EU approved the first extension. This extension was flexible and would end either in April or June. On 29 March 2019, Theresa May suffered her third and final defeat in Parliament and thus offered to resign later in the year. She also secured a second extension of the Brexit process until 31 October 2019. Theresa May resigned as prime minister on 24 July 2019 and Boris Johnson assumed the role immediately thereafter. In his first speech, Boris Johnson set out that the UK would leave the EU on 31 October 2019 with or without a deal and authorised spending on preparing for 'no deal'. After the summer of 2019, in August Boris Johnson sought to prorogue Parliament from 10 September 2019 until 14 October 2019, the longest ever prorogation. The reason for such an excessive prorogation was not explicitly given but it was widely assumed to be to prevent Parliament from preventing no deal. Various **judicial review** cases were instituted against this prorogation and the Supreme Court unanimously declared that the prorogation was unlawful and thus of no legal effect (see **Chapter 6** on judicial review and the case of *Cherry/Miller 2* [2019] UKSC 41).

Notwithstanding this case, on 17 October 2019, Boris Johnson secured amendments to Theresa May's deal with the EU such that only Northern Ireland and not the rest of the UK would stay within the EU's customs union in the default backstop position if the UK and EU failed to agree a future trade agreement. However, Boris Johnson stuck to his timeline of leaving the EU by the end of October 2019 and gave the UK Parliament insufficient time to scrutinise this revised Withdrawal Agreement. Therefore, under the terms of the European Union (Withdrawal) (No 2) Act 2019, in the absence of parliamentary approval of a deal between the UK and the EU, the prime minister was forced to seek a new extension to the Art 50 TEU period. Thus, Boris Johnson sought and was granted an extension until 11 pm on 31 January 2020.

Given these significant political and legal defeats, the inherited problems of a divided Parliament and a number of defections further eroding his power in Parliament, Boris Johnson then sought again to have a general election. A supermajority of MPs granted his wish and the subsequent general election took place on 12 December 2019. This election saw Boris Johnson returned as prime minister but this time with an 80-seat majority in Parliament. This emphatic result allowed Boris Johnson to easily gain parliamentary approval for his deal that had previously eluded him and his predecessor Theresa May.

10.2.3 The transition period

The UK therefore finally left the EU at 11 pm on 31 January 2020 (exit day) and entered a transition period until 11 pm on 31 December 2020. The approval of the revised Withdrawal Agreement effectively deferred the terms of the 2018 Act such that the UK entered an implementation period, whereby the UK left the EU but voluntarily agreed to accept the full force of the vast majority of relevant EU law within the UK legal space until the terms of a newly negotiated UK–EU legal relationship came into force, superseding the terms of the implementation period. Thus, EU law continued to have legal effect in the UK for the transition period largely as it had done for the past 47 years.

The UK's near half-century of membership of what is now the EU, with its legal requirement to integrate the UK legal system into the EU ecosystem, invariably meant that extricating the UK from the orbit of the EU legal system would be a complex and lengthy process.

The desire of the UK government to leave the single market and customs union of the EU and with it the jurisdiction of the ECJ is diametrically opposed to, and incompatible with, the avoidance of a hard border between Northern Ireland and the Republic of Ireland, the desire of Scotland and Northern Ireland to remain in the EU and the fact that devolution across the UK was predicated upon continuing UK membership of the EU.

Brexit thus threw up numerous legal, factual, economic, social and political problems, problems that will subsist for the foreseeable future.

10.3 The terms of the Withdrawal Agreement

The UK–EU Withdrawal Agreement is divided into six broad sections and is accompanied by three protocols concerning Northern Ireland, Cyprus and Gibraltar respectively.

The Withdrawal Agreement first addresses a number of common provisions that set out the general aspects of the operation of the agreement and places the agreement in context. This Part One deals with definitions to be used throughout the agreement, the principles to be applied to the agreement and the territorial extent of the agreement.

Part Two of the Withdrawal Agreement deals with the issue of citizens' rights. It is estimated that there are over four million EU citizens who have chosen to live in the UK and over a million UK nationals who live and work across the 27 countries of the EU. This part provides generally that these UK and EU citizens can stay in their chosen territory and thus contribute to the communities of those countries.

Part Three of the Withdrawal Agreement deals with a number of important issues concerning the separation of the UK from the EU. In particular, this part deals with the question of goods placed on the market before Brexit, allowing them to continue to their destination, continues the protection available under intellectual property law to goods, such as the law on geographical indicators, the treatment of pre-existing procedures and cooperation such as police and judicial cooperation in criminal matters, the issue of use and protection of data and information exchange and matters relating to Euratom as regards nuclear materials.

Part Four of the Withdrawal Agreement provided for the 11-month transition period that started on 31 January 2020 and ended on 31 December 2020. This part of the agreement essentially treated the UK, for most purposes, as if it was still a Member State of the EU. The main exception to this was the fact that the UK was excluded from participating in the EU institutions and governance structures. This transition period was an opportunity for the UK and the EU to negotiate the UK–EU Trade and Cooperation Agreement.

Part Five of the Withdrawal Agreement sets out the framework for the financial settlement that equitably and fairly ensures that the UK and EU both honour their financial obligations arising during the UK's membership of the EU.

The final part, Part Six, deals with the governance of the Withdrawal Agreement. This part deals with the issue of the effective management, implementation and enforcement of the agreement and sets out the process for settling disputes that may arise from the agreement.

Attached to the agreement are three legally binding protocols dealing with Northern Ireland and the Sovereign Base Areas in Cyprus and Gibraltar.

The Northern Ireland Protocol is designed to avoid the imposition of a hard border on the island of Ireland, protect North–South cooperation and the entire economy of the island of Ireland, protect and respect the terms of the Good Friday Agreement of 1998 and safeguard the integrity of the single market of the EU.

The Sovereign Base Areas (SBA) Protocol is designed to ensure the application of EU law in the SBAs of Cyprus following the UK's departure from the EU and to promote the continued cooperation between the UK and the Republic of Cyprus.

The Protocol on Gibraltar is designed to facilitate close cooperation between Spain and the UK on ensuring the terms of Part Two of the Withdrawal Agreement on citizens' rights.

10.3.1 Status of the Withdrawal Agreement under UK law

Section 7A of the European Union (Withdrawal) Act 2018 provides that the rights, powers, liabilities, obligations, restrictions, remedies and procedures created by the Withdrawal Agreement and those that may arise in the future under the agreement are to be accorded supremacy over inconsistent UK law and are automatically part of the law of the UK. Thus, the Withdrawal Agreement is generally to have a similar status in UK law to that given to EU law when the UK was a member of the EU. Thus, it binds the three parts of the state and is accorded priority even over future UK law. The Withdrawal Agreement also overrides 'assimilated law' as explained later.

10.3.2 **Jurisdiction of the Court of Justice of the European Union under the Withdrawal Agreement**

Notwithstanding the desire of the UK government to completely expunge the role of the Court of Justice of the European Union (CJEU) from the UK legal system, the Withdrawal Agreement tolerates a limited role for the Court, as set out below.

10.3.2.1 Pending cases

Under the Withdrawal Agreement, the CJEU continues to have jurisdiction over certain cases that were initiated prior to the end of the transition period. Thus, the CJEU has jurisdiction in pending cases that were brought before it either by the UK or were taken against the UK and requests for preliminary rulings under Art 267 TFEU. As an example of a case under Art 267 TFEU, see the case of *R (on the application of Association of Independent Meat Suppliers and another) v Food Standards Agency* [2021] UKSC 54.

10.3.2.2 Cases relating to alleged transition breaches

The CJEU is competent, for four years after the transition period, to receive infringement proceedings brought by the European Commission against the UK under the terms of Art 258 TFEU. Such cases can be brought where the Commission considers that the UK is in breach of either certain EU Treaty obligations or the terms of Part Four of the Withdrawal Agreement concerning the transition period. As an example of this jurisdiction, see the CJEU's judgment that the UK failed to fulfil its EU obligations in respect of the incompatibility between the UK Supreme Court case of *Micula v Romania* [2020] UKSC 5 and that of the ECJ in Case C-638/19 P, *Commission v European Food* SA, EU:C:2022:50 (Case C-516/22, *Commission v United Kingdom* EU:C:2024:231). In the event of a Member State's (or the UK's) non-compliance with an adverse judgment of the CJEU as to the failure to fulfil obligations, the Commission can subsequently bring a case against the Member State or the UK under Art 260 TFEU (as to this jurisdiction, see Case C-692/20, EU:C:2023:707).

Similarly, where a decision of the EU has been taken regarding the UK, the CJEU has jurisdiction to hear actions against the legality of that decision under Art 263 TFEU for four years from the date of that decision. For examples of this jurisdiction, see Case T-56/22, *United Kingdom v Commission*, EU:T:2024:51 and Case C-555/22 P, *United Kingdom v Commission*.

10.3.2.3 Cases regarding the Northern Ireland Protocol

As regards the Northern Ireland Protocol, the Commission has the power to issue infringement proceedings against the UK for alleged violation of aspects of the protocol and thereafter to bring the matter to the CJEU. The relevant parts of the protocol are the provisions requiring Northern Ireland to align with EU law as regards the free movement of goods on issues such as customs and the need for monthly information exchanges between the UK and the EU, various technical aspects, VAT and excise matters, the single electricity market and provisions on state aid.

More generally, as regards these aspects of the protocol, the EU institutions, bodies, offices and agencies are to be given their normal powers under EU law as regards the UK, and natural and legal persons within the jurisdiction of the UK. This extends to the normal jurisdiction of the CJEU. Thus, questions on the interpretation of the protocol can be sent to the Court from UK courts under Art 267 TFEU.

In addition to legal actions before the ECJ, the terms of the Northern Ireland Protocol have given rise to a plethora of domestic litigation before the Northern Irish and UK courts (see, eg, *Northern Ireland Human Rights Commission's Application for Judicial Review* [2024] NIKB 35; *Dillon's Application for Judicial Review, Re* [2024] NIKB11; *Allister's application for Judicial Review, Re* [2023] UKSC 5; *Chuinneagain* [2021] NIQB 79 and *SPUC* [2023] NICA 35).

EXAMPLE

Under the Northern Ireland Protocol to the Withdrawal Agreement, the UK committed itself to inspecting goods that enter Northern Ireland from the UK to ensure that they comply with EU law. However, the UK and the EU mutually agreed a set of grace periods, whereby the full extent of the checks would be delayed. The UK and the EU agreed a three-month grace period for authorised traders like supermarkets and their trusted suppliers concerning products of animal origin, composite products, food and feed of non-animal origin and plants and plant products (collectively agri-foods), a six-month grace period for chilled meats and a 12-month phasing-in period of regulatory rules for medicines. In early March 2021, the UK government confirmed that it would unilaterally extend the three-month grace period for agri-foods that would expire at the end of March 2021 by six months to the end of September 2021. Thus, the European Commission considered this to be a breach of the Northern Ireland Protocol since any extension to the grace periods must be determined jointly by the UK and the EU through the Joint Committee and a breach of the Withdrawal Agreement requirement for the EU and the UK to act in good faith and as such had instituted an Art 258 TFEU infringement proceeding against the UK. The Commission then suspended the legal action to allow for further negotiations. These negotiations ultimately led to the Windsor Agreement (https://www.gov.uk/government/collections/the-windsor-framework-further-detail-and-publications) between the UK and the EU. Under this framework, the free movement of goods has been simplified and become less bureaucratic. The terms of the Windsor Framework are discussed below.

10.3.2.4 Cases concerning citizens' rights

Given the fact that EU citizens already living in the UK may opt to continue to live in the UK for a significant period of time post-Brexit, the Withdrawal Agreement provides that questions concerning interpretation of the relevant law, that is Part Two of the Withdrawal Agreement, can be sent to the CJEU from a UK court or tribunal under Art 267 TFEU for a maximum period of eight years from the end of the transition period. Certain questions on the issuance of residence permits issued during the transition period will be subject to a slightly earlier deadline.

In order to provide greater confidence to EU and EEA citizens living in the UK that their rights will be protected, the Independent Monitoring Authority (IMA) was set up. As an example of its work, the IMA, in December 2021, instituted a judicial review action against the Home Office, alleging that it is unlawful for the Home Office to consider that EU/EEA citizens who fail to apply for Settled Status before their pre-Settled Status expires automatically lose their free movement rights. The English High Court subsequently agreed with the IMA and declared the Home Office's stance to be unlawful (*R (on the application of the IMA) v Secretary of State for the Home Department* [2022] EWHC 3274 (Admin)).

As regards domestic litigation, see for example the case of *Akinsanya v Secretary of State for the Home Department* [2021] EWHC 11535 (Admin).

Alongside the hearing of cases drawn from the UK, the ECJ also receives numerous cases from the domestic courts of the EU Member States and direct actions concerning the rights of UK citizens based in the EU (see, eg, joined cases of C-501/21 *Shindler and Price v Council*).

10.3.2.5 Cases on the financial settlement

Legal questions may arise over the exact meaning and extent of the financial commitments agreed to by the UK and the EU concerning their 'divorce'. Thus, the CJEU can receive requests from UK courts for an interpretation of these provisions under Art 267 TFEU. The European Commission is also authorised to bring infringement proceedings against the UK in cases of alleged non-compliance and thereafter bring the matter to the CJEU.

10.3.2.6 Cases relating to dispute settlement

Given the desire of the UK to be free from the jurisdiction of the CJEU post-Brexit, Part Six of the Withdrawal Agreement provides for a broad dispute settlement procedure. Under this part of the Withdrawal Agreement, a Joint Committee was set up to be responsible for the implementation and application of the Withdrawal Agreement. If the Joint Committee cannot reach a mutually acceptable solution to the issue within three months, the issue may be resolved via arbitration. The Withdrawal Agreement provides that an arbitration panel can be set up to adjudicate on the matter. However, where the issue raises a question on the interpretation of EU law, the panel must refer that question to the CJEU. The resultant CJEU ruling is binding on the panel, and in turn the arbitration panel's ruling binds the UK and the EU.

10.4 The UK–EU relationship after Brexit

After the UK left the EU at 11 pm on 31 January 2020 and entered an 11-month implementation period, the UK and EU were locked in a frantic race to agree the terms of the future trading and cooperation relationship between them. The negotiations took place against a background of the global pandemic of Covid-19 and increasing distrust between the two protagonists. Nevertheless, the UK and EU did finally agree a Trade and Cooperation Agreement (TCA) on Christmas Eve 2020, a week before the UK exited the implementation period. Alongside the TCA, the EU and UK also agreed provisions on nuclear materials (EU–UK Agreement for cooperation on the safe and peaceful uses of nuclear energy) and on the security of classified information (EU–UK Security of Information Agreement).

The European Union (Future Relationship) Act 2020 was rapidly passed by the UK Parliament to provide for the incorporation of these international agreements into UK law and to allow ministers to pass secondary laws to give effect to the agreements and to amend domestic law in light of these arrangements.

10.4.1 The UK–EU Trade and Cooperation Agreement

The TCA is similar in approach, content and format to Association Agreements that the EU signs with neighbouring states that have stated an intention to join the EU in the future. The TCA sets out a number of preferential arrangements for both the UK and the EU in a wide range of areas of competence.

The TCA comprises three main legal agreements: the Free Trade Agreement, a close partnership on security of citizens and a comprehensive framework for governance. The agreement contains seven sections, several protocols and a number of technical annexes.

Part One of the TCA deals with general institutional aspects, including legal definitions, principles of interpretation and the applicable framework. Part Six deals with the general settlement of disputes that arise from the agreement. Part Two is entitled Trade, Transport and Fisheries. Part Three refers to law enforcement and judicial cooperation in criminal matters. Part Four relates to thematic UK-EU cooperation on matters such as cybersecurity and health security. Part Five sets out the conditions for continued UK participation in certain EU programmes and activities. Part Seven addresses final provisions relating to the TCA.

The three TCA protocols deal with administrative cooperation and combating fraud in the field of VAT and on mutual assistance for the recovery of claims relating to taxes and duties, mutual administrative assistance in customs matters and social security coordination.

It is a broad relationship, although not as extensive as the one the UK had as a member of the EU or the one that members of the European Economic Area (Iceland, Lichtenstein and Norway) have with the EU.

Nevertheless, the TCA covers the following areas of activity: the traditional areas of free trade of goods and services and a number of important extraneous matters such as investment, competition law and policy, laws and rules on public procurement or state aid and tax transparency; digital aspects of trade such as cybersecurity; intellectual property laws and policy; agreement on continued and sustainable air, road, rail and maritime transport connectivity; rules on open and competitive energy markets and provisions on renewable energy; issues related to fisheries, particularly the joint management and conservation of species; continued coordination of certain social security matters for EU citizens in the UK and UK citizens in the EU; the issue of visas for short-term visits; the question of law enforcement and judicial cooperation in relation to criminal matters, including arrangements for extradition, measures for fighting and prosecuting cross-border crime and terrorism and continued UK involvement in Europol and Eurojust and for general cooperation in matters such as data exchange under the Prüm Treaty, Passenger Name Records data and measures on asset-freezing; general aspects of UK–EU regulatory cooperation across a number of broad areas of mutual interest like health and cyber security; issues of sustainable development; continued UK participation in, and funding of, various EU programmes and provisions such as Copernicus, Horizon Europe, research and training under Euratom, the International Thermonuclear Experimental Reactor and access to the EU's Space Surveillance and Tracking services on the settlement of disputes.

In terms of goods, the TCA provides for zero tariffs and quotas on goods moving between the EU and the UK, subject to rules of origin provisions that require a set percentage of components and parts to be of UK and EU origin.

The TCA is underpinned by measures designed to ensure a level playing field between the EU and the UK and a requirement for both sides to adequately respect fundamental rights. For example, EU–UK security cooperation on fighting terrorism and cross-border crime could be suspended if the UK violates its international law obligations under the ECHR (see **Chapter 8** on the Human Rights Act 1998). In terms of level playing field commitments, the UK and EU have agreed to maintain high levels of protection of the environment, including commitments in respect of climate change and carbon pricing, high levels of social and labour rights, transparency requirements on taxes levied and robust rules limiting state aid.

Settlement of disputes is set out in Part Six of the TCA. Generally, the settlement provisions of the TCA are horizontal in nature, applying to the whole agreement. However, the TCA also provides for a number of specific dispute mechanisms for certain sections of the TCA.

Part Six of the TCA provides for the creation of a Joint Partnership Council and the creation of a number of specialised committees. The Joint Partnership Council will oversee the proper application and interpretation of the entire TCA. It is essentially a diplomatic consultative forum for settling disputes that will act by consensus. It is made up of a representative from the European Commission and the UK government. If the Council fails to resolve the dispute, the dispute can be sent to an independent arbitration tribunal specially set up for the dispute. The tribunal will then have up to 160 days to reach a decision. If one side of the TCA fails to comply with the ruling of the arbitration tribunal, the other side is entitled to engage in retaliatory measures such as suspending its participation in other parts of the TCA.

This general approach to dispute settlement does not apply in a number of key areas of the TCA such as certain provisions on the level playing field, fisheries and law and justice cooperation. Violation of level playing field conditions allows the other side to institute retaliatory measures quickly, with review of these measures being undertaken by an arbitration tribunal or expert panel after the event.

Alleged violations of the provisions of law and justice cooperation will be resolved by the Specialised Committee on Law Enforcement and Judicial Cooperation. This section of the TCA also allows for the suspension of cooperation in the event of non-compliance.

Discussion of fisheries issues can be raised in the Specialised Committee on Fisheries, however both sides may unilaterally suspend or limit access to their waters or end preferential tariffs on fishery products in cases of alleged violation, with such actions reviewable by an arbitration tribunal after the event. Ultimately, the fisheries agreement may be terminated by either side, although resort to this action of last resort will have serious repercussions since it will also terminate the trade, aviation and road transport sections of the TCA.

More generally, the TCA allows for the imposition of rebalancing, remedial, compensatory and safeguarding measures. So, for example, either side, in the event of alleged non-compliance with the TCA, may engage in such behaviour as placing punitive tariffs on the importation of selected high-value, popular goods.

Unlike the Withdrawal Agreement, the TCA makes no provision whatsoever for involvement of the CJEU, a key requirement of the UK negotiating team. Where non-compliance may also extend to international trade obligations, these disputes may be heard under the World Trade Organisation (WTO) settlement procedure.

The agreement is reviewable at five-yearly intervals and can be terminated at the instance of either the UK or the EU on one year's notice. The TCA was only provisionally applicable for the first four months of 2021, pending approval by the EU Parliament. The EU Parliament approved the TCA on 28 April 2021, allowing the TCA to come into force on 1 May 2021.

Although comprehensive in scope, the TCA does not cover a range of important sectors. For example, foreign policy, external security and defence cooperation are excluded from the terms of the agreement. The TCA does not deal with decisions of the EU as to equivalence of financial services, the adequacy of data protection laws and policy or the assessment of sanitary and phytosanitary measures in relation to food products.

Questions on the legality of the provisions of the TCA have been raised in actions before the ECJ (eg Case C-285/22 P, *Julien v Council*, EU:C:2023:551 and Case C-479/21 PPU, SN and SD and Governor of Cloverhill Prison, EU:C:2021:929.

10.5 From retained EU law to assimilated law

The transition period provided legal continuity for the UK and the EU as the two sides negotiated their TCA to regulate their future relationship. Most EU law applied to the UK during this period as a matter of international law. In order to avoid a cliff edge in legal continuity, avoid a legal vacuum and to provide for a functioning statute book, UK law in the form of the European Union (Withdrawal) Act 2018 ensured that EU law would continue to apply in the UK after the end of the transition period. The 2018 Act originally created a new species of UK law, known as 'retained EU law'. This law was a snapshot of relevant EU law as it existed at the end of the transition period. This body of law was saved and incorporated into UK law via ss2–4 of the 2018 Act.

However, this species of law has now been significantly amended under the terms of the Retained EU Law (Revocation and Reform) Act 2023. In particular, the 2023 Act has renamed 'retained EU law' to 'assimilated law', and this new corpus of law has seen its special status under UK law revoked. The main legal impacts of the 2023 Act on 'assimilated law' are set out below.

Section 2 of the 2018 act refers to the saving of EU-derived domestic legislation. This mostly relates to UK secondary legislation previously made by UK ministers and ministers of the devolved executives under s2(2) of the European Communities Act 1972. These UK secondary laws are made to give effect to EU Directives.

Section 3 saved a significant amount of relevant directly applicable EU law such as EU Regulations and EU Decisions addressed to the UK and converted them into UK law as 'retained direct EU legislation'. The main focus of this section was on directly applicable EU law required under Part Four of the Withdrawal Agreement as regards the transition period. EU law is *sui generis* and as such is not easily categorised according to domestic classifications of law. Nevertheless, UK law sub-categorised this element of 'retained EU law' into 'retained direct principal EU legislation' and 'retained direct minor EU legislation'. The term 'principal' referred to EU Regulations, whilst the term 'minor' related to EU decisions and EU tertiary legislation. This distinction was important as regards the power to amend this retained EU law since the original terms of the 2018 Act made it easier to amend minor law. Minor law was treated in a similar way to UK secondary law whilst principal law was treated akin to UK primary legislation. A swathe of these laws have now been expunged from the statute book by virtue of Sch 1 of the Retained EU Law (Revocation and Reform) Act 2023.

Section 4 of the 2018 act applied to most of the EU rights, powers, liabilities, obligations, restrictions, remedies and procedures that were available in UK law under the terms of s2(1) of the European Communities Act 1972. These varied EU law provisions were saved and converted into UK law. However, s4 has now been repealed and with it these special features of EU law have disappeared, as discussed below.

The concept of 'retained EU law' expressly excluded the Charter of Fundamental Rights of the EU under s5 of the European Union (Withdrawal) Act 2018.

The 11-month transition period gave the UK time to prepare for exit day. Therefore, although 'retained EU law' would be a snapshot of the law existing on 31 December 2020, there would still be a danger of legal confusion, so a large number of UK primary and secondary legislation was enacted in advance of exit day, designed to alter this new species of UK law (s8 European Union (Withdrawal) Act 2020). Under this power, 'retained EU law' was simply modified to remove references to EU bodies and institutions that would no longer have power over this law.

More substantively and significantly, alterations were also imperative in order to 'take back control' from the EU. Deviation from EU law rules was the *raison d'être* of Brexit and the EU referendum and as such 'retained EU law', once incorporated into UK law, would require fundamental modification or indeed revocation to reflect changed UK priorities. Thus, EU policies based on EU exclusive and shared competences need to be replaced with bespoke UK policies now that the UK is no longer bound by EU law constraints.

Conversely, if the UK had not explicitly decided upon a new policy by the time of exit day, then the extant EU policy would subsist until it was subsequently replaced by a new UK policy.

EXAMPLE

The UK has enacted a number of Acts of Parliament dealing with policy areas that were previously the preserve of the EU, either on an exclusive or shared basis in relation to the Member States of the EU.

Agriculture Act 2020: this Act replaces the system of agriculture in the UK that was previously governed by the Common Agricultural Policy (CAP) of the EU.

Fisheries Act 2020: In a similar vein to the Agriculture Act 2020, the Fisheries Act 2020 replaces the old system governing fisheries in the UK that was dominated by the rules of the Common Fisheries Policy. This Act provides the legal framework for the new status of the UK as an independent coastal state under the terms of the United Nations Convention on the Law of the Sea 1982. However, aspects of the old rules subsist given the peripatetic nature of fish and historical fishing patterns and shared cooperation of the coastal states of the North Sea.

Private International Law (Implementation of Agreements) Act 2020: this Act provides a framework for the exercise of the UK's extended power to enter into international law agreements that formalise rules on the conflict of laws. A significant part of this competence was previously exercised by the EU on the UK's behalf when the UK was a Member State of the EU.

Taxation (Post-transition Period) Act 2020: This law sets out the taxation rules applicable to goods in Northern Ireland.

United Kingdom Internal Market Act 2020: this Act is controversial from the perspective of the devolved nations of Scotland and Wales since it is designed to protect and preserve the internal market of the UK by legislating for areas of EU competence that were exercisable by the devolved nations to be repatriated back to central government in London and not the capitals of the devolved nations. The aim of the Act is to ensure that goods, people and services can be delivered and accessed across the entire territory of the UK. The uncertainty around this Act has resulted in domestic litigation (see *R (on the application of Counsel General for Wales) v Secretary of State for Business, Energy and Industrial Strategy* [2022] EWCA Civ 118).

Under this rectifying and modifying power, over 100,000 amendments were made to the corpus of retained EU law via the promulgation of over 1,000 pieces of secondary legislation.

The Retained EU Law (Revocation and Reform) Act 2023 further significantly amends the nomenclature, scope and treatment of retained EU law. A whole swathe of retained EU law was expunged from the statute book on 31 December 2023 by virtue of this act. The EU derived law that remains is now known as 'assimilated law' and possesses no special features. (The UK government has produced and maintains an assimilated law dashboard tracker that allows citizens and corporations to find relevant assimilated law (https://www.gov.uk/government/publications/retained-eu-law-dashboard).)

In particular, domestic judges are now given greater latitude to depart from assimilated case law and no longer interpret assimilated law in light of EU interpretative principles and tenets.

The original concept of 'retained EU law' was augmented by the interpretation of that law by the UK courts. The UK courts, in determining the validity, meaning or effect of 'retained EU law', were to be guided by pre-exit case law of the CJEU ('retained case law') and retained general principles of EU law. The UK courts were also able to take into account future case law of the CJEU if they considered it relevant to the case. The UK courts could also take into account decisions of EU institutions and bodies where they considered it relevant.

Given the fact that a vast volume of laws were expedited through Parliament in time for the end of the implementation period, it was inevitable that some legislative drafting errors would occur. In such instances, there was a presumption that the domestic courts should adopt a rectifying construction of that law, but only where the intention of Parliament could be readily inferred. In the case of doubt, however, the more appropriate response was for the court to defer to the relevant Secretary of State and await rectification of the error via statutory instrument (see *R (SSE Generation v OFGEM* [2022] EWCA Civ 1472 and **Chapter 2** on legislation).

Section 5 of the European Union (Withdrawal) Act 2018 originally provided for the status of both 'retained EU law' and EU law post-Brexit. Section 5 originally stated that priority was to be given to 'retained EU law' made under ss3 and 4 of the 2018 Act over pre-existing UK, that is law made prior to the end of the transition period (see, eg, *R (Liberty) v Home Secretary* [2022] EWHC 1630 (Admin)). However, once the transition period ended, no priority was generally to be given to 'retained EU law' or EU law subject to a number of exceptions.

Section 5 also contained provisions on interpretation. So, for example, in the case of UK law made prior to the end of the transition period, particularly in the case of UK law passed to give effect to an EU Directive, that law should still have been interpreted in accordance with that Directive. Similarly, EU law could be given supremacy where it would be relevant to do so when considering the interpretation, disapplication or quashing of any pre-existing UK law.

Notwithstanding the general diminished status of assimilated law in the UK after the promulgation of the Retained EU Law (Revocation and Reform) Act 2023, UK separation agreement law still has a pre-eminent place in the UK legal system. Thus, in the event of a conflict between 'retained EU law' and separation agreement law, that is, the Withdrawal Agreement, that conflict should still be resolved in favour of the separation agreement law (as an example, see *Dillon's application for Judicial Review, Re* [2024] NIKB 11, discussed below).

Section 6 of the European Union (Withdrawal) Act 2018, as amended by the 2023 Act will, once fully in force, provide for a significantly narrower interpretative power for the UK courts as regards assimilated law.

At present, the Supreme Court is not bound by any assimilated EU case law. Nevertheless, for the sake of legal certainty, the Supreme Court will only depart from retained EU case law using the same test it applies to deciding whether to depart from its own case law.

Similarly, the Court of Appeal, the Court Martial Appeal Court and the Lands Valuation Appeal Court are also generally not bound by any assimilated EU case law. However, to provide legal certainty, these courts will only depart from assimilated EU case law using the same test the Supreme Court applies in deciding whether to depart from its own case law.

In addition, the Court of Appeal, the Court Martial Appeal Court and the Lands Valuation Appeal Court are currently bound by post-transition case law which alters or applies EU case law.

In the cases of *TuneIn Inc v Warner Music UK Ltd and Another* [2021] EWCA Civ 441 and *Lipton v BA City Flyer* [2021] EWCA Civ 454, the Court of Appeal refused to depart from the relevant CJEU jurisprudence.

More generally, as regards the position involving non-retained EU case law, where that case law is in point, it remains of persuasive authority (*Lidl GB Ltd v Tesco Stores Ltd* [2023] EWHC 873 (Ch)). These provisions on departure from assimilated EU case law are without prejudice to the normal rules of precedence governing decisions of UK courts such that no court or tribunal is bound by any assimilated domestic case law over and above that which it would be bound by under the rule of *stare decisis* (see **Chapter 3** on the courts and precedent).

Under the future version of s6 of the 2018 Act, the Supreme Court and the higher courts will find it much easier to depart from assimilated case law. When deciding to depart from assimilated EU case law, the Supreme Court and the higher courts will be guided by three factors, namely, the fact that foreign court judgments are generally not binding on UK courts, the existence of any relevant changes of circumstances that effect the assimilated EU case law and the extent to which the assimilated EU case law is restricting the proper development of domestic law. In addition, the future version of s6 of the 2018 Act provides that higher courts may depart from their own assimilated domestic case law if they consider it is the right thing to do, taking into account the extent to which the assimilated domestic case law is determined or influenced by assimilated EU case law that the court has already departed from or would depart from, any relevant changes of circumstances and the extent to which the assimilated domestic case law is restricting the proper development of domestic law.

10.6 Future developments in UK and EU relations and the Windsor Agreement

The operation of the Northern Ireland Protocol (the Windsor Agreement) has been contentious for the UK government ever since the end of the transition period. During this time, the UK government has been attempting to effectively renegotiate the terms of the Northern Ireland Protocol. In the summer of 2021, the UK government issued a Command Paper setting out a number of key changes it wishes to see integrated into a new bilateral agreement between the UK and the EU. Throughout 2021, a series of protracted meetings took place between the UK and the EU to try and avoid either side triggering Art 16 of the Protocol, which allows for unilateral trade sanctions to be imposed in the event of non-compliance with the terms of the Protocol. The UK government also proposed the Northern Ireland Protocol Bill in order to unilaterally alter the terms of the Protocol. This Bill would have undermined the international agreement agreed with the EU and was roundly condemned. However, Prime Minister Rishi Sunak managed to secure a revised international law agreement with the EU in late February 2023. This new agreement, the Windsor Framework, deals with a number of contested issues and negates the need for passage of the Northern Ireland Protocol Bill. As a consequence, in return for removing the Bill from the UK legislative process, the EU agreed to drop various legal cases in relation to the bill.

In particular, the Windsor Framework introduces a new system for customs in Northern Ireland, namely a 'Green' customs lane with simplified and reduced checks on goods destined for the Northern Ireland market, a 'Red' lane for EU destined goods with full customs checks, a simplified system for agri-foods, changes to zero and reduced VAT rated goods, no checks on individuals sending parcels to Northern Ireland, reduced administration for online businesses sending parcels and regulation of medicines in Northern Ireland to be undertaken by the Medicines and Healthcare products Regulatory Agency (MHRA) of the UK. (Detailed arrangements of the Windsor Framework are set out in the House of Commons Library Research Paper of 21 March 2023 and the supplementary Research Paper from 2024 (https://commonslibrary.parliament.uk/research-briefings/cbp-9548/)). In the event of identified problems with the operation of the Framework, particularly as regards the free movement of goods, the Windsor Framework introduced a 'Stormont Brake' mechanism whereby 30 members of the Northern Ireland Assembly, drawn from at least two parties, may object to the application of new EU laws by submitting a 'petition of concern' to the UK government. The UK government would then be able to challenge the EU laws in the EU–UK Joint Committee, with a further option of invoking arbitration.

The unique legal status of the Withdrawal Agreement and the accompanying Windsor Framework means that it can be used as a sword to challenge and ultimately disapply inconsistent national law (see the discussion of *Dillon* below and the case of *Northern Ireland Human Rights Commission's Application for Judicial Review* [2024] NIKB 35, challenging the terms of the UK's Illegal Migration Act 2023 https://nihrc.org/news/detail/illegal-migration-act-challenge-factsheet

EXAMPLE

Dillon's application for Judicial Review, Re [2024] NIKB 11

On 18 September 2023, the Northern Ireland Troubles (Legacy and Reconciliation) Act 2023 received royal assent. This Act of the UK Parliament is designed to address the legal legacy issues arising from the tumultuous historical period of UK–Irish conflict during the Troubles, that is, between the late 1960s and the passing of the Belfast Good Friday Agreement in 1998. The Good Friday Agreement provides for a number of rights for victims of the Troubles and their family members. Alongside these provisions, the European Union promulgated the Victims' Directive in 2012 (Directive 2012/29/EC (http://data.europa.eu/eli/dir/2012/29/oj)). Under EU law, directives, in certain circumstances, can create rights for individuals which become part of their legal heritage (see C-26/62, *Van Gend en Loos*, EU:C:1963:1).

This UK act has proved to be highly controversial, particularly as regards the question of immunity for individuals accused of illegal conduct during the Troubles. As such, a number of individuals elected to bring an application for judicial review of the act to the High Court of Justice of Northern Ireland. This legal action alleged that various provisions of the 2023 act violated the ECHR. In the event of a breach of the ECHR, such a breach then results in a breach of the Good Friday Agreement and in turn, these breaches may constitute a breach of the Northern Ireland Protocol/Windsor Framework. Such a finding is significant, since s7A of the European (Withdrawal Agreement) Act 2018 provides that the Withdrawal Agreement must be given the same status under UK law as EU law had when the UK was a member of the European Union. Thus, the Windsor Framework has supremacy over inconsistent national law. Further, the Withdrawal Agreement has direct effect in the UK legal system, must be interpreted according to the interpretative canons of the EU and in light of the general principles of EU law and by reference to relevant jurisprudence of the Court of Justice of the European Union (see *Secretary of State for Work and Pensions v AT* [2023] EWCA Civ 1307). Where an apparent inconsistency between the Withdrawal Agreement and inconsistent national law cannot be resolved by way of purposive interpretation, the offending terms of that domestic law must be disapplied in order to resolve that conflict. The High Court of Justice of Northern Ireland proceeded to investigate the terms of the 2023 Act under the test set out in *SPUC* [2023] NICA 35. In *SPUC*, it was held that in order to establish a breach of Art 2 of the Windsor Framework, a number of conditions had to be satisfied. First, a relevant right or obligation of opportunity under the Belfast Good Friday Agreement had to be engaged and that right or obligation had to have existed prior to 31 December 2020, the date of Brexit. Next, the Northern Ireland law had to be underpinned by EU law and that underpinning has been removed as a consequence of Brexit. Finally, that loss of underpinning has led to a diminution of the right and such a reduction of the right would not have happened but for Brexit. The High Court considered these conditions in turn as regards the position of the rights set out in the EU Victims Directive (Directive 2012/29/EC (http://data.europa.eu/eli/dir/2012/29/oj) and concluded that all six conditions were satisfied. As a result the court declared that ss7(3), 8, 12, 19, 20, 9, 21, 22, 39, 41 and 42(1) of the Northern Ireland Troubles (Legacy and Reconciliation) Act 2023 be disapplied.

KEY POINT SUMMARY

- Membership of the European Union fundamentally altered the constitution of the UK.
- EU law, during the UK's membership of the EU, was supreme over inconsistent domestic law, could produce direct effects, could be directly applicable, gave rise to an interpretative obligation on domestic courts and generated claims of state liability.
- Questions of EU law could be sent to the Court of Justice of the European Union from UK courts.
- Extricating the UK from the EU proved to be a complex undertaking.
- Simple extrication of the UK from the EU would lead to legal uncertainty and a legal vacuum.
- Leaving the EU required the negotiation of two international agreements; that is, a Withdrawal Agreement and an agreement on future UK–EU cooperation, the EU–UK Trade and Cooperation Agreement.
- A significant amount of UK law had to be passed to ensure legal certainty post-Brexit and to provide incorporation of the Withdrawal Agreement and the EU–UK Trade and Cooperation Agreement into UK law.
- Elements of EU law still have (diminishing) legal effect within the UK legal system, notwithstanding Brexit.

PART D
Legal Services

CHAPTER 11

Regulatory Role of the SRA

FUNCTIONING LEGAL KNOWLEDGE

This chapter covers the following functional knowledge required to pass the SQE 1 assessments:

The regulatory role of the SRA:

- principles and risk-based regulation
- jurisdiction and sanctions of the Solicitors Disciplinary Tribunal
- reserved legal activities
- professional indemnity insurance
- other regulated providers of legal services

AUTHORITIES UNDERPINNING PRACTICE

The key authorities that underpin this area of practice are listed below. Note that for legislation you are linked to legislation.gov.uk.

Although much of the legislation on this government website is available in its amended form, the incorporation of new amendments into the text of legislation can be delayed. You should refer to legal databases to ensure you are referencing the most up-to-date legislation.

- Legal Services Act 2007
  https://www.legislation.gov.uk/ukpga/2007/29/contents
- SRA Principles 2019
  https://www.sra.org.uk/solicitors/standards-regulations/principles/
- SRA Code of Conduct for Solicitors, RELs and RFLs 2019
  https://www.sra.org.uk/solicitors/standards-regulations/code-conduct-solicitors/
- SRA Code of Conduct for Firms 2019
  https://www.sra.org.uk/solicitors/standards-regulations/code-conduct-firms/
- Solicitors Act 1974
  https://www.legislation.gov.uk/ukpga/1974/47/contents
- Solicitors (Disciplinary Proceedings) Rules 2019
  https://www.legislation.gov.uk/uksi/2019/1185/contents/made
- SRA Regulatory and Disciplinary Procedure Rules
  https://www.sra.org.uk/solicitors/standards-regulations/regulatory-disciplinary-procedure-rules/
- SRA Indemnity Insurance Rules
  https://www.sra.org.uk/solicitors/standards-regulations/indemnity-insurance-rules/
- SRA Assessment of Character and Suitability Rules
  https://www.sra.org.uk/solicitors/standards-regulations/assessment-character-suitability-rules/
- SRA Enforcement Strategy
  https://www.sra.org.uk/sra/corporate-strategy/sra-enforcement-strategy/

11.1 Introduction

The effective operation of the legal system is dependent on all individuals who work within it upholding the highest standards of integrity and professional ethical behaviour to ensure that the **rule of law** is upheld and that clients, as users of legal services, are appropriately safeguarded and protected.

All solicitors, Registered European Lawyers (RELs) and Registered Foreign Lawyers (RFLs), whether in private practice or in-house and whether acting as sole practitioners, working freelance, in not-for-profit organisations, in law firms or anywhere else are subject to authorisation and regulation by the Solicitors Regulation Authority (SRA). In addition, all authorised law firms and their managers and employees (including trainee solicitors, legal assistants and paralegals, as well as support staff) are subject to the SRA's regulatory regime.

In addition, the standards expected of those mentioned above don't just apply in a working context; they can also apply to behaviour that contravenes the standards even in a personal capacity. The SRA's Enforcement Strategy clearly states that: '. . . our Principles set out the core ethical values we require of all those we regulate and apply at all times and in all contexts—and apply both in and outside of practice (as the context permits). We are concerned with the impact of conduct outside of legal practice including in the private lives of those we regulate if this touches on the risk to the delivery of safe legal services in future. The closer any behaviour is to professional activities, or a reflection of how a solicitor might behave in a professional context, the more seriously we are likely to view it.' In addition, the introduction to the SRA's Code of Conduct for Solicitors provides that: 'Conduct does not need to take place in a workplace in order to relate to your practice – these requirements capture conduct which touches realistically upon your practice of the profession, in a way that is demonstrably relevant.' There are serious implications for individuals or firms that fail to uphold these standards or comply with regulations.

This chapter will provide detail of the SRA's regulatory role and its relationship with the **Solicitors Disciplinary Tribunal**. There will be some overlap with the **Ethics, Professional Conduct and Client Care** chapter as solicitor's ethical obligations are regulated and governed by the SRA, however this chapter focuses more broadly on the role of the SRA. It will also cover **reserved legal activities** and the requirements relating to **professional indemnity insurance** for solicitors.

11.2 Regulatory background: introduction

The legal profession has been subject to formal regulation since at least 1275, when the Statute of Westminster forbade 'deceit or collusion' by lawyers. Ethical principles continued to evolve over the centuries, leading to the publication of the Law Society's *Guide to Professional Conduct and Etiquette of Solicitors* in 1960.

In 2004, Sir David Clementi completed an independent review of the regulation of legal services in England and Wales, highlighting the need for a central body to oversee the regulation of lawyers, bring consistency and clarity to regulation and bring greater focus to protecting the interests of users of legal services.

The Legal Services Act 2007 (LSA) addressed the needs identified within the Clementi review. The LSA brought about significant changes to the regulation of legal services, in furtherance of the eight regulatory objectives set out in s1(1) of the Act.

The regulatory objectives are:

(a) protecting and promoting the **public interest**;

(b) supporting the constitutional principle of the rule of law;

(c) improving access to justice;

(d) protecting and promoting the interests of consumers;

(e) promoting competition in the provision of services;

(f) encouraging an independent, strong, diverse and effective legal profession;

(g) increasing public understanding of the citizen's legal rights and duties;

(h) promoting and maintaining adherence to the professional principles.

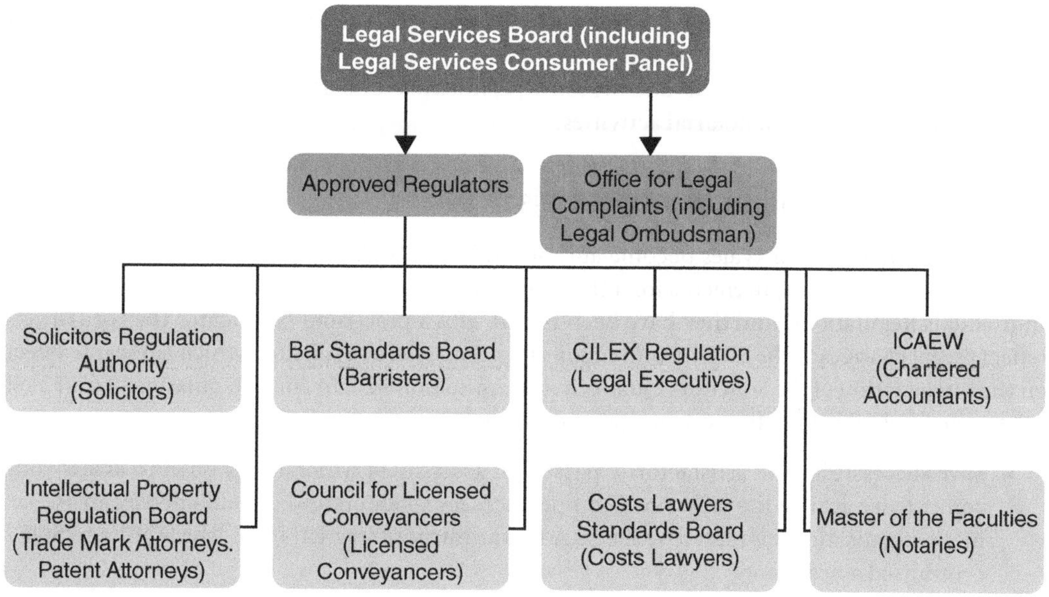

FIGURE 11.1 The regulatory oversight of the Legal Services Board.

The LSA established the **Legal Services Board** (LSB) under s2 of the LSA as the body with responsibility for the regulatory oversight of **approved regulators** of legal services, the Solicitors Disciplinary Tribunal (SDT) and the Office for Legal Complaints (the body responsible for administering the **Legal Ombudsman** scheme). **Figure 11.1** provides a basic map of the LSB's regulatory oversight. 'Approved regulators' are defined in Sch 4, para 1 to the LSA, but in practice regulation of specific types of lawyers is carried out by the independent regulatory bodies listed in **Figure 11.1**, on behalf of the approved regulators.

The LSA also introduced a statutory definition of 'reserved legal activity' and legislation surrounding the provision of any such activity (see **11.6**). It is important that you understand what constitutes a 'reserved legal activity' because if you carry out a 'reserved legal activity' and you are not authorised to do so pursuant to s13 of the LSA, then under s14 of the Act you are committing a criminal offence which can lead to a custodial sentence.

In addition, the LSA removed certain restrictions on competition within the legal profession, providing more flexibility for law firms in terms of their management, structure and ownership. This included the introduction of **Alternative Business Structures** (ABS), which allowed for non-lawyer management and ownership of legal services businesses (see **11.10**).

As a result of the wide-ranging changes within the LSA, the SRA was formed as an independent regulatory arm of the Law Society in January 2007, replacing the previous Law Society Regulation Board, to authorise and regulate solicitors in England and Wales. The LSB has regulatory oversight of the SRA.

11.3 The Solicitors Regulation Authority

The SRA authorises and regulates individuals and firms in England and Wales. It is therefore the regulatory body for solicitors. The Law Society is the representative body for solicitors.

11.3.1 Authorisation

The SRA provides authorisation to individuals (as practising solicitors, RELs and RFLs) and to firms (meaning recognised bodies, licensed bodies and recognised sole practices) to provide specified legal services (known as 'reserved legal activities', see **11.6**).

For the purposes of SRA authorisation and regulation, a '**recognised body**' means a legal services body in which all managers and interest holders are legally qualified—effectively meaning a traditional law firm. A 'licensed body' is generally used to refer to an ABS (**11.10**), as a body with at least one manager who is an SRA-authorised individual. A recognised sole practice refers to a solicitor or REL who is the sole principal in a practice.

Upon authorisation, individuals and firms are permitted to undertake 'reserved legal activities' (**11.6**) with the exception of notarial activities.

11.3.1.1 Authorisation of individuals

Solicitors in England and Wales become authorised by the SRA at the point at which they have met the SRA's current requirements for admission to the Roll (set out in the SRA Authorisation of Individuals Regulations) and they have been issued with a practising certificate. The regulations reflect recent changes to the SRA's requirements for admission as a solicitor, which came into effect on the introduction of the Solicitors Qualifying Examination SQE in 2021. Regulations 1 and 2 set out that to be eligible for admission individuals must:

- have successfully and satisfactorily passed an assessment which is designed to assess your competence against the prescribed competences for solicitors and is conducted by an assessment organisation appointed by the SRA for the purpose (reg 1.1(a)) *i.e.* The SQE1 and SQE2 centralised assessments.
- hold a degree or qualifications or experience which the SRA is satisfied are equivalent to a degree (reg 1.1(b));
- have completed qualifying work experience (reg 1.1(c) and defined in reg 2); and
- have satisfied the SRA of their character and suitability to be admitted as a solicitor (reg 1.1(d)).

The SRA Authorisation of Individuals Regulations also set out the process for RELs and RFLs to become authorised and contain details of the eligibility requirements for admission of individuals who have completed an earlier or alternative route to legal qualification, before the introduction of the SQE.

Of note, are the SRA's Assessment of Character and Suitability Rules, which provide that all individuals applying for admission 'must be of satisfactory character and suitability'. You should familiarise yourself with these rules. They set out the types of factors that the SRA will take into account when assessing an individual's character and suitability, and the obligations on that individual to provide relevant information to the SRA both at the outset and on an ongoing basis throughout their careers. Obviously, the type of factors include criminal offences but also include any other 'conduct or behaviour' which relate to 'integrity and independence' or 'financial conduct', for example. Further information, and details of how to complete the pre-screening process, can be found on the SRA's website.

11.3.1.2 Authorisation of firms

Firms become authorised by the SRA when they have applied for and been granted authorisation. The SRA Authorisation of Firms Rules set out the requirements for authorisation of firms. Rule 8 specifies a requirement for authorised firms to have designated **compliance officers at all times**, being individuals approved by the SRA to hold the role of compliance officer for legal practice (COLP) and compliance officer for finance and administration (COFA). In practice, these roles may be held by the same person. The individual in these roles may also be the Money Laundering Reporting Officer (MLRO).

The rules also set out some conditions relating to the operation and management of authorised firms.

11.3.2 The SRA's regulatory functions

The SRA sets the principles and codes of conduct which all solicitors and law firms in England and Wales must abide by. All practising solicitors, RELs and RFLS *and* all authorised firms and employees of authorised firms in England and Wales are subject to regulation by the SRA. This means that the SRA's regulation will apply to non-lawyer managers of law firms, to paralegals, legal assistants and trainee solicitors within law firms, and to any other staff who may not be legally qualified, including support staff. It is important to note that any barristers or chartered legal executives working within SRA-regulated law firms must comply with both the SRA's regulatory regime and with the regime set out by their own regulator (being the Bar Standards Board for barristers and CILEX Regulation for Chartered Legal Executives).

The SRA's regulatory regime also applies to any solicitors who work outside traditional law firms, including in-house solicitors, freelance solicitors and solicitors working in pro bono organisations or in other types of firm, such as conveyancing or probate services firms.

The SRA carries out its regulatory functions in a variety of ways, including:

1. through setting the standards and requirements for qualifying as a solicitor, and remaining on the roll of solicitors;
2. through creating and maintaining rules of professional conduct—including the Codes of Conduct and Principles;
3. through administering the roll (register) of solicitors, including through issuing practising certificates to new solicitors (either as individuals who pass the SQE, complete their qualifying work experience and satisfy the SRA's character and suitability rules, or who qualify through the previous routes during the transitional period), and through the annual renewal of practising certificates;
4. through authorising firms to carry out 'reserved legal activities' (**11.6**);
5. through taking enforcement action against individuals or firms who contravene provisions of the Codes of Conduct and Principles.

The SRA's approach to regulation is guided by its public interest purpose. It seeks to regulate in a way that maintains and builds public trust and confidence in solicitors and supports the proper administration of justice and the operation of the rule of law. The SRA seeks to ensure that consumers of legal services are protected through setting and enforcing high professional standards of competence, skill, integrity and ethical behaviour.

EXAMPLE

Amelia is a History graduate. She has never studied law before but is exploring the legal profession as a career option and has taken an entry-level role as an assistant paralegal at an SRA-regulated high street law firm, which she hopes will contribute towards her required legal work experience if she subsequently decides to take the SQE centralised assessments.

Even though Amelia has never studied law, and is not legally qualified, because she is working within an SRA-regulated law firm she will be subject to the SRA's regulatory regime, as an 'employee' and should ensure that she is aware of the content of the regime and of the ethical and professional standards expected of her. In practice, the law firm will have proper procedures, policies and/or training in place to ensure that Amelia is aware of the SRA's regulatory regime and how this applies to her role. Under the SRA Code of Conduct for Firms (9.1) the COLP should ensure that this takes place and is responsible in ensuring this happens.

11.3.3 The SRA's regulatory framework

The SRA's regulation of solicitors was initially set out within its first Code of Conduct, established in 2007. In 2011, the SRA introduced a new Handbook, which in turn introduced the concept of Outcomes Focused Regulation (OFR) with the intention of providing solicitors with greater flexibility in how they assisted clients to achieve their objectives. The 2011 Handbook incorporated a Code of Conduct containing mandatory principles, mandatory outcomes and 'indicative behaviours' designed to assist solicitors in demonstrating that the mandatory outcomes had been achieved.

On 25 November 2019, the SRA amended its regulatory regime and the SRA Standards and Regulations (STARS) came into effect, replacing the previous Handbook in its entirety.

The 2019 Standards and Regulations presented a new slimmed down regulatory regime, with seven Principles (**11.3.4**) and two new Codes of Conduct (**11.3.5**). The Code of Conduct for Solicitors was last updated in December 2023 and the Code of Conduct for Firms was last updated in April 2023.

11.3.4 The Principles

The SRA's Principles are the fundamental tenets of ethical behaviour required and expected from anyone who is regulated by the SRA, including solicitors, RELs and RFLs as well as authorised firms and the managers and employees of such firms. The Principles underpin the entirety of the SRA's Standards and Regulations. The Principles require that any individual or entity regulated by the SRA must act:

1. in a way that upholds the constitutional principle of the rule of law and the proper administration of justice;
2. in a way that upholds public trust and confidence in the solicitors' profession and in legal services provided by **authorised persons**;
3. with independence;
4. with honesty;
5. with integrity;
6. in a way that encourages equality, diversity and inclusion;
7. in the best interests of each client.

The SRA's introductory guidance to the Principles sets out that if any of the Principles ever come into conflict, those which safeguard the wider public interest (eg upholding the rule of law and public confidence in the profession) take precedence over an individual client's interests.

EXAMPLE

A solicitor is asked by their client to lie to the court to support their case, that is, to act dishonestly and without integrity. Clearly, if the solicitor followed those instructions they would be complying with Principle 7 because if the lie supports the client's case, it would be acting in the best interests of the client. However, the solicitor acting in that way would invoke Principles 1, 2, 3, 4 and 5 and therefore those Principles would take precedence over the individual client's interests, and the solicitor must act in accordance with those Principles that take precedence, and refuse to act on those client's instructions.

The introductory guidance also makes clear that solicitors must inform their clients of the circumstances in which their duty to the court and other professional obligations will outweigh their duty to clients. It is best practice to set this out in writing to the client at the outset of the retainer so they understand precisely the limitations and the circumstances in which the solicitor's professional obligations will outweigh the duties owed to them.

11.3.5 The Codes of Conduct

The SRA's Codes of Conduct are made up of the Code of Conduct for Solicitors, RELs and RFLs (referred to in this chapter as the 'Individual Code') and the Code of Conduct for Firms (referred to in this chapter as the 'Firms Code').

The full Codes of Conduct can be found on the SRA's website. This chapter provides an overview of the regulatory regime rather than detailed consideration of the specific provisions of the Codes of Conduct. You must ensure that you are familiar with the full content of the Codes of Conduct, but some of the provisions of the Codes that specifically relate to regulation are addressed within the chapter.

A serious failure to meet the SRA's standards or a serious breach of the SRA's regulatory requirements may lead to the SRA taking enforcement action against a regulated individual, a firm or anyone employed within a firm.

CONDUCT POINT

It is essential for all solicitors and employees within SRA-regulated firms to be aware of the content of the Codes of Conduct and of how provisions of the Codes impact on their practice. Ignorance of the Codes will not be a defence to failing to comply with them.

11.3.5.1 The Individual Code

The Individual Code applies to conduct and behaviour relating to the individual practice of any person authorised and regulated by the SRA as a solicitor, REL or RFL. The Code provides a framework for ethical and competent practice which applies irrespective of the individual's role or the organisation in which they work.

Regulated individuals are personally accountable for compliance with the Individual Code and must be prepared to justify their decisions and actions in accordance with the Code and the Principles. This highlights the importance of keeping detailed file notes and confirming client's instructions in writing. Individuals may be challenged on a breach of the Individual Code many years after the event, and having contemporaneous written evidence of what was done and why it was done may provide the necessary justification to avoid sanctions. Any failure by an individual to meet the standards within the Individual Code may result in the SRA instigating regulatory action against an individual.

11.3.5.2 The Firms Code

The Firms Code sets out the standards and business controls that the SRA expect from firms that they authorise and regulate. The provisions of the Firms Code aim to ensure the delivery of competent and ethical legal services to clients. The Firms Code applies to the way that authorised firms run their businesses and to all professional activities that firms undertake.

Certain provisions of the Firms Code apply specifically to managers and compliance officers (**11.3.1.2**) within firms; but otherwise the provisions of the Firms Code apply to all employees working within SRA-regulated firms.

A failure to meet the provisions of the Firms Code may lead to the SRA taking regulatory action against a firm itself, or against its managers or compliance officers. The SRA may also take action against individual employees within firms in respect of any breaches for which they are personally responsible.

11.3.6 Cooperation and accountability

Part 7 of the Individual Code and part 3 of the Firms Code provide details on how regulated individuals and firms must cooperate with the SRA, how they are accountable to the SRA and circumstances in which they must provide information to the SRA. You should ensure that you are familiar with these parts, as you could breach the Code by not informing the SRA about something they should know, but some key provisions are addressed in this section.

Pursuant to part 7.6 of the Individual Code and part 3.6 of the Firms Code, there are certain events which *must* be **promptly** notified to the SRA. These include if an insolvency event occurs in relation to a firm or a solicitor (eg a firm entering into administration or liquidation or a solicitor being made bankrupt), or if a regulated individual is subject to any criminal charge, conviction or caution (subject to the Rehabilitation of Offenders Act 1974) (para 7.6(a) Individual Code). Matters which must always be notified to the SRA are referred to as 'notifications', and Sch 1 to the SRA's Reporting and Notification Guidance summarises what these include.

Further to part 7.7 of the Individual Code and part 3.9 of the Firms Code, the SRA must also be 'promptly' informed of 'any facts or matters' that a regulated individual or a regulated firm 'reasonably believe are capable of amounting to a serious breach' of the SRA's regulatory arrangements. Whether a report should be made is a matter of individual judgement based on the circumstances of a matter but there is guidance in the SRA's Enforcement Strategy on what should be considered when deciding if a breach is serious. Schedule 2 to the SRA's Reporting and Notification Guidance summarises the wider reporting obligations that firms and individuals have.

It is important to note that a solicitor or a firm's obligation is to report 'facts or matters' which ***could*** constitute a serious breach; meaning that solicitors or firms do not themselves need to determine whether there *has* been a serious breach – that will be decided by the SRA. However, in the event of an apparent breach of the standards or regulations, in practice firms may conduct their own investigations as well as making a report to the SRA and cooperating with the SRA's investigations.

On receiving a report of any events or 'facts or matters', the SRA will investigate as appropriate and determine whether there has been a serious breach of standards or regulations and, if so, what action should be taken. The SRA provides a specific form which can be used to make a report; though reports can be made in any format.

Part 7 of the Individual Code and part 3 of the Firms Code requires solicitors and firms to cooperate with the SRA and other bodies in relation to investigations and to respond **promptly** to any queries raised by the SRA. These parts also require solicitors and firms to act **promptly** to take any remedial action requested by the SRA.

Individual solicitors may satisfy their reporting obligations towards the SRA by reporting any matters to one of their firm's designated compliance officers, where appropriate, on the understanding that they will make a report to the SRA (under part 7.12 of the Individual Code). The compliance officer will then use their expertise and professional judgement to determine whether a report should be made to the SRA. However, if an individual disagrees with their firm's compliance officer's assessment, that individual may still make a report to the SRA themselves and should carefully consider whether they should do so.

EXAMPLE

Roisin is a newly qualified solicitor in a large commercial firm. Recently, an issue has arisen that Roisin is concerned may constitute a breach of confidentiality. Roisin immediately reports the issue to her firm's compliance officer for legal practice (COLP), who considers the circumstances very carefully and decides that the matter is very minor in nature and is not something that warrants a report to the SRA.

Roisin has discharged her reporting obligations (and acted correctly) by reporting the issue to her firm's compliance officer. However, if Roisin disagrees with the compliance officer's assessment, she should still make a report to the SRA herself.

11.3.7 Breaches which may warrant SRA investigation

Any 'facts or matters' which are 'capable of amounting to a serious breach' of the SRA's standards and regulations, whether in respect of a regulated individual, a regulated firm or an employee of a regulated firm, must be promptly reported to the SRA and may result in an SRA investigation. The SRA's introduction to both Codes of Conduct makes it clear that a breach may be considered to be serious 'either in isolation or because it comprises a persistent or concerning pattern of behaviour'. The SRA Enforcement Strategy makes clear that breaches which are minor or technical in nature, or allegations which are without merit or frivolous, do not need to be reported, as this is not in anyone's interest. They make it clear that they only want to receive reports 'where it is possible that a serious breach of our standards or requirements has occurred' (SRA Enforcement Strategy).

Some examples of facts or matters which may constitute a serious breach may include (but are not limited to):

1. discriminating unfairly against a client based on your own personal views (part 1.1 Individual Code and Principle 6);
2. taking unfair advantage of someone (part 1.2 Individual Code);
3. breach of an undertaking (part 1.4 Individual Code);
4. bullying, harassing or discriminating unfairly against colleagues (part 1.5 Individual Code);
5. Misleading the Court, generating false evidence or tampering with evidence (part 2 Individual Code);

6. knowingly acting in a situation in which there is a significant risk of conflict (parts 6.1 and 6.2 Individual Code and the Firms Code);
7. breaches of provisions of the Solicitors Accounts Rules;
8. failure to appropriately handle client complaints (parts 8.2–8.5 Individual Code);
9. breach of client confidentiality either in writing or orally (part 6.3 Individual Code);
10. failure to report what could constitute a serious breach of the regulations to the SRA (part 7.7 Individual Code).

EXAMPLE

Rupesh is employed as a paralegal within a high street firm. In a busy working week, he decides to take some client files home with him to work on in the evening. He stops at a shop on his way home and accidentally leaves his bag, containing the client files, on the shop counter.

He realises and returns to the shop within 45 minutes. He notices that his bag is still on the counter so collects it and returns home.

Rupesh must promptly report this issue to either his firm's compliance officers or to the SRA. Whilst Rupesh is not a solicitor, he is nonetheless subject to the provisions of the Firms Code as an employee of a regulated firm. The circumstances described are capable of constituting a serious breach of part 6.3 of the Firms Code on confidentiality, particularly as what happened to the bag is not known to Rupesh while it was out of his possession, for example someone may have looked at the contents and/or taken documents (or a copy/photograph of documents) but the consequences could have been serious even if the bag was untouched, and a report to the SRA should be made promptly.

11.3.8 **Powers of the SRA**

The SRA can investigate any concerns which are reported to them by clients, members of the public, the judiciary or by solicitors and firms themselves. The SRA can take action against firms or individuals.

11.3.8.1 Investigation

Upon receiving a report of a possible serious failure to meet the SRA's standards, or of facts that could constitute a serious breach of the SRA's regulatory requirements, the SRA may commence investigations or in the most serious cases may take immediate steps to protect clients or the public, by imposing conditions on a practice or closing a firm down by way of an intervention.

The SRA will assess all complaints and reports that it receives and decide whether an investigation is required. The SRA will act in accordance with the SRA's Regulatory and Disciplinary Procedure Rules in making this assessment.

The SRA applies a three-stage test known as the 'Assessment Threshold Test' in deciding whether to investigate a complaint or report. The three stages considered are:

1. Has there been a potential breach of the SRA's Standards and Regulations?
2. Is the potential breach or risk sufficiently serious that, if proved, the SRA would take action?
3. Is the breach or risk capable of being evidenced to the required standard of proof? Rule 8.7 of the SRA Regulatory and Disciplinary Procedure Rules provide that the civil standard of proof applies to all decisions made under the rules, that is, on the balance of probabilities *or* more likely than not.

If the answer to all three stages of the test is 'yes', the SRA will investigate the reported breach or failure to meet standards further. If the answer to any of these questions is 'no', the SRA is unlikely to investigate.

Detailed guidance on how the SRA conducts investigations and gathers evidence is available on its website.

The SRA will direct any complaints which appear to solely relate to poor service to the Legal Ombudsman (**11.7**).

11.3.8.2 Enforcement

The SRA's current Enforcement Strategy makes it clear that the SRA regulates 'in the public interest, protecting consumers, setting and enforcing high professional standards, and supporting access to affordable legal services, the rule of law and the administration of justice'. Accordingly, the SRA will focus enforcement action on serious issues that present a risk to the public.

The SRA has a range of enforcement powers available to address any failure to meet its prescribed standards. The SRA's powers are not designed to be punitive—but rather to focus on protecting users of legal services by controlling or limiting the risk of harm to clients and upholding the rule of law and the administration of justice. Enforcement action may also seek to prevent or deter future wrongdoing by an individual or firm or by other individuals or firms that the SRA regulates. Of course, the individual solicitor or firm subject to any enforcement action *may* see sanctions as harsh, but it is about the protection of the public.

11.3.8.2.1 When will the SRA take enforcement action?

The SRA focuses enforcement actions on the most serious issues—meaning serious breaches, misconduct or conduct that is improper and falls short of ethical standards either when taken in isolation or when demonstrating a persistent failure to comply. Full details are provided in the SRA's Enforcement Strategy.

In deciding what (if any) action to take, the SRA will consider all the relevant circumstances breach, including any aggravating or mitigating factors, while ensuring that the wider public interest is upheld. Accordingly, if the SRA is satisfied that there is no underlying public interest concern, it may close matters without further investigation or action. Alternatively, the SRA may close a case after providing advice or a warning to an individual or a firm about conduct, making clear that any further breaches may result in more serious future sanctions.

In considering the seriousness of a breach and what enforcement action to take, the SRA will consider past conduct and behaviour of an individual or firm and the risk of future breaches. The SRA may consider mitigating features including an apology or expression of regret or remorse or where there is no evidence of a pattern of misconduct. The SRA may also consider the background, character and circumstances of an individual or firm and any factors or features of the environment in which a solicitor was working.

As detailed within the Enforcement Strategy, the SRA may also consider other factors including:

- *Intention or motivation:* including whether a breach was because of a genuine mistake or whether an individual or firm demonstrated deliberate or reckless disregard for their obligations. The reputation of the legal profession is dependent on trust and therefore any conduct or behaviour which brings the integrity or trustworthiness of the profession into doubt will be treated seriously. In *Bolton v The Law Society* [1993] EWCA Civ 32, the court made it clear that any solicitor who is shown to have discharged their professional duties with anything less than complete integrity and trustworthiness must expect severe sanctions.
- *Harm and impact:* referring to any harm caused to a **victim** by the solicitor's conduct or firm's action. This may include financial loss or physical or mental harm that has occurred or that could have occurred because of the breach.
- *Vulnerability:* the SRA requires the same standards from solicitors irrespective of the nature of their clients but recognises that some clients are more vulnerable than others and therefore at a higher risk of being taken advantage of. In deciding whether to take action, the SRA may consider the personal attributes of the victim of a solicitor's breach (eg whether they had a health issue or learning **disability**) or any circumstances of the client's matter which made them particularly vulnerable (eg whether their legal matter was one which may have resulted in loss of personal liberty). This ties in with part 1.2 of the Individual Code which provides that you 'do not abuse your position by taking unfair advantage of clients or others', and could potentially breach Principle 6 which provides that you act 'in a way that encourages equality, diversity and inclusion', as well as potentially breaching other Principles and parts of the Codes of Conduct.
- *Role, experience and seniority:* the SRA requires compliance with the Codes of Conduct from all individuals and firms that it regulates, but the level of seniority or experience of an individual may be considered in respect of the control or influence that they may have had over a situation. However, inexperience will never excuse serious misconduct such as dishonesty.

- *Regulatory history and patterns of behaviour:* whether an individual or firm has a history of misconduct or breaches will be considered.
- *Remediation:* the SRA may take account of whether an individual or firm has been able to take remedial action to ensure that a breach will not happen again.
- *Criminal convictions:* the SRA will always investigate criminal convictions or cautions (which *must* be reported (including any criminal charges), as set in the Codes of Conduct and detailed at **11.3.6**) but will take a proportionate approach to this. For example, minor motoring offences are unlikely to warrant investigation or action by the SRA but more serious offences such as dishonesty offences such as theft, drink-driving or assault are likely to result in regulatory action. Offences resulting in custodial sentences and any offences relating to dishonesty will always result in SRA enforcement action.

11.3.8.2.2 Who is enforcement action taken against?

In any investigation, the SRA may consider the actions of a firm itself and of any individuals within it to determine whether enforcement action should be taken at all, and if so against whom. The contents of the Individual Code and the Firms Code may assist in determining this; though where obligations apply equally to firms and to individuals, the SRA is able to take enforcement action against both. Also note that breaches of the Codes of Conduct are likely to come hand-in-hand with breaches of the SRA Principles.

Investigations and actions will be taken against individuals where they are personally responsible for a breach.

11.3.9 What enforcement action can be taken?

At the conclusion of an investigation into a breach of its regulatory requirements, the SRA has various options available to it. Full details of the sanctions and controls available to the SRA, and the circumstances in which the SRA may impose sanctions, can be found within the Enforcement Strategy and particularly at Appendix A: Sanctions and Controls, which sets out the sanctions and controls in tabular format. The intention behind sanctions is to discipline the person to prevent similar misconduct, maintain standards and uphold public confidence. The intention behind the available controls is to protect the public and clients by 'controlling or limiting the risk of harm'.

These include:

1. *Closing* a case if it would be disproportionate to take action.
2. *Taking regulatory action, including*:
   - In the least serious cases, providing advice and warnings by way of a letter. This will include advising a firm or individual that they have breached the SRA's standards and warning them that more serious action may result if conduct or behaviour is repeated. This would be in response to a minor regulatory breach.
   - Issuing a rebuke—sanctioning a firm or individual for a moderately serious breach of standards with a view to upholding public confidence and deterring similar behaviour in the future. This is for a breach of moderate seriousness and do not require a higher level of response to maintain standards and uphold public confidence.
   - Imposing conditions on an individual or firm. Conditions could prevent the individual or firm from being involved in certain activities or require them to take certain steps to enable careful monitoring by the SRA to ensure the interests of the public are protected.
   - Issuing financial penalties to sanction a firm or individual. This would be appropriate in respect of a serious breach of standards but where suspension or strike-off would not be required to protect the public. For an individual solicitor, traditional law firm and individuals who work within them, the SRA can impose a financial penalty, since 2022 of up to £25,000. Prior to 2022 the SRA's fining powers were limited to £2,000. For licensed bodies (ABSs) and individuals working for them, the SRA can impose fines of up to £50 million for an individual or £250 million for an entity. The SRA's approach to financial penalties can be found online.

- Suspending or revoking a firm's authorisation either temporarily or permanently, if necessary to protect the public. Guidance on when the SRA will intervene into a practice, and the implications of an intervention, is available on the SRA website.

3. *Issuing disciplinary proceedings before the Solicitors Disciplinary Tribunal (SDT).* In cases involving serious breaches of standards and requirements, the SRA may refer matters to the SDT to consider suspension or strike-off of an individual. The SRA may refer a matter to the SDT even if they believe a fine of up to £25,000 is appropriate. This action will be taken where it is deemed necessary to protect the public and the public interest. Before bringing proceedings to the SDT, the SRA must be satisfied, following its own investigations, that it is in the public interest to make a referral and that there is a realistic prospect of the SDT making an order (under rule 6.1 Regulatory and Disciplinary Procedure Rules 2019). The SRA provides guidance on its website as to how it will decide whether to refer a matter to the SDT. The SRA will give notice to any person or firm that it is intending to refer to the SDT, providing an opportunity for representations to be put forward and considered by the SRA before a referral is made. The SRA makes some (but not all) regulatory and disciplinary decisions against regulated individuals and firms publicly available. Individual solicitor's records can be checked on the SRA's website, which also contains records of the most recent SRA regulatory decisions. In essence, therefore, disciplinary matters against solicitors and law firms, are in the public domain.

11.4 Solicitors Disciplinary Tribunal: introduction

The SDT is a Statutory Tribunal under s46 of The Solicitors Act 1974. It is subject to regulation by the LSB and is completely independent from the SRA. Its primary purpose is to adjudicate on alleged breaches of the rules and regulations applicable to solicitors and to the firms in which they work. The SDT has a range of sanctions available to it but does not have power to award compensation.

The SDT is made up of members appointed by the Master of the Rolls. There is no limit on the maximum number of members. Members include solicitors and lay members drawn from a wide range of backgrounds, seeking to represent the diversity of the profession and the public. Solicitor members of the SDT have no connection with the SRA (other than themselves being regulated as solicitors).

The SDT's jurisdiction extends beyond solicitors to include former solicitors, recognised bodies, RELs and RFLs. In some circumstances, the SDT also has jurisdiction in respect of individuals who are not qualified solicitors but who are employed or remunerated by solicitors (under s43 Solicitors Act 1974).

11.4.1 Solicitors Disciplinary Tribunal: proceedings

Most cases dealt with by the SDT are referred to it by the SRA. The remaining cases are commenced by members of the public. The SDT does not investigate cases itself or collect evidence in support of any applications; it simply decides cases based on the evidence put before it, which will generally consist of evidence obtained during the SRA's investigations. Applications to the SDT must be made in a prescribed form, supported by a statement setting out the allegations that the respondent is required to answer and the facts and matters in support of the application.

Applications to the SDT are considered in accordance with the Solicitors (Disciplinary Proceedings) Rules 2019. When an application is received by the SDT, its first duty is to consider whether there is a case for the respondent to answer (under rule 13). If an application shows that there is a case to answer, the application will be listed for a substantive hearing and directions will be given (rule 20).

Hearings before the SDT take place before a panel made up of two solicitors and one lay member. Hearings will usually be held in public (rule 35) and can now be watched via Zoom links on the SDT's website. The SRA always has legal representation before the SDT and a respondent may choose to be legally represented. Legal aid is not available to pay for a legal representative. The SDT's decision will be announced in public either at the end of the hearing or at a later date (rule 40). The SDT's judgments are accessible on its website.

In 2020 and 2021, due to the Covid-19 pandemic, the SDT conducted many hearings by way of video conferencing.

The SDT may make such order that it sees fit in respect of the costs of proceedings (rule 43). Where the SDT finds against a solicitor, the solicitor will usually be ordered to pay the costs of the proceedings (taking into account considerations such as the conduct of the parties, the amount of time spent on the matter, including the SRA's investigation costs, and the solicitor's personal financial means).

In November 2019 the standard of proof for first instance decisions in the SDT changed from the criminal standard (beyond reasonable doubt) to the civil standard (on the balance of probabilities *or* more likely than not). However, for cases certified prior to 25 November 2019, the standard of proof will be the criminal standard. That said, you should appreciate by now that the civil standard of proof is a much lower standard of proof than the criminal standard, and therefore since 2019 it is easier for the prosecution to succeed.

11.4.2 SDT powers and decisions

The SDT's powers are set out in s47 of the Solicitors Act 1974 and include powers to order:

- *That a solicitor be struck off the roll.* Strike-off is likely in the most serious of cases, particularly those involving dishonesty. Solicitors must be 'trusted to the ends of the earth' (*Bolton v Law Society* [1993] EWCA Civ 32) to ensure that the public are protected and to uphold the rule of law. Accordingly, any SDT findings of dishonesty are likely to result in strike-off.
- *That a solicitor be suspended from practice indefinitely or for a specified period.* Suspension may be appropriate in cases which do not warrant strike-off, but where serious sanctions are required for the protection of the public.
- *Fines.* Fines may be imposed for any breaches or to take away any financial advantage gained through misconduct.
- *The exclusion of a solicitor from* ***legal aid*** *work* (either permanently or for a specified period). This may be appropriate where specific rules and regulations relating to the Legal Aid Agency have not been complied with.
- A direction prohibiting the restoration of a solicitor's name to the Roll except by order of the tribunal.
- The payment by any party of costs or a contribution towards costs of such amount as the tribunal may consider reasonable. This may include the SRA's investigation costs.

The SDT's sanctions may be combined as appropriate (eg a solicitor may be fined and suspended).

Decisions of the SDT may be appealed to the High Court.

EXAMPLE

Jordan is an in-house solicitor. He had sought to register several charges at Companies House for the benefit of his employer. He initially completed the documentation incorrectly and by the time he resubmitted the charges he realised that he would be out of time to register them. He therefore redated the documents using correction fluid, to bring them within the time limit for registration, and resubmitted them. He states that he did so to protect his employer's interests. This would certainly constitute a 'serious breach'.

The matter was reported to the SRA, which has investigated and made a referral to the SDT.

Notwithstanding that Jordan was working as an in-house solicitor and that he intended his actions to be for the protection of his employer's interests, his actions were misleading and dishonest. Jordan is likely to be struck off.

11.4.3 Recent SDT decisions

The SDT publishes an annual report each July, available online, providing detail of its activities, hearings and decisions during the previous year. Decisions of the SDT are also available on their website. However, the last annual report available on their website was published in 2022.

11.5 SRA criminal proceedings

The SRA may commence criminal proceedings against individuals who are not regulated by the SRA but who either pretend to be solicitors or undertake reserved activities that require authorisation (**11.6**); or against regulated persons who take steps that undermine the SRA's regulatory role.

Examples of criminal proceedings that the SRA may bring include action under the Solicitors Act 1974 if an unqualified person acts as a solicitor (s20) or pretends to be or wrongly implies that they are a solicitor (s21) and against individuals or firms which knowingly or recklessly provide false information, or which falsify, conceal or destroy documents which would be relevant to an SRA investigation (s44BC). In addition, the SRA may bring criminal proceedings against individuals or firms that carry out reserved activities (see **11.6**) when not entitled to do so (pursuant to section 14 of the Legal Services Act 2007).

In deciding whether to commence criminal proceedings, the SRA must be satisfied that a case would pass a two-stage test; the 'evidential test' (that there would be sufficient evidence to provide a realistic prospect of conviction against an individual) and the 'public interest test' (that it would be in the public interest to bring a prosecution to protect the public and support the rule of law).

If the SRA is not satisfied that the test for bringing criminal proceedings is satisfied, it may take regulatory action or disciplinary action as an alternative.

11.6 Reserved legal activities

Legal services can be divided into two distinct categories—'reserved' and 'unreserved' activities.

Section 12(1)(a)–(f) of the Legal Services Act 2007 sets out the six specific 'reserved' legal services activities which (subject to extremely limited exceptions) only individuals and businesses that are authorised by an approved regulator may carry out. Authorisation of individuals and firms is discussed at **11.3.1**.

Authorisation to carry out reserved legal activities must be provided by one of the 'approved regulators' working under the oversight of the LSB (**Figure 11.1**).

The SRA is the approved regulator which authorises firms and individuals to carry out 'reserved legal activities'.

When the SRA provides authorisation to a firm, that firm can undertake reserved activities through individuals who are personally entitled to undertake those activities (which would include solicitors who hold current practising certificates, RELs and RFLs; but would not include trainee solicitors, former or non-practising solicitors or any person who has passed the SQE but is yet to obtain a practising certificate).

Table 11.2 sets out the 'Reserved Activities' under s12(1)(a)–(f) of the Legal Services Act 2007.

TABLE 11.2 Reserved legal activities

Activity	Explanation
Exercise of a right of audience	The right to appear before and address a court, and to call and examine witnesses. Note: Solicitors can only exercise their right of audience in certain courts after admission to the roll and while in receipt of a practising certificate. In order to exercise the right of audience in the senior courts (High Court, Crown Court, Court of Appeal) and Supreme Court, solicitors must pass an additional qualification (Higher Rights of Audience) and register that right with the SRA.
Conduct of litigation	Issuing proceedings before any court in England or Wales—commencing, prosecuting and defending proceedings and performing any ancillary functions in relation to those proceedings.

TABLE 11.2 Continued

Activity	Explanation
Reserved instrument activities	Preparing any instruments of transfer or charge for the purposes of the Land Registration Act 2002, making any applications or lodging documents for registration under that Act and preparing any instruments relating to real or personal estate for the purposes of the law of England and Wales. 'Instruments' includes a contract for sale or disposition of land but excludes wills or other testamentary instruments, letters or powers of attorney and transfers of stock containing no trusts or limitations of the transfer.
Probate activities	Preparing any probate papers on which to found or oppose a grant of probate or letters of administration. As set out above, preparing a will is not a reserved activity.
Notarial activities	Any activities which, prior to the LSA, were carried out by notaries under the Public Notaries Act 1801; though reg 9.1 of the SRA's Authorisation of Individuals Regulations and rule 5.1 of the SRA's Authorisation of Firms Rules make clear that authorisation from the SRA does not entitle a firm or an individual to carry out notarial activities.
The administration of oaths	The exercise of any powers conferred on a commissioner for oaths under the Commissioners for Oaths Act 1889, the Commissioners for Oaths Act 1891 and s24 of the Stamp Duties Management Act 1891.

Activities falling outside the scope of reserved legal activities detailed above are known as 'unreserved'.

'Unreserved activities' can be provided by individuals or organisations which are not authorised by one of the LSB's approved regulators, and are therefore unregulated providers of legal services. Examples could include individuals or businesses providing will-writing services or anyone providing general legal advice verbally or in writing (which may include most university law clinics).

It is an offence under s14(1) of the LSA for any person to knowingly carry out a reserved legal activity unless they are entitled to do so. A person guilty of an offence under s14 may be liable to imprisonment or a fine or, in respect of conduct of litigation, to proceedings for contempt of court.

EXAMPLE

Harvey has owned a will-writing business for several years, undertaking unreserved activities. He decides that he would like to expand the business by offering the additional service of applying to obtain grants of probate. Harvey is not a solicitor, REL or RFL and his business is not authorised by any of the authorised regulators, but he feels that he has developed excellent knowledge and understanding of all probate matters during the course of his business and he feels that he would be well placed to provide this additional service.

However, preparing papers on which to found or oppose a grant of probate is a reserved legal activity. If he expands the business as he suggests, it is likely that Harvey will be committing a criminal offence under s14(1) LSA. Harvey may have a defence if he can show that he did not know, or could not reasonably be expected to know, that an offence was being committed (s14(2) LSA); but in view of Harvey's previous involvement in will-writing services, it seems unlikely that Harvey will be able to argue this defence.

11.7 Legal Ombudsman

Whilst this chapter focuses on the SRA's regulatory regime, the Legal Ombudsman is also relevant to the regulation of solicitors. Brief information on the role of the Legal Ombudsman is provided below, with full details of its role and functions available on its website.

The Legal Ombudsman was established pursuant to the LSA. Its role is to help to resolve complaints made by consumers against regulated providers of legal services (including solicitors and law firms as well as barristers, legal executives and any other regulated providers of legal services).

The Legal Ombudsman investigates complaints relating to the standard of service provided to consumers, which could include complaints relating to the provision of costs information, unexplained delays in the progression of matters or poor information being provided to clients. Matters may be brought to the Legal Ombudsman after a law firm's own complaints procedure has been exhausted (see part 8 of the Individual Code). The Ombudsman's powers include asking firms to apologise for poor service and recommending that a firm refund or reduce its fees, or pay compensation for a client's losses or poor treatment (though the Ombudsman does not investigate or adjudge allegations of professional negligence, only of poor service).

Complaints dealt with by the Legal Ombudsman may (but will not always) relate to breaches of the SRA's regulatory regime, in which case matters may be investigated by the SRA as well as by the Ombudsman. The SRA and the Ombudsman may therefore refer matters between each other.

11.8 Professional indemnity insurance: introduction

All SRA-authorised bodies must have valid professional indemnity insurance (PII) in place to be able to carry on in practice, pursuant to the SRA Indemnity Insurance Rules.

The purpose of compulsory PII is to provide financial protection to clients in the event of unexpected events or circumstances, such as negligence or breach of duty on the part of a solicitor, which cause financial loss to the client.

Examples of events or circumstances that could cause loss to a client may include a solicitor giving wrong advice, missing a court deadline resulting in a client's claim being struck out or failing to act on a client's instructions. Together, these circumstances are known as professional negligence. However, a client will only be successful in a professional negligence action if they have suffered loss, therefore if there is no loss there is no claim, *but* a solicitor may still be subject to disciplinary action over their conduct.

PII also provides protection to firms and solicitors themselves, as it provides financial cover for the costs that a firm may otherwise incur in responding to or defending actions brought against it.

PII must be obtained by all new SRA-authorised firms before they start practising and must be renewed annually. Firms are required to demonstrate that they have PII in place at the time that they renew practising certificates and at all times while practising.

The premium payable for PII will be calculated considering relevant factors including a firm's previous claims history, the type of work it carries out and the number of principals and employees within the firm.

In the event of any SRA-authorised body being unable to renew its PII, insurance will continue to be provided by the firm's last-named insurer for up to 90 days. The firm will enter into what is known as the Extended Policy Period (EPP), a period of up to 30 days. During the EPP, the firm may continue to practise for existing clients and may take on new work but must seek to obtain new insurance and must draw up plans to close in an orderly fashion if it is unable to obtain cover. The SRA must be notified within five business days of a firm entering the EPP.

If, at the end of the EPP, a firm has been unable to obtain qualifying insurance (detailed in **11.8.1**), it will enter into the 'cessation period' (CP) during which it will still be able to carry out work on existing instructions but must seek to cease practice promptly (and by not later than 90 days from the commencement of the EPP).

11.8.1 Minimum terms of insurance

SRA-authorised firms must take out and maintain 'qualifying insurance' with a 'participating insurer'. 'Qualifying Insurance' refers to a policy of insurance that meets the SRA's minimum terms and conditions of PII (known as the MTC), which are set out in Annex 1 to the SRA Indemnity Insurance Rules. A 'participating insurer' refers to an insurer which has a current and valid participating insurer's agreement with the SRA.

The MTC set out that the insurance must provide indemnity against any amounts payable on the basis of recommendations by the Office for Legal Complaints (including the Legal Ombudsman) or any other regulatory body, as well as against any civil liability.

Under the MTC, the minimum sum insured for any one claim (exclusive of defence costs) must at the time of writing be £3 million. There must be no monetary limit on the cover for defence costs.

11.8.2 **Implications of non-compliance**

It is a serious regulatory breach for any authorised individual or authorised body to practise without sufficient insurance.

The responsibility to ensure compliance with the Indemnity Rules rests with each authorised body and with any principal of such body. A principal would include a sole practitioner in respect of a recognised sole practice, a partner in a partnership, a director or beneficial owner in a company and a member or owner in an LLP.

If a client suffers a loss because of the acts or omissions of a solicitor within an authorised firm which should have had PII but did not, the client may have recourse to the SRA Compensation Fund to be compensated for their losses.

11.8.3 **Solicitors outside SRA-authorised bodies**

The SRA Indemnity Insurance Rules apply to all SRA-authorised bodies but they do not apply to solicitors, RELs or RFLs who are in practice *outside* SRA-authorised bodies.

However, pursuant to part 5.6 of the Code of Conduct for Solicitors, RELs and RFLs, any solicitor, REL or RFL who carries on reserved legal activities in a 'non-commercial body' (as defined in s23(2) LSA and including charities and not-for-profit organisations) must ensure that the body takes out and maintains indemnity insurance that is adequate and appropriate to the services that it provides. What is considered to be 'adequate and appropriate' will depend on the nature of the individual business and circumstances.

Freelance solicitors providing reserved legal services must also maintain adequate and appropriate insurance, but freelance solicitors providing only non-reserved legal activities will not require PII.

11.9 **Other regulated providers of legal services**

As is noted throughout this chapter, the SRA's regulatory regime applies to all individual solicitors, RELs and RFLs, whether they work in private practice (either as sole practitioners or within firms), in not-for-profit organisations, as in-house solicitors or in businesses that provide a range of professional services in addition to legal services (sometimes known as multi-disciplinary practices or MDPs). The SRA's regulatory regime also applies to all SRA-regulated firms—including regulated law firms and ABS businesses.

Any other legally qualified professional such as a barrister, chartered legal executives or licensed conveyancer who works within an SRA-regulated practice will be subject to both SRA regulation and to regulation by their own regulator. Similarly, any solicitor practising in any entity outside a law firm will remain subject to SRA regulation.

Some organisations and individuals provide legal services that fall outside the remit of the Authorised Regulators under the LSA, such as immigration advisors, who are authorised and regulated by the Office of the Immigration Services Commissioner. However, any solicitor working within such an organisation will still also be subject to regulation by the SRA.

11.9.1 **CILEX**

CILEX members who are employed by and work under the supervision of an authorised person (including a solicitor either within a law firm or in-house) may carry out the reserved legal activities that their supervisor is entitled to carry out (by virtue of being an employee). This is pursuant to exemptions set out in Sch 3 to the LSA. CILEX members who are qualified as CILEX practitioners in specific areas of law (and have gained 'practice rights') can undertake reserved activities in their specific areas of practice without supervision, though they can only conduct advocacy in the lower courts and in chambers.

11.9.2 **Barristers**

In any legal matter, but most frequently in litigious matters when representation at court will be required, it may be necessary for a solicitor, REL or RFL to instruct a barrister on behalf of their client. In accordance with a solicitor's duties to their client under the SRA Principles and Individual Code, a solicitor must ensure that they act in the client's best interests in instructing a barrister, which will necessitate finding an appropriately experienced and qualified barrister and providing detailed instructions on the client's matter. Failure to act in their client's best interests in selecting and instructing a barrister may constitute a breach of the SRA's regulatory regime.

Conversely, if a client chooses to select and instruct a barrister independently of their solicitor, through the Direct Access scheme, the client will have separate legal relationships with the solicitor and the barrister and any complaints relating to the barrister's service or conduct would need to be directed to the barrister and their regulator.

11.10 **Alternative Business Structures**

The LSA makes provision for law firms to be owned or managed by people other than lawyers, and for businesses which are not law firms but provide some legal services—known as Alternative Business Structures.

Operating as an ABS and being authorised by the SRA (**11.3.1**) means that a business may provide regulated and reserved legal services alongside other professional services, such as insurance or financial services, and that it may employ the expertise of owners and managers who are not legally qualified.

The SRA has power to grant licences to any entity that wishes to become an ABS and meets its requirements. If the SRA grants authorisation, it will have power to regulate the ABS in the same way as it would regulate any other individual or firm.

ABS are still relatively uncommon in the legal sector, though some large law firms have converted to the structure to enable innovation and investment from non-lawyers, and some other organisations such as university law clinics have adopted the structure in order to offer reserved legal activities.

KEY POINT SUMMARY

- The primary purposes of the SRA's regulatory regime are to protect the public, uphold standards in the legal profession and ensure the administration of justice.
- All solicitors (whether in private practice, in-house or in any other organisations), all regulated firms and all employees within regulated firms must comply with the SRA's regulatory regime including the Principles and the Codes of Conduct (Individual and Firms).
- Solicitors must review the contents of the regulatory regime frequently and must take appropriate action to report any serious breaches to their firm's compliance officers or to the SRA directly.
- Failure to comply with the SRA's regulatory regime can have serious consequences for individuals and for firms, which may include complaints, professional negligence claims or disciplinary action by the SRA or SDT.
- Only authorised bodies or individuals may provide reserved legal activities.
- Law firms must have appropriate professional indemnity insurance in place to provide protection to their clients.

CHAPTER 12
Financial Services

FUNCTIONING LEGAL KNOWLEDGE

This chapter covers the following functional knowledge required to pass the SQE 1 assessments:

Financial services:

- the financial services regulatory framework including authorisation and how it applies to solicitors' firms
- recognition of relevant financial services issues including the identification of specified investments, specified activities and relevant exemptions
- application of the Financial Services and Markets Act 2000 and related secondary legislation to the work of a solicitor

Money laundering:

- purpose and scope of anti-money laundering legislation including the international context
- circumstances encountered in the course of practice where suspicion of money laundering should be reported in accordance with the legislation
- the appropriate person or body to whom suspicions should be reported, the appropriate time for such reports to be made and the appropriate procedure to be followed
- direct involvement and non-direct involvement offences, and defences to those offences under Proceeds of Crime Act 2002
- due diligence requirements

AUTHORITIES UNDERPINNING PRACTICE

The key authorities that underpin this area of practice are listed below. Note that for legislation you are linked to legislation.gov.uk.

Although much of the legislation on this government website is available in its amended form, the incorporation of new amendments into the text of legislation can be delayed. You should refer to legal databases to ensure you are referencing the most up-to-date legislation.

- Financial Services Act 2012
  http://www.legislation.gov.uk/ukpga/2012/21/contents/enacted
- Financial Services and Markets Act 2000
  http://www.legislation.gov.uk/ukpga/2000/8/contents
- Financial Services and Markets Act 2000 (Regulated Activities) Order 2001/544
  https://www.legislation.gov.uk/uksi/2001/544/contents/made
- Terrorism Act 2000
  https://www.legislation.gov.uk/ukpga/2000/11/contents
- Proceeds of Crime Act 2002
  https://www.legislation.gov.uk/ukpga/2002/29/contents
- Financial Services Act 2012
  https://www.legislation.gov.uk/ukpga/2012/21/part/2/crossheading/financial-conduct-authority-and-prudential-regulation-authority/enacted

- Serious Crime Act 2015
  https://www.legislation.gov.uk/ukpga/2015/9/contents/enacted
- Criminal Finances Act 2017
  https://www.legislation.gov.uk/ukpga/2017/22/contents/enacted
- Money Laundering, Terrorist, Financing and Transfer of Funds (Information on the Payer) Regulations 2017 (SI 2017/692)
  https://www.legislation.gov.uk/uksi/2017/692/contents/made
- The Money Laundering Regulations (As Amended)
  https://www.legislation.gov.uk/uksi/2022/137/made
- The Financial Services and Markets Act 2023
  https://www.legislation.gov.uk/ukpga/2023/29/pdfs/ukpga_20230029_en.pdf
- Economic Crime and Corporate Transparency Act 2023 (ECCTA)
  https://www.legislation.gov.uk/ukpga/2023/56/contents/2024-03-04
- SRA Financial Services (Scope) Rules
  https://www.sra.org.uk/solicitors/standards-regulations/financial-services-scope-rules/
- SRA Financial Services (Conduct of Business) Rules
  https://www.sra.org.uk/globalassets/documents/sra/consultations/phase-two-financial-services-cob-rules.pdf?version=4a1ac8

12.1 Introduction

This chapter covers the regulation of solicitors in relation to financial services and money laundering. Understanding these topics is an essential part of practising as a solicitor where the consequences for any breaches can be severe, including criminal sanctions. This chapter will consider the relevant legislation in context to the role of a solicitor so that it can be more easily applied to situations within practice.

Most solicitors will provide work in relation to financial services at some point in their career. If they do, they must be able to comply with the regulations set out by the Financial Conduct Authority (FCA) and the Solicitors Regulation Authority (SRA).

The FCA Handbook contains a glossary of terms which can be accessed via the FCA's website. You should familiarise yourself with this glossary and refer to this when you need clarification of any terms relating to financial services. It is easy to use online and has a search function.

Below are some examples of the type of work which a solicitor may advise, manage, safeguard or arrange in relation to financial services:

(a) in business law when making arrangements to purchase or start up a business;
(b) in probate when executors are disposing of the deceased's assets;
(c) in conveyancing when a client may need assistance in obtaining a mortgage or the solicitor is arranging implementation of a Legal Indemnity Insurance Policy;
(d) in employment law if helping a client to invest damages received;
(e) in private client work, including obtaining a life insurance police, tax planning etc;
(f) in litigation when the client requires After the Event Insurance to protect against any adverse costs risks;
(g) in corporate law when dealing when drafting certain documents;
(h) in family work when looking at financial issues on divorce, family business, life insurance etc.

12.2 Background to financial services

The first significant comprehensive legislation relating to the provision of financial services was the Financial Services Act 1986. It received royal assent in November 1986 and came into force in April 1988. Prior to this Act the provision of financial services was mostly self-regulated and one of the driving forces behind the call for regulation was several financial scandals, one such scandal involved the mis-selling of private pensions. The Act mainly sought to protect investors by regulating 'investment business' which included giving investment advice or establishing collective investment schemes. Only those who were authorised, exempt or excluded were entitled to carry on investment business.

The Financial Services Act 1986 was repealed by the Financial Services and Markets Act 2000 (Consequential Amendments and Repeals) Order 2001 on 1 December 2001 with the introduction of the Financial Services and Markets Act 2000 (FSMA) which came into force on the same day. FSMA 2000 (as amended) along with FSMA (Regulated Activities) Order 2001 remain the key legislation in the provision of financial services.

FMSA 2000 established the Financial Services Authority as the single regulator for financial services in the UK. The Financial Services Authority was described as 'the independent, non-governmental regulator of the financial services industry in *R (on the application of Davies) v Financial Services Authority* [2003] EWCA Civ 1128.

The Financial Services Authority was abolished by the Financial Services Act 2012 (FSA 2012) which established two new regulators, the Financial Conduct Authority (FCA), who regulate financial services firms and financial markets in the UK, and the Prudential Regulation Authority (PRA), who are responsible for the prudential regulation and supervision of banks, building societies, insurers and major investment firms. FSA 2012 also established the Financial Policy Committee (FPC) which monitors and takes action to improve financial stability after the financial crisis in 2008.

There have been other key amendments to FSMA which will be identified in this chapter, and means when viewing the legislation, you should use a legal database to ensure you are viewing the current version of the statute.

You should also be aware that there are several planned amendments to FSMA, which are not yet in force, under the following statutes:

- Bank of England and Financial Services Act 2016
- Financial Services Act 2021
- Financial Services and Markets Act 2023

The Financial Services and Markets Act 2023 will signal major reforms for financial services within the UK, including seeking to address the issues following Brexit.

12.3 **Financial Conduct Authority**

The FCA took over most of the FSA's regulatory functions when it was formed in 2013. It regulates the conduct of all firms and dual-regulated firms.

The FCA's general duties, taken from s1B of the Financial Services Act 2012 are:

To act in a way which

(a) is compatible with its strategic objective, and

(b) advances one or more of its operational objectives.

One of the main aims of the FCA is to secure the appropriate degree of protection for consumers when making investments.

The FCA Handbook is an extensive and useful tool which can be accessed online.

12.4 **Prudential Regulation Authority**

The PRA is a financial services regulatory body, part of the Bank of England. The PRA generally supervises financial institutions which manage significant financial risks. Examples of these institutions are banks, building societies, credit unions, insurers and major investment firms. These institutions are known as dual-regulated as they are also regulated by the FCA.

Policy created by the PRA for the firms they regulate to follow is enacted through the PRA Rulebook.

12.5 The general prohibition

The general prohibition is a very important area for solicitors who carry out work in relation to financial services to be aware of and understand so they avoid breaching the prohibition and committing an offence. Section 19 FSMA 2000 prohibits a person from carrying on a regulated activity unless that person is authorised under the Act, is excluded or is an exempt person. However, the general prohibition should be in the mind of all practising solicitors, as any inadvertent breach can have severe penalties. Practising solicitors must understand that they cannot provide these regulated financial activities unless they are authorised or exempt. For example, a solicitor, ignorant of the rules, who discusses investment opportunities with a client who has just received a large personal injury settlement, may breach the general prohibition.

The two main areas in which this would be relevant to solicitors are:

(a) carrying out a regulated activity, for example advising on investments in shares;

(b) making a financial promotion.

Breach of the general prohibition is a criminal offence under s23 FSMA 2000. It is important that you can identify situations where you may be asked to act in a way which contravenes the general prohibition and ensure that you properly follow the relevant rules and regulations to ensure you can act, before doing so. In this respect, it is important that you keep a detailed written note of the factors that you have considered, the decision and the reasons. A person who breaches the prohibition is guilty of a criminal offence and is liable to:

- A custodial sentence of up to six months or a fine, or both, on summary conviction,
- A custodial sentence of up to two years or a fine, or both, following conviction on indictment.

12.5.1 Regulated activity

Solicitors carrying out business in the UK should establish whether they are required to apply for authorisation to carry on regulated activities. As stated by the SRA on their website: 'As a firm you need to determine whether or not you need to be authorised by the FCA or can rely on Part 20 of FSMA.' To establish whether a person is carrying out a regulated activity and therefore needs to have authorisation, the activities and specified investments which constitute 'regulated activities' are set out generally under s22 FSMA 2000, as amended by the FSA 2012.

> (1) An activity is a **regulated activity** for the purposes of this Act if it is an **activity of a specified kind** which is carried on **by way of business** and—
>
> (a) relates to an **investment of a specified kind**; or
>
> (b) . . . is carried on in relation to property of any kind.

12.5.2 By way of business

Generally, this is referred to as the 'business test' and it will be obvious if the 'by way of business' element is satisfied. As such, if the business test is not satisfied, authorisation will not be necessary. FCA guidance on this provides that 'whether or not an activity is carried on by way of business is ultimately a question of judgement that takes account of several factors (none of which is likely to be conclusive)' (PERG 2.3.3). The guidance continues and lists a number of factors that can be taken into account;

i. 'The degree of continuity'

ii. 'The existence of a commercial element'

iii. 'The scale of the activity'

iv. 'The proportion which the activity bears to other activities carried on by the same person but which are not regulated'

In *Smith v Anderson* (1880) 15 Ch D 247 (at 277 and 278) it was stated that:

> 'the expression 'carrying on' implies a repetition of acts, and excludes the case of an association formed for doing one particular act which is never to be repeated. That series of acts is to

be a series of acts which constitute a business . . . The association . . . must be formed in order to carry on a series of acts having the acquisition of gain for their object.'

Under the provisions of the act the Treasury have the power to amend the meaning of 'by way of business'. This power has been exercised in the Financial Services and Markets Act 2000 (Carrying on Regulated Activities by Way of Business) Order 2001, for example. The outcome of this is that the business element of the consideration is modified in respect of certain activities.

12.5.3 Specified activities

In addition to the description of specified activities, within FSMA 2000, the Financial Services and Markets Act 2000 (Regulated Activities) Order 2001 (SI 2001/544) (RAO) lists specified activities in Part II as including the following:

- dealing in investments as an agent (art 21);
- arranging investments (art 25);
- managing investments (art 37);
- safeguarding investments (art 40);
- advising on investments (art 53);
- entering as provider into a funeral plan contracts (art 59);
- additional more specific activities.

12.5.3.1 Dealing in investments as an agent

This covers buying, selling, subscribing for or underwriting designated, pure protection contracts, general insurance contracts or structured deposits as agent. An example of this could be selling shares for a client due to a financial consent order made on divorce.

12.5.3.2 Arranging deals in investments

This covers making arrangements for another person (whether as principal or agent) to buy, sell, subscribe for or underwrite a particular investment. It must be something more than simply introducing the client to the investment.

12.5.3.3 Managing investments

This involves managing assets belonging to another person in circumstances which involve the exercise of discretion. For example, making decisions on issuing dividends on shares which form part of a trust fund which the solicitor is administering.

12.5.3.4 Safeguarding and administering investments

This involves the safeguarding of assets belonging to another and the administration of those assets, or arranging for one or more other persons to carry on that activity. This will be common in firms that undertake trust and probate work.

12.5.3.5 Advising on investments

This does not cover generic advice; it covers more specific advice and requires advising a person if the advice is given to an investor or potential investor and they are providing advice as to the merits of their investments. Generic advice would be something like advising on the advantages and disadvantages between repayment and endowment mortgages and does not fall under advice on investments.

12.5.3.6 Entering as provider into a funeral plan contract

This covers rights under a contract under which a person makes one or more payments to another person and the other person undertakes to provide a funeral in the UK for the customer (or some other person) on their death. The only exclusion to this is if, at the time of entering the contract, both persons intend or expect the funeral to occur within one month.

12.5.4 **Excluded activities under the RAO**

In addition to exemptions for those supervised by a **designated professional body**, there are several additional **exclusions** from art 25(1) arrangements. This means that a solicitor does not need to be authorised when carrying out certain work.

The exclusions are set out fully in the RAO 2001 (arts 26–36) and the first four are listed as follows:

- arrangements not causing a deal (art 26);
- enabling parties to communicate (art 27);
- arranging transactions to which the arranger is a party (art 28);
- arranging deals through **authorised persons** (art 29).

These exclusions fall into two main types:

- exclusions which apply depending on the investment which is subject to the activity; and
- exclusions of a general application, which apply regardless of the investment.

For solicitors, there are three main exclusions within art 36 which would be the most relevant. These are listed and explained below.

12.5.4.1 Trustees and personal representatives

Trustees and personal representatives can be excluded from the general prohibition. Therefore, solicitors acting in this way can carry out activities such as arranging, managing, safeguarding and advising without being authorised.

12.5.4.2 Activities in the provision of non-investment services

Solicitors carrying out the provision of non-investment services are excluded as long as they are dealing as agent, arranging, safeguarding and advising and are doing it within the course of their profession.

EXAMPLE

Kenny instructs a solicitor to carry out probate. He has also instructed her to arrange for the sale of all assets to pay inheritance tax. They would be providing advice and preparing all the necessary documentation in connection with this.

In this instance, the solicitor is acting 'by way of business' as they are doing this work in their role as a solicitor within their firm. The preparation of documentation relating to probate, arranging for sale of assets is a specified investment and by the solicitor arranging it they would be carrying out a specified investment activity. In order to avoid breaching the general prohibition and committing an offence, the solicitor must only act if there is an exclusion or an exemption. In relation to probate and the arrangement of sale of assets, this is classed as an exclusion in the RAO as it is an activity in the course of non-investment services.

12.5.4.3 Activities in relation to the sale of a body corporate

Solicitors are excluded when they are arranging, advising and dealing as agent in relation to transactions to buy or sell shares in a body corporate where, generally:

(a) the transaction involves the acquisition or disposal of a least 50% of the voting shares in the body corporate; or

(b) the object of the transaction is the acquisition of day-to-day control of the affairs of the body corporate.

12.5.5 **Specified investments**

FSMA 2000 does not define what investments are specified investments, however the RAO lists several investments in Part III to be included, which include:

(a) deposits (these include ISAs and money held in bank or building society accounts);
(b) contracts of insurance (including life policies, defective title indemnity insurance, buildings and household insurance, after-the-event legal expenses insurance);
(c) company stocks and shares etc;
(d) instruments creating or acknowledging indebtedness;
(e) government and public securities such as gilts, but excluding National Savings products;
(f) instruments giving entitlement to investments;
(g) certificates representing certain securities;
(h) units in a collective investment scheme;
(i) rights under a stakeholder pension scheme;
(j) options;
(k) futures;
(l) contracts for differences etc;
(m) Lloyd's syndicate capacity and syndicate membership;
(n) funeral plan contracts;
(o) regulated mortgage contracts; and
(p) rights to or interests in investments.

There are some investments that are not included in this list and are therefore not regulated by FSMA 2000. These are interests in land, currency and tangible assets such as cars, boats etc.

However, it is important to note that the Financial Services and Markets Act 2023 (s69) has extended the definition of regulated activities to those involving cryptoassets. Section 417 FSMA 2000 was also amended by s69 of the Financial Services and Markets Act 2023 to include a definition for cryptoassets being 'any cryptographically secured digital representation of value or contractual rights that (a) can be transferred stored or traded electronically and (b) uses technology supporting the recording or storage of data'.

EXAMPLE

Ms Bridges has received a £40,000 lump sum as part of a divorce settlement, using a solicitor in the family department. She states to her solicitor in the corporate and commercial department that she wishes to purchase shares in a company and would like some advice on which company she should invest in. She also asks for some generic advice on the advantages and disadvantages of a repayment mortgage and endowment mortgage.

This would be a regulated activity under s22 FSMA because the solicitor satisfies the business test and is being asked to carry out an activity relating to an activity of a specified kind (Advising on Investments, art 53 RAO Part II) and relating to an investment of a specified kind (Shares, art 76 RAO Part III).

In order to provide Ms Bridges with advice on this, the solicitor will need to determine whether they are excluded or exempt. If they are not excluded or exempt and provide her with advice, then the solicitor would be in breach of the general prohibition and could be liable for committing a criminal offence. The advice on the mortgages would not fall under advice on investments as it is general advice and is therefore outside the regulations of FSMA 2000. However, the solicitor would be prudent to keep a detailed file note of the advice given and confirm the same in writing.

12.6 Solicitors and their designated professional body

FSMA 2000 allows law firms to carry out certain financial activities without being regulated by the FCA if the criteria under s327 FSMA is satisfied. In relation to solicitors, the SRA states that each firm must fall under one of the following criteria:

(a) be authorised and regulated by a designated professional body (DPB), such as the SRA, under Pt 20 FSMA 2000; or

(b) be able to rely on a statutory exclusion, meaning that the activity is not a **regulated financial activity**. Examples include debt collecting where the activities are undertaken by a solicitor while also providing advocacy services or litigation services.

Each solicitor's firm needs to determine whether they need to be authorised by the FCA or can rely on the exemption in s327 FSMA 2000 (pursuant to the SRA (Financial Services) Scope Rules which is the starting point once a solicitor has decided that they have been asked to advise on a regulated financial activity and for considering whether they are exempt from the general prohibition). In many situations, a solicitors' firm would be able to rely on point (a) above as they are authorised by the SRA, which is the DPB for solicitors.

12.6.1 Exemption from the general prohibition under s327 FSMA 2000 (Pt 20)

In your capacity as a solicitor, you should be aware of the DPB/SRA exemption under s327 FSMA 2000. Note that under the provisions of the SRA (Financial Services) Scope Rules, solicitors only need to satisfy s327(2) *to* (5). In order to understand where the general prohibition does not apply, you must look at whether the following conditions are satisfied:

(a) a person is a member of a profession or is controlled or managed by such members;

(b) a firm must not receive from a person other than their client any pecuniary reward or other advantage, which they do not account to their client;

(c) the manner of the provision in the course of carrying on the activities must be incidental to the provision of professional services;

(d) a person must not carry on, or hold themselves out as carrying on, a regulated activity apart from one in relation to which he is an exempt person.

In point (c), incidental should be considered in relation to the proportion of the firm's work relating to regulated activities. This needs to be looked at in comparison with the other professional services that it provides and should not be a major part of the firm's activities. It must also be closely connected to the business. As such, if the activity is not incidental to the provision of professional services, it will not satisfy the relevant criteria under s327 FSMA 2000.

12.7 Regulation of solicitors

The SRA is the independent regulatory body which supervises and regulates the way in which non-mainstream regulated activities are carried on. **Figure 12.1** outlines the regulatory regime.

12.7.1 The Scope Rules

The SRA Financial Services (Scope) Rules and the SRA Financial Services (Conduct of Business) Rules set out the main framework for carrying out regulated financial services under s327 FSMA 2000 for solicitors. These rules are relatively straightforward and provide the basis for when the general prohibition on carrying out a regulated activity does not apply. Solicitors' firms must comply with these regulatory arrangements when seeking to use the DPB exemption.

In essence, the Scope Rules tell you *when* you can carry out a regulated financial service. Rule 2 of the Scope Rules sets out the criteria that must be satisfied for a solicitor to carry out any regulated

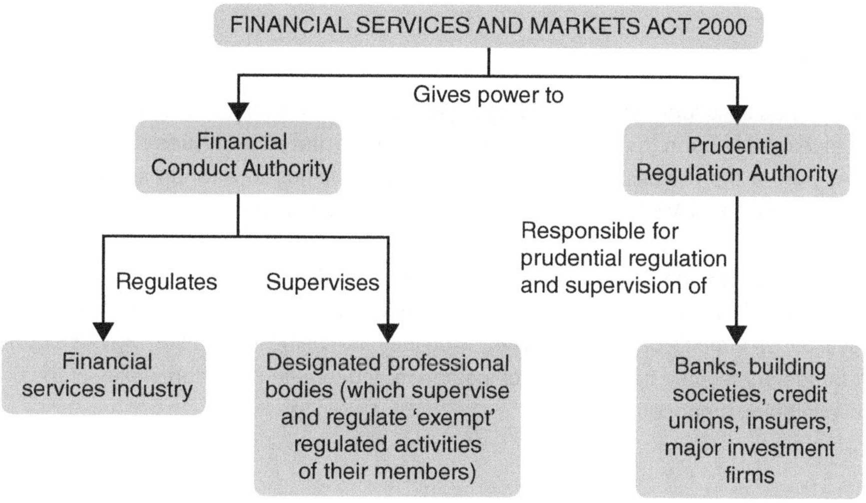

FIGURE 12.1 Regulatory regime

financial services activity. Rule 2.1(a) stipulates that the conditions in s327(2)–(5) of FSMA must be satisfied (see above).

The wording of Rule 2.1(b) can cause some confusion with reference to the regulated financial service being 'complementary' to the provision of a professional service to a particular client. In addition, the use of this term should not be confused with the term 'incidental' in s327 FSMA 2000. In order to make a decision on this, you should consider whether the financial activity is an unrelated new instruction or whether the need for the activity arises from current instructions.

For example, if a solicitor is acting for a client in a conveyancing matter and the client asks the solicitor to advise on whether they should invest in some shares in a construction company, those instructions have not arisen from the conveyancing transaction and are completely unrelated. In these circumstances, the request to provide a regulated financial service cannot be said to be complimentary. The activity is being requested in isolation to the conveyancing instructions.

Now consider a solicitor acting for a client in civil litigation where the client should have the benefit of an insurance product to protect against any adverse cost orders. The need for the solicitor to arrange that product for the client has arisen out of the instructions in the civil proceedings. It can therefore be said to be 'complimentary' and is not something the solicitor is doing in isolation to what they are instructed to do.

Other examples taken from the SRA's website include:

- Providing debt counselling in respect of joint credit card debts in a matrimonial matter
- Advising a client on how they should invest monies when advising on a will or probate matter

The Scope Rules are clearly drafted and can be found on the SRA's website.

12.7.2 The Conduct of Business Rules

The Conduct of Business (COB) Rules come into play once a firm can provide a regulated financial activity to a client, that is, the Scope Rules have been satisfied. In essence, the COB Rules dictate the *way* in which the firm will carry out that activity. Amongst other things, the rules set out what information must be provided to the client in writing (Rule 2), that where it has been decided to effect a transaction then this should be done as soon as possible (Rule 3), what records must be kept in respect of any transaction (Rule 4), that steps must be taken to safeguard assets entrusted by the client (Rule 6) and that records should be kept for six years (Rule 8). Of particular interest is Rule 15 which relates to renumeration in insurance distribution activities. Rule 15 provides that you must not be renumerated or renumerate or assess the performance of a firm's employee in a way which conflicts with their duty to act in each client's best interest (SRA Principle 7). In essence, this is a prohibition on providing any incentive to a firm or its employees in recommending a particular contract of insurance to a client when a different contract of insurance may better suited to the client's needs.

The full Conduct of Business Rules can be found on the SRA's website.

EXAMPLE

An unauthorised solicitors' firm is providing some legal services for a client, Mr Green. The solicitor has managed to bring the work within the **exempt regulated activities** regime (s327 FSMA 2000). As part of the professional service, the solicitor wishes to arrange some Warranty and Indemnity insurance for Mr Green. The firm has an insurance distribution officer who is registered with the FCA.

In accordance with the Conduct of Business Rules, the firm can provide this insurance to the client but must follow rule 11. This means the firm must provide a 'demands and needs statement' which sets out Mr Green's demands and needs on the basis of the information provided by him, the reason for recommending that contract of insurance and to reflect the complexity of the contract of insurance being proposed.

12.7.3 What to look out for

As a solicitor, it is crucial to understand the financial services legislation and whether it applies to your work. Failure to follow this can lead to sanctions. There are signs to look for which could alert you to when this is necessary.

The main questions to ask yourself are:

- Does this activity involve a specified investment?
- Is this activity a regulated activity under the RAO?
- If it is, does it fall within any of the exclusions in the RAO?
- If it does not, is this activity capable of being an exempt regulated activity under s327 of FSMA 2000?
- Does this activity comply with the Scope Rules and Conduct of Business Rules?

EXAMPLE

Miss Chen has received £12,000 from an unfair dismissal claim in which one of the solicitors from the employment law department represented her. Miss Chen has asked for advice on where she should invest the money. Can you advise?

(a) Does the activity involve a specified investment?
Yes, and to advise properly you need to be able to cover all types of investment as some will be specified investments.

(b) Is the activity capable of being a regulated activity under the RAO?
Yes, advising on investments.

(c) If so, does it fall within any of the exclusions in the RAO?
No, it does not fall within any of the exclusions. Article 67 (Provision of non-investment services) is not available as the activity could not be reasonably regarded as a necessary part of the other services provided to Miss Chen; that is, representing in the employment law claim. However, please note that the exclusion under Art 67 only applies when dealing with certain regulated activities, not all of them.

(d) Does this activity comply with the Scope Rules and Conduct of Business Rules?

Even if the activity is incidental to the professional services offered by the firm, it cannot be said to be complementary to the provision of legal services under the Scope Rules.

You cannot advise Miss Chen. If you did, then you would be in breach of the financial services legislation and potentially commit a criminal offence. The only thing you could do would be to provide generic advice on the different types of investments and their different characteristics, but again it would be best practice for a solicitor to refer the client to a regulated financial advisor or advise them to seek independent financial advice. Even general advice could be misinterpreted by the client as specific investment advice.

12.8 The UK leaving the EU and the impact on financial services

The UK formally left the EU on 31 January 2020. The Treasury made over 50 EU Exit Statutory Instruments under the European Union (Withdrawal) Act 2018 prior to this. Part of the aim was to make sure that the financial services regulatory regime within the UK would be prepared for a variety of scenarios which could occur upon exit.

The UK left the EU and entered a transition period which ended on 31 December 2020. The European Union (Withdrawal Agreement) Act 2020 delayed parts of the EU Exit Statutory Instruments so that they came into force at the end of the transition period rather than at exit on 31 January 2020.

The Treasury retained the regulators' 'Temporary Transitional Power' (TTP), which was introduced via the Financial Services and Markets Act 2000 (Amendment) (EU Exit) Regulations 2019. This was used by UK regulators for a period of two years from the end of the transition period. After this, legislation introducing UK policies in areas previously within EU competence (including anti-money laundering) came into effect. This allowed the Bank of England, PRA and FCA to develop changes to UK regulatory requirements so that firms can adjust to the changes in an orderly way and alongside the objectives already set by Parliament.

12.9 Financial promotions

On their website, the FCA state that financial promotions are 'how firms communicate financial services and products to consumers'. It is important that safeguards are put in place in respect of these financial promotions because they can 'significantly influence a consumer's decision when choosing a financial product or service' (source: FCA website).

FSMA 2000 contains controls on financial promotions. The relevant provisions are in s21(1) of FSMA 2000. It is important to note that s21 FSMA 2000 was amended by s20 of the Financial Services and Markets Act 2023. Section 21 FSMA 2000 provides:

A person ('A') must not, in the course of business, communicate an invitation or inducement to (a) engage in investment activity...

If caught by this provision, the communication can only be made if the person is authorised by the FCA or the content of the communication is approved by an authorised person (s21(2) FSMA 2000). An authorised person cannot, under any circumstances, give approval of the financial promotion unless they have permission to do so by the FCA (s55NA FSMA 2000).

Guidance on financial promotions from the FCA can be found in PERG 8 which provides detailed guidance on whether a communication is subject to the provisions of the Act. It is, however, important to note that FCA guidance only represents the views of the FCA, and is not binding upon courts.

The Financial Services and Markets Act 2023 added to the definition of investment in s21(14) of FSMA 2000 cryptoassets.

There are four main conditions that must be satisfied to be caught by s21(1), namely:

i. A person must be acting in the *course of business*, and
ii. there must be a *communication*, and
iii. that communication must *invite or induce*,
iv. engagement in investment activity.

The following three statutes are also relevant when considering financial promotions;

i. The Financial Services and Markets Act 2000 (Regulated Activities) Order 2001.
ii. The Financial Services and Markets Act 2000 (Financial Promotion) Order 2005.
iii. The Financial Services and Markets Act 2023.

12.9.1 The 'Invitation or Inducement' element

There is no statutory definition as to what amounts to an 'invitation or inducement'. The FCA do provide guidance that an objective test, rather than a subjective test, should be applied and stipulates that 'the essential elements of an invitation or an inducement... must both have the purpose or intent of leading a person to engage in investment activity'. As such, when looking at the surface of the communication, it must be seeking to persuade or incite. In this respect, a communication that says a consumer should definitely buy shares in a specifically named company would be seen as an invitation or incitement to engage in investment activity.

If communications contain purely factual information with no indication that they are seeking to invite or induce, then they will not be caught by the regulations. In this respect, a communication that advises that a certain company has shares for sale, would not be seen as an invitation or incitement. However, this will always be a question of fact. There could be an argument that, why would a company advertise that they had shares for sale if they were not inviting or inducing individuals to engage in investment activity? In other words, is the company trying to generate future business? By way of further example, consider 'Tombstone' adverts. Whether a 'Tombstone' advert is an invitation or inducement will depend on the contents. The FCA say it will depend 'on the extent to which their contents seek to persuade or incite persons to contact the advertiser for details of its services or to do business with it' (PERG 8.4.10).

Overall, when looking at whether a communication seeks to invite or induce a person to engage in investment activity will be a question of fact. Analyse the communication being made and consider whether it seeks to persuade individuals to do business in respect of a transaction, for example buy shares in a company.

12.9.2 In the course of business

The definition here is distinct to the business test that was considered above in relation to regulated activities. Here, there needs to be a commercial interest on behalf of the person making the communication and the definition is intended to exclude genuine non-business communications.

EXAMPLE

A solicitor is invited to a private party by some close friends. At the party the solicitor has a conversation with another guest who they have not met before. The other guest mentions that they have recently made a substantial profit by selling some 'buy-to-let' properties and is looking to invest the profit. The solicitor says that the other guest should buy shares in a specific company which they have recently invested in because their shares have already made a profit and are continuing to rise in value. The 'invitation or inducement' element would certainly be satisfied, but the solicitor *would not* be acting in the course of business. This would be considered a genuine non-business communication.

However, consider if the solicitor had provided this advice after the other guest had come to see them in their office and had asked for professional advice on where they should invest their money. This would involve the solicitor acting in the course of business.

Another important consideration is whether or not the business actually exists. If an individual has an idea for a business and asks others to be involved with the business venture, or invest in the business, prior to the business existing, then this would not be acting in the course of business, unless the individual in question is in the business of setting up new businesses. However, contrast this with a situation where an individual has already established a business, and makes an offer to others to invest on the basis that the business will become a limited company. Even though the identity of the company will change, this would still be considered as acting in the course of business because the business already exists.

12.9.3 Communicate

You should note that the general prohibition in s21 FSMA also includes causing a communication to be made (s21(13)). The FCA provide some useful guidance on what constitutes a communication that 'a person is communicating where he gives materials to the recipient or where, in certain circumstances, he is responsible for transmitting the material on behalf of another person' (PERG 8.6). Communications can be via oral or written means.

12.9.4 Engage in Investment Activity

This has a statutory definition which is found in s21(8) FSMA which provides that:

'engagement in investment activity means—

(a) entering or offering to enter into an agreement the making or performance of which by either party constitutes a controlled activity; or

(b) exercising any rights conferred by a controlled investment to acquire, dispose of, underwrite or convert a controlled investment.'

'Controlled activities' are set out in Sch 1 of the Financial Services and Markets Act 2000 (Financial Promotion) Order 2005. They include, for example, accepting deposits, effecting or carrying out contracts of insurance, debt-counselling, arranging deals in investments, managing investments and advising on investments. 'Controlled investments 'are set out in P II of Sch 1 and include, amongst other things, futures, options, rights under a contract of insurance and shares or stock.

12.10 Money laundering

It is essential that you are able to recognise circumstances in which an individual is attempting to launder money through a law firm; have knowledge of the legislation and the safeguards that can be deployed in order to prevent and/or detect money laundering; and know who you should report any suspicions of money laundering to. Not least, because acting contrary to the anti-money laundering legislation can result in criminal prosecution and a custodial sentence.

Money laundering is a process by which dirty money becomes clean money. By dirty money we mean funds that have been generated from an illegal source, such as a crime. When these dirty funds become clean, the funds appear to be from a legitimate or trustworthy source, for example a solicitor's client account or a bank *rather than* from the sale of drugs, fraud, tax evasion, for example. Criminals launder money because it can make the funds easier to spend and the more transactions there are between the original illegal source (the crime that has been committed) and the funds, the less likely it can be that crime agencies will be able to correlate the funds with the original illegal origin. This means that criminals can evade justice. It is important to note that clean money can also become dirty, for example by funding a terrorist situation (Terrorism Act 2000).

As solicitors are so heavily regulated and are expected to operate ethically in accordance with the SRA Principles and Code of Conduct, they can be a target for money launderers as money received from a solicitor's account will be regarded as originating from a trustworthy source. Junior lawyers are likely to be targeted by criminals as being seemingly less experienced than more senior staff. It is important that regardless of your seniority within a firm you take money laundering seriously.

It is no surprise that the SRA expect firms to comply with anti-money laundering responsibilities at all times and have issued a number of 'warning notices' on money laundering to remind members of the profession of the obligations and requirements that firms must have, for example a written and up to date firm-wide risk assessment identifying the risks of money laundering and terrorist financing that are relevant to the firm, providing and recording suitable training for staff within the organisation and appointing a Money Laundering Reporting Officer (MLRO).

It is also important to note that while a solicitor could facilitate money laundering deliberately for a client, they can also be unwittingly involved. This could arise from not understanding the money laundering legislation, circumstances in which money laundering may arise or because the solicitor has not kept themselves up to date on developments in the novel ways criminals launder money or the relevant legislation/guidance. Remember, even if a solicitor is unwittingly involved in money laundering, the sanction could still be custodial.

12.10.1 Three stages in a money laundering transaction

You should be aware of the three stages in a money laundering transaction in order to look out for these during your day-to-day work as a solicitor. If you see any evidence of these activities, you should inform your firm's '**nominated officer**' (discussed further in **12.10.8.1**). The 'nominated officer' may also be referred to as the Money Laundering Reporting Officer (MLRO).

12.10.1.1 Placement

This is the most difficult stage of money laundering. It is where the cash proceeds from the crime are used to purchase something, such as property, or paid into various bank accounts. It is sometimes paid into offshore accounts in an attempt at layering. For a law firm, this could be the payment of criminal cash into the firm's client account.

12.10.1.2 Layering

This is the second stage and involves moving the money several times in order to avoid it being easily traced. The property bought with the money may be sold or the money taken out of the bank and reinvested. This cycle is often repeated. There may also be an attempt to pass money through a solicitor's client account by a bank transfer from another account. Therefore, the Law Society provides detailed guidance about holding client money and advises that it should only be held for a genuine legal transaction.

12.10.1.3 Integration

This is the final stage and is where the money is attempted to be moved into a legitimate place such as a business, property or investment. At this point, the money is usually very difficult to associate with its criminal source.

12.10.2 **Money laundering legislation**

There are various pieces of legislation which cover money laundering. It is important to be aware of all of these and any amendments which are made to them, as this area is rapidly changing in order to adapt to the fast-paced growth of technology. The six pieces of legislation that you need to be aware of are:

- Terrorism Act 2000;
- Proceeds of Crime Act 2002;
- Counter-Terrorism Act 2008;
- Serious Crime Act 2015;
- The EU's Fifth Money Laundering Directive, which came into force on 10 January 2020, amending the Money Laundering, Terrorist Financing and Transfer of Funds (Information on the Payer) Regulations 2017 (SI 2017/692) (MLRs).
- Criminal Finances Act 2017.
- The Money Laundering, Terrorist Financing and Transfer of Funds (Information on the Payer) Regulations 2017 (as amended). The most recent change to this important statute was made by the Money Laundering and Terrorist Financing (Amendment) (No 2) Regulations 2022. This highlights the importance of using a legal database to view rules, regulations and legislation to ensure you are viewing the most up-to-date version.
- Economic Crime and Corporate Transparency Act 2023.

12.10.3 **Terrorism Act 2000**

The Terrorism Act 2000 covers offences of money laundering relating to terrorist property.

Section 18 of the Act states that:

> A person commits an offence if he enters into or becomes concerned in an arrangement which facilitates the retention or control by or on behalf of another person of terrorist property—
>
> (a) by concealment,
>
> (b) by removal from the jurisdiction,
>
> (c) by transfer to nominees, or
>
> (d) in any other way.

It is a defence for a person charged with an offence under subsection (1) to prove that he did not know and had no reasonable cause to suspect that the arrangement related to terrorist property.

These offences carry a sentence of up to 14 years' imprisonment.

12.10.4 Counter Terrorism Act 2008

The Counter-Terrorism Act 2008 gives the Treasury powers to issue directions to firms to take certain action in respect of business relationships or transactions with people in non-EEA (European Economic Area) countries or territories. This is usually when it has concerns about money laundering, terrorist financing and the proliferation of weapons.

12.10.5 Proceeds of Crime Act 2002

The main offences of money laundering are found within the Proceeds of Crime Act 2002 (POCA). The offence of money laundering is defined as an act which constitutes an offence under ss327, 328 and 329 of the POCA, or a conspiracy or attempt to commit such an offence. Money laundering also includes counselling, aiding or abetting or procuring. These are all offences you need to understand and be aware of while working within a law firm, in order to be able to report any concerns or suspicions you may have. It is important to be aware that dishonesty is not required to commit these offences. These offences are discussed in further detail at **12.12**.

12.10.5.1 Criminal property

Under the POCA, the laundered proceeds must be 'criminal property', as defined in s340 of POCA, which states that the property constitutes a person's benefit from criminal conduct. It is critical to understand what criminal property is in order to understand the main money laundering offences. Criminal property is not criminal property unless the offender knows or suspected that it is derived from criminal conduct.

'Criminal conduct' is all conduct which constitutes an offence in any part of the UK or would constitute a criminal offence if it occurred in the UK (s340(2)).

In order to be 'criminal property', the property must:

- constitute a benefit from criminal conduct or that it represents such a benefit (in whole or part and whether directly or indirectly); and
- the alleged offender must know or suspect that it constitutes or represents such a benefit (s340(3)).

In *R v GH* [2015] UKSC 24, [2015] All ER (D) 155 (Apr), the Supreme Court provided a summary of the relevant law and authorities on what constitutes criminal property. There was clarification of previous confusion as to exactly when property becomes criminal and how this relates to POCA. The facts of the case were that B set up fake websites appearing to sell cheap car insurance. The plan, however, was to take money from customers and not to provide any insurance. The Supreme Court found that the respondents were entering into or becoming concerned in an arrangement which they knew or suspected would facilitate the retention, use or control of criminal property, contrary to s328(1) of POCA. The court clarified that in the present case the character of the money, although lawful at the moment of payment, changed on being paid into the bank accounts. It was not the arrangement between the parties that made the stolen monies 'criminal property' but rather the fact that the monies were obtained by deception.

12.10.6 Serious Crime Act 2015

The Serious Crime Act 2015 (SCA) amended a number of statutes, including POCA. Several of the provisions of the SCA 2015 were brought into force on 1 June 2015. The stated principal objective of the SCA 2015 was to ensure that law enforcement agencies had effective legal powers to deal with the threat from serious and organised crime.

Changes to POCA included the authorised disclosure regime in Pt 1 Ch 4 of the SCA 2015. Prior to this, when money laundering was suspected, the particular transaction could not be completed. An authorised disclosure had to be made to the relevant authorities; however, the individual could not inform their client of their disclosure as to do so would amount to the offence of tipping off. This resulted in the organisation making the disclosure potentially open to a civil claim about their failure to complete the transaction. This issue has seen a lot of litigation. The SCA 2015 inserts new provisions into s338 of POCA so that where an authorised disclosure is made, and that disclosure was made in good faith, no civil liability arises.

12.10.7 Money laundering regulations

The Money Laundering, Terrorist Financing and Transfer of Funds (Information on the Payer) Regulations 2017 (SI 2017/692) came into force on 26 June 2017. These have been amended by subsequent statutory instruments, the most recent being The Money Laundering and Terrorist Financing (Amendment) (No 2) Regulations 2022. Please note, the Money Laundering Regulations 2007 are now repealed by subsequent statute.

The regulations apply to all people acting 'in the course of business' which is carried out in the UK. Most legal professionals who undertake 'relevant business' will be subject to these regulations. All beneficial owners, officers or managers of a firm, as well as sole practitioners, must apply to the SRA for approval under the regulations. Failure to comply with the regulations is a criminal office which may result in a fine, imprisonment or both (reg 26). These regulations will be discussed further in **12.11** on client due diligence.

12.10.8 The Money Laundering and Terrorist Financing (Amendment) Regulations 2019 (MLRs)

The 2019 MLRs included amendments to reg 28, relating to **customer due diligence measures**. They now require firms to update their records relating to the beneficial ownership of corporate clients. Firms must also take reasonable measures to understand the ownership and control structure of that legal person, trust, company, foundation or similar legal arrangement and record any actions or difficulties encountered in identifying beneficial ownership.

Regulation 30A is a new requirement for firms to report to Companies House any discrepancies between the information the firm holds on their customers compared with the information held in the Companies House Register.

Amendments to reg 33 require firms to include new additional high-risk factors when assessing the need for enhanced due diligence and seek additional information and monitoring in certain cases. Examples where this may occur are:

- there are relevant transactions between parties based in high-risk third countries;
- the customer is the beneficiary of a life insurance policy;
- the customer is a third-country national seeking residence rights or citizenship in exchange for transfers of capital, purchase of a property, governments bonds or investment in corporate entities;
- there is a transaction related to oil, arms, precious metals, tobacco products, cultural artefacts, ivory or other items related to protected species or items of archaeological, historical, cultural and religious significance or of rare scientific value.

The amendments to reg 38 regarding electronic money include that firms can only forego customer due diligence measures in situations where the maximum amount which can be stored electronically is €150 (previously it was €250).

As of 10 September 2020, the new regulations require that a central automated mechanism be established. This is to enable law enforcement agencies to request customer information from banks, building societies and credit unions and information about safe deposit boxes, and for institutions to respond to these requests.

12.10.8.1 Internal controls and reporting

Regulation 21 states that there must be several internal controls in place within a firm.

There must be a person appointed, who is at senior management level, to be responsible for compliance with the regulations (reg 21(1)). That person must carry out screening of relevant employees appointed by the relevant person, both before and during employment. They must also establish an independent audit function with the responsibility to examine and evaluate the adequacy and effectiveness of the policies, controls and procedures (PCPs) adopted by the relevant person, in order to comply with the requirements of the regulations. This includes risk management practices and client due diligence.

A firm must also have a 'nominated officer' to receive reports from within the firm of anything which may be suspicious in relation to money laundering and to communicate with the National Crime Agency, if relevant (reg 21(3)). The National Crime Agency replaced the Serious Organised Crime Agency in October 2013. It is the main body within the UK which is responsible for receiving and analysing any suspicious activity reports relating to money laundering.

Where a disclosure is made to the nominated officer, that officer must consider it in the light of any relevant information available and determine whether it gives rise to knowledge or suspicion that a person is engaged in money laundering or terrorist financing (reg 21(5)).

A firm must establish these controls in order to be able to respond to any enquiries relating to any business relationship within the last five years and the nature of that relationship (reg 21(8)).

12.10.9 **Criminal Finances Act 2017**

The Criminal Finances Act 2017 came into force on 30 September 2017. It amends POCA and introduces the corporate offence of failure to prevent the facilitation of criminal tax evasion. Professional firms that fail to prevent associated persons criminally facilitating tax evasion can be held to account and this includes law firms.

In March 2018, the Legal Sector Affinity Group (LSAG), which includes the Law Society and all the legal sector supervisors named in the anti-money laundering regulations, published guidance on anti-money laundering. This can be found on the Law Society's website and is to assist firms in complying with the Money Laundering Regulations 2017 (as amended).

12.10.10 **Economic Crime and Corporate Transparency Act (ECCTA) 2023**

In relation to money laundering, the ECCTA 2023's aim was to strengthen anti-money laundering powers. In the government's fact sheet on the legislation, it was stated that 'The Act will strengthen anti-money laundering powers, enabling better information sharing on suspected money laundering, fraud and other economic crimes' (https://assets.publishing.service.gov.uk/media/65df57cf-cf7eb1e5f4f57fdf/01.+ECCT+Bill+Overarching+Fact+Sheet.pdf). The relevant provisions relating to money laundering are contained in Part 5 of the ECCTA 2023 between ss182 and 187. These provisions have now come into force, with the exception of ss185 and 186 which are partially in force. The ECCTA 2023 also makes some legislative changes to the money laundering offences under POCA 2002 by providing further exemptions. Where relevant, these are considered below.

Importantly in the modern age, the ECCTA brings cryptoassets into the realms of both money laundering and terrorist financing with amendments to POCA 2002, the Anti-terrorism, Crime and Security Act 2001 and the Terrorism Act 2000 (ss179 to 181 ECCTA 2023 – note, these provisions are only partially in force at the time of writing).

12.11 **Client due diligence**

Money laundering is more likely to occur in organisations that fail to promote good practice and values. Even if this is direct or indirect, these acts can bring harsh penalties for law firms and individual solicitors, who may face a prison sentence.

Client due diligence essentially means identification of the client. Most law firms are required to verify the identity of their clients in a process referred to in the MLRs as 'customer due diligence'. This verification should usually take place prior to the business relationship beginning or any transactions made in relation to the client.

Regulation 27 sets out that a relevant person must apply due diligence checks if the person:

- establishes a business relationship (for solicitors this means instructing the firm as a client or creating a retainer);
- carries out an occasional transaction that amounts to a transfer of funds within the meaning of art 3(9) of the funds transfer regulation exceeding €1,000;
- suspects money laundering or terrorist financing; or
- doubts the veracity or adequacy of documents or information previously obtained for the purposes of identification or verification.

Regulation 28(12) provides that when complying with the requirement to take client due diligence measures, which may differ from case to case, you must reflect on:

- the practice's risk assessment required under reg 18; and
- your assessment of the level of risk arising in any particular case.

Regulation 28(13) provides that in assessing the risk you must take account of factors including:

- the purpose of a transaction or business relationship;
- the size of the assets or of the transactions undertaken;
- the regularity and duration of the business relationship.

There are therefore different ways in which a solicitor will verify the identity of a client and this depends on the type of client, the area of law and the risk of money laundering. These are:

- simplified due diligence;
- standard due diligence;
- enhanced due diligence.

12.11.1 Simplified due diligence

Simplified due diligence is generally allowed when the transaction presents a low risk of money laundering or terrorist financing. In order to determine this, a firm must take into account its own general risk assessment, the relevant information provided and the associated risk factors (reg 37(1)). Risk factors to consider would include customer risk factors, product, service or delivery risk factors and geographical risk factors, including the country in which the customer is resident or operates.

An example of a customer who would be eligible for simplified due diligence would be a customer who is an independent legal professional, resident in the UK and there is a pooled account which has certain provisions.

12.11.2 Standard due diligence

Standard due diligence will apply to most clients and involves verifying the identity of the client by a document or information from a reliable, independent source (reg 28). This is often by way of a passport or a driving licence. However, it may be best practice to obtain two forms of identification from the client which confirm the client's name, current address and date of birth. For non-limited liability partnerships, it is usually necessary to obtain information on the individuals who make up the partnership. For companies, it is necessary to verify the company and so the information usually required is confirmation of the firm name, company number and registered office address or main place of business.

Regulation 28(3) states that when a customer is a body corporate, the relevant person must obtain and verify:

- the name of the body corporate;
- its company number or other registration number;

- the address of its registered office and, if different, its principal place of business;
- the law to which the body corporate is subject, and its constitution;
- the full names of the board of directors and the senior persons responsible for the operations of the body corporate.

The Law Society recommends considering whether the person providing the instructions is authorised to do so. This should be best practice. As such, the solicitor may need to clarify this with other individuals involved with the company. The solicitor must also establish the beneficial owner if the beneficial owner is not the client.

12.11.3 Enhanced due diligence

Enhanced due diligence is when a solicitor must take additional due diligence measures and additional ongoing monitoring in high-risk situations.

Regulation 33 sets out the circumstances where enhanced due diligence must be carried out. These include where:

- the case has been identified as one where there is a high risk of money laundering or terrorist financing by the relevant person in its risk assessment or in information made available to the relevant person;
- the business relationship is in a high-risk third country;
- the customer or potential customer is a politically exposed person (PEP) or a family member or known close associate of a PEP;
- the customer has provided false or stolen identification documentation or information and the relevant person proposes to continue to deal with that customer;
- in any case where a transaction is complex or unusually large, there is an unusual pattern of transactions or the transaction or transactions have no apparent economic or legal purpose;
- in any other case which by its nature can present a higher risk of money laundering and terrorist financing.

EXAMPLE

Jones & Jones Ltd instruct a solicitors' firm to carry out an additional office purchase for them. The firm would have to obtain confirmation of the name, company number, address and additional information set out in reg 28. Most of this information would be provided from Companies House. The beneficial owner of the company would also have to be identified, usually from looking at the share ownership and voting rights within the company.

12.12 Money laundering offences

In your capacity as a solicitor, you are likely to come across these offences and so must be aware of your responsibilities.

12.12.1 Direct money laundering offences

There are three main direct money laundering offences and each of these offences requires that a person does something with criminal property with the requisite *mens rea*. For example, they:

- conceal, disguise, convert or transfer what they know or suspect to be criminal property or remove what they know or suspect to be criminal property from the jurisdiction (s327 POCA);
- enter into or become concerned in an arrangement that they know or suspect facilitates (by whatever means) the acquisition, retention, use or control of criminal property, by or on behalf of another person (s328 POCA);

- acquire, use or possess what they know or suspect to be criminal property (s329 POCA).
- The ECCTA 2023 (s182 – exiting and paying away exemptions) has added some exemptions to the direct offences in ss327–329 POCA 2002). In respect of s327, for example, the amendment to the legislation provides that a person would not commit an offence under subsections (c) and (d) of s327 if;
  i. the person is carrying on business in the regulated section that is not an excluded business, and
  ii. the person does the act of transferring the money or assets in the course of business for the purpose of termination of the business relationship, and
  iii. the total value is less than the threshold amount, which is currently £1,000 (s339A POCA 2002), and
  iv. before the transaction is carried out, the person has complied with the customer due diligence duties.

The provisions are similar in respect of the offences under ss328 and 329. You should also be aware that there are further exemptions for mixed property transactions which were added by s183 ECCTA 2023.

12.12.2 Indirect money laundering offences

There are also indirect offences which include:

- failure to disclose when you know, suspect or have reasonable grounds to suspect a person is money laundering and you do not disclose it to a nominated officer or other authorised person as soon as practicable (ss330, 331 and 332 POCA);
- tipping off a person that you suspect is money laundering about an investigation or suspicious activity report (s333A POCA);
- failure to disclose using the correct form prescribed (s339 POCA).

Please note that there are also exemptions to these offences, with some recent amendments to the legislation by the ECCTA 2023 (see s184).

12.13 Money laundering defences

There are several defences to money laundering offences which are found in POCA.

12.13.1 Disclosure defence

POCA provides for three types of disclosure defences:

- a protected disclosure;
- an authorised disclosure; and
- voluntary disclosures.

12.13.1.1 Authorised disclosure defence

In law firms, it is more likely that an authorised disclosure would need to be carried out. A solicitor may have a defence to breaching s327 or 328 if they made an 'authorised disclosure' as soon as practically possible prior to the transaction taking place, and the authorisation of the nominated officer or National Crime Agency (NCA) was obtained to complete the transaction.

Once the 'nominated officer' has made a suspicious activity report to the NCA, they cannot give consent for the transaction until they either receive consent from the NCA and hear nothing for seven working days or, if consent is refused by the NCA, within 31 days they receive consent or hear nothing further.

If there was a reasonable excuse for not making a disclosure despite the person intending to do so, then this may also be a defence. This excuse has not been defined and the Law Society guidance states that a solicitor should document their reasons for not making the disclosure.

Liability when a disclosure is made during the prohibited act can only be avoided if the provisions of s338(2A) are satisfied:

- the disclosure was made while the alleged offender was doing the prohibited act;
- the alleged offender began to do the act at a time when they did not then know or suspect that the property constituted or represented a person's benefit from criminal conduct; and
- the disclosure was made on their own initiative and as soon as is practicable after they first knew or suspected that the property constituted or represented a person's benefit from criminal conduct.

If disclosure occurs after the prohibited act, the person must show that they had a reasonable excuse for their failure to make the disclosure before they did the act and that the disclosure was made on their own initiative and as soon as it is practicable for them to make it (reg 338(3)).

12.13.1.2 Overseas defence

Another defence is the 'overseas' defence. This means that if the offence occurred outside the UK and the offence was not unlawful where it happened, then no offence would be committed under s328. It is not, however, available if the offence in the UK would give a sentence of imprisonment of over 12 months' imprisonment, apart from limited exceptions. These can be found in the Proceeds of Crime Act 2002 (Money Laundering: Exceptions to Overseas Conduct Defence) Order 2006.

12.13.1.3 Adequate consideration defence

A solicitor may have a defence to breaching s329; the defences are set out in s329(2). The same defences as apply to offences under s327 and s328 are also provided for by s329(2)(a) and (b). However, in addition, a person does not commit an offence under this section if they acquired, used or had possession of the property for 'adequate consideration'. An example of this is in the case of tradespeople who are paid for goods and services in money that comes from crime. This defence will also apply where professional advisors (eg solicitors or accountants) receive money for or on account of costs. This defence would not be available to a professional where the value of the work carried out was significantly less than the money received on account of costs.

12.13.1.4 Tipping-off defence

There are some defences to the tipping-off offence: one is that the person making the disclosure did not know or suspect that the disclosure would prejudice an investigation into money laundering (s333D(3) and (4)) and also if the disclosure is made to the client in order to attempt to dissuade them from conduct amounting to a money laundering offence (s333D(2)).

There are some permitted disclosures which are disclosures within an undertaking or group etc (s330B) and disclosures between institutions (ss330C and 330D).

You must remain vigilant in order to ensure that you will not commit any of these offences.

12.14 **Penalties**

- A person guilty of an offence under ss327, 328 or 329 is liable to imprisonment for a term not exceeding 14 years or to a fine or to both.
- A person guilty of an offence under ss330, 331, 332 or 342 is liable to imprisonment for a term not exceeding five years or to a fine or to both.
- A person guilty of an offence under s333A is liable to imprisonment for a term not exceeding two years or to a fine or to both.
- A person guilty of an offence under s339(1A) is liable to a fine.

EXAMPLE

Jane is a property solicitor. If she transferred a house to the relative of a client when she suspected that the house was purchased with money from the proceeds of crime, then she would be involved in a 'money laundering arrangement'. Jane would not, however, commit an offence if she made an authorised disclosure to the firms 'nominated officer' as soon as it was practically possible before the transaction took place, or in certain circumstances (as discussed earlier), while the act was ongoing after the transaction.

If Jane were about to complete on a property purchase that day but received information regarding money being obtained from the proceeds of crime one hour beforehand, then she would have to postpone the purchase until she received consent that she could continue. She would not, however, be able to disclose the reason for the delay to her client, as this would be 'tipping off'.

12.15 Law Society warnings

There is detailed guidance about money laundering as well as Anti-Money Laundering Guidance on the Law Society website. There have previously been warnings issued regarding what client behaviour to look out for.

12.15.1 What to look out for

As a solicitor, recognising warning signs of money laundering is an ongoing challenge. Criminals continually adapt to changing markets and opportunities; however, there are signs to look for which could alert you to possible money laundering.

The Law Society has provided a detailed practice note which provides information on types of behaviours to look out for and questions to consider if you are concerned about money laundering. These behaviours include funds coming from third parties, clients instructing you who are based out of the geographical area, sudden changes of instructions and large money transactions. This practice note is important to read on quite a regular basis in order to be as up to date with the guidance as possible.

KEY POINT SUMMARY

- A solicitor needs to determine if the activity they are carrying is a regulated activity under s22 of FSMA 2000, as amended by the FSA 2012.
- If so, they must then look at whether it falls within the exclusions of the RAO or if it is an exempt regulated activity under s327 of FSMA 2000.
- If the activity is an exempt regulated activity, then a solicitor needs to comply with the Scope Rules and Conduct of Business Rules.
- Money laundering is an illegal practice and a solicitor must be aware of their responsibilities in order to avoid the risk of facilitating this crime.

CHAPTER 13
Funding Options for Legal Services

FUNCTIONING LEGAL KNOWLEDGE

This chapter covers the following functional knowledge required to pass the SQE 1 assessments:

Funding options for legal services:

- private retainer
- conditional fee agreements
- damages-based agreements
- fixed fees
- eligibility for criminal and civil legal aid
- third party funding
- legal expenses insurance

AUTHORITIES UNDERPINNING PRACTICE

The key authorities that underpin this area of practice are listed below. Note that for legislation you are linked to legislation.gov.uk.

Although much of the legislation on this government website is available in its amended form, the incorporation of new amendments into the text of legislation can be delayed. You should refer to legal databases to ensure you are referencing the most up-to-date legislation.

- Courts and Legal Services Act 1990
  https://www.legislation.gov.uk/ukpga/1990/41/contents
- Legal Aid, Sentencing and Punishment of Offenders Act 2012
  https://www.legislation.gov.uk/ukpga/2012/10/contents/enacted
- The Consumer Contracts (Information, Cancellation and Additional Charges) Regulations 2013
  https://www.legislation.gov.uk/uksi/2013/3134/contents/made
- Solicitors' Guideline Hourly Rates
  https://www.gov.uk/guidance/solicitors-guideline-hourly-rates
- Civil Legal Aid (Financial Resources and Payment for Services) Regulations 2013
  https://www.legislation.gov.uk/uksi/2013/480/contents/made
- Civil Legal Aid (Merits Criteria) Regulations 2013
  https://www.legislation.gov.uk/uksi/2013/772/contents/made
- Conditional Fee Agreements Order 2013
  https://www.legislation.gov.uk/ukdsi/2013/9780111533437
- Criminal Legal Aid (General) Regulations 2013
  https://www.legislation.gov.uk/uksi/2013/9/contents/made
- Criminal Legal Aid (Contribution Orders) Regulations 2013
  https://www.legislation.gov.uk/uksi/2013/483/contents/made
- Criminal Legal Aid (Financial Resources) Regulations 2013
  https://www.legislation.gov.uk/uksi/2013/471/contents/made

- Damages-Based Agreement Regulations 2013
  https://www.legislation.gov.uk/uksi/2013/609/contents/made
- SRA Standards and Regulations 2019
  https://www.sra.org.uk/solicitors/standards-regulations/
- SRA Transparency Rules 2019
  https://www.sra.org.uk/solicitors/standards-regulations/transparency-rules/

13.1 Introduction

One of the most important considerations for anyone using legal services will be what those services will cost and how costs will be met. Providing appropriate advice on funding options is therefore an essential component of professional conduct for solicitors and there are specific sections in the Code of Conduct for Solicitors, RELs and RFLs that you should be aware of.

The rules around fees and costs in different areas of practice are lengthy and complex. The purpose of this chapter is to provide a summary of the information that clients should be given about costs generally and of the main funding types which may be available.

Some of the funding options introduced in this chapter are particularly relevant to civil litigation and will be covered in further detail in the *Dispute Resolution in Contract & Tort* manual (**Chapter 6** on costs).

13.2 Funding legal services: professional conduct considerations

When a client instructs a solicitor in relation to any matter, the retainer between them will be a formal binding contract. It is important that the costs that a solicitor will charge to the client, and how those costs will be charged, are agreed as part of that contract.

Agreements between solicitors and their clients in respect of fees and charges are governed by law and by rules of professional conduct. Giving thorough information on costs to clients is therefore essential both at the time of engagement and throughout the client's instructions, which means that costs need to be kept under review both to advise the client on the amount of costs incurred at appropriate intervals and to advise on any changes to the overall estimate to conclusion.

13.2.1 Best possible information

The SRA requires all individuals and firms that it regulates to act 'in the best interests of each client' (Principle 7). This principle applies to all aspects of a solicitor's service to their client, including advice on funding options.

Solicitors must ensure that their clients are provided with clear information to enable them to make decisions about their legal matter:

> You will give clients information in a way that they can understand. You ensure they are in a position to make informed decisions about the services they need, how their matter will be handled and the options available to them.
>
> (SRA Code of Conduct for Solicitors, RELs and RFLs, para 8.6)

In addition, solicitors are specifically required to provide the 'best possible information' to their clients about the costs of legal services throughout the client's matter:

> You ensure that clients receive the best possible information about how their matter will be priced and, both at the time of engagement and when appropriate as their matter progresses, about the likely overall cost of the matter and any costs incurred. This means that costs must be kept under review, and the client updated where necessary.
>
> (SRA Code of Conduct for Solicitors, RELs and RFLs, para 8.7)

To demonstrate compliance with these provisions, and with many other provisions within the Principles and the Code of Conduct for Solicitors, a solicitor must discuss all viable funding options with their client and assist their client to come to an informed decision about the services that they require and the most appropriate means by which they can fund those services.

A solicitor should be able to evidence that they have provided thorough information on different funding options that may be available to their client and that they have advised on what they consider to be the most appropriate funding mechanism for their client's matter. Furthermore, that where any funding arrangement relates to a complicated legal document, for example a Conditional Fee Agreement, that the client has been afforded ample time to consider (and has been advised on) the components of that arrangement.

Any funding agreement between a solicitor and their client will be regulated by law and may be open to scrutiny and to challenge at a later stage, this could be many years after the start of a matter, for example in complex and lengthy dispute resolution. Solicitors should therefore maintain detailed records of the costs and funding information provided both at the time of engagement and throughout the client's instructions. If the funding arrangement is later discovered to be void, or the client was not properly advised on funding options at the outset, this could have a significant impact upon the recovery of any costs.

CONDUCT POINT

As a matter of best practice, to show compliance with paras 8.6 and 8.7 a solicitor should sit down with each client at the start of their matter to discuss with them what funding options exist and to explain which options may be appropriate for the client's needs. Solicitors should give reasons as to why particular options may or may not be available to or appropriate for clients. It is best practice to ensure that all discussions are followed up in writing to the client and recorded in writing on the client's file. This is evidence that the client was advised on all available and viable funding options, the advice given on the best funding option and the reasons for that advice. It can also be best practice to get the client to sign the funding advice letter to confirm that they have read, understood and accept the advice given. Usually, issues with funding are not raised until conclusion of a matter – taking these steps with hopefully avoid, but at least mitigate, against any issues.

13.2.2 **SRA Transparency Rules**

In December 2018, the SRA Transparency Rules came into force. They were last updated in November 2019. The Transparency Rules require authorised firms (and anyone providing services to the public from outside authorised firms) to display prices and service information to clients and potential clients in particular practice areas.

The practice areas falling within the Transparency Rules are:

- conveyancing (residential) which comprise freehold or leasehold sales or purchases, or mortgages or re-mortgages;
- probate matters (uncontested);
- immigration services (excluding asylum);
- motoring offences within the magistrates' court (summary offences dealt with at a single hearing);
- employment tribunals (unfair/wrongful dismissal, for employees or employers);
- debt recovery for businesses (up to the value of £100,000);
- licensing applications (for business premises).

Rule 1.1 of the Transparency Rules requires that specific costs information must be published on the websites of authorised firms working in the above practice areas. Rule 1.5 states that the information that must be provided includes:

(a) the total cost of the service or, where not practicable, the average cost or range of costs;

(b) the basis for charges, including hourly rates or fixed fees;

(c) the experience and qualifications of anyone carrying out the work, and of their supervisors;

(d) a description of, and the cost of, any likely disbursements, and where the actual cost of a disbursement is not known, the average cost or range of costs;

(e) whether any fees or disbursements attract VAT and, if so, the amount of VAT they attract;

(f) details of what services are included in the price displayed, including the key stages of the matter and likely timescales for each stage, and details of any services that might reasonably be expected to be included in the price displayed but are not; and

(g) where **conditional fee** or **damages-based agreements** are used, the circumstances in which clients may have to make any payments themselves for legal services (including from any damages).

Rule 1.6 states that costs information published under this rule must be *clear and accessible and in a prominent place* on a firm or solicitor's website. If a firm does not have a website, the information must be made available in other formats.

Solicitors working within the practice areas covered by the Transparency Rules must be aware of the obligations that they and their firms have in respect of them.

13.2.3 Contractual basis of legal services and client care letter

The contract between a solicitor and client is usually evidenced within a **client care letter** sent by a solicitor to their client, which may be accompanied by a separate terms of business document. The SRA regulatory regime applies to this contract in addition to general principles of contract law but is more commonly referred to as a 'retainer' in the legal profession.

The client care letter assists in providing clarity and certainty on what has been agreed between a solicitor and their client. It provides written evidence of the contract between the solicitor and their client and of the terms agreed within that contract—including any terms that set out the solicitor's right to be paid for the services that they provide and how and when they are entitled to be paid. It will also clearly evidence any limitations on the scope of the retainer, for example where the retainer only covers preliminary investigations and not the issue of proceedings.

In respect of costs, solicitors should ensure that sufficient information to comply with paras 8.6 and 8.7 of the Code of Conduct for Solicitors is contained within the client care letter.

As a matter of best practice, a client care letter should always be provided at the start of a client's instructions, irrespective of the funding method used in the matter. The client should be asked to sign and return a copy of the client care letter to confirm their agreement to its terms and therefore to the terms of the contract between the solicitor and the client. However, the simple fact that a client care letter has been sent to a client (even if the client does not sign and return it) may suffice as evidence of the contract between a solicitor and their client. A client may be deemed to have accepted the terms if they have received the client care letter and not objected to the terms. This is important as it means that a solicitor would still be entitled to be paid even if the client had not signed and returned the letter.

If a client chooses to terminate their instructions at any stage (which they may do at any time and for any reason), the client care letter should provide clarity on what the client will be liable to pay to their solicitor for the work carried out up to that point. If a client has instructed their solicitor on the basis of a **private retainer** (13.4), they will usually be liable to pay all fees up to the point at which they withdraw their instructions to the solicitor, so long as the solicitor has complied with all of their contractual obligations. Similarly, if circumstances arose in which the solicitor was unable or unwilling, for good reason, to continue to act for a client, the solicitor would ordinarily be entitled to be paid for work carried out up to the point of termination of the contract.

It is important to note that even if a solicitor has good reason to terminate a contract with a client they must still pay regard to their duties under the SRA Code of Conduct and Principles. They must ensure that they act in the best interests of their client (Principle 7), and therefore before terminating the contract they should provide the client with reasonable written notice of their intention to do so and to take any necessary steps to ensure their client's interests are protected.

Circumstances may occasionally arise in which a solicitor undertakes urgent work at the request of a client before having the opportunity to send a client care letter. In such circumstances, the solicitor will still be legally entitled to make a reasonable charge for work undertaken, even if the client subsequently withdraws their instructions.

13.2.4 Consequences of failing to advise appropriately

Failing to advise fully and appropriately on funding options either at the start of or throughout a client's instructions can have serious implications for firms and for individual solicitors, including a risk of disciplinary action from the SRA, client complaints or actions for negligence. Some types of funding agreements (namely, conditional fee agreements and damages-based agreements) may be unenforceable against a client if a solicitor has failed to comply with legal or regulatory requirements, for example where the stringent provisions of the Consumer Contracts (Information, Cancellation and Additional Charges) Regulations 2013 have not been complied with. Further, if a solicitor has acted on the basis of a private retainer when the client may have had more appropriate options to pay for their legal costs (eg legal expense insurance or trade union membership), the solicitor may be unable to recover their costs from their client because there was a better funding option available to the client. In other words, the agreed retainer was not in the best interests of the client.

The Code of Conduct for Solicitors makes clear that clients must be informed in writing at the time of engagement of a firm's complaints procedure, of their right to complain about services and charges and of any right that they have to make complaints to the **Legal Ombudsman** if they are dissatisfied with any aspect of the solicitor's service (para 8.3).

The Legal Ombudsman has power to reduce or disallow fees, and to order a firm to apologise or to pay compensation to a client, if service has been unsatisfactory—which would include circumstances in which inadequate advice was provided on funding options.

The introductory notes to the Code of Conduct for Solicitors make clear that a serious failure to meet the SRA's standards or a breach of regulatory requirements may result in the SRA taking regulatory action against a solicitor. This could include breaches relating to information provided on funding options and costs.

Chapter 11 on the regulatory role of the SRA provides more details of disciplinary sanctions available to the SRA for a breach of the SRA Standards and Regulations.

Claims for professional negligence or breach of professional duty could be brought against a solicitor if a client can establish that they have suffered loss because of the solicitor's failure to appropriately advise on funding options or costs. This may result in a solicitor or firm being ordered by a court to pay damages to their client.

Complaints claims or disciplinary actions of this nature may result in reputational damage to solicitors or to the firms that they work for and in increased premiums for **professional indemnity insurance**. In addition, disputes over fees can be costly and time-consuming for firms and may result in solicitors having to take legal action against their own clients to seek recovery of unpaid costs.

By ensuring that they consider funding options and costs carefully with their clients at the start of and throughout every matter, solicitors will minimise the risks of these consequences arising. The Legal Ombudsman has prepared a guide to the provision of a good costs service. In the introduction it sets out that in 2018–2019 13% of the complaints accepted by the Legal Ombudsman included a complaint about costs. In 2019–2020 15% of all complaints were about costs, and in 2020–2021 this percentage fell slightly to 14%. Complaints about costs therefore factor in a significant number of complaints to the Legal Ombudsman. The Legal Ombudsman publishes an annual report in which these statistics can be obtained and provides advice on what solicitors can do to mitigate against complaints.

13.3 Options for funding legal services

The most appropriate options for funding legal services will depend on numerous factors including the nature of a client's matter, the area of law involved (including whether the matter is criminal, civil or family), the client's own personal and financial circumstances and the legal representative or law firm's own approach to risk and funding.

Some methods of funding will only be appropriate to specific types of instructions—for example, civil **legal aid** is available in only very limited prescribed circumstances set out in Sch 1 of the Legal Aid, Sentencing and Punishment of Offenders Act 2012; and conditional fee agreements will only be appropriate to contentious matters.

The information that follows is intended to provide a general introduction to funding options for legal services but is not intended as a comprehensive guide to all funding options in all areas of law. You should also be aware that legal funding arrangements and legal costs are subject to case law analysis and interpretation. Any challenge to a funding arrangement, including the amount of costs claimed under that arrangement, can be scrutinised by the Court. You can access decisions of the Senior Courts Costs Office via this link: BAILII - England and Wales High Court (Senior Courts Costs Office) Decisions.

13.4 Private retainers

For many types of matter, it will be appropriate for solicitors and their clients to agree that the client will pay the solicitor privately as their matter progresses—known as a private retainer. This is the traditional way of paying for legal services.

Full details of the basis upon which the client will be charged, and the solicitor will be entitled to be paid, should be set out in writing at the outset of the client's instructions, within the client care letter and the solicitor's terms of business documents (see 13.2.3).

Private retainers usually involve clients paying legal fees either based on hourly rates or an agreed fixed fee.

13.4.1 Hourly rates

Hourly rates are a common charging method for solicitors in many areas of practice.

As the name suggests, this simply means that clients are charged for the time that is actually spent on their matter by fee earners, on the basis of hourly rates notified to the client at the start of their instructions within the client care letter. Time is recorded by the fee earner in 6-minute units, meaning there are 10 units in every hour.

Hourly rates can be used in both contentious and non-contentious matters.

Understandably, this method of charging is not always viewed favourably by clients due to concerns about overall costs, which can escalate very quickly, and perceptions of poor value for money.

Nevertheless, hourly rates are still used by many law firms. To ensure compliance with professional conduct obligations and to minimise the risk of client dissatisfaction, it is important that solicitors who charge on the basis of hourly rates provide detailed information to their clients about how they will be charged. As a minimum, the client care letter should specify the roles (and where possible the names) of the fee earners who are likely to work on the matter; and the hourly rates of those fee earners including VAT. However, simply informing a client of the names and hourly rates of fee earners working on their matter is unlikely to be compliant with para 8.7 of the Code of Conduct for Solicitors. This would not provide clients with the 'best possible information' about costs and does not indicate the likely overall cost of the matter.

Therefore, to demonstrate compliance with para 8.7, within their client care letter to a privately paying client a solicitor should also consider the following.

- Providing an estimate of costs with clear details of how they will be calculated. Depending on the type of matter, this could be an estimate for the whole of the matter or for specific stages or tasks. This estimate should include a breakdown of fees and VAT.
- Providing details of the nature and cost of any likely disbursements that may arise and any VAT that will be payable on them, for example expert fees.
- Agreeing a costs limit with their client—meaning a maximum initial figure for costs. When that limit is reached, the client's instructions should be sought before any further costs are incurred.
- Agreeing whether the client will pay any of the fees up front—on account of costs.
- Agreeing a time frame for either interim bills or interim statements of costs to be sent to the client. This could be either when a particular costs figure is reached or after a specified amount of time (often monthly).
- In contentious matters, providing an indication of what the client may be able to recover from their opponent if they are successful and what any shortfall may be between what the client has paid or will pay to the solicitor and what they may be able to recover. Whilst the usual rule in civil litigation (with some limited exceptions) is that the losing party will be ordered to pay

the successful party's costs, in practice those costs are usually either assessed by the court or agreed between the parties and will rarely equate to the actual sum claimed by the solicitor or the amount their client is required to pay. When assessing costs, judges will often use the Senior Courts Costs Office Guideline Hourly Rates as a start point. These rates will often be much lower than hourly rates that are charged by firms. Details of the current guideline hourly rates for the summary assessment of costs can be found on the government website. These were last updated in January 2024. Furthermore, in terms of civil litigation/dispute resolution, you should also be aware of the considerations contained within the Civil Procedure Rules regarding the factors to be taken into account in determining appropriate costs, including the rules on conduct and proportionality.

Paragraph 8.7. of the Code of Conduct for Solicitors makes clear that solicitors have a continuing professional duty to provide information on costs. To comply with that continuing duty, solicitors charging hourly rates should ensure that any changes that arise throughout the retainer are notified to the client. This could include (but is not limited to):

- changes to the fee earners working on the matter or their hourly rates;
- changes to VAT rates;
- changes to the nature and cost of likely disbursements;
- changes in the nature of the case which means it may go on for longer than originally anticipated or a conclusion could be achieved sooner;
- changes in the amount of work that needs to be done; for example in civil litigation an accurate estimate of costs may not be possible until it is known what the defendant will require the claimant to prove in their defence, but best estimates should still be provided;
- any other changes to the amount and nature of costs specified in an estimate or quotation.

This information should be provided to the client in writing wherever possible. If any earlier costs estimates provided to a client are no longer accurate, the client's instructions should be sought before further costs are incurred.

13.4.2 **Fixed fees**

For some types of instruction, it may be appropriate for solicitors to charge based on fixed fees agreed at the time of engagement. Fixed fees for individual clients are most often encountered in conveyancing, private client matters (eg wills) or private family law matters (particularly straightforward divorces). Firms providing services to business clients with regular instructions of a particular nature (eg debt recovery actions) may also agree fixed fees for such work. However, these are now becoming increasingly applicable in civil litigation work; see for example the new rules relating to the 'intermediate track' and the fixed costs regime that relates to cases that run under that track.

A fixed fee can be specified as inclusive or exclusive of VAT and disbursements. A fixed fee may be for part of a client's instructions (eg the initial meeting), may be for the whole matter (eg the sale of a residential property) or may be for any instructions of a particular type (eg debt recovery work).

Fixed fees are often more attractive to clients than hourly rates. They provide more certainty and may be perceived as better value for money. Firms may therefore make a business decision to accept some specific types of instructions on a fixed fee basis to give them a competitive advantage in the legal market.

Fixed fees may also be attractive to firms, as if a fee is agreed but a matter takes less time to conclude than expected, the firm may receive more fees than if it had acted on hourly rates. Conversely, some matters will inevitably become more complex and time-consuming than first anticipated. If a fixed fee has been agreed but a matter takes longer than expected, the client will still only be liable to pay the sum agreed. As such, some firms may only use them where there is certainty on the amount of work they will be carrying out.

Therefore, before offering a fixed fee for any matter, solicitors should carefully consider the likely complexity of the matter and the amount of time that it may take to complete. Solicitors should ask their client to provide all information and documentation that is relevant to their matter in an agreed format and by an agreed date. Solicitors may also wish to inform their clients that the fixed fee is based on an assumption that the matter will conclude by a specified date—which will necessitate the client doing everything that may be required of them to ensure that the time frame is kept to.

Solicitors must carefully and thoroughly set out to the client, in writing, what is and is not covered by the fixed fee that is offered to avoid any uncertainty later.

Solicitors who work on a 'fixed fee' basis must also ensure compliance with the Transparency Rules (**13.2.2**) where applicable.

13.4.3 Payment on account

When a solicitor is providing legal services to a client on the basis of a private retainer, they may wish to request advance payment on account of the costs and disbursements that they expect to incur throughout the matter.

Any payments made by clients to their solicitors on account of costs or disbursements must be dealt with in accordance with the SRA Accounts Rules.

In contentious matters, a solicitor may require a client to pay a sum on account of costs within a reasonable time and may terminate the retainer upon giving reasonable notice to the client if they do not do so (s65(2) Solicitors Act 1974).

In non-contentious matters, any requirement for a client to make a payment on account of costs should be made clear as a term of the retainer between them and therefore included within the client care letter.

13.4.4 Disbursements

As well as paying for the time that solicitors spend on their matter, clients may also be required to pay for disbursements.

Disbursements are fees or expenses paid by a solicitor to a third party in respect of a client's legal matter. Clients will usually be required to repay their solicitor for any disbursements that are incurred on their case. In non-contentious matters, typical disbursements could include Land Registry fees or Probate Registry fees; and in contentious matters they may include court fees, expert fees or counsel's fees.

It is essential for solicitors to provide as much information as possible to their clients in relation to potential disbursements both at the time of engagement and as a matter progresses. This applies irrespective of the funding method used by a client.

By providing detailed information on the likely nature, cost, timing and frequency of disbursements, solicitors will evidence their compliance with paras 8.6 and 8.7 of the Code of Conduct for Solicitors. It is best practice to break down disbursements to give the client absolute certainty. A solicitor may also require the client to put them in cleared funds before any disbursements are incurred to ensure they receive payment, for example if an expert is instructed in civil litigation who forms an opinion adverse to the client's case, the client may be reluctant to pay but the solicitor would still be liable for the fee.

If the likely cost or nature of disbursements change during a matter, the solicitor must notify the client in writing and take further instructions as necessary.

13.5 Conditional fee and damages-based agreements

13.5.1 Background

In some matters, solicitors and their clients may enter into funding agreements in which the payment of the solicitor's fees is dependent on the outcome of the matter. It is important to note, however, that such agreements **are not permitted** for the payment of certain disbursements e.g., an agreement with an expert that they will only be paid if the case is successful. Such agreements may take the form of a 'conditional fee agreement' (CFA) or a 'damages-based agreement' (DBA).

Statutory provision for CFAs was first made within the Courts and Legal Services Act 1990, though CFAs were not made available for use as a funding option until 1998. Originally, conditional fee agreements were required to be signed by the client under the provisions of the Conditional Fee Agreements Regulations 2000, but this entire statutory instrument has now been repealed and signature by the client is no longer a requirement. However, it is best practice to get the client to sign the CFA to evidence that they have agreed to the terms, after all it is a binding contract.

DBAs were first introduced, for use in employment law matters, in 2009 pursuant to s58AA of the same Act (as amended). In April 2013, on the implementation of the Legal Aid, Sentencing and Punishment of Offenders Act 2012 (LASPO) and following recommendations made in Lord Justice Jackson's 2010 Review of Civil Litigation Costs: Final Report, DBAs became permitted in all contentious matters with the exception of criminal law and most family law cases. However, in practice DBAs are still rarely encountered other than in employment matters.

The 2013 Civil Justice Reforms on Costs and LASPO also led to other significant changes in respect of CFAs, DBAs and **after the event (ATE) insurance**, particularly in respect of the recoverability of success fees and ATE premiums, as addressed later in this chapter.

13.5.2 **CFAs**

The use of CFAs is governed by:

- the Courts and Legal Services Act 1990 (CLSA 1990), as amended by the Access to Justice Act 1999 and LASPO;
- the Conditional Fee Agreements Order 2013.

13.5.2.1 What is a CFA?

A CFA is defined in s58(2)(a) of the CLSA 1990 as:

> an agreement with a person providing advocacy or litigation services which provides for his fees and expenses, or any part of them, to be payable only in specified circumstances.

The 'specified circumstances' will generally mean that a client is only liable to pay their solicitor's fees when and if the client's claim (or in some circumstances their defence) is successful.

CFAs can be used by both claimants and defendants in litigation, though providing a definition of 'success' will be easier in CFAs relating to claims or counterclaims than in CFAs solely relating to a defence but could be specified as 'successfully defending the claim or part of the claim'.

CFAs can be used by litigants even if they could afford to pay their litigation costs on a private basis, as confirmed by the House of Lords in *Campbell v MGN Ltd* [2005] UKHL 61 and even when a client could be entitled to civil legal aid, providing the client has been properly advised as to the advantages and disadvantages of both methods and been able to make an informed decision.

A CFA can be entered into prior to or during litigation and can take several forms; but the most common is the CFA with success fee.

13.5.2.2 CFA with success fee

This type of CFA is a binding agreement between a solicitor and their client that the client will not be required to pay any legal costs to their solicitor throughout the case or if they lose their case; but if the client is successful the solicitor will be entitled to be paid their 'base costs' (meaning their normal fees usually calculated on an hourly rate basis) *and* an agreed percentage uplift on those fees, known as a 'success fee'.

The usual rule in most civil litigation is that a losing party will be ordered to pay the winning party's costs. This means that if a client funded by a CFA is successful in their claim, their opponent is likely to be ordered to pay the client's solicitor's reasonable base costs and disbursements, to be subject to detailed assessment (where costs are considered by the court) if not agreed. However, the client may still be liable to their solicitor under the CFA for any shortfall that arises if the base costs and disbursements cannot be recovered in full from the opponent. The important point is that the CFA must clearly state what the client may have to pay and in what circumstances, and this must be set out in a way the client can understand (SRA Code of Conduct for Solicitors, RELs and RFLs 8.6).

To ensure compliance with paras 8.6. and 8.7 of the Code of Conduct for Solicitors, a solicitor must ensure that their client is aware that they may be liable for this shortfall before entering into the CFA.

In addition, the client will usually be personally liable to pay the success fee, and it is essential that solicitors ensure that their clients are aware of this before entering into a CFA. Before 1 April 2013, if a successful litigant had a CFA with success fee, the success fee would have been recoverable from their opponent (alongside the base costs and disbursements). However, recommendations for the abolition of the recoverability of success fees within the Jackson Review were accepted by the government and implemented through LASPO. As a result, in almost all CFAs encountered today, the losing party in litigation will *not* be liable to pay the 'success fee' (other than in *extremely* limited circumstances such as specific claims relating to diffuse mesothelioma). In almost all CFAs with success fees now, payment of the success fee will be the client's own responsibility along with any premium for an After the Event insurance policy.

A success fee is expressed as a percentage uplift of the base costs that a client would have been liable to pay to their solicitor if there were no CFA in place. Pursuant to the Conditional Fee Agreements Order 2013, the maximum uplift on those base costs is 100% in most cases which is calculated by reference to a risk assessment mainly relating to the prospects of success. However, in personal injury litigation the amount of the success fee actually paid by the client cannot be more than 25% of the damages recovered at first instance (excluding future pecuniary loss and net of any sums recoverable by the Compensation Recovery Unit). This is an important point because while the success fee can be set at more than 25%, the maximum that the client would pay is 25% of damages recovered at first instance. The 25% is not automatically the amount the client will pay, it is a cap on the amount the client can pay—if the success fee is calculated at a sum lower than 25% of the damages recovered at first instance, they will only pay that lower amount.

EXAMPLE

Siobhan, a solicitor, enters a valid and enforceable CFA with their client, Alice, a claimant in a personal injury matter. The case is complex, and significant investigations need to be undertaken before the prospects of success can be accurately predicted. Siobhan sets the success fee at 100% due to the risks and uncertainty involved at the outset.

Alice recovers £100,000 at first instance. Siobhan's base costs under the CFA are £125,000 *plus* VAT at £25,000, a total of £150,000. This means the actual success fee should be £125,000 *plus* VAT at £25,000. However, Siobhan can only recover a maximum of £25,000 from the client being 25% of the damages recovered at first instance.

The percentage of the success fee must be recorded within the CFA itself. It is calculated by the solicitor after a careful assessment of the prospects of the client's case, based on all information and documentation available. In calculating the success fee, solicitors will assess the risks of losing the case and their costs of funding the case to trial or earlier settlement, without being paid anything in the interim.

If a client funds their matter under a CFA and is unsuccessful, they will not be required to pay anything in respect of their own solicitor's costs but, depending on the wording of the CFA, they may still be liable for disbursements. They may also be required to pay their opponent's legal costs. Solicitors must ensure that their client is aware of this possible adverse cost liability and advise them of options that may exist to minimise that liability, such as ATE insurance (see **13.5.2.5** and **13.9.2**).

EXAMPLE

Jamie, a solicitor, enters a valid and enforceable CFA with their client, Anita, the claimant in a commercial dispute. The CFA provides for a success fee of 60%, calculated after a careful assessment of Anita's matter.

Anita is successful at court. Jamie's base costs for legal services under the CFA are £30,000 *plus* VAT at £6,000.

Anita will be required to pay £18,000 *plus* VAT at £3,600 to Jamie in respect of the success fee (60% of £30,000 *plus* VAT). This success fee will not be recoverable from the opponent.

13.5.2.3 Discounted CFAs

Some forms of CFA provide for clients to pay partial sums towards their solicitor's costs, based on a discounted hourly rate, as their litigation progresses and regardless of the outcome. This is known as a 'discounted CFA'.

Under a discounted CFA, if the client is unsuccessful, the client will only be required to have paid their solicitor at the discounted hourly rate set out in the CFA document. However, if the client is successful, the solicitor will be entitled to payment of their base costs at the usual (undiscounted) rate and to the success fee (if the CFA provides for one). The usual rule on costs will apply (meaning costs should be recoverable from the unsuccessful opponent), but if there is any shortfall between the costs that are recoverable from the opponent and the amount of their solicitor's (undiscounted) base costs, the client will be liable for that shortfall. If the discounted CFA contains a success fee, the client will also be liable to pay that as it will not be recoverable from the opponent.

13.5.2.4 Requirements for all solicitor/client CFAs

To be enforceable, a CFA must comply with the legal requirements set out in s58(3) and (4) of the CLSA 1990:

- it must be in writing;
- it must not relate to proceedings which cannot be the subject of a CFA;
- for CFAs with success fee, the CFA must expressly state the success fee.

As well as meeting these mandatory requirements, to ensure that they are providing the best possible information to their clients as required under paras 8.6 and 8.7 of the Code of Conduct for Solicitors, solicitors will also need to:

- consider other methods of funding which may be available and more suitable for all or part of a client's legal costs, which may include BTE insurance (13.9.1) or **trade union funding** (13.7);
- carefully consider whether a CFA would be a suitable method of funding for clients with a low-value claim, where the amount of damages recovered from the opponent may not be sufficient to cover the success fee. In such circumstances, it would not be in the client's best interests to enter a CFA;
- carefully explain when the client may become liable to pay their solicitor's costs or success fee. The client must be specifically informed if they will be liable to pay a success fee if their case is successful, and that they may be required to contribute towards base costs as well if they cannot be recovered in full from the unsuccessful party;
- explain how and when the client may become liable for adverse costs. This may necessitate advising on the availability of ATE insurance (13.9.2);
- explain who will be responsible for paying and disbursements and when they will need to be paid. Many CFAs require clients to pay for disbursements as and when they arise throughout the case;
- ensure that the client understands all provisions of the CFA. CFAs can be complex documents so, as a matter of best practice, the solicitor should fully discuss the CFA with their client and follow up on that discussion in writing;
- if a CFA contains a success fee, explain the reasons for the calculation of the success fee. This is particularly advisable on the basis that a client may request assessment of their solicitor's CFA success fee or base costs under the Solicitors Act 1974.

13.5.2.5 Additional considerations

13.5.2.5.1 Non-compliance

If a CFA is found to be invalid for non-compliance with the legal requirements for CFAs, the client would have no liability to pay the solicitor for any of the costs covered by the CFA (including any success fee). Costs would similarly be irrecoverable from the opponent because of the Indemnity Principle—this means that a successful party must not recover more for their legal costs than they are liable to pay their solicitor.

In addition, if a solicitor fails to comply with regulatory requirements when entering a CFA, for example if they failed to advise the client of alternative, more appropriate methods of funding their matter, the CFA may be unenforceable, or may give grounds for the client to make a complaint to the SRA. If a client has **before the event (BTE) insurance** (13.9.1) or trade union funding (13.7), either may be a preferable funding option for the client. Either method may mean that a client would not be required to pay anything to their solicitor from any damages that they receive, whereas funding through a CFA would require the client to pay the success fee.

In addition, when agreeing a CFA with a client, the solicitor must comply with the stringent provisions of the Consumer Contracts (Information, Cancellation and Additional Charges) Regulations 2013. These regulations provide different criteria that must be satisfied depending on whether the contract was agreed at a 'distance', for example by correspondence; 'on-premises', for example at the solicitor's office or 'off-premises', for example at a client's home. Non-compliance with these regulations will render a CFA invalid and unenforceable.

13.5.2.5.2 CFAs, adverse costs and ATE

CFAs will be an appropriate way for some clients to fund their own legal costs in litigation; but consideration must also be given to a client's potential liability for adverse costs. The losing party in litigation will often be required to pay their opponent's costs, and it is essential for a solicitor to make their client aware of that adverse costs risk and of options available to minimise that risk.

Clients are often advised to take out a policy of ATE insurance for adverse costs alongside entering a CFA in respect of their own legal costs. Solicitors must ensure that clients are advised that, following the implementation of LASPO, the premium payable for ATE insurance will be irrecoverable from their opponent in a successful matter and will be payable by the client (save for in extremely limited circumstances such as claims for diffuse mesothelioma).

More information on ATE insurance and on a solicitor's responsibilities in relation to ATE insurance is provided at 13.9.2.

In personal injury matters, qualified one-way costs shifting (QOCS) may mean that a claimant will not be liable for adverse costs in an unsuccessful claim (where the claim has been struck out as disclosing no reasonable grounds for bringing the claim, where there is evidence of **abuse of process** or poor conduct on the part of the claimant or where the claimant fails to beat a defendant's Part 36 offer). This could negate the need for ATE insurance to be taken out in personal injury cases, though a solicitor must still consider the circumstances of each case individually and advise their client appropriately. In particular, while the claim may be one for personal injury, an insurance policy may be appropriate to protect the claimant against the risks of failing to beat a Part 36 offer which was rejected on sound legal advice.

13.5.2.5.3 Model CFA document

The Law Society provides a model CFA and guidance for solicitors. At the time of writing, the model CFA and guidance was being revised by the Law Society to take account of current changes in legislation and case law, in particular, the case of *Belsner v CAM Legal Services* [2022] EWCA Civ 1387.

13.5.3 **DBAs**

The use of DBAs is governed by:

- the Courts and Legal Services Act 1990, as amended by LASPO;
- the Damages-based Agreements Regulations 2013.

13.5.3.1 What is a DBA?

DBAs are contingency fee arrangements in which a client will only be required to make a payment to their solicitor if they recover damages in their case. The amount that the client will be required to pay to their solicitor is calculated as a percentage of the damages that they receive.

DBAs were initially introduced as a means of funding employment law matters but became available in a wider range of contentious matters in 2013 following LASPO. However, they are still rarely used in practice outside employment law, due in part to uncertainties within the regulations governing their use.

The Damages-based Agreement Regulations 2013 (DBA Regulations) set out the requirements that a DBA must comply with to be enforceable. The regulations refer to legal 'representatives' rather than solicitors and refer to any sum payable by a client to their representative from their damages as a 'payment'.

There are proposals for significant reform to the regulations surrounding the use of DBAs to provide clarity to the regime.

13.5.3.2 How do DBAs operate?

Under a DBA, a client who recovers damages will be required to pay an agreed percentage of their damages to their solicitor, in respect of their legal costs. If the client does not recover any damages in their case, the client will not be required to pay anything to their solicitor.

The maximum payment that a client will be required to make is capped under the DBA Regulations at different percentages depending on the type of claim (see **Table 13.1** for caps in different types of matter).

TABLE 13.1 Caps on DBA Recovery Rates

Personal injury claims	25% of sum recovered by client (excluding damages for future care and loss and net of any sums recoverable by the Compensation Recovery Unit of the DWP): reg 4(2)(a) and (b)
Employment claims	35% of the sum recovered by the client: reg 7
Any other civil claim	50% of the sum recovered by the client: reg 4(3)

Clients may be required to pay expenses (eg court fees) in addition to the cap, but the capped amount is inclusive of VAT. The caps do not apply to appeals.A client will only be required to make payment from sums that they actually recover. If a client obtains judgment but is unable to enforce payment of that judgment from their opponent, they will not be liable to pay their solicitor.

Therefore, before a DBA is offered to any client, the financial position of the opponent must be carefully considered to determine whether they are likely to be able to satisfy any judgment made against them. This should assist in assuring the solicitor that they will be paid.

Outside employment tribunal matters, if a client wins their case and is awarded damages, they should be able to claim some or all their costs and disbursements from the losing party. However, the client will not be able to recover more by way of costs from their opponent than the amount payable by the client under the DBA.

In practice, the solicitor would keep any base costs recovered from the opponent and the client would be required to pay any shortfall between the costs recovered from the opponent and the payment due under the DBA. This shortfall would usually be paid from the client's damages.

In an unsuccessful case funded by way of a DBA, a client would have no liability to pay their solicitor's costs but would ordinarily still be liable for any disbursements that fall outside the DBA; which may include the costs of any ATE insurance taken out by the client (13.9.2).

EXAMPLE

Kallias, the claimant and their solicitor, Pravin, enter a DBA with a 50% cap in a commercial litigation matter.

Kallias recovers £100,000 in damages and £20,000 in costs from the defendant, being a total of £120,000.

Pravin can recover a maximum of £50,000 as a DBA fee (50% of the damages recovered). If Pravin receives £20,000 in costs from the defendant, Kallias will be liable to pay £30,000 from their damages to Pravin. Kallias therefore has a net recovery of £70,000 and Pravin receives £50,000—being the amount that they were entitled to under the DBA (50% of the amount of the damages recovered).

Pravin is *not* entitled to the full £50,000 DBA fee in addition to the £20,000 recovered from the defendant—as the maximum payment that the Kallias was liable to make under the DBA was 50% of the amount of the damages recovered.

13.5.3.3 Requirements of DBAs

A DBA is a legally binding document between a solicitor and their client. To be enforceable, any DBA must be recorded in writing and must comply with reg 3 of the DBA Regulations. The agreement must therefore detail:

- the claim or proceedings or parts of them to which the agreement relates;
- the circumstances in which the representative's payment, expenses and costs, or part of them, are payable; and
- the reason for setting the amount of the payment at the level agreed.

Additional requirements apply to DBAs in respect of employment matters under reg 5, which states that before a DBA is entered into, a solicitor must provide information on:

- the circumstances in which the client may seek a review of costs and expenses of the representative and the procedure for doing so;
- the dispute resolution service provided by the Advice, Conciliation and Arbitration Service (ACAS) in relation to actual and potential claims;
- whether other methods of pursuing the claim or financing the proceedings are available and, if so, how they apply to the client and the claim or proceedings in question including:
  - advice under arrangements made for the purposes of Pt 1 (legal aid) of LASPO;
  - legal expenses insurance;
  - pro bono representation; or
  - trade union representation;
- the point at which expenses become payable; and
- a reasonable estimate of the amount that is likely to be spent on expenses, inclusive of VAT.

Under reg 6, any amendment to a DBA in an employment matter to cover additional causes of action, must be in writing and signed by the representative and the solicitor. In practice, solicitors should ensure that amendments to a DBA in *any* matter are evidenced in writing and signed by the client and the representative.

To demonstrate compliance with professional conduct requirements, a solicitor considering a DBA with their client in any matter should also advise their client of:

- the definition of 'success' under the DBA;
- who will be responsible for paying any disbursements and when they must be paid;
- how any liability for adverse costs could be covered (which may include ATE insurance);
- any alternative funding methods which may be available, particularly if any options exist which would mean a client would not be required to make any payment out of damages that they recover (eg BTE insurance (**13.9.1**) or trade union funding (**13.7**) which may be common in employment matters);
- how and when the DBA can be terminated by either the client or the representative and what the implications of termination may be;
- the fact that the amount payable by the client to the solicitor under the DBA (from damages or any settlement that a client recovers) will be payable even if the litigation settles at any early stage. The solicitor must be able to evidence that funding by way of a DBA is in their client's best interests and that there is no conflict between the solicitor's and the client's interests, even if early settlement is possible.

These points should be discussed with the client and followed up in writing.

13.5.3.4 Additional considerations

13.5.3.4.1 Non-compliance

As with a CFA, if a DBA is found to be invalid or non-compliant with the DBA Regulations it will be unenforceable. The solicitor would not be entitled to a payment from the client or (in applicable matters) to recover costs from the defendant.

If a solicitor fails to comply with regulatory requirements when entering into a DBA, for example if they fail to advise the client on alternative funding options, the DBA may be unenforceable against the client or the client may have grounds for a complaint to the SRA. BTE insurance or trade union funding may be more advantageous to a client as it may mean they are not required to make payment to their solicitor from any damages that they recover.

Again, as with CFAs, the DBA is a contract between the solicitor and the client, so the solicitor must ensure they comply with the Consumer Contracts (Information, Cancellation and Additional Charges) Regulations 2013).

13.5.3.4.2 DBAs, adverse costs and ATE

As with a CFA, before entering a DBA a solicitor must advise their client of their possible liability for adverse costs if they are unsuccessful in their litigation.

In matters other than employment tribunal matters (in which the usual rule is that each party bears their own legal costs), it is likely to be appropriate for a client to take out ATE insurance (13.9.2) to cover possible adverse costs.

Clients must be informed that, subject to limited exceptions, an ATE insurance premium will be irrecoverable from their opponent and will be payable by the client personally. Whilst the DBA Regulations are unclear, it appears that an ATE premium would be viewed as an 'expense' of litigation and therefore be payable outside the cap on fees (and therefore in addition to the percentage of damages that the client is required to pay under the DBA). Future DBA regulations may provide certainty on this.

13.5.3.4.3 Can a defendant use a DBA?

The current DBA Regulations make references to a sum 'recovered'. In a recent High Court decision (*Tonstate Group Ltd v Wojakovski and others* [2021] EWHC 1122 (Ch)), the court found that this wording meant that a defendant could not validly use a DBA unless they had a counterclaim (in which the Defendant would become the counterclaimant) in which they were seeking to make a recovery from their opponent. Future regulations may provide certainty on this point.

13.5.4 **Business implications of CFAs and DBAs**

CFAs and DBAs can be risky and impact on a firm's cash flow, particularly when the firm has agreed to fund the client's disbursements during the course of the matter. In unsuccessful cases, it is likely that no fees will be recovered by the solicitor. A solicitor may undertake a significant amount of work and receive nothing for it. Solicitors must carefully consider the merits of any matter and the prospects of success before offering to fund a client's case by way of a CFA or a DBA. This may mean that a client can only find representation under this funding method if their case meets the firm's risk profile for accepting cases on a CFA.

Even in successful cases, legal fees will generally only be paid once a case has concluded and a recovery is made from the opponent. Therefore, solicitors must also carefully consider the financial position of their client's opponent and the prospects of making a recovery of either damages or costs from the opponent if their client's case is successful. In some cases, however, the client will have appropriate insurance to enforce any judgment against.

Firms may wish to limit the number of CFAs and DBAs that they offer to ensure that they are not exposed to excessive irrecoverable fees.

Solicitors must ensure that their CFAs and DBAs comply with all statutory requirements and that any CFA success fees or DBA payments are reasonable and properly explained to clients, to avoid being unenforceable or challenged by clients.

13.5.5 **CFAs with counsel**

Funding agreements may be entered into with barristers, meaning that their fees will not be payable as and when they arise but will instead be dependent on the outcome of the matter. Detailed consideration of CFAs with barristers is outside the scope of this chapter.

13.6 Legal aid

13.6.1 Background

Legal aid in England and Wales is administered by the Legal Aid Agency (LAA), an executive agency of the Ministry of Justice. Only firms that have a contract with the LAA can undertake legally aided work. The LAA produces a directory of providers (updated monthly and available online).

The basic framework setting out the availability of and eligibility for legal aid is contained within Pt 1 of LASPO.

To ensure compliance with paras 8.6 and 8.7 of the Code of Conduct for Solicitors, solicitors working in relevant areas of law should always consider whether their clients may be eligible for legal aid funding, even if their own firm does not have a contract with the LAA. If a solicitor considers that their client may be eligible for legal aid in a particular case, they should inform their client that they may wish to take advice from a practice that has an LAA contract in order to benefit from funding that may be available.

The rules surrounding eligibility for legal aid and the bases upon which legal aid will be provided are lengthy and complex and as such are beyond the scope of this chapter. The following information is intended to provide a summary of considerations which may be relevant in determining whether a client will be eligible for legal aid. It is not intended to be a comprehensive guide to legal aid.

13.6.2 Civil legal aid

LASPO significantly reduced the availability of public funding in civil matters, with the objectives of discouraging unnecessary litigation at public expense, making costs savings, delivering better value to the taxpayer and targeting legal aid to people most in need.

Different forms of civil legal services may be available to a client who secures legal aid, including legal help (where solicitors will provide advice but will not issue or conduct court proceedings), family mediation (including an assessment of whether mediation would be suitable and, if so, providing mediation) and legal representation (providing legal services to someone who is or wishes to be a party to legal proceedings).

There are three criteria which must generally be satisfied for a client to be eligible for any form of legally aided civil legal services, though there are some exceptions. **Figure 13.1** shows the usual eligibility criteria for civil legal aid.

Scope

- Does the client's matter fall within the scope of civil legal aid (determined in Sch 1 to LASPO)?

Merits criteria

- Does the client's matter meet the merits criteria for legal aid (pursuant to the Civil Legal Aid (Merits Criteria) Regulations 2013)?

Means criteria

- Is the client financially eligible for legal aid, taking into account their income and capital (pursuant to the Civil Legal Aid (Financial Resources and Payment for Services Regulations) 2013)?

FIGURE 13.1 Eligibility for civil legal aid

13.6.2.1 Scope of civil legal aid

The areas of law for which civil legal aid may be available are known as areas which are 'in scope'. LASPO removed certain areas of law from the scope of civil legal aid, including most private family law matters, employment matters (other than discrimination), some immigration matters and most clinical negligence matters.

Schedule 1 to LASPO sets out the matters that remain 'in scope' for civil legal aid; which include private family matters where there is evidence of domestic violence or some matters in respect of children, public family law proceedings (eg care proceedings), discrimination matters and cases where a person is at risk of homelessness.

As well as the matters listed in Sch 1 as being in 'scope', civil legal aid may also be available in other very limited exceptional circumstances (by way of 'exceptional cases funding' under s10 of LASPO).

If a client requires assistance with a matter that falls 'in scope' for civil legal aid (or is an exceptional case), before they will be entitled to access legal aid they must usually also satisfy tests relating to the merits of their case and their financial means; though some matters are not subject to merits testing or means testing such as legal aid for parents or children in respect of care proceedings.

13.6.2.2 Merits criteria for civil legal aid

A solicitor should consider the merits of a client's case before making an application for civil legal aid.

The Civil Legal Aid (Merits Criteria) Regulations 2013 and subsequent amendments to those regulations provide guidance on how merits will be considered by the LAA. An assessment of merits will depend on the nature of a client's individual case and the area of law that it involves, but will usually include consideration of:

- prospects of success;
- **proportionality**;
- whether the case is a matter of significant **public interest**;
- whether alternative methods of funding may be available (such as a CFA);
- likely damages;
- whether a case is of overwhelming importance to the client.

13.6.2.3 Means criteria for civil legal aid

In most cases, even if a client's issue falls within the scope of civil legal aid and satisfies the merits test, a solicitor will still need to consider whether their client is financially eligible to receive legal aid.

When assessing a client's financial means both their income and the value of assets that they own (their 'capital') may be relevant. In some circumstances, the income and capital of a client's partner will also be considered when determining the client's financial means.

The Civil Legal Aid (Financial Resources and Payment for Services) Regulations 2013 and subsequent amendments set out the provisions for determining financial eligibility for civil legal aid and prescribe the financial limits for the income means and capital means tests.

Full information on means testing for civil legal aid and on current prescribed income and capital limits can be found at https://www.gov.uk/guidance/civil-legal-aid-means-testing. At the time of writing, in most cases if a client has a gross monthly income of £2,657 or less, disposable income of £733 a month or less and disposable capital of a value of under £8,000, they may be financially eligible for civil legal aid for some or all of their legal costs. These financial limits are reviewed in April each year and are contained within the LAA 'Keycard' each year, which provides a quick reference point for determining financial eligibility for civil legal aid.

13.6.2.4 Passporting in civil legal aid

If a client is in receipt of certain benefits, they are 'passported' through the income means test for civil legal aid. This means that they will automatically meet the means test in respect of the limits of their income, but their financial eligibility must still be assessed under the capital means test.

Benefits that would enable a client to be 'passported' through the income means test include:

- Income Support;
- Income-based Jobseeker's Allowance;
- Universal Credit;
- Guarantee Credit element of Pension Credit;
- Income-related Employment and Support Allowance.

The client's matter would still need to be in scope and meet the merits test.

EXAMPLE

Harry is seeking a divorce from his husband. There are no allegations or evidence of domestic violence, and he and his husband have no children. Harry is in receipt of Income Support and has no savings or assets of value. He has approached your firm because you have a contract with the Legal Aid Agency.

Whilst Harry would appear to be financially eligible for civil legal aid under the means test, his matter would not fall within the scope of civil legal aid as a private family law matter. He will not therefore be entitled to legal aid in respect of his divorce and other funding options would need to be considered.

13.6.2.5 Exceptional cases funding

Cases that are out of scope for civil legal aid might still be eligible to receive exceptional case funding (ECF) from the LAA. A client would usually still need to pass the merits and means tests on eligibility.

ECF will only be available in matters where a lack of legal advice and representation would breach an individual's convention rights (within the meaning of the Human Rights Act 1998) or retained enforceable EU rights (s10 of LASPO). This could include cases in which a client would be unable to have a fair hearing without legal aid (Art 6 ECHR); if their right to private and family life would be impacted without legal aid (Art 8 ECHR); or under Art 2 ECHR in circumstances where there was potential state accountability for a death (eg a death in custody) and the deceased's family required funded representation at the inquest.

A request to the LAA for ECF must be supported by evidence as to why ECF is required.

13.6.2.6 Contributions and statutory charge

Civil legal aid does not automatically entitle a client to completely free representation. It is intended to put legally aided clients into the same position as non-legally aided clients would have been. This means that dependent on their disposable income, clients may be required to make contributions towards their costs of legal representation. Section 23 of LASPO provides detail on payments for civil legal services.

Further, if a client receives money (eg by way of damages) in a matter which is funded by legal aid, the client may be required to repay some or all of the costs of their solicitor's fees from the money that they receive. Similarly, if a client receives any real property (eg a house), that property may be subject to a legal charge in favour of the LAA and registered at the Land Registry in respect of the costs of the solicitor's fees, until such time as the fees are repaid. This is known as the 'statutory charge'. Section 25 of LASPO provides more detail in respect of this.

Any solicitor acting for a client with civil legal aid funding must ensure that they carefully explain the basis upon which the client may be liable to pay legal costs and what the statutory charge might mean in their case. The client should be provided with regular information as to the amount of the solicitor's costs (and therefore the possible amount of the statutory charge) throughout their matter.

The LAA publishes a detailed Statutory Charge Manual setting out full details of the statutory charge, and also publishes an explanatory leaflet for clients.

13.6.3 Criminal legal aid

The rules determining eligibility for criminal legal aid are set out in LASPO and in the Criminal Legal Aid (General) Regulations 2013. The LAA also publishes a lengthy criminal legal aid manual to assist in determining eligibility.

To determine whether a client qualifies for criminal legal aid for their defence costs, a solicitor will usually need to consider the merits of the matter and their client's financial means.

The criminal legal aid regime is currently undergoing review due to significant concerns regarding funding and provision. This review may lead to changes in the availability of and eligibility for criminal legal aid in the near future.

13.6.3.1 Merits criteria for criminal legal aid

In the context of criminal legal aid eligibility, merits are determined based on the 'interests of justice' test. This may include consideration of the client's previous convictions, the nature of the offence that they are accused of and the risk of a custodial sentence. The more serious the charge against a client, the more likely that they will qualify for legal aid.

The criteria used to establish whether the interests of justice test is met are set out in s17(2) of LASPO; and are sometimes referred to as the 'Widgery criteria'.

The criteria which must be considered include the following.

- Whether it is likely that the client will lose their liberty or livelihood or suffer serious damage to their reputation.
- Whether the proceedings may involve consideration of a substantial question of law.
- Whether the client may be unable to understand the court proceedings or state their own case.
- Whether the proceedings may involve the tracing, interviewing or expert cross-examination of witnesses on behalf of the client.
- Whether it is in the interests of another person that the client is represented (eg if the complainant is a vulnerable person and it would be inappropriate for the client to cross-examine the complainant without representation).

If the LAA rejects a request for criminal legal aid based on the interests of justice test, an appeal can be made to the LAA. If the solicitor or client is still unsatisfied with the decision made after an appeal, they may ask the LAA to put the decision to the court to review.

In any cases involve Crown Court trials (other than appeals to the Crown Court against conviction or sentence), the interests of justice test will be automatically satisfied. However, any such cases are still subject to the means test. Clients under the age of 18 will also usually automatically pass the interests of justice test.

13.6.3.2 Means criteria

To assess whether a client is eligible for criminal legal aid for all or part of their defence costs, their financial position must also be considered, as set out in the Criminal Legal Aid (Financial Resources) Regulations 2013. This may take into account income and capital.

Full information on means testing for criminal legal aid and on current prescribed income and capital limits can be found on the UK government website.

The initial means test for criminal legal aid involves consideration of a client's gross annual income and their family circumstances. Their gross income could include wages or salary, pension payments, student loan payments, interest on savings and some benefits such as child benefit, tax credit and incapacity benefit. If the client has a partner, their partner's gross income may also be considered. The client's gross income is then 'weighted' based on their family circumstances including the number and ages of any children that they have.

If a client has an annual household disposable income over a prescribed limit, they may be ineligible for criminal legal aid or they may be required to make contributions towards their legal aid from their income.

If a client has over a prescribed limit in capital and equity (including savings, equity in properties or shareholdings) and is convicted of an offence, they may have to contribute towards the balance of their final defence costs from their capital assets. Conversely, if a client is found not guilty, contributions that they made towards legal aid costs may be refunded.

13.6.3.3 Passporting in criminal legal aid

If clients are under the age of 18 or if they are in receipt of certain benefits, they will be 'passported' through the means test. The applicable benefits are:

- Income Support;
- Income-based Jobseeker's Allowance;
- Universal Credit;
- Guarantee Credit element of Pension Credit;
- Income-based Employment and Support Allowance.

Even if a client is 'passported' through the means test, they must still have passed the interests of justice (merits) test to be eligible to receive legal aid.

EXAMPLE

Ivan is 15 and is a child actor. He had an income of £250,000 last year following a lead role in a film. He was arrested recently at a party after an argument got out of hand and he has now been charged with attempted murder. He has approached you seeking representation on a legally aided basis.

Despite his income, Ivan will be eligible for legal aid. Because of his age and the severity of the charge against him, he will be passported through both the means and merits test.

13.7 Trade union funding

Some trade unions have legal assistance schemes which enable their members to obtain advice and representation from solicitors, funded by the union through the contributions made by members. It is usual that the client will need to have been a member of the trade union at the time the cause of action accrued.

In some legal disputes, particularly work-related matters such as employment law or health and safety issues, a member of a trade union will be referred by the union to a solicitor or firm of solicitors for legal advice. Trade unions will often engage several different firms as their 'panel' of approved solicitors.

The 'panel' solicitor will assess the prospects of success in the matter and, if the prospects are deemed to be reasonable, the trade union may cover all or part of the client's legal fees in respect of the dispute. In addition, some trade unions may also provide or pay for insurance for adverse costs in disputes.

To demonstrate compliance with paras 8.6. and 8.7 of the Code of Conduct for Solicitors, solicitors should ask their clients if they have trade union membership which could cover their legal costs. If a client has trade union cover but has sought advice from a solicitor who is not on the union's panel, the solicitor must advise the client that it would be in their financial interests to contact a firm that is on the union's panel in order to benefit from the funding available. Trade union funding would generally be more advantageous to a client than an alternative arrangement such as a CFA or DBA as trade union funding would not generally require the client to make payment towards costs from any damages that they are awarded.

EXAMPLE

Mo is seeking advice on making a constructive dismissal claim against his former employer, a major transport company. Mo has approached your firm as he knows that you offer to pursue employment law claims on a DBA basis.

Before advising Mo, you must make enquiries as to other possible options by which he could fund his legal costs. Given the nature of Mo's employment, it is possible that may be a member of a trade union and therefore entitled to trade union funding towards his legal costs.

Your firm is not on any trade union panels. Notwithstanding this, if Mo is a union member, you must advise him to make enquiries of his union to see if funding would be available for his matter, as if so it is likely to be a better funding option for him than a DBA. If you fail to do so and enter into a DBA regardless, it may be unenforceable and you may be considered to have acted in breach of the Code of Conduct for Solicitors.

13.8 Third party funding

Third party funding refers to ways in which a client's legal costs are paid by someone other than the client, who may have no prior connection with or pre-existing interest in a matter, including:

- pure funding or crowdfunding;
- **litigation funding** (commercial funders).

In the past, third party funding of litigious matters was viewed as champertous. Champerty refers to an arrangement in which a person agrees to fund the costs of litigation in return for a share of the proceeds if the litigation is successful. This was historically considered as unlawful or immoral due to concerns that the third party might try to exert control over litigation, exaggerate claims or interfere with the proper administration of justice. However, third party funding is now considered to be an acceptable method of funding legal costs in some circumstances and was specifically identified in the Jackson Review as providing an additional means of funding litigation and promoting access to justice.

Third party funding, even in return for a share of the damages in litigation, will not generally be considered champertous (and will not be invalid as a funding arrangement) unless there is evidence of improper conduct.

13.8.1 Pure funders or crowdfunding

Perhaps as a result of changing times and the reduction in the scope of legal aid, there has been a recent increase in third party funding by individuals or companies that have no control of or financial interest in a legal matter; known as 'pure funders' or 'crowd funders'. This type of funding may be found in cases that are a matter of public interest and is generally provided to facilitate access to justice.

Pure funders and crowdfunders contribute towards the costs of litigation without any expectation of or entitlement to a refund of their contribution. In some exceptional cases, if costs are recovered from an opponent, funders may receive some of their contribution back, but will never profit from the funding.

Funding can be raised privately (perhaps by clients asking family or friends for contributions towards legal costs) or through sites such as Crowdjustice.com.

Pure funders and crowdfunders who have no financial interest in or control over a matter are unlikely to have any legal liability beyond the amount that they donate towards legal costs. These funding arrangements are unlikely to be successfully challenged by an opponent. However, it is important to remember that the court has discretion to make any funder liable for costs by way of a non-party costs order under s51 of the Senior Courts Act 1981.

When advising clients with legal matters that are of public interest or where assistance in accessing justice is required, solicitors should be aware that it may sometimes be appropriate to consider 'pure funding' or 'crowdfunding' as a method by which a client could fund legal costs. Solicitors should be prepared to discuss how the funding works and what the possible benefits and risks may be.

13.8.2 Litigation funders

In contrast to pure funders, commercial third parties known as 'litigation funders' are prepared to pay the costs of litigation with the specific aim of financially benefiting from it. Funding is provided under an agreement that the client who receives the funding will repay the litigation funder's contributions, with an element of profit, from any damages that the client recovers.

There are numerous litigation funding companies in the UK, many of which are members of the Association of Litigation Funders (ALF). ALF is an independent body which delivers self-regulation of litigation funding; but membership of ALF is not compulsory for ligation funders. ALF administers a Code of Conduct of litigation funding for its members, setting out required standards of practice and behaviour in litigation funding. The code prescribes details such as the financial resources that a litigation funder must have, the restrictions on a funder seeking to control litigation and the limited circumstances in which a funder may withdraw litigation funding.

13.8.2.1 Litigation funding: availability

Litigation funding is available in arbitration and litigation and generally only encountered in high-value commercial disputes with good prospects of success. Litigation funding may be a desirable funding option for clients for a number of reasons, for example if they would be financially unable to pursue an action by any other means or if they do not wish to bear the full risk of pursuing litigation personally.

Litigation funders seek a return from damages paid in a case, meaning litigation funding is only usually available to claimants; though it may be available to defendants who have a significant counterclaim. The return that funders seek could be calculated as a percentage of damages recovered, or as an uplift on the amount of funding that they have provided or set aside for the litigation.

Litigation funders have criteria for deciding which matters they are prepared to fund. This is likely to include consideration of the anticipated costs of the action, the prospects of success (with most litigation funders requiring prospects of at least 60%, based on counsel's opinion), the damages that may be awarded, the recoverability prospects and the probable timescales for the litigation.

Litigation funding may be used in conjunction with a CFA and ATE insurance, with the latter minimising the funder's potential exposure to adverse costs.

13.8.2.2 Litigation funding and champerty

If a litigation funding arrangement is found to be champertous, it will be void and unenforceable. against the funded client. In addition, the unsuccessful opponent to litigation would not be liable to make any payment of costs to the successful funded party. The litigation funder may themselves be subject to a non-party costs order pursuant to s51 of the Senior Courts Act 1981.

Factors that may lead to a court making such a finding could include the funder having excessive control over the litigation or circumstances where there has been a risk of misrepresentation or distortion of evidence or exaggeration of claims. The court may also consider whether the litigation funder is regulated or voluntarily adheres to the ALF Code of Conduct and the amount of profit that the litigation funder stands to make from the litigation.

Solicitors can minimise the risk of a challenge to the validity of a litigation funding arrangement by ensuring that their client, rather than their client's funder, remains in control of the litigation, and by only using or recommending funders who are members of ALF and fully comply with ALF's Code of Conduct.

In practice, a funding agreement provided by a litigation funder that is a member of ALF (and therefore fully complies with the ALF Code of Conduct) is unlikely to be found to be champertous.

13.8.2.3 Litigation funding and adverse costs

As noted above, a litigation funder may be liable for costs by way of a non- party costs order.

In *Arkin v Borchard Lines* [2005] EWCA Civ 655, [2005] 1 WLR 3055, the defendant to an unsuccessful claim that had been funded through litigation funding sought an order that the litigation funder should be held liable for the defendant's full defence costs. The application was unsuccessful, with the Court of Appeal finding that the litigation funder was only liable up to the amount of its own contribution (a limit which became known as the '*Arkin* cap').

However, in the 2020 decision in *Chapelgate Credit Opportunity Master Fund Ltd v Money & Ors* [2020] EWCA Civ 246, the Court of Appeal found that the decision in *Arkin* was not a binding rule and that the *Arkin* approach did not necessarily have to be followed when determining a litigation funder's liability for costs. In *Chapelgate*, based on the circumstances of matter, the litigation funder of the claimant's unsuccessful claim was held liable for the defendant's costs in full.

In practice, litigation funders are likely to insist that a client takes out adequate ATE insurance to cover adverse costs risks, therefore reducing the litigation funder's risk.

13.8.2.4 Advising a client on litigation funding

If it appears that litigation funding may be appropriate for a client, to demonstrate compliance with paras 8.6 and 8.7 of the Code of Conduct for Solicitors, a solicitor will need to carefully explain to the client how the funding operates and what the risks and possible benefits are when compared to other funding options. Any advice should be recorded in writing.

The client may then instruct the solicitor to approach litigation funders, or a broker, to try to source funding.

If any funding offers are made, the solicitor must ensure that their client is able to make an informed decision on the offer. Solicitors must ensure that their client fully understands the funding offer, including the basis upon which the litigation funder would be entitled to be paid.

13.8.2.5 Professional conduct considerations in litigation funding

Solicitors must be careful to comply with all professional conduct obligations when dealing with litigation funders.

They must ensure that their duties to their client and to the court are not compromised, and that there are no conflicts of interest or significant risks of conflict. They must ensure that control of the matter remains with their client.

Litigation funders are likely to request detailed information in respect of funded matters, before making funding offers, meaning solicitors must also pay careful regard to their duties of confidentiality under para 6.3 of the Code of Conduct for Solicitors. They must ensure that they have their client's informed consent before providing any information to the funder. It may be appropriate for the solicitor to request that the litigation funder signs a confidentiality agreement before any information or documentation is provided.

13.9 Legal expenses insurance

Legal expenses insurance (LEI) is a way in which some clients may be able to fund all or part of their legal services, advice and representation in contentious matters. Dependent on the type of LEI, it may be used to cover a client's own costs or adverse costs.

There are broadly two types of LEI—before the event insurance and after the event insurance. Although, after the event insurance is not a type of litigation funding.

13.9.1 BTE insurance

BTE insurance is a form of insurance against possible future legal costs in contentious matters. It is often purchased through paying an additional, optional premium when taking out insurance policies such as home insurance or motor insurance (though cover may be included as standard in some policies). Cover may sometimes be provided through bank accounts, car or home insurance policies or credit card providers.

If a client has an insurance policy, bank account or credit card that includes BTE cover and an event which could give rise to legal action occurs, they may be entitled to claim for legal advice and representation or occasionally cover for possible adverse costs. The method for making a claim would usually involve the client contacting their insurer (or bank or credit card provider) to notify them of the legal issue. The matter would then usually be referred to a specified firm of solicitors (known as 'panel solicitors') for an initial assessment. Insurers and banks may have several different firms on their 'panel' at any one time. Occasionally, the terms of the BTE may enable a client to instruct any solicitor of their choosing from the initial assessment of their matter. If legal proceedings are required, the client will be able to use a solicitor of their choosing.

The client may be unsure whether they have BTE insurance; therefore it would be best practice to ask the client for a copy of any insurance policies they hold and review the terms.

13.9.1.1 BTE insurance: limitations

The terms of an insurance policy may limit the types of dispute that the BTE insurance will cover. For example, when BTE is attached to motor insurance, the cover could be limited to negligence claims brought by or against the insured party as a road user. Similarly, the amount of cover available is usually limited to a specific sum (between £25,000 and £100,000 of LEI cover is standard in most home or motor policies).

BTE insurance cover will only be provided if the insured's dispute is assessed by the panel solicitors as having reasonable prospects of success. This assessment may depend on numerous factors including consideration of all the evidence that is available, how much time has passed since the legal issue arose and the likely legal costs of pursuing the matter compared to the amount that the insured might expect to recover as damages.

13.9.1.2 BTE insurance: professional conduct

To ensure compliance with paras 8.6 and 8.7 of the Code of Conduct for Solicitors, at the start of any contentious matter a solicitor should ask their client if they have any form of BTE insurance in place. If so, they should advise their client that in some circumstances that insurance may be the best way for the client to fund the legal services that they require. BTE may be preferrable to a client using a CFA or DBA, as it would not require the client to make any payment to their solicitor out of damages that they receive.

If a client is unsure as to whether they have BTE insurance or whether their BTE insurance would cover their matter, the solicitor should recommend that the client contacts their insurer or bank for guidance. In some cases, it may be appropriate for a solicitor to review a client's insurance policies to check for the existence of appropriate BTE insurance cover.

When acting on the basis of BTE insurance, solicitors must ensure that they advise their client as to exactly how the insurance will cover their legal costs and disbursements, of any limits on the amount or availability of the insurance cover and of any costs for which the client may become liable.

If the cover is not likely to be sufficient, BTE can be combined with other funding methods (eg hourly rates or a CFA or DBA).

CONDUCT POINT

Solicitors should ensure that any discussions with clients about the availability or limitations of BTE are clearly explained to the client and are carefully recorded in writing.

13.9.2 **ATE insurance**

ATE insurance is a specific type of insurance product that is taken out after a dispute has arisen.

ATE insurance usually covers a client for their potential liability to pay their opponent's costs and disbursements in the event of the client losing their case. It is often used in addition to another form of funding arrangement which covers a client's own legal costs, such as a CFA or DBA. In some circumstances, ATE insurance may also be used to cover the costs of the client's own disbursements in the event of them losing their case.

ATE insurance is available to claimants and defendants.

13.9.2.1 ATE premiums

Before 2013, the successful party in litigation could seek to recover the cost of an ATE premium from their opponent, in addition to their other legal costs. However, following the Civil Justice Reform on Costs 2013 and the implementation of LASPO, premiums payable for ATE insurance are no longer recoverable from an opponent (save for in very limited prescribed cases such as claims for damages for diffuse mesothelioma). A client who takes out ATE insurance will therefore usually have to bear the cost of the ATE premium themselves.

The availability of ATE insurance and the rate of the premium will depend on factors such as:

- The prospects of success in a matter (ATE insurers will usually require prospects of at least 51%–60% and will often require counsel's opinion to confirm this).
- The value of the claim or counterclaim.
- The financial position of the client (ie that they will be able to pay the premium if they are required to do so).

Some ATE policies may require payment of the insurance premium either up-front or by way of staged premiums throughout the matter (with the premium increasing proportionately to the adverse costs that the client and insurer are potentially exposed to).

Some premiums will be deferred until the outcome of a case (and payable whether the case is successful or unsuccessful).

Some policies of ATE insurance provide 'self-insuring' premiums; meaning that the premium will only be payable by the client if they are successful in their case. However, self-insuring premiums are sometimes payable on success irrespective of whether or when a recovery of damages is made by the insured client.

13.9.2.2 ATE practicalities and professional conduct

In any contentious matter, it would be good practice to discuss the possibility of taking out ATE insurance with a client, particularly if they do not have BTE insurance cover for adverse costs. This will be especially important if a client is funding their case through a CFA or DBA, as that funding arrangement will cover their own legal costs but leave them potentially exposed to their opponent's costs.

Having ATE insurance in place may be sufficient to defeat any security for costs application that may be made in litigation. Further, whilst it is not a legal requirement for an opponent to be notified of the existence of ATE insurance, choosing to notify them may provide an incentive for settlement as it indicates that a case has been carefully analysed, and considered to have good prospects of success.

To comply with professional conduct requirements, solicitors must ensure that their clients are advised of the benefits and possible detriments of taking out ATE. They must also be made aware of the specific circumstances in which their ATE insurance premium will become payable—particularly if a client could become liable to pay the premium before they have recovered any damages. Solicitors must also ensure that clients are aware of any circumstances that might affect the client's ATE insurance cover or their ability to discontinue or settle their matter.

ATE insurance is generally entered into as a contract between the client and the insurer but a client may require advice and assistance in choosing an insurer and in putting ATE insurance into place. If solicitors recommend a policy or arrange insurance on behalf of their client, they will be undertaking insurance distribution activities and must carefully consider all applicable provisions of the SRA Standards and Regulations 2019 in that regard. They must also consider their professional obligations in respect of potential for conflicts of interest between themselves, the insurer and their client.

A solicitor may be required to provide updates to the insurer at various stages of a matter; particularly if offers of settlement are made or received, or if prospects of success change. Solicitors must ensure that their clients are aware of this obligation and must ensure that they comply with their professional conduct obligations regarding confidentiality.

See **Table 13.2** for an overview of funding options.

TABLE 13.2 Funding options: summary

Funding option	Notes
Private retainer: hourly rates	Available to any client who can afford it, in any legal matter where no other more appropriate sources of funding exist.
Private retainer: fixed fee	Often used in respect of one-off, non-contentious instructions (eg will-writing or conveyancing), or for commercial clients with repeat instructions of the same type (eg debt recovery actions).
CFA	No win, no fee agreement used in contentious matters. The solicitor will be entitled to payment of their fees in the event of success and will often recover some of their base costs from the unsuccessful party. However, if the CFA includes a success fee, the successful client will be liable to pay that fee—it cannot be recovered from the opponent. CFAs are often used in conjunction with ATE insurance to protect against adverse costs. They are available to claimants and defendants.

(Continued)

TABLE 13.2 Continued

Funding option	Notes
DBA	No win, no fee agreement in which a successful party will pay an agreed proportion of any damages that they recover to their solicitor in respect of their legal fees. Available in a variety of civil matters but only usually encountered in employment cases.
Civil legal aid	Available to clients who have matters which fall within scope, and who satisfy the merits and means criteria specified in law. May be available in other limited circumstances through Exceptional Cases Funding. Financial contributions may be required from clients in some cases
Criminal legal aid	Available to clients who satisfy the interests of justice and means tests. Financial contributions may be required from clients in some cases.
Trade union	Available to members of trade unions in respect of legal matters specified by the union (often employment-related matters).
Third party funding: litigation funding	Most often encountered in high-value commercial litigation with good prospects of success. Funding is provided by a third party in return for a specified financial benefit.
Third party funding: pure funding and crowdfunding	Occasionally available for matters of public interest or to facilitate access to justice. Funding is provided by third parties either on a purely charitable basis or on the basis that they will only be entitled to be repaid what they have contributed.
BTE insurance	An optional extra in many car or home insurance policies, providing cover for legal expenses in certain types of matter and up to specified financial limits.
ATE insurance	Insurance in litigation, generally providing cover for possible adverse costs. Usually used in conjunction with a CFA or DBA.

KEY POINT SUMMARY

- Solicitors must identify possible methods of funding that may be available to each client and evaluate the suitability of those methods for their matter.
- Solicitors must provide their clients with the best possible information on funding options and on the cost of legal services both at the time of engagement and throughout any matter.
- Solicitors must ensure that information in respect of costs is provided in a way that clients can understand, to enable clients to make informed decisions.
- The appropriate methods of funding legal services will depend largely on the nature of a client's instructions—including whether the matter is contentious or non contentious or of a civil or criminal nature.
- Solicitors must keep detailed written records of all discussions with clients regarding funding options, and of all decisions made.

APPENDIX
Guides and Useful Websites

Here is a list of web links to the guides and useful websites mentioned in this manual.

Guides and useful websites

- Action Fraud
  https://www.actionfraud.police.uk
- Administrative Court Judicial Review Guide 2023
  https://www.gov.uk/government/publications/administrative-court-judicial-review-guide
- Administrative Justice Council
  https://ajc-justice.co.uk/
- Advisory, Conciliation and Arbitration Service
  https://www.acas.org.uk/dispute-resolution
- Attorney General
  https://www.gov.uk/government/ministers/attorney-general
- BAILII
  https://www.bailii.org/
- Bar Standards Board
  https://www.barstandardsboard.org.uk/
- Cabinet
  https://www.gov.uk/government/ministers
- Cabinet Committees and sub-committees
  https://www.gov.uk/government/publications/the-cabinet-committees-system-and-list-of-cabinet-committees
- Cabinet Manual 2011
  https://assets.publishing.service.gov.uk/government/uploads/system/uploads/attachment_data/file/60641/cabinet-manual.pdf
- Chartered Institute for Legal Executives
  https://www.cilex.org.uk/about_cilex
- Civil Justice Statistics Quarterly, England and Wales, Ministry of Justice.
  https://assets.publishing.service.gov.uk/government/uploads/system/uploads/attachment_data/file/889851/civil-justice-statistics-quarterly-Jan-Mar-2020-accessible-.pdf
- Civil legal aid: means testing
  https://www.gov.uk/guidance/civil-legal-aid-means-testing
- Civil Procedure Rules, Part 54
  https://www.justice.gov.uk/courts/procedure-rules/civil/rules/part54
- Civil Service: Introduction to Devolution
  https://assets.publishing.service.gov.uk/government/uploads/system/uploads/attachment_data/file/770300/IntroductionToDevolution.pdf
- Code for Crown Prosecutors
  https://www.cps.gov.uk/publication/code-crown-prosecutors
- Code for Crown Prosecutors, 'Public Protests'
  https://www.cps.gov.uk/legal-guidance/public-protests

- Code for Crown Prosecutors, 'Public Order Offences incorporating the Charging Standard' https://www.cps.gov.uk/legal-guidance/public-order-offences-incorporating-charging-standard
- College of Police operating manuals https://www.app.college.police.uk/app-content/public-order/core-principles-and-legislation/
- Competition and Markets Authority https://competitionandmarkets.blog.gov.uk/2019/09/06/how-the-cma-investigates-cartels/
- Confidence motions https://researchbriefings.files.parliament.uk/documents/SN02873/SN02873.pdf
- Council of Europe https://www.coe.int/en/web/sarajevo/objectives-mission
- Council of Europe, 'The Rule of Law' https://www.coe.int/en/web/portal/rule-of-law
- County Court https://www.judiciary.uk/you-and-the-judiciary/going-to-court/county-court
- Court of Appeal https://www.judiciary.uk/you-and-the-judiciary/going-to-court/court-of-appeal-home/
- CPS Jurisdiction Legal Guidance (September 2020) https://www.cps.gov.uk/legal-guidance/jurisdiction
- Customs union https://ec.europa.eu/taxation_customs/facts-figures/eu-customs-union-unique-world_en
- Criminal Legal Aid Manual https://assets.publishing.service.gov.uk/government/uploads/system/uploads/attachment_data/file/926398/criminal-legal-aid-manual_October_2020.pdf
- Criminal legal aid: means testing https://www.gov.uk/guidance/criminal-legal-aid-means-testing.
- Crown Court https://www.gov.uk/courts/crown-court
- Crown Prosecution Service https://www.cps.gov.uk/
- Declaration of Delhi, 'The Rule of Law in a Free Society' (1959) https://www.icj.org/wp-content/uploads/1959/01/Rule-of-law-in-a-free-society-conference-report-1959-eng.pdf
- Devolution of powers to Scotland, Wales and Northern Ireland https://www.gov.uk/guidance/devolution-of-powers-to-scotland-wales-and-northern-ireland
- Directory of providers https://www.gov.uk/government/publications/directory-of-legal-aid-providers
- English Votes for English Laws (EVEL) https://www.parliament.uk/business/publications/research/key-issues-parliament-2015/decentralisation/the-english-question/
- Environment Agency https://www.gov.uk/government/publications/environment-agency-enforcement-and-sanctions-policy/environment-agency-enforcement-and-sanctions-policy#enforcement-options
- Equality and Human Rights Commission https://www.equalityhumanrights.com/guidance/business
- Erskine May https://erskinemay.parliament.uk/
- EU Association Agreements https://ec.europa.eu/trade/policy/countries-and-regions/negotiations-and-agreements/index_en.htm

- EU Regulations, Directives and Decisions
  https://europa.eu/european-union/law/legal-acts_en
- EU–UK Agreement for cooperation on the safe and peaceful uses of nuclear energy
  https://commission.europa.eu/strategy-and-policy/relations-non-eu-countries/relations-united-kingdom/eu-uk-trade-and-cooperation-agreement/eu-uk-agreement-cooperation-safe-and-peaceful-uses-nuclear-energy_en#:~:text=Finally%2C%20the%20EU%2DUK%20Agreement,and%20promote%20the%20improvement%20of%2C
- EU–UK Security of Information Agreement
  https://commission.europa.eu/strategy-and-policy/relations-non-eu-countries/relations-united-kingdom/eu-uk-trade-and-cooperation-agreement/eu-uk-security-information-agreement_en
- EU–UK Withdrawal Agreement
  https://commission.europa.eu/strategy-and-policy/relations-non-eu-countries/relations-united-kingdom/eu-uk-withdrawal-agreement_en
- European Convention on Human Rights 1950
  https://www.echr.coe.int/documents/convention_eng.pdf
- European Court of Human Rights
  http://www.echr.coe.int
- Explanatory Notes to the Equality Act 2010
  https://www.legislation.gov.uk/ukpga/2010/15/notes/division/3/2/2/7/3
- FCA's glossary of terms
  https://www.handbook.fca.org.uk/handbook/glossary/?page=1
- FCA Handbook
  https://www.handbook.fca.org.uk/handbook
- Financial Conduct Authority
  https://www.fca.org.uk/
- Financial Policy Committee
  https://www.bankofengland.co.uk/financial-stability
- Freedom of Information Request: Applications for a Banning Order under the Public Order Act 1986
  https://www.gov.uk/government/publications/applications-for-a-banning-order-under-section-13-of-the-public-order-act-1986
- Government guidance, 'Living in Europe'
  https://www.gov.uk/guidance/living-in-europe
- Guidance on how the SRA conduct investigations
  https://www.sra.org.uk/solicitors/guidance/investigations-gathering-evidence/
- Guide to the Family Law Courts
  https://assets.publishing.service.gov.uk/government/uploads/system/uploads/attachment_data/file/462915/guide-to-family-law-courts.pdf
- Health and Safety Executive
  https://www.hse.gov.uk/enforce/enforcement.htm
- Her Majesty's Court and Tribunal Service
  https://www.gov.uk/government/organisations/hm-courts-and-tribunals-service
- High Court
  https://www.judiciary.uk/you-and-the-judiciary/going-to-court/high-court/
- HM Government Note on the investigation and prosecution of crimes of universal jurisdiction
  https://assets.publishing.service.gov.uk/government/uploads/system/uploads/attachment_data/file/709126/universal-jurisdiction-note-web.pdf
- House of Commons
  https://www.parliament.uk/business/commons/
- House of Commons briefing paper, 'Constituency Boundary Reviews and the number of MPs'
  https://researchbriefings.files.parliament.uk/documents/SN05929/SN05929.pdf

- House of Commons briefing paper, 'Police powers: protest'
  http://researchbriefings.files.parliament.uk/documents/SN05013/SN05013.pdf
- House of Commons briefing paper, 'Prisoners' Voting Rights? Developments since 2015'
  https://researchbriefings.files.parliament.uk/documents/CBP-7461/CBP-7461.pdf
- House of Commons briefing paper, 'Public Bodies 2018'
  https://www.civilservant.org.uk/library/2018-HoC-public_bodies.pdf/
- House of Commons Departmental Select Committees
  https://www.parliament.uk/about/how/committees/select/
- House of Commons Political and Constitutional Reform Committee Report on the UK Constitution, March 2015
  https://www.parliament.uk/globalassets/documents/commons-committees/political-and-constitutional-reform/The-UK-Constitution.pdf
- House of Lords
  https://www.parliament.uk/business/lords/
- House of Lords Appointment Commission
  https://lordsappointments.independent.gov.uk/
- House of Lords briefing on Membership
  https://www.parliament.uk/globalassets/documents/lords-information-office/lords-briefing-papers/15595HoLBriefing-membership.pdf
- House of Lords membership
  https://members.parliament.uk/parties/Lords
- House of Lords Select Committees
  https://www.parliament.uk/business/lords/work-of-the-house-of-lords/lords-select-committees/
- Housing Ombudsman
  https://www.housing-ombudsman.org.uk/
- How government works
  https://www.gov.uk/government/how-government-works
- HUDOC database
  https://www.echr.coe.int/Pages/home.aspx?p=caselaw/HUDOC&c
- Human Rights Council of the UN, 'Human rights, democracy and the rule of law'
  https://ap.ohchr.org/documents/dpage_e.aspx?si=A/HRC/RES/19/36
- Human Rights Council of the UN, 'Integrity of the judicial system'
  https://ap.ohchr.org/documents/dpage_e.aspx?si=A/HRC/RES/19/31
- Incorporated Council of Law Reporting for England and Wales
  https://www.iclr.co.uk/
- Independent Office for Police Conduct
  https://www.policeconduct.gov.uk/
- Independent report: Leveson Inquiry
  https://www.gov.uk/government/publications/leveson-inquiry-report-into-the-culture-practices-and-ethics-of-the-press
- Independent Review of Administrative Law 2021
  https://assets.publishing.service.gov.uk/government/uploads/system/uploads/attachment_data/file/970797/IRAL-report.pdf
- Independent Review of Administrative Law Panel
  https://www.gov.uk/government/groups/independent-review-of-administrative-law#membership
- Individual Ministerial Responsibility, 'Issues and examples'
  https://researchbriefings.files.parliament.uk/documents/RP04-31/RP04-31.pdf
- Judicial Appointment and Conduct Ombudsman
  https://www.gov.uk/government/organisations/judicial-appointments-and-conduct-ombudsman

- Judicial Appointments Commission (JAC)
https://www.judiciary.uk/about-the-judiciary/the-judiciary-the-government-and-the-constitution/jud-acc-ind/jud-appts/
- Judicial Committee
https://www.jcpc.uk/
- Judicial Conduct Investigations Office (JCIO)
https://www.judiciary.uk/about-the-judiciary/the-judiciary-the-government-and-the-constitution/jud-acc-ind/jud-conduct/
- Judicial review
https://www.judiciary.uk/you-and-the-judiciary/judicial-review/
- Judicial Review Reform
https://www.gov.uk/government/consultations/judicial-review-reform
- Judiciary
https://www.judiciary.uk/
- LAA 'Keycard'
https://assets.publishing.service.gov.uk/government/uploads/system/uploads/attachment_data/file/899469/Eligibility-keycard_56.pdf
- Law Society's Anti Money Laundering Guidance
https://www.sra.org.uk/solicitors/standards-regulations/transparency-rules/
- Law Society Guidance on the Equality Act 2010
https://www.lawsociety.org.uk/topics/hr-and-people-management/equality-act-2010
- Legal Aid Agency
https://www.gov.uk/government/organisations/legal-aid-agency
- Legal Aid Agency explanatory leaflet
https://assets.publishing.service.gov.uk/government/uploads/system/uploads/attachment_data/file/860909/Client_Legal_Aid_Leaflet.pdf
- Legal Ombudsman
https://www.legalombudsman.org.uk/
- Local Government and Social Care Ombudsman
https://www.lgo.org.uk/
- Lord Chief Justice
https://www.judiciary.uk/about-the-judiciary/who-are-the-judiciary/judicial-roles/judges/lord-chief-justice/
- Lord Justice Jackson's 2010 Review of Civil Litigation Costs: Final Report
https://www.judiciary.uk/wp-content/uploads/JCO/Documents/Reports/jackson-final-report-140110.pdf
- Lords Spiritual
https://churchinparliament.org/about-the-lords-spiritual/
- Magistrates' courts
https://www.judiciary.uk/you-and-the-judiciary/going-to-court/magistrates-court/
- Memorandum of Understanding from 2012
https://www.gov.uk/government/publications/devolution-memorandum-of-understanding-and-supplementary-agreement
- Ministerial Code
https://www.gov.uk/government/publications/ministerial-code
- Monetary Policy Committee
https://www.bankofengland.co.uk/about/people/prudential-regulation-committee
- National Crime Agency
https://www.nationalcrimeagency.gov.uk/
- Northern Ireland Protocol
https://assets.publishing.service.gov.uk/government/uploads/system/uploads/attachment_data/file/840230/Revised_Protocol_to_the_Withdrawal_Agreement.pdf

- Office of the Independent Adjudicator for Higher Education in England
  https://www.oiahe.org.uk/
- OSCOLA
  https://www.law.ox.ac.uk/oscola
- Panel on Takeovers and Mergers
  https://www.thetakeoverpanel.org.uk/
- Parliament Live TV
  https://www.parliamentlive.tv
- Practice Direction 3 of the Supreme Court (Applications for Permission to Appeal)
  https://www.supremecourt.uk/docs/practice-direction-03.pdf
- Practice Statement (Judicial Precedent) [1966] 1 WLR 1234
  https://publications.parliament.uk/pa/ld199697/ldinfo/ld08judg/redbook/redbk45.htm
- Pre-Action Protocol for Judicial Review
  http://www.justice.gov.uk/courts/procedure-rules/civil/protocol/prot_jrv
- Press Recognition Panel
  https://pressrecognitionpanel.org.uk/
- Press gangs
  https://www.parliament.uk/about/living-heritage/transformingsociety/private-lives/yourcountry/overview/pressgangs-/
- Prisons and Probation Ombudsman
  https://www.ppo.gov.uk/
- Prorogation Dispute of 2019: One Year on
  https://researchbriefings.files.parliament.uk/documents/CBP-9006/CBP-9006.pdf
- Protests and marches: letting the police know
  https://www.gov.uk/protests-and-marches-letting-the-police-know
- Private Bills in Parliament: House of Commons Background Paper
  https://researchbriefings.files.parliament.uk/documents/SN06508/SN06508.pdf
- Prudential Regulation Authority
  https://www.bankofengland.co.uk/prudential-regulation
- Prudential Regulation Committee
  https://www.bankofengland.co.uk/about/people/prudential-regulation-committee
- Research Briefing, 'Press regulation after Leveson'
  https://commonslibrary.parliament.uk/research-briefings/cbp-7576/
- Royal prerogative
  https://researchbriefings.files.parliament.uk/documents/CBP-9877/CBP-9877.pdf
- Senedd
  https://senedd.wales/
- Senior Salaries Review Body
  https://www.gov.uk/government/organisations/review-body-on-senior-salaries
- Serious Fraud Office
  https://www.sfo.gov.uk/
- Service Prosecuting Authority
  https://www.gov.uk/guidance/service-prosecuting-authority
- Seven Nolan standards of professional life
  https://www.gov.uk/government/publications/the-7-principles-of-public-life
- Sewel Convention
  https://commonslibrary.parliament.uk/research-briefings/sn02084/
- Single market
  https://ec.europa.eu/growth/single-market_en
- Solicitor General
  https://www.gov.uk/government/ministers/solicitor-general

- Solicitor's record check
  https://www.sra.org.uk/consumers/solicitor-check/
- Solicitors Disciplinary Tribunal Annual Report
  https://www.solicitorstribunal.org.uk/about-us/annual-reports
- Solicitors Disciplinary Tribunal Judgment Search
  https://www.solicitorstribunal.org.uk/judgment-search-results#search
- Solicitors' guideline hourly rates
  https://www.gov.uk/guidance/solicitors-guideline-hourly-rates
- Solicitors Regulation Authority (SRA)
  https://www.sra.org.uk/
- SRA 50 most recently published regulatory decisions
  https://www.sra.org.uk/consumers/solicitor-check/recent-decisions/
- SRA Authorisation of Firms Rules
  https://www.sra.org.uk/solicitors/standards-regulations/authorisation-firms-rules/
- SRA Authorisation of Individuals Regulations
  https://www.sra.org.uk/solicitors/standards-regulations/authorisation-individuals-regulations/
- SRA Code of Conduct
  https://www.sra.org.uk/solicitors/standards-regulations/code-conduct-solicitors/
- SRA Compensation Fund
  https://www.sra.org.uk/solicitors/standards-regulations/compensation-fund-rules/
- SRA enforcement strategy
  https://www.sra.org.uk/sra/corporate-strategy/sra-enforcement-strategy/
- SRA Financial Services (Conduct of Business) Rules
  https://www.sra.org.uk/solicitors/standards-regulations/financial-services-conduct-business-rules/
- SRA Financial Services ('Scope') Rules
  https://www.sra.org.uk/solicitors/standards-regulations/financial-services-scope-rules/
- SRA Guidance Issuing Solicitors Disciplinary Tribunal proceedings
  https://www.sra.org.uk/solicitors/guidance/disciplinary-issuing-solicitors-disciplinary-tribunal-proceedings/
- SRA Indemnity Insurance Rules
  https://www.sra.org.uk/solicitors/standards-regulations/indemnity-insurance-rules/
- SRA Regulatory and Disciplinary Procedure Rules
  https://www.sra.org.uk/solicitors/standards-regulations/regulatory-disciplinary-procedure-rules
- SRA Reporting and Notification Guidance summarises
  https://www.sra.org.uk/solicitors/guidance/reporting-notification-obligations/#schedules
- SRA Standards and Regulations
  https://www.sra.org.uk/solicitors/standards-regulations/code-conduct-solicitors/
- SRA Transparency Rules
  https://www.sra.org.uk/solicitors/standards-regulations/transparency-rules/
- Statutory Charge Manual
  https://assets.publishing.service.gov.uk/government/uploads/system/uploads/attachment_data/file/670213/legal-aid-stat-charge-manual.pdf
- State Opening of Parliament
  https://www.parliament.uk/about/how/occasions/stateopening/
- Statute of the Council of Europe
  https://www.coe.int/en/web/conventions/full-list/-/conventions/rms/0900001680935bd0
- Supreme Court
  https://www.supremecourt.uk/

- Trade and Cooperation Agreement (TCA)
  https://ec.europa.eu/info/relations-united-kingdom/eu-uk-trade-and-cooperation-agreement_en
- Tribunals Organisation Chart
  https://www.judiciary.uk/wp-content/uploads/2020/09/tribunals-chart-updated-April-2021.pdf
- United Nations Universal Declaration of Human Rights 1948 (UDHR)
  https://www.un.org/en/universal-declaration-human-rights/
- Venice Commission of the Council of Europe: Rule of Law Checklist
  https://www.venice.coe.int/images/SITE%20IMAGES/Publications/Rule_of_Law_Check_List.pdf
- Whip system
  https://www.parliament.uk/about/mps-and-lords/principal/whips/

Glossary

Abuse of process In the context of judicial review, this means the unreasonable use of civil procedure for the purpose of gaining an unfair advantage over an opponent in a legal dispute.

After the event (ATE) insurance Insurance often taken out in litigation to protect a client against the risk of being ordered to pay their opponent's costs (adverse costs). Often used in conjunction with a CFA, DBA or litigation funding.

Alternative Business Structure (ABS) An entity created pursuant to Pt 5 of the Legal Services Act 2007, which is essentially a business that is authorised to provide regulated and reserved legal services alongside other services, and/or has some non-lawyer owners and managers.

Approved regulators The regulators set out in Sch 4, para 1 of the Legal Services Act 2007. The Law Society is the approved regulator and representative body for solicitors and the SRA is the independent regulatory body for solicitors.

Associative discrimination Associative discrimination is where a person is directly discriminated against due to their association with a friend or partner with a protected characteristic.

Authorised person A person who is authorised by the FSA to conduct regulated activities under the Financial Services and Markets Act 2000.

Before the event (BTE) insurance Insurance cover, often an optional extra on motor or household insurance, which enables a client to obtain legal advice and/or representation for free under the terms of their insurance in relation to certain legal issues arising during the period of their insurance.

Client care letter A letter providing information about the services that a solicitor will provide to a client, usually including key information on costs, timescales and complaints procedures. The client care letter provides clarification and certainty of what has been agreed between a solicitor and a client. It may be accompanied by a separate 'terms of business' document providing further, more detailed information.

Collective Cabinet responsibility Any policy decision reached by the Cabinet has to be supported thereafter by all members of the Cabinet whether they approve of it or not, unless they feel compelled to resign.

Combined discrimination Where a person discriminates against another because of a combination of two relevant protected characteristics treating them less favourably than they would treat a person with either of the two protected characteristics.

Common law The common law is made up of judge-made rules applied in decided cases which apply throughout England and Wales.

Compliance officers A term used to refer to either or both of a practice's Compliance Officer for Financial Affairs (COFA) or Compliance Officer for Legal Practice (COLP), which are roles required pursuant to rule 8 of the SRA's Authorisation of Firms Rules. The COLP and COFA roles may be held by the same person or by two separate people.

Conditional Fee Agreement (CFA) An agreement between a client and a solicitor in litigation pursuant to which the solicitor will only be entitled to payment for their legal services in 'specified circumstances', usually if the client is successful.

Conduct Conduct which is 'related to' a relevant protected characteristic captures any conduct engaged with because of the protected characteristic and any conduct which is connected to it.

Constitutional practices or conventions Informal political rules adopted by those who participate in the process of government, which are considered binding to a varying extent but which are not enforceable in the courts.

Convention right In the Human Rights Act 1998, 'Convention right' means: (a) the rights contained in Arts 2–12 and 14 ECHR; (b) Arts 1–3 First Protocol; and (c) Arts 1 and 2 Sixth Protocol.

Customer due diligence measures Identifying the customer and verifying the customer's identity on the basis of documents, data or information obtained from a reliable and independent source.

Damages-based agreement (DBA) An agreement between a client and a solicitor in litigation pursuant to which the solicitor will only be entitled to payment for their legal services if the client receives a specified financial benefit (usually damages). The payment that the solicitor will be entitled to will be expressed as a percentage of the damages that the client recovers in the litigation.

Declaration of incompatibility A declaration of incompatibility in UK constitutional law is a declaration issued by a UK judge that a statute is incompatible with the European Convention of Human Rights under the Human Rights Act 1998.

Delegated legislation Regulations and other laws made by government ministers empowered to do so by statute. The empowering statute may require such regulations to be scrutinised and approved by Parliament before they come into effect.

Designated professional body Professional bodies that have supervisory responsibility for their own members.

Detriment The test as to what constitutes a detriment is a subjective one and can include not only acts which are positively done to another person but also those where there is an omission.

Direct disability discrimination This is discrimination against a disabled person if the unfavourable treatment is because of something arising in consequence of that disability and the discrimination is not a proportionate means of achieving a legitimate aim.

Direct discrimination Where a person discriminates against another person because of a protected characteristic.

Directive A Directive is a legislative act of the European Union which requires Member States to achieve a particular result without dictating the means of achieving that result. It can be distinguished from EU Regulations which are self-executing and do not require any implementing measures. Directives can be adopted by means of a variety of legislative procedures depending on the subject matter.

Disability This a mental or physical impairment which has a substantial and long-term adverse effect on a person's ability to carry out normal day-to-day activities.

Equality of arms This principle ensures that both parties to a case, whether in civil or criminal proceedings, are not placed at a procedural disadvantage.

Excluded activity Certain specified activities listed in the Financial Services and Markets Act 2000 (Regulated Activities) Order 2001 (SI 2001/544) (RAO) which are excluded from having to be authorised by the Financial Conduct Authority.

Exempt activity Activity which means a person does not have to be authorised by the Financial Conduct Authority, when the following are met: (a) the designated body must be a professional body (DPB); and (b) the professional body must also supervise and regulate the way in which its members carry on non-mainstream investment business.

Gender reassignment Where a person is proposing to undergo, is undergoing or has undergone a process of reassigning their sex by changing a physiological or other attribute of sex.

General prohibition The prohibition imposed by s19 of FSMA 2000, which states that no person may carry on a regulated activity in the UK, or purport to do so, unless they are an authorised person or an exempt person.

Harassment Where a person engages in unwanted conduct related to a relevant protected characteristic and this has the 'purpose or effect' of violating the dignity of another or creating an intimidating, hostile, degrading, humiliating or offensive environment for that person.

Horizontality Before Brexit, UK courts were under a duty to interpret national laws consistently with EU law and where these interpretations affected the legal rights and duties of both private parties to a case this was called horizontal effect.

Illegality In Lord Diplock's words, this ground means that the decision-maker must understand correctly the law that regulates their decision-making power and must give effect to it.

Impairment This can include physical or mental impairments and there is no requirement that the mental impairment be clinically recognised.

Indirect discrimination Where a person applies a provision, criterion or practice to another which is discriminatory in relation to a protected characteristic.

Injunction This is a discretionary court order which can be used to stop something being done or require something to be discontinued. It can also be used to order something to be done.

Judicial review According to the Pre-Action Protocol on Judicial Review, judicial review allows people with a sufficient interest in a decision or action of a public body to ask a judge to review the lawfulness of an enactment or a decision, action or failure to act in relation to the exercise of a public function.

Jurisdictional error At common law, jurisdictional error developed as a ground of review which was available where a tribunal or inferior court (as opposed to an administrator such as a minister or public servant) purported to exercise jurisdiction in excess of that which had been conferred upon it, or failed to exercise jurisdiction which it properly had.

Justiciability This means that a matter is capable of being decided by a court.

Legal aid Public funding available to pay for criminal and civil legal advice and representation in some circumstances. Usually only available subject to a client meeting complex criteria relating to their financial means and the merits of their case.

Legal Ombudsman The Ombudsman established pursuant to the Legal Services Act 2007 to assist in the resolution of issues arising between providers and users of legal services, after a provider's complaints procedure has been exhausted.

Legal Services Board (LSB) The oversight regulator of legal services in England and Wales. The LSB was established pursuant to s2 of the Legal Services Act 2007 and has regulatory oversight of 'approved regulators' of legal services (including the Law Society and its regulatory body the SRA), the Solicitors Disciplinary Tribunal and the Office for Legal Complaints and Legal Ombudsman scheme.

Litigation funding An arrangement in which a commercial third party provides funding for legal costs in litigation in return for a specified financial benefit.

Long-term effect If it has lasted or is likely to last for at least 12 months or is likely to last for the rest of the person's life.

Margin of appreciation This allows the European Court of Human Rights to take into account cultural, historic and philosophical differences between Strasbourg and the particular national authority, which may mean the Convention is interpreted differently thereby giving a national authority a degree of flexibility in fulfilling its obligations under the Convention.

Ministers of the Crown A minister of the Crown is the formal constitutional term used to describe a member of His/Her Majesty's Government. Secretaries of State are ministers of the Crown. The term indicates that the person appointed serves in theory at His/Her Majesty's Pleasure, and advises the monarch. In practice, all ministers of the Crown are members of and are accountable to Parliament.

Money laundering Money laundering is an illegal practice in which money generated from criminal activities is disguised and made to appear to have come from a legitimate source in order to make it easier to spend the money and avoid suspicion.

Nominated officer A person who is nominated to receive disclosures under Part 7 of the Proceeds of Crime Act 2002 (money laundering) or Part 3 of the Terrorism Act 2000 (terrorist property).

Objective justification Where a respondent to a claim can show that the discrimination complained of is proportionate, appropriate and reasonably necessary.

Ouster clause Any provision of an Act of Parliament which purports to limit or exclude the supervisory jurisdiction of the High Court.

Parliamentary sovereignty Parliamentary sovereignty is absolute sovereignty and Parliament is supreme over all other government institutions, including executive or judicial bodies.

Positive action This is more favourable treatment due to a protected characteristic and is generally unlawful under the Act.

Preliminary ruling To ensure the effective and uniform application of EU legislation and to prevent divergent interpretations, national courts may, and sometimes must, turn to the European Court of Justice and ask that it clarify a point concerning the interpretation of EU law in order, for example, to ascertain whether their national legislation complies with that law. Post Brexit, the CJEU can still receive preliminary ruling requests from UK courts concerning citizens' rights under the Withdrawal Agreement.

Private Members' Bills Private Members' Bills are public Bills introduced by MPs and Lords who are not government ministers. As with other public Bills, their purpose is to change the law as it applies to the general population.

Private retainer An agreement between a solicitor and their client pursuant to which the client will pay the solicitor privately for services provided. Solicitors will charge either on the basis of time spent on a matter (calculated by reference to hourly rates) or will charge an agreed fixed fee.

Procedural impropriety A decision of a public body suffers from procedural impropriety if, in the process of its making a decision, the procedures prescribed by statute have not been followed or if the 'rules of natural justice' have not been adhered to.

Professional indemnity insurance Compulsory insurance for all SRA-authorised bodies, providing protection for clients against losses caused by a solicitor's negligence or breach of duty. PII must meet minimum terms specified by the SRA.

Proportionality Proportionality is a requirement that a decision is proportionate to the aim that it seeks to achieve.

Protected acts The Equality Act 2010 sets out a broad list of 'protected acts' which includes giving of evidence in support of an allegation or making an allegation.

Protected characteristics These are as set out in s4 of the Equality Act 2010: age, disability, gender reassignment, marriage and civil partnership, race, religion or belief, sex, sexual orientation, pregnancy and maternity.

Public Accounts Committee The Committee of Public Accounts is appointed by the House of Commons to examine the accounts showing the appropriation of the sums granted by Parliament to meet public expenditure, and of such other accounts laid before Parliament as the Committee may think fit.

Public authority According to s6(3) of the Human Rights Act 1998, 'public authority' includes: (a) a court or tribunal; and (b) any person certain of whose functions are functions of a public nature; but does not include either House of Parliament or a person exercising functions in connection with proceedings in Parliament.

Public body Any organisation whose functions are of a governmental nature and whose powers are not wholly based on agreement.

Public interest This is a wide subjective principle usually referring to the safety and welfare of the state.

Public interest immunity (PII) This is a principle of English common law under which the English courts can grant a court order allowing one litigant to refrain from disclosing evidence to the other litigants where disclosure would be damaging to the public interest. This is an exception to the usual rule that all parties in litigation must disclose any evidence that is relevant to the proceedings. In making a PII order, the court has to balance the public interest in the administration of justice (which demands that relevant material is available to the parties to litigation) and the public interest in maintaining the confidentiality of certain documents the disclosure of which would be damaging.

Reasonable adjustments These are reasonable adjustments to eliminate barriers to access and participation for disabled people.

Recognised body A body recognised by the SRA under s9 of the Administration of Justice Act 1985, and for the purposes of SRA authorisation and regulation referring to a legal services body in which all managers and interest holders are legally qualified.

Recurring conditions Where the effect of the condition is likely to recur even where there are episodic effects of less than 12 months' impairment.

Regulated financial activity An activity of a specified kind that is carried on by way of business and relates to a specified investment or property of any kind (s22 FSMA 2000).

Regulation A Regulation is a legislative act of the EU which becomes immediately enforceable as law in all Member States simultaneously. Regulations can be distinguished from Directives which, at least in principle, need to be transposed into national law.

Republic A country which has an executive or non-executive president as head of state.

Reserved legal activity Specific types of legal activity, defined in s12(1) of the Legal Services Act 2007, which may only be carried out where authorisation has been provided by an 'approved regulator'.

Royal assent The monarch's acceptance of a parliamentary Bill which has either received the necessary assents of the House of Lords and the House of Commons or has received the assent of the House of Commons under the Parliament Acts 1911 and 1949. Royal assent is also an essential step in creating Acts of the Scottish Parliament, Senedd Cymru and the Northern Ireland Assembly.

Royal Commissions A Royal Commission is a major government public inquiry into an issue.

Royal prerogative The judicially accepted definition of royal prerogative is that it represents the residue of arbitrary and discretionary power possessed by the Crown.

Rule of law The rule of law implies the equal subordination of governmental bodies to the substantive and procedural requirements of the law so as to prevent them exercising purely arbitrary and discretionary power. It also embodies the idea that everyone is equally subject to the law and that the rights of citizens are protected by the legal system.

Secretaries of State Senior ministers who lead most, but not all, central government departments. They are members of the Privy Council and the Cabinet.

Separation of powers The separation of powers is capable of meaning that: the same persons should not form part of more than one of the three organs of government; one organ of government should not control or interfere with the work of another; and one organ of government should not exercise the functions of another.

Sexual harassment Sexual harassment occurs where there is 'unwanted conduct of a sexual nature' and the conduct has the 'purpose or effect' as set out earlier under 'Harassment'.

Solicitors Disciplinary Tribunal (SDT) The statutory tribunal regulated by the Legal Services Board, and independent of the SRA, which adjudicates on alleged breaches of the rules and regulations applicable to solicitors and the firms in which they work.

Substantial disadvantage A substantial disadvantage is one which is more than minor or trivial and is in comparison to a non-disabled person as opposed to a person whose circumstances are the same as those of the disabled person.

Supremacy of law In this context it means that governmental power is based on law rather than arbitrary force exercisable with absolute discretion.

Trade Union funding An arrangement through which members of a trade union may be entitled to seek legal advice and representation funded by their Union.

Ultra vires This is a Latin phrase that literally means 'beyond the powers'.

Unreasonableness Under Lord Diplock's classification, a decision is irrational if it is so outrageous in its defiance of logic or of accepted moral standards that no sensible person who had applied their mind to the question could have arrived at it.

Victim Under s7(7) of the Human Rights Act 1998, a person is a victim of an unlawful act only if they would be a victim for the purposes of Art 34 ECHR if proceedings were brought in the European Court of Human Rights in respect of that act.

Victimisation Where a person subjects another to a detriment because they believe rightly or wrongly that that person has or may commit a protected act, this will constitute victimisation.

Whip system The aim of the whip system is to maintain party discipline within Parliament. Whips are MPs or peers appointed by each party to maintain party discipline. In a sense, they are personnel managers who convey information between party leaders and backbench members. Part of their role, however, is to encourage members of their party to vote in the way that their party would like.

Index

Introductory Note

References such as '178–9' indicate (not necessarily continuous) discussion of a topic across a range of pages. Wherever possible in the case of topics with many references, these have either been divided into sub-topics or only the most significant discussions of the topic are listed. Because the entire work is about 'public law', the use of this term (and certain others which occur constantly throughout the book) as an entry point has been restricted. Information will be found under the corresponding detailed topics. Cross-references in a form such as 'ombudsmen *see also individual titles*' direct the reader to headings in a particular class (e.g. in this case 'Parliamentary and Health Service Ombudsman') rather than a specific '*individual titles*' entry.